Corporate Governance and Statutory Derivative Actions: Comparative Approach to Shareholder Litigation

This book is the first comprehensive study of the statutory derivative action in Australia, using the Australian model as a reference point and comparing it with the United Kingdom, Canada, Singapore, New Zealand, Hong Kong and USA counterparts. The book includes an empirical study covering over a 20-year period from the date the statutory framework came into operation, coupled with extensive case law analysis and comparisons with other jurisdictions. It informs the world about the uniqueness of Australia's statutory derivative action, and what other countries can learn from it as shareholder protection and promotion of good corporate governance. While some countries have statutory derivative action, there are still countries that do not have the statutory framework that are considering introducing it into their corporate law. This book is also useful for countries that already have their local variants of the statutory derivative action that are considering revising their existing provisions. This book provides insights and suggestions for lawmakers, judges, litigation practitioners and corporate law and litigation researchers worldwide in reforming their existing model.

Dr Lang Thai is an established corporate law academic with over 20 years of university research and teaching experience in Australia and the UK. She has published widely in corporate law, including shareholders remedies, derivative actions, class actions and other forms of corporate litigation. She published her first comparative article on statutory derivative action in 2002 in a well-respected journal and has since been following the developments in this area of law.

Routledge Research in Corporate Law

Available titles in this series include:

Employee Rights in Corporate Insolvency
A UK and US Perspective
Hamiisi Junior Nsubuga

Shareholder Protection Reconsidered
Derivative Action in the UK, Germany and Greece
Georgios Zouridakis

Corporate Takeover, Management Discipline and the Law
Francis Okanigbuan Jnr

Shareholder Activism and the Law
The Future of US Corporate Governance
Ekrem Solak

The Law and Governance of Decentralised Business Models
Between Hierarchies and Markets
Edited by Roger M Barker and Iris H-Y Chiu

The Enlightened Shareholder Value and Corporate Social Responsibility
A theoretical and qualitative analysis
Taskin Iqbal

Adjudicating Global Business in and with India
International Commercial and Investment Disputes Settlement
Leïla Choukroune and Rahul Donde

Business, Law and Human Rights in Africa
Oyeniyi Abe

Small and Medium Enterprises, Law and Business
Uncertainty and Justice
Jan Winczorek and Karol Muszyński

Corporate Governance and Statutory Derivative Actions: Comparative Approach to Shareholder Litigation

Lang Thai
PhD (Monash); LLM (Monash); GradDipEd (Melbourne); BSc/LLB (Monash)
Senior Lecturer in Law, University of Lincoln

Routledge
Taylor & Francis Group
LONDON AND NEW YORK

First published 2024
by Routledge
4 Park Square, Milton Park, Abingdon, Oxon OX14 4RN

and by Routledge
605 Third Avenue, New York, NY 10158

Routledge is an imprint of the Taylor & Francis Group, an informa business

British Library Cataloguing-in-Publication Data
A catalogue record for this book is available from the British Library

Library of Congress Cataloging-in-Publication Data
A catalog record has been requested for this book

ISBN: 978-1-032-55311-5 (hbk)
ISBN: 978-1-032-55313-9 (pbk)
ISBN: 978-1-003-43006-3 (ebk)

DOI: 10.4324/9781003430063

Typeset in Optima
by Deanta Global Publishing Services, Chennai, India

Dedicated to my mother

Contents

Table of cases

Australia:

Canada:

Hong Kong:

New Zealand:

Singapore:

United Kingdom:

United States of America:

Table of legislation

New Zealand:

Singapore:

United Kingdom:

Others:

Preface

This book informs the world about the uniqueness of Australia's statutory derivative action as a mechanism for shareholder protection and for promoting good corporate governance. Derivative action is the only type of private enforcement action a shareholder can bring on behalf of the company to enforce a corporate right and remedy a wrong done to the company, even where shareholders will only be entitled to a pro rata benefit of the total recovery. There is no other type of action by which a company can obtain relief in circumstances where the board of directors fails to take appropriate action.

The book provides a comprehensive study of statutory derivative action in Australia, using the Australian model as a reference point and comparing it with counterparts in the United Kingdom, Canada, New Zealand, Singapore, Hong Kong and the US. Other countries that do not yet have the statutory framework are considering introducing it into their corporate law – for example, Greece, Brazil and Cyprus. This book provides practical suggestions for lawmakers, judges, litigation practitioners and corporate law and litigation researchers in their jurisdictions who seek to introduce statutory derivative action or to reform their existing derivative action model. It also provides arguments as to why and how statutory derivative action is in need of reform. Statutory derivative action plays an important role in maintaining good corporate governance.

The book is approached from the perspective of empirical research coupled with extensive case law analysis and international comparisons. No other scholars have written on statutory derivative action in Australia with such depth. The book includes a comprehensive empirical study of statutory derivative action covering a period of more than 20 years since the statutory framework came into operation.

I published my first article on comparative statutory derivative action in 2002, at a time when Australia had just introduced the statutory model. Since then, I have followed the developments in the law in this area, and later took on a study of the statutory derivative action by way of doctoral research at Monash University Law Faculty in Melbourne, from which this book has developed and expanded.

I am grateful to many friends and colleagues who have provided their assistance and support, and to those who are eager to see this book published. Without them, this book would not have been possible. My sincere thanks to those who have taken their time to provide their comments on earlier drafts of this work, in different portions, and special mention goes to Associate Professor John Duns, Professor Bruce Dyer, Professor Jennifer Hill, Professor Andrew Keay, Associate Professor Matthew Berkahn, Dr Benjamin Hayward, and to both Professors John Farrar and Lynne Taylor who suggested that I should get my thesis published. My thanks also go to Michelle Bendall and Kay Tucker for their advice on how to manage and keep track of large volumes of cases. Chapter 4 repeats part of the material and arguments drawn from an article by Lang Thai, "Reconsideration of the "Good Faith" Requirement in Statutory Derivative Actions in Australia" (2020) 37 *Company and Securities Law Journal* 403. I acknowledge too the financial support I received from the Australian Government Research Training Scholarship, which enabled me to pursue and complete my study.

To friends, relatives and colleagues who have shown their encouragement and support in numerous other ways, my sincere thanks to you all, including Abe Herzberg who introduced me to the topic of statutory derivative action, Professors Richard Cullen, Paul Latimer, Ian Ramsay AO (from Melbourne) and Richard Krever AM for their advice on all things academic, my dear friend George Thomas for his patience and kindness in reading through earlier drafts of this work, Dr Paul McDonough, Dr Firew Tiba, Dr John Guo, Dr Nuannuan Lin and Andrew Francis for their friendship and encouragement, and my corporate law students who took part in the discussions in my lectures and tutorials. I wish to also convey my thanks to colleagues at Lincoln Law School at University of Lincoln, UK, including Associate Professor Martyn Heathcote and Dr Mike Varney. The law stated is current as at 31 December 2022.

Lang Thai
England, UK

Glossary of abbreviations

A-G	Attorney-General's Department
ALRC	Australian Law Reform Commission
ASIC	Australian Securities and Investment Commission
CA	*Corporations Act* 2001 (C'th)
CASAC	Companies and Securities Advisory Committee
CLERP Act	*Corporate Law Economic Reform Program Act* 1999 (C'th)
CLERP Bill	*Corporate Law Economic Reform Program Bill* 1998 (C'th)
CLERP Proposal	Corporate Law Economic Reform Program Proposal
CLSTF	Corporations Law Simplification Task Force
CSLRC	Companies and Securities Law Review Committee
C'th	Commonwealth
EM	*Explanatory Memorandum to* the *CLERP Bill* 1998 (C'th)
FC	Federal Court
FCAA	*Federal Court of Australia Act* 1976 (C'th)
HK	Hong Kong
HCA	High Court of Australia
LCA	Legal and Constitutional Affairs
NSW	New South Wales
NZ	New Zealand
PJC on CFS	Parliamentary Joint Committee on Corporations and Financial Services
SA	South Australia
SC	Supreme Court
SDA	Statutory Derivative Action
SSC on LCA	Senate Standing Committee on Legal and Constitutional Affairs
UK	United Kingdom
USA	United States of America
VLRC	Victorian Law Reform Commission
WA	Western Australia

1 Introduction

Statutory derivative action is a court action brought by a shareholder or an officer on behalf of and in the name of the company to remedy a wrong done to the company where the company is unwilling or unable to do so. While many countries, such as Australia, New Zealand, Canada, Singapore, the United Kingdom, Hong Kong, China, Malaysia and Vietnam, have already adopted the local variants of the statutory framework for derivative action, there are still many countries that do not have the statutory framework that are considering introducing it into their corporate law, for example, Brazil, Greece and Cyprus.

The main purpose of this book is to inform the world about the uniqueness of Australia's statutory derivative action, and what other countries can learn from it as shareholder protection and promotion of good corporate governance. This book considers the Australian model as an example, a reference point for discussion and to compare it with the United Kingdom, Canada, New Zealand, Singapore, the US and Hong Kong counterparts. The objective in this book is, therefore, to analyse whether the statutory derivative action framework is in need of reform in Australia and if so, why and how. To understand and appreciate the importance of this topic, one has to understand what a statutory derivative action is and why its continued existence is important in the context of corporate law.

This chapter commences by explaining the nature of the statutory derivative action and where it fits within the broad public/private enforcement framework. This introductory chapter then provides a roadmap for the remainder of the book, which will seek to show how the statutory derivative action, which constitutes an important private enforcement tool, could be strengthened to provide shareholders with an appropriate remedy, particularly those in small private and closely held companies. Australia is one of the first countries that adopted the *statutory* derivative action from Canada, its birthplace.[1]

1 Canada invented the statutory derivative action in 1971, followed by Singapore in 1993 with some variants, then New Zealand in 1994 with some variants, Australia in 2000 and again with some variants. A few other countries followed suit. The United Kingdom introduced its statutory framework in 2007.

DOI: 10.4324/9781003430063-1

1.1 Meaning of statutory derivative action and its importance

A derivative action is a special type of court action brought by a shareholder or an officer of a company on behalf of and in the name of the company against a person for a wrong done to the company, in circumstances where the company itself is unwilling or unable to bring the necessary action. In early cases,[2] the courts acknowledged the derivative action at common law as a means of providing an exception to the general rule in the famous case of *Foss v. Harbottle*,[3] that the company is the "proper plaintiff" in legal proceedings to defend the company's rights. Generally, a decision on whether a company will bring an action against a wrongdoer lies in the power of the board of directors,[4] and in small privately owned or closely held companies,[5] these directors also tend to be the controlling shareholders.[6] The board of directors or the majority directors acting as a company organ are usually the ones to cause the company to bring a court action against a wrongdoer.

However, there may be circumstances where the directors may be unwilling or unable to cause the company to sue a wrongdoer.[7] The wrongdoer could, for example, be a director (or directors) who has committed a breach of directors' duties, and who may be the controlling director and shareholder in the company.[8] A wrongdoer could also be a person outside the company who has close ties with the board of directors or the controlling shareholders and, as a result, those people may be unwilling or unable to bring the necessary action against their "mate".

2 See, for example, *Burland v. Earle* [1902] AC 83; *Edwards v. Halliwell* [1950] 2 All ER 1064, 1066–1069. For an Australian decision, see *Mesenberg v. Cord Industrial Recruiters Pty Ltd* (1996) 14 ACLC 519.

3 *Foss v. Harbottle* (1843) 2 Hare 461.

4 For commentaries, see K.W. Wedderburn, "Shareholders' rights and the rule in *Foss v. Harbottle*" (1957) 15 *Cambridge Law Journal* 194 and (1958) 16 *Cambridge Law Journal* 93; G. R. Sullivan, "Restating the scope of the derivative action" (1985) 44 *Cambridge Law Journal* 236.

5 Ryan J. Turner, "Directors' fiduciary duties and oppression in closely held corporations" (2013) 31 *Company and Securities Law Journal* 278, at 279–282 (explaining the concept of closely held companies, such as a quasi-partnership or joint-venture type, including small family-owned companies).

6 Ian M. Ramsay and Ben Saunders, "Litigation by shareholders and directors: An empirical study of the Australian statutory derivative action" (2006) 6 *Journal of Corporate Law Studies* 397, at 402–403; James Corkery, *Directors' Powers and Duties* (Longman Professional, Melbourne, 1987), at 172.

7 Wedderburn, n 4. See also Sullivan, n 4.

8 A classic example is the case of *Cook v. Deek* [1916] AC 554, where three of the four directors who were all equal shareholders decided to divest their lucrative corporate opportunities away from the existing company and place them into their newly incorporated company, in exclusion and at the expense of the fourth minority director/shareholder. This was a case of a breach of directors' duties against the *company* and a "fraud on the minority" *shareholder* as a relevant exception for the fourth minority shareholder to be permitted to bring a court action on behalf of the company against those three offending directors. The court declared the profits to be held on constructive trust and made an order for their return to the original company.

A derivative action is one way of overcoming improper inaction by the board. In other words, an alternative way for a company to sue a wrongdoer would be for a shareholder or an individual director to step in and assist the company by bringing a "derivative" suit.[9] A successful applicant will be acting on behalf of and in the name of the company.[10] The importance of a derivative suit in corporate law is succinctly described in *Metyor Inc v. Queensland Electronic Switching Pty Ltd*, where McPherson AJ in the Queensland Court of Appeal states:[11]

> "It is because one group of members are in control of the management or affairs of the company and refuse to permit it to take proceedings that there is a dispute between the two groups of shareholders or members here. It is only by permitting proceedings to be taken on behalf of the company that the dispute in question can be resolved at all and that the complaint of one set of members against the others can be remedied. Otherwise the majority will be able to prevent the minority and through them the company from obtaining redress against the actions of the majority."

It might be asked why corporate law would not simply allow any individual shareholder to bring an action to enforce a wrong done to the company. However, the courts' traditional reluctance to permit shareholders to enforce corporate rights, except via a derivative suit, is not without good reason. Policy justifications for the rule in *Foss v. Harbottle*, and for restricting the ability of individual shareholders to sue, include the following. A restrictive approach arguably avoids the problem of a multiplicity of actions by shareholders.[12] It has been argued, for example, that it would be inefficient and a waste of resources if shareholders, particularly those with small holdings, were permitted to sue management.[13] Another justification for the law's

9 Hereinafter, where reference is made that a derivative action may be brought by a shareholder, it is also possible that an individual director could bring a similar suit.

10 *Corporations Act* 2001 (C'th), s.236(2).

11 *Metyor Inc (formerly Talisman Technologies Inc) v. Queensland Electronic Switching Pty Ltd* (2002) 42 ACSR 398; [2002] QCA 269, at [11].

12 On the other hand, there are some arguments suggesting that the fear of a multiplicity of actions is largely unfounded. For example, shareholders who have only a small stake, which is often the case in large public companies, usually will not have the incentive to bring a legal action. See *Joy v. North* 692 F.2d 880 (1982), at 886 (Winter J). There is the problem of collective action, in terms of both organisation and costs, for a large number of geographically dispersed shareholders to bring a legal action. See Tim Bowley and Jennifer G. Hill, "Stewardship and Collective Action: The Australian Experience" (Working Paper No. 491/2020, ECGI Working Paper Series in Law, European Corporate Governance Institute, January 2020); Bernard S. Black, "Shareholder passivity re-examined" (1990) 89 *Michigan Law Review* 520, 527–528. Finally, the high cost of litigation, the problem of free riding and the uncertainty of recovery can all operate as disincentives to shareholder litigation.

13 *Joy v. North* 692 F.2d 880 (1982), at 886 (Winter J).

reluctance to entertain suits by individual shareholders is that it minimises disruption to the company's business, and avoids the internal affairs of the company spilling into the public domain in a way that results in unwanted publicity and negative effects on the company, such as falling share prices.

In the light of these restrictions, the derivative action is important because it is effectively the only type of action a shareholder can bring on behalf of the company to enforce a corporate right and remedy a wrong done to the company. There is no other type of action where the company can obtain relief in circumstances where the board improperly fails to take action. To be sure, other forms of private enforcement, such as oppression and class action suits,[14] are potentially available to shareholders; however, these actions are strictly personal actions, including class actions; that is, they are not actions brought on behalf of the company.

1.2 The great public/private enforcement debate

Where do derivative suits fit within Australia's broad enforcement framework relating to directors' duties and wrongs done to the company?

Generally, there are two types of enforcement regime. The first is public enforcement, in which a corporate regulator, such as the Australian Securities and Investments Commission ("ASIC"), has responsibility for investigating and bringing legal actions for alleged breaches of directors' duties. Since 1993, ASIC has had broad powers to issue civil penalties and to seek civil penalty orders for contraventions of certain provisions of the Australian *Corporations Act* 2001 (C'th), including for breach of statutory directors' duties.[15] The second regime is privately funded enforcement by individual shareholders or minority directors, of which the derivative suit is a prime example.

There is extensive and ongoing debate on the roles, and relative merits, of public and private enforcement.[16] The following segments discuss some of

14 Although a class action is a collective shareholder action brought by a representative, it is usually brought against, not on behalf of, the company. The differences between a class action and a derivative action will be discussed further in Chapter 7. See also, Lang Thai, "Class action procedure in Australia: Issues and challenges", in Colin B. Picker and Guy I. Seidman (eds.), *The Dynamism of Civil Procedure – Global Trends and Developments* (Ius Gentium: Comparative Perspectives on Law and Justice, Springer International Publishing, Switzerland, 2016), 215–236.

15 Michelle Welsh, "Realising the public potential of corporate law: Twenty years of civil penalty enforcement in Australia" (2014) 42 *Federal Law Review* 217, at 224–225.

16 See, for example, Olivia Dixon and Jennifer G. Hill, "Australia: The protection of investors and the compensation for their losses", in Pierre-Henri Conac and Martin Gelter (eds.), *Global Securities Litigation and Enforcement*, at 1063–1100 (Cambridge University Press, 2019); Jennifer G. Hill, "Images of the shareholder - shareholder power and shareholder powerlessness" (pp. 53–73) in Jennifer G. Hill and Randall S. Thomas (eds.), *Research Handbook on Shareholder Power* (Edward Elgar, 2015); Welsh, n 15; Belinda Gibson and Diane Brown, "ASIC's expectations of directors" (2012) 35 *University of New South Wales Law Journal* 254; Howell E. Jackson and Mark J. Roe, "Public and private enforcement of securi-

the advantages and disadvantages of each of public and private enforcement. They examine the differences between these two enforcement regimes and their salient features for the purposes of understanding the critical importance of private shareholder enforcement by means of the derivative suit.

1.2.1 Advantages and disadvantages of public enforcement

Some scholars have asserted that the public enforcement regime is superior to private enforcement as a means of deterring corporate misconduct, promoting corporate compliance and maintaining investor confidence and market stability.[17] If, for example, a public enforcement agency, such as ASIC or the Commonwealth Director of Public Prosecutions ("DPP"),[18] successfully prosecutes a case involving breaches of directors' duties, that case can potentially serve to deter future misconduct by those directors and by directors in other companies.

Another argument for supporting public enforcement stems from the fact that shareholders are often diverse and scattered in large public companies, and small individual shareholders may not have the incentives to bring a private action,[19] even for their own benefit. In addition to the cost of bringing a private action, individual shareholders may face deterrents, such as lack of access to inside information and free rider problems.[20] In such circumstances, a public enforcement agency plays an extremely valuable role in enforcing directors' duties and promoting public confidence.[21]

Despite these undoubted benefits, a public enforcement regime can also have certain downsides. First, a public enforcement agency may lack an understanding of the particular business, and such an understanding is vital to the effective enforcement of corporate rights and duties. Public enforcement action, such as an investigation by ASIC, where it has reason to suspect a contravention of the directors' duties, might be undertaken with little regard to the interests of the company involved or its shareholders.[22] The mere

ties laws: Resource-based evidence" (2009) 93 *Journal of Financial Economics* 207–238; Matthew Berkahn and Lindsay Trotman, "Public and private enforcement of company law in New Zealand 1986–1990" (2000) 7 *Canterbury Law Review* 516; Ian Ramsay, "Enforcement of corporate rights and duties by shareholders and the Australian Securities Commission: Evidence and analysis" (1995) 23 *Australian Business Law Review* 174.

17 Renee M. Jones and Michelle Welsh, "Toward a public enforcement model for directors' duty of oversight" (2012) 45 *Vanderbilt Journal of Transnational Law* 343; Gibson and Brown, n 16.

18 Jasper Hedges, Helen Bird, George Gilligan, Andrew Godwin and Ian Ramsay, "An Empirical Analysis of Public Enforcement of Directors' Duties in Australia: Preliminary Findings" (Working Paper No. 105/2016, Centre for International Finance and Regulation, Melbourne Law School, March 2016), at 7.

19 Jenifer Varzaly, "The enforcement of directors' duties in Australia: An empirical analysis" (2015) 16 *European Business Organisation Law Review* 281, at 290. See also Welsh, n 15.

20 Berkahn and Trotman, n 16, at 518–519.

21 Jones and Welsh, n 17; Gibson and Brown, n 16; Berkahn and Trotman, n 16, at 518.

22 Berkahn and Trotman, n 16, at 519.

appointment of an inspector by ASIC to carry out the investigations could severely damage the company's prospects and thereby injure its members.[23] A public enforcement agency is typically tasked with inquiry and penalisation, rather than the recovery of the company's losses. It has been argued, for example, that ASIC's main remedial priority is not to obtain compensation for individual shareholders who have suffered loss, but instead to protect the public interest by securing "maximum voluntary compliance".[24]

Second, a public enforcement agency may have limited resources and funding,[25] which restrict its ability to pursue all cases involving breaches of directors' duties. A public enforcement agency such as ASIC tends to concentrate its energy on high-profile cases involving breaches of directors' duties in large public companies.[26] In this way, it is able to send a message to the business community, discouraging and deterring other directors from wrongdoing and promoting greater corporate compliance.[27] Due to resource constraints, a public enforcement agency is less likely to take a keen interest in pursuing litigation involving small privately owned companies.[28]

1.2.2 Advantages and disadvantages of private enforcement

With their limited resources, public agencies such as ASIC and the Commonwealth DPP will therefore be unable to litigate all issues involving alleged breaches of directors' duties, particularly in the context of small privately owned companies (such as those managed by family members and those in quasi-partnership arrangements). In these instances, it is paramount for shareholders to have a clear set of rules to enable them to bring a private action.

Private enforcement by shareholders can provide a number of advantages. First, in small private companies where there is often no significant separation of ownership and control,[29] a shareholder litigant may be in a better position

23 H. H. Mason, "Possible alternatives to an Australian Securities and Exchange Commission: Contingent fees and derivative actions by shareholders" (1976) 50 *Australian Law Journal* 26, at 27–28.

24 Welsh, n 15, at 240.

25 It should be noted that a new Act for an industry funding model has been passed on 15 June 2017, *ASIC Supervisory Cost Recovery Levy Act* 2017 (No.43, 2017), enabling ASIC to call upon a company to pay the costs of ASIC's activities. The effectiveness of this Act remains to be seen.

26 Hill, n 16, at 61–64; Gibson and Brown, n 16; Brian R. Cheffins and Bernard S. Black, "Outside director liability across countries" (2006) 84 *Texas Law Review* 1385, at 1437–1440; Jones and Welsh, n 17.

27 Cheffins and Black, n 26, at 1465. See also Gibson and Brown, n 16.

28 Varzaly, n 19, at 285–286; Ramsay, n 16, at 175 and 180–183 where the author found that in the 3.5-year study, ASIC (equivalent to then ASC) had taken on far more actions to enforce corporate rights and duties than the shareholders had and concluded that "such enforcement is more typically undertaken by a regulatory agency".

29 Robert B. Thompson and Randall S. Thomas, "The public and private faces of derivative lawsuits" (2004) 57 *Vanderbilt Law Review* 1747, at 1755.

than a public enforcement agency to know what would be in the interests of the company. A shareholder litigant will in some circumstances have a superior understanding of the nature of the company's business and might be better able to avoid further damage to the company's goodwill than a public enforcement agency, whose enforcement action might attract unwanted and harmful publicity. Second, private enforcement can be more effective than public enforcement in providing monetary compensation to aggrieved shareholders who have been injured by wrongdoing. Third, it has been argued that shareholders' ability to assert their corporate rights can potentially operate as a useful deterrent and regulatory check on corporate management.[30] Shareholders can, in this way, act as a quasi-regulator.[31] Fourth, private enforcement may be a comparatively inexpensive way of ensuring that directors comply with their duties to the company,[32] compared with the public enforcement regime.

While public enforcement of directors' duties on behalf of a company may be necessary in some instances, particularly in the context of large public companies, it is also important that shareholders in small privately owned companies should be able to enforce their corporate rights. Indeed, this becomes critical in circumstances where a public enforcement agency is not prepared to become involved in an enforcement action.

Nonetheless, just as there are disadvantages and limitations in relation to public enforcement, so too there are hurdles in the operation of the private enforcement regime. The extent of these hurdles can vary depending on the specific type of private enforcement involved. Generally, however, all private enforcement regimes require shareholder litigants to bear their own costs in pursuing a court action, including a derivative action.[33] There are also issues relating to gathering evidence, due to the shareholder's restricted access to company information, if he or she is not also a company director.[34]

The statutory derivative action, which is the focus of this book, has far more hurdles than any other type of private enforcement regimes. The book will examine those hurdles, and how the current private enforcement regime embodied in the statutory derivative suit affects shareholders' enforcement of their rights and access to justice.

It might be argued that in the 21st century, the need for private enforcement to protect shareholder rights has been superseded by the growth of

30 Hill, n 16, at 65–68 where the author refers to the concept of stewardship and the rule relating to shareholders' vote on executive pay as an example of shareholders' private enforcement of corporate rights.

31 Hill, n 16, at 67.

32 Ramsay, n 16, at 178.

33 Chapter 6 in this book will discuss the costs issue relating to statutory derivative action.

34 Applying for inspection of company books and documents as a shareholder is not a smooth process and generally, there is no certainty in the outcome of that application. Shareholders' restricted access to company books and documents will be canvassed further in Chapter 7.

investor activism in many countries, including Australia, as an effective check on managerial power.[35] Shareholder activism comes in a variety of forms. One such example is the adoption of the self-regulatory Stewardship Codes in Australia in 2017.[36] Another example is Australia's distinctive "two-strike rule",[37] providing shareholders with stronger rights in relation to executive remuneration.[38] Investor activism of this kind enables shareholders to assert their corporate rights and power to influence the behaviour of the company's managers.[39] However, as in the case of public enforcement by ASIC, investor activism of this kind will be much more relevant in large public companies than in small private, family-owned or closely held companies.[40]

Private enforcement therefore matters, and one of the claims of this book is that the private enforcement regime in Australia is weak and does not go far enough in providing adequate protection for shareholders, particularly in small private companies.

1.3 Transformation from common law derivative action to statutory derivative action

As already noted, the derivative action constitutes a quintessential form of private enforcement. However, the derivative suit under Australian corporate law underwent a dramatic change in 2000, when a statutory derivative action ("SDA") was introduced in Part 2F.1A of the Australian *Corporations Act* 2001 (C'th) to replace the common law derivative action.

35 Tim Bowley and Jennifer G. Hill, "Stewardship and Collective Action: The Australian Experience" (Working Paper No. 491/2020, ECGI Working Paper Series in Law, European Corporate Governance Institute, January 2020), at 3; Gaia Balp and Giovanni Strampelli, "Institutional investor collective engagements: Non-activist corporation vs activist wolf packs" (2020) 14(2) *Ohio State Business Law Journal* 135; Iris H.-Y. Chiu, *The Foundations and Anatomy of Shareholder Activism* (Hart Publishing, 2010); Jennifer G. Hill, "Subverting shareholder rights: Lessons from News Corp's migration to Delaware" (2010) 63 *Vanderbilt Law Review* 1.

36 Bowley and Hill, n 35c, at 4–9. See also Jennifer G. Hill, "Good Activist/Bad Activist: The Rise of International Stewardship Codes" (Working Paper No. 368/2017, ECGI Working Paper Series in Law, European Corporate Governance Institute, September 2917), at 12.

37 *Corporations Act* 2001 (C'th), ss.250U-250W, as introduced in 2011. The "two-strike rule" is a short form reference to provisions of the *Corporations Act* 2001 (C'th) relating to limiting executive remuneration by way of shareholders passing at least 25% resolution on a no-vote on the remuneration report in two consecutive annual general meetings, and at the end of the second meeting, the company is required to put to the shareholders to vote on whether to hold a further shareholder meeting for the purposes of requiring all company directors to stand for reelection.

38 Hill, n 16, at 19–22.

39 See Dionysia Katelouzou, *The Rhetoric of Activist Shareholder Stewards* (European Corporate Governance Institute – Working Paper No. 636/2022, King's College London Law School Research Paper, March 2022), available at https://papers.ssrn.com/sol3/papers.cfm?abstract_id=4057118 (viewed 12 July 2022)

40 *Corporations Act* 2001 (C'th), ss.250U and 250W concern executive remuneration and apply only in public listed companies.

Prior to its enactment, there was intense debate as to whether Australia should adopt a statutory version of the derivative action.[41] Some scholars welcomed the introduction of the SDA without reservation.[42] Others, however, although agreeing that codification of the derivative suit was a valuable idea in theory, remained sceptical as to whether the Australian SDA would have any positive impact on shareholders' willingness to pursue litigation as an enforcement option.[43]

Nonetheless, it was widely considered that the rules relating to the common law derivative action were too restrictive, too complex and were lacking consistency in application. There were numerous obstacles that a shareholder needed to overcome in order to bring a derivative suit at common law.

Criticisms about the operation of the common law derivative suit at that time may be conveniently grouped into three categories – namely, ratification, standing and costs.[44] These criticisms may be summarised as follows.[45]

First, the mere possibility of ratification by the general meeting was sufficient to prevent a shareholder from bringing a common law derivative action. This radically reduced the circumstances in which a shareholder could bring an action.

Second, only registered shareholders had standing to bring a common law derivative action. Such shareholders would then be required to show that

41 See, for example, John Kluver, "Derivative actions and the rule in *Foss v. Harbottle*: Do we need a statutory remedy?" (1993) 11 *Companies and Securities Law Journal* 7; Stephen Bottomley, "Shareholder derivative actions and public interest suits: Two versions of the same story?" (1992) 15 *University of New South Wales Law Journal* 127; Ian M. Ramsay, "Corporate governance, shareholder litigation and the prospects for a statutory derivative action" (1992) 15 *University of New South Wales Law Journal* 149. See also the list of government law reform reports in the Bibliography; for example, Companies and Securities Advisory Committee, *Statutory Derivative Action* (Report, 1993); Corporate Law Economic Reform Program Proposal Paper No. 3, *Proposals for Reform: Directors' Duties and Corporate Governance* (1997).

42 Lynden Griggs and J.P. Lowry, "Minority shareholder remedies: A comparative view" (1994) *Journal of Business Law* 463, at 474 (saying that "the introduction of the statutory derivative action would greatly enhance the range of remedies available to the minority shareholder"); James McConvill, "Ensuring balance in corporate governance: Parts 2F.1 and 2F.1A of the Corporations Law" (2001) 12 *Australian Journal of Corporate Law* 293, at 296 (saying that the reform was a "vast improvement on the previous position").

43 Keith Fletcher, "CLERP and minority shareholder rights" (2001) 13 *Australian Journal of Corporate Law* 290, at 295 and 300 (saying that Part 2F.1A had "significantly weakened the legal position of minority shareholders" and "shareholders have been short changed by these legislative developments"); Peter Prince, "Australia's statutory derivative action: Using the New Zealand experience" (2000) 18 *Company and Securities Law Journal* 493, at 510–511 (arguing that the Australian SDA is "harder to use than its New Zealand equivalent"; Lang Thai, "How popular are statutory derivative actions in Australia? Comparisons with USA, Canada, and New Zealand" (2002) 30 *Australian Business Law Review*, 118.

44 House of Representatives, *Explanatory Memorandum to the Corporate Law Economic Reform Program Bill* (1998) (C'th) ("*CLERP Bill* 1998"), at para 6.14–6.15.

45 Thai, n 43, at 133–135.

their individual circumstances fell within one of five recognised "situations",[46] entitling them to bring a common law derivative action.[47] Three of these situations related to bringing a common law derivative action were about "fraud on the minority", "special majority" vote[48] and "interests of justice".[49] These exceptions were unworkable in most cases because directors could easily ratify their breaches at a general meeting, and as noted, such ratification would prevent a shareholder from taking any action.

Third, the lack of financial support from the company and the potential for free riding by other members provided strong disincentives for a shareholder to bring a derivative action. No automatic right existed for a shareholder litigant to recover costs from the company. A shareholder would need to apply to the court to require the company to fund the action and such approval would only be given in extreme circumstances, if, for example, the shareholder were destitute or "financially handicapped".[50]

It was clear that different branches of the Australian government considered that the introduction of an SDA to replace the common law derivative suit would serve two valuable purposes.[51] The first of these was providing shareholders with an "effective remedy", given the view that the common law approach was "inadequate" and "deficient". The intention was to replace the common law derivative suit with a simplified statutory version to give a shareholder greater opportunity to sue a wrongdoer and recover property belonging to the company. The second purpose was to promote directors' accountability and improve corporate governance, by requiring wrongdoers to compensate the company appropriately and bringing about deterrence of managerial misconduct.

An interesting aspect of the SDA is its relationship with Australia's business judgment rule ("BJR"). In 2000, when the Australian government passed legislation to introduce the SDA,[52] it simultaneously enacted a statu-

46 As described in Wedderburn, n 4.

47 *Edwards v. Halliwell* [1950] 2 All ER 1064.

48 There were some doubts as to whether the special majority exception could be truly an exception for a common law derivative action, as this would depend on other circumstantial facts.

49 Chapter 2 in this book will explain these situations. There were two other recognised situations, namely relating to an "infringement of personal rights" and the application of the "ultra vires" principle, but these were for bringing personal or oppression actions.

50 *Farrow v. Registrar of Building Societies* [1991] 2 VR 589.

51 House of Representatives, *Explanatory Memorandum to the CLERP Bill* 1998, at [20–21]. See also Companies and Securities Law Review Committee ("CSLRC"), *Enforcement of the Duties of Directors and Officers of a Company by means of a Statutory Derivative Action* (Report No. 12, Nov 1990); at [6]; Companies and Securities Advisory Committee ("CSAC"), *Statutory Derivative Action* (Report, 1993), at page 4; Corporate Law Economic Reform Program Proposal ("CLERP Proposal") Paper No. 3, *Proposals for Reform: Directors' Duties and Corporate Governance* (1997), at pages 30, 32–33.

52 *Corporate Law Economic Reform Program Act* 1999 (C'th) ("*CLERP Act* 1999"), as now contained in Part 2F.1A of the *Corporations Act* 2001 (C'th).

tory BJR.[53] The plan was to provide a balance between, on the one hand, allowing shareholders to assert their corporate rights through bringing an SDA, and on the other hand, providing directors with the freedom to make business judgments without fear of being sued by shareholders; thus, the operation of the BJR may have an indirect effect in minimising vexatious or frivolous suits.[54] However, it is arguable that the balance sought has not been achieved. While directors receive protection as a result of the statutory BJR, the SDA has not become the effective "self-help measure" that it was intended to be,[55] due to the presence of a series of demanding hurdles, see below, that a shareholder applicant is required to satisfy the court for permission to be granted to bring an SDA.[56] In addition, there remains considerable uncertainty in relation to recovery of costs[57] and free riding problems.

Although the transformation of the common law derivative action into a statutory framework represented a promising policy reform to enhance managerial accountability, this book suggests that ultimately its effectiveness has been undermined. As will be argued in later chapters, the SDA merely constitutes a reformulation of the common law position with no major improvements to enhance Australia's private enforcement regime.

1.4 Aims of the book and research questions

The introduction of the SDA potentially represented a major development in Australian corporate law by establishing a basic legal framework for proceedings to be brought to remedy harm done to a company. However, twenty years on, it is questionable whether the SDA has achieved its intended purposes.

This book aims to investigate the effectiveness of the SDA and assess whether there has been a significant improvement from the previous common law position. As noted at the onset, the book's main objective is to analyse whether the SDA is in need of reform in Australia, and if so, why and how.

The related research questions to be answered in this book are:

(1) Has the SDA been effective as a shareholder remedy and as a tool for deterring corporate wrongdoings, with a view to bringing about enhancement of directors' accountability and corporate governance as intended by the legislation?

53 *Corporations Act* 2001 (C'th), s.180(2) and the presumption referred to in s.237(3) relating to an application for a statutory derivative action to be brought against a third party.

54 House of Representatives, *Explanatory Memorandum to the CLERP Bill* 1998 (C'th), at [6.32–6.33, 6.16, 6.41, 2.4–2.5, 6.4 and 6.9].

55 House of Representatives, *Explanatory Memorandum to the CLERP Bill* 1998 (C'th), at [6.33].

56 *Corporations Act* 2001 (C'th), s.237(2). This provision, and other provisions in Part 2F.1A are reproduced in Appendix A.

57 *Corporations Act* 2001 (C'th), s.242 provides the court with complete discretion in deciding on the costs question.

(2) Which of the SDA provisions might benefit from reform to achieve the intended purposes?

The argument advanced in this book will be twofold. First, the leave criteria under s.237(2) are too onerous for an applicant to satisfy, particularly in relation to two particular aspects of the leave requirement – (i) the "good faith" element; and (ii) the need to demonstrate that the proposed derivative action "is in the best interests of the company".[58] Second, the costs provision in s.242 is too uncertain, as there is no guarantee that a successful applicant will be able to recover the costs of bringing the approved action.

1.4.1 The leave requirement

As will be argued in this book through empirical research and case analysis, applicants generally have difficulties establishing the "good faith" and "in the best interests of the company" requirements. There is no clear or practical way of understanding and appreciating the scope of these requirements. Nowhere in the Act are these terms defined, and given their subjective nature, these terms are almost impossible to describe with precision.

In the current state of the law, there are a large number of judicial decisions on the interpretation of "good faith" and "best interests". In relation to "good faith" under s.237(2)(b), the court is required to consider: (a) whether the applicant honestly believes that a good cause of action exists and has a reasonable prospect of success; and (b) the applicant must not have an ulterior motive for bringing the derivative action that would amount to an abuse of process.[59] It is worth noting that not all jurisdictions have the "good faith" requirement in their legislation. It is absent, for example, in analogous legislation in New Zealand and Hong Kong.

While this test of "good faith" has been applied with some inconsistency, the most difficult part for an applicant to satisfy the court relates more to the need to demonstrate under s.237(2)(c) that the proposed derivative action "is in the best interests of the company" – a test that is almost impossible to fulfil. One cannot possibly predict what the outcome of a court case will be. In reference to "best interests", it is the financial state of the company and its welfare that the courts are concerned with.[60] For example, where a company is still operating and is still financially sound, the best interests of the company would be the best interests of all shareholders as a whole.[61] Where the company becomes insolvent, its best interests may turn to reflect its creditors.[62] It

58 Paragraphs (a), (d) and (e) of s. 237(2) do not seem to have any major issue in court.

59 *Swansson v. RA Pratt Properties Pty Ltd* (2002) 42 ACSR 313, [2002] NSWSC 583, at [36].

60 *Charlton v. Baber* (2003) 47 ACSR 31; [2003] NSWSC 745.

61 *Goozee v. Graphic World Group Holdings Pty Ltd* (2002) 42 ACSR 534; [2002] NSWSC 640, at [73].

62 *Charlton v. Baber* (2003) 47 ACSR 31; [2003] NSWSC 745, at [53].

is worth noting that Australia has a much higher standard of proof than the Canadian, New Zealand and Singapore counterparts, which only require that the proposed action "appears" to be "in the interests of" the company.

In circumventing these issues, the courts have adopted a general approach that if an applicant undertakes to pay for the proposed action, this could be an indication that the applicant has satisfied both the "good faith" and "in the best interests of the company" requirements.[63] If a company is not required to pay for the action, and if there is nothing for the company to lose regardless of the outcome of the derivative action, this could be a strong indication that the proposed action "is in the best interests of the company".[64] In some cases, even where the applicant has successfully demonstrated good faith and the proposed action appears to be in the best interests of the company, the applicant is still required to bear the costs of the derivative action; that is, the court would not allow the company to finance the derivative action. In *Li v. Dao*, for example, Connock J confirms the general position that an applicant undertaking to bear the costs of the proposed action is a "consideration *material* to the satisfaction of the good faith and best interests of the company requirements".[65] Regrettably, not all shareholder applicants can afford to pay for the action. In *Cooper v. Myrtace Consulting Pty Ltd*, there was no issue with the applicant's good faith,[66] except that the applicant was unable to offer adequate indemnity and this was noted by the court as posing "a significant difficulty", which led the court to decide against the grant of leave.[67] The judicial approach in this case and in many other cases appears to be harsh, all because of the strict leave criteria in s.237(2).

1.4.2 The costs issue

The other difficulty relates to the uncertainty in the recovery of the applicant's costs. Under s.242, the court has complete discretion in deciding when, how and against whom costs are to be awarded. There is no clarity as to whether and to what extent an applicant can recover their costs in bringing the proposed action. There are two types of costs: costs associated with the leave application and costs of bringing the substantive derivative proceedings. In nearly all leave applications, the courts have reserved their power until the conclusion of the substantive derivative action to decide who pays for the

63 *Robash Pty Ltd v. Gladstone Pacific Nickel Pty Ltd* [2011] NSWSC 1235, at [58]; *Zhu v. Orico Australia Pty Ltd* [2019] VSC 313.

64 *Zhu v. Orico Australia Pty Ltd* [2019] VSC 313; *Connective Services Pty Ltd v. Slea Pty Ltd* [2018] VSCA 229; *Fiduciary Ltd v. Morningstar Research Pty Ltd* (2005) 53 ACSR 732; [2005] NSWSC 442.

65 *Li v. Dao* [2018] VSC 530, at [183] (Connock J) (emphasis added).

66 *Cooper v. Myrtace Consulting Pty Ltd* [2014] FCA 480, at [18] (Davies J).

67 *Cooper v. Myrtace Consulting Pty Ltd* [2014] FCA 480, at [32] (Davies J). See also, *Re Fishinthenet Investments Pty Ltd and Coastal Waters Seafood Pty Ltd* [2014] NSWSC 260.

derivative action and the leave application, which means in the interim, a successful applicant may have to bear the costs of bringing the approved action.[68] There is no certainty that any of these costs are recoverable.

Generally, applicants have been unsuccessful in getting their costs reimbursed, irrespective of the outcome of the leave application. There have been only three cases over the past twenty years where the successful applicant has taken the approved SDA all the way to final judgment, and none of these applicants was successful in obtaining an indemnity, regardless of the outcome.[69] This low number is a serious cause for concern. The uncertainty in the recovery of costs and the issue relating to free riding are arguably the main obstacles to shareholder litigation in derivative action, as will be discussed further in Chapter 6.

1.4.3 The entanglement between the leave requirement and costs

It is not surprising that there is a considerable overlap between the leave criteria in paragraphs (b) and (c) in s.237(2) and the costs provision in s.242; and because of this entanglement, the courts' reasoning process appears to have been circular, resulting in inconsistent and conflicting outcomes. Shareholders who are financially constrained are less likely to consider applying for leave, and even if they have successfully applied for leave, it does not necessarily mean that they will commence a derivative action.[70] This is because there is no certainty that they can obtain leave and no certainty that their legal fees and court costs are recoverable – arguably, these have been the main drawback for some shareholders seeking leave to bring an SDA. A further related problem is that there is no provision dealing with the free riding issue, which means that if there is a successful outcome in the derivative action, any compensation awarded by the court will go to the company, with the successful shareholder applicant receiving only a *pro rata* benefit.

As noted above, the first argument advanced in this book is that the SDA provisions and the courts' interpretations have not greatly improved the shareholders' position. The other argument advanced in this book is that the

68 *Cf. Wood v. Links Golf Tasmania Pty Ltd* [2010] FCA 570, which is the only case in Australia where the court ordered the company to fund the SDA.

69 In *Maher v. Honeysett and Maher Electrical Contractors Pty Ltd* [2009] NSWSC 445, the applicant was successful in the final judgment in the SDA, but only a modest amount in compensation was awarded in favour of the company, which led the court to make an order requiring the defendant to pay only half of the applicant's costs, with the overall effect that the company had lost nothing. Comparing with *Reale v. Duncan* [2006] NSWSC 227 *Duncan Reale v. Cameda Investments* [2006] NSWSC 1099, the applicant who was successful in the leave application ultimately lost in the substantive derivative action, and on the costs issue, the court would not allow the company to pay for any of the action, and thus both the applicant and the defendant bore their own legal fees.

70 There is no compulsion for a successful applicant to bring a derivative action when the court has granted leave.

SDA is in need of reform, and in making this argument, this book will attempt to offer some suggestions for reform in the hope that these will be taken into consideration in future law reform.

1.4.4 Statutory derivative action and corporate governance

One of the goals of the SDA was to promote directors' accountability and improve corporate governance.[71] It is worth noting that whether SDA is a valuable tool for achieving this goal is partly dependent on the outcome of the SDA, that is, whether the shareholder compensation purpose has been fulfilled, and partly dependent on the directors' responsiveness. A successful outcome in the form of a large compensation awarded in favour of a company may have some effect in deterring breaches of directors' duties and other corporate misconduct; it could over time improve corporate compliance and bring about enhanced corporate governance. Some certainty in the applicant's recovery of costs could facilitate this process.

However, it is worth noting too that there is no guarantee that a large compensation ordered against a director for breach of directors' duties will bring about future corporate compliance in all cases. A successful outcome with a large compensation ordered against directors may have some deterrent effect but not all directors will care about having to pay compensation (for example, very wealthy directors). To truly foster good corporate governance, both public and private enforcement regimes are necessary. SDA, as a private enforcement tool, if amended appropriately to allow greater protection to shareholders, can complement the work of public enforcement agencies to achieve the desired corporate governance outcome.

1.5 Importance of this research

This research is important for a number of reasons. First, it adds significant depth to our understanding of how the statutory derivative action has been operating in Australia since coming into effect in 2000. Literature on the Australian SDA remains scarce.[72] No amendment has taken place since the

71 House of Representatives, *Explanatory Memorandum to the CLERP Bill* 1998, at pp. 20–21. See also CSLRC, *Enforcement of the Duties of Directors and Officers of a Company by means of a Statutory Derivative Action* (Report No. 12, Nov 1990); at [6]; CSAC, *Statutory Derivative Action* (Report, 1993), at page 4; CLERP Proposal Paper No. 3, *Proposals for Reform: Directors' Duties and Corporate Governance* (1997), at pages 30, 32–33.

72 Peter Prince, "Australia's statutory derivative action: Using the New Zealand experience" (2000) 18 *Company and Securities Law Journal* 493; Keith Fletcher, "CLERP and minority shareholder rights" (2001) 13 *Australian Journal of Corporate Law* 290; Lang Thai, "How popular are statutory derivative actions in Australia? Comparisons with USA, Canada, and New Zealand", (2002) 30 *Australian Business Law Review* 118; Lynden Griggs, "The statutory derivative action: Lessons that may be learnt from its past" (2002) 6 *University of Western Sydney Law Review* 64; James McConvill, "Part 2F.1A of the Corporations Act: Insert a new

enactment of the statutory procedure, but this is not to say that amendment is unnecessary. This research provides a comprehensive and detailed study of the operation of the SDA in Australia since its codification. It presents arguments based on the empirical research into the entire twenty-year period of the SDA's operation, together with detailed case law analysis and on comparative analysis with other countries. This research will be the first of its kind in Australia as no other scholars in Australia have attempted a similar approach on SDA in such depth and detail (i.e., empirical, case law and comparisons with other jurisdictions).[73] It will also attempt to provide suggestions for law reform in order to provide shareholders with better access to justice.

Those few scholars who have published in this area have generally been negative about the current operation of the SDA. For example, Egert et al. note that there are "still issues relating to the application of Part 2F.1A that require resolution" and discuss the courts' conflicting views on the application of Part 2F.1A to company liquidation as one example.[74] Monichino, a legal practitioner, refers to the costs provision in s.242 and the leave requirement in s.237(2) as an entanglement.[75] Duffy refers to the uncertainty in the recovery of costs as a dilemma affecting the use of the SDA.[76] Thus, the detailed and comprehensive research contained in this book will make a significant contribution to knowledge in the area of SDA.

The research in this book is also important for law reform. It provides a foundation for encouraging and inspiring lawmakers in Australia to consider reforming the SDA. Furthermore, while many countries, such as New Zealand, Singapore, the United Kingdom, Hong Kong, Malaysia, Israel, Taiwan, Vietnam, China and South Africa,[77] have already adopted local vari-

---

s.242(2) or give it the boot?" (2002) 30 *Australian Business Law Review* 309; Michael Duffy, "Procedural dilemmas for contemporary shareholder remedies – Derivative action or class action" (2004) 22 *Company and Securities Law Journal* 46; Ian M. Ramsay and Benjamin Saunders, "Litigation by shareholders and directors: An empirical study of the Australian statutory derivative action" (2006) 6 *Journal of Corporate Law Studies* 397; Matthew Broderick, "Statutory derivative actions in company liquidations" (2008) 16 *Insolvency Law Journal* 7; Geoffrey Egert, Colin Anderson and Scott Kiel-Chisholm, "The application of the statutory derivative action in Pt 2F.1A of the Corporations Act to companies in liquidation under Ch 5: Well-oiled machine or is Pt 2F.1A in need of a tune up?" (2011) 25 *Australian Journal of Corporate Law* 318; Lang Thai, "Calling for reform to the statutory derivative action in Australia: Critical analysis and suggestions for reform" (2013) 21 *Insolvency Law Journal* 242; Albert Monichino, "Costs in statutory derivative actions: The lingering ghost of Wallersteiner" (2015) 33 *Company and Securities Law Journal* 104, at 127.

73 An earlier study by Ramsay and Saunders, n 6, was limited to the first six years of the SDA's operation. Their work will be referred to in Chapter 3 of this book.

74 Egert, Anderson and Kiel-Chisholm, n 72, at 318. See also Broderick, n 72.

75 Monichino, n 72, at 115.

76 Duffy, n 72, at 67–68.

77 For other countries in Europe with SDA, see Martin Gelter, "Why do shareholder derivative suits remain rare in Continental Europe?" (2012) 37 *Brooklyn Journal of International Law* 843. For countries with SDA in South America, see Mathias Siems, "Private enforcement of

ants of the SDA, there are still a number of countries that consider adopting the statutory model. It is therefore clear that the SDA is here to stay. This detailed research of the SDA will be of interest not only to lawmakers in countries that are planning to adopt the SDA but also to those other countries wishing to gain an insight into the operation of the Australian counterpart for the purposes of reforming their existing model. As will be discussed in detail in later chapters, Australia has the most demanding SDA procedure, making it extremely difficult for shareholders to obtain leave to bring an SDA. Thus, this research informs the world about the uniqueness of the Australian SDA, and what other countries can learn from it.

The SDA is the only type of private enforcement that enables a shareholder to bring an action on behalf of the company to remedy a wrong done to it. It is the only means by which a shareholder or a minority director can enforce corporate rights on behalf of the company, even where it means that shareholders will only be entitled to a *pro rata* benefit of the total recovery. This research is important in providing empirically based reform proposals, which could result in bringing about managerial accountability and good corporate compliance.

1.6 Method, approach, scope and limitations

This book is focused on law reform. As noted above, the aim is to assess how effective the SDA has been as shareholder protection in the past two decades and to assess areas that might benefit from reform. The book will answer the two research questions identified above.

This book comprises a combination of literature review (including review of law reform reports), empirical study, case law analysis and jurisdictional comparisons to investigate whether there is a need for reform to the SDA in Australia. The book seeks to answer *why* and *how*, first, by using the empirical study approach to identify areas that the applicants have most difficulty with when applying for leave to bring an SDA and to assess the outcomes of the costs provision, whether the applicants have been able to recover their costs under s.242. The book will then progress to analysing cases as to why reform is necessary in certain areas, supported by the findings in the empirical study. The empirical study has identified "good faith" in s.237(2)(b), "in the best interests of the company" in s.237(2)(c) and uncertainty in the recovery of costs in s.242 as the key areas that require special consideration, and further case law analysis appears in subsequent chapters. For each area, suggestions for law reform will also be given.

There will be some comparison with other jurisdictions (Canada, New Zealand, Singapore, US, United Kingdom and Hong Kong) wherever possible

directors' duties: Derivative actions as a global phenomenon" in Stefan Wrbka, Steven van Uytsel and Mathias Siems (eds.), *Collective Actions: Enhancing Access to Justice and Reconciling Multilayer Interests?* (Cambridge University Press, 2015), at 106–110.

for the purposes of making suggestions for law reform. These countries are chosen because they have a more lenient approach to SDA than Australia. For example, in Canada, New Zealand, Singapore and Hong Kong, the criteria for leave are less strict. In Canada, New Zealand and the United Kingdom, to an extent, it is possible for a successful applicant to get some of their costs recovered. In the US, the derivative plaintiff can recover their costs through the common fund and lodestar approach and based on a contingency fees arrangement.

This book is predominantly about SDA, with a brief discussion of other types of shareholder remedies in Chapter 7. The main focus will be on the uncertainty in obtaining leave of the court under s.237(2), in particular, the "good faith" and "in the best interests of the company" requirements, and in the costs provision in s.242, also expressed in uncertain terms. These areas, as identified in the empirical research to be most problematic, will be considered extensively with the aim of suggesting amendment to s.237(2)(b) and (c) and s.242. The view is that amendment in these three areas, *as a minimum*, would significantly improve the utility of the SDA as shareholder remedy and as protection for shareholders.

Other SDA provisions will be referred to in passing only, for example, standing of applicant in s.236, effect of shareholder ratification under s.239 and leave to discontinue compromise or settle approved proceedings under s.240. The author is not of the view that an expansion of the standing provision in s.236 (for example, including employees as an eligible applicant) would have any significant improvement to the operation of the SDA. It is submitted that an ordinary employee, who is not a shareholder and unrelated to other shareholders in the company and has no financial interest in the success of the SDA, is unlikely to have a keen interest in pursuing a derivative action for other people.

Under s.239, shareholder ratification or approval of any improper conduct is no longer a bar to a minority shareholder seeking leave to bring an SDA, which is a big improvement from the common law position. Reported decisions on s.240 are extremely limited, with one possible explanation being that many of the successful leave applicants did not go on to commence the approved derivative action.

Other areas not covered or receiving only minimal discussion in this book are these. The law relating to directors' duties will receive some consideration only where there is overlap with the SDA; discussion of the law relating to insolvency will be confined to illustrating the uncertainty in the application of Part 2F.1A to company liquidation. This chapter has covered extensively the differences between public and private enforcements and their respective advantages and disadvantages, and for this reason, there will be no further coverage on these in the remainder of the book.[78]

78 The dichotomy between public and private enforcements has received extensive coverage in recent years, as noted earlier in this chapter.

This book is approached from the perspective of empirical research and case law analysis. No attempt will be made to discuss the social and economic utility of the SDA or the history and political aspects of SDA other than those already covered in this chapter; also, as other scholars have covered these areas. For example, a book edited by Puchniak, Baum and Ewing-Chow focuses on the social and economic challenges in the SDA and its functionality, advantages and disadvantages in the Asian context.[79] Reisberg in his book discusses the history, jurisprudence, theoretical and political aspects of the SDA, at the time when the United Kingdom was introducing its SDA.[80] Similarly, Zouridakis's book focuses on the history, role and functionality in formulating his argument as to why Greece is in need of the SDA, using the United Kingdom and German models as a discussion point.[81] Lin in his book focuses on how the SDA model in China could be improved by considering implantation of models from the western countries, with some discussion of the political restrictions in China.[82] Safari in her thesis focuses on the inclusion of corporate social responsibility by suggesting employees and other stakeholders should have a right to bring an SDA in the United Kingdom.[83]

Because "good faith" and "in the best interests of the company" are simple expressions that appear in the context of directors' duties, some scholars may feel they have other ideas on the topic of this book. Some scholars may think that the law does not need changing because these expressions have a long history and are clear enough to represent the law as they are. The author will attempt to explain why and how the law in SDA needs some refinement. It is not the plan to suggest a significant shift from the current model but to suggest a few minimal but significant changes for the purposes of providing shareholders with better protection in the company.

1.7 Structure of the book

This book presents as follows, with eight chapters.

This chapter, which is **Chapter 1**, has explained the objectives and aims of the book, including providing backgrounds to SDA as a private enforcement regime, setting out the research questions, the importance of this research and its scope and limitations.

79 Dan Puchniak, Harald Baum and Michael Ewing-Chow (eds.), *The Derivative Action in Asia: A Comparative and Functional Approach* (Cambridge University Press, 2012).

80 Arad Reisberg, *Derivative Actions and Corporate Governance* (Oxford University Press, 2007).

81 Georgios Zouridakis, *Shareholder Protection Reconsidered: Derivative Action in the UK, Germany and Greece* (Routledge, 2021).

82 Shaowei Lin, *Derivative Actions in Chinese Company Law* (Kluwer Law International, The Netherlands, 2015).

83 Neshat Safari, *Reconsidering the role of the derivative claim in the United Kingdom: A comparative study with the United States and New Zealand* (PhD thesis, School of Law, City University of London, May 2018).

Chapter 2 discusses the need for the SDA and its current defects. The chapter reviews the historical development of the common law derivative action and the reasons for its abolition, including the debate on why the common law position was perceived as inadequate and deficient and why the statutory framework was considered necessary to overcome these problems and provide shareholders with better protection in the company. The objective is to explain the government's intention for introducing the SDA, namely, to provide shareholders with "an effective remedy" and to bring about directors' accountability by deterring improper conduct. The important purpose of this chapter is to point out areas in which Part 2F.1A has eliminated the common law problems, areas that have not been addressed properly that need further attention and areas that have not been addressed at all that also need attention.

Chapter 3 focuses on the empirical study of the SDA in Australia. The chapter describes the empirical research methodology and reports on the outcomes of that study, covering the period from 13 March 2000 to 28 December 2019 with a total of 449 reported judgments collected, narrowing down to 168 *relevant* leave application cases. The purpose of the empirical study is to assess the utility of the SDA and its patterns of use. The two broad purposes of this chapter are these. First, it sets out to identify which of the criteria in s.237(2) that the applicants found most difficult in satisfying the court in their leave applications, and the number of applicants that have been successful in obtaining leave to bring an SDA. Second, the chapter assesses the number of successful cases for a costs indemnity order, whether the successful applicant has also been able to obtain a costs indemnity order for the leave application and whether the company has been required to fund the applicant's costs of bringing the approved derivative action.

The empirical study shows that the applicants have most difficulty in establishing the "good faith" and "in the best interests of the company" requirements. It was unexpected to discover that the number of costs orders made in favour of the successful applicants has been extremely low. These areas form the subject of further analysis in Chapters 4, 5 and 6.

Chapter 4 provides a critical analysis of the "good faith" requirement in s.237(2)(b). In particular, the chapter considers the relevance of "good faith" and queries whether "good faith" is necessary as a prerequisite for an SDA. In suggesting the removal of "good faith" from the legislation, the chapter argues that the term is unclear and has no precise definition due to its subjective nature, and consequently, judicial approaches to "good faith" have been inconsistent, and other prerequisites for leave are already adequate. In further support for the removal, the chapter also considers other jurisdictions and notes that New Zealand and Hong Kong have chosen not to include "good faith" as an express requirement in their SDAs and both appear to be functioning well without any issue of abuse to the SDA procedure. The United Kingdom has "good faith" only as a discretionary factor for the court to take into account. Singapore and

Canada have "good faith" as a requirement in their legislation, but while the courts in Canada have taken a more lenient approach, the Singapore Court of Appeal has recently overturned its original approach.

Chapter 5 focuses on the requirement that the applicant must demonstrate to the court that the proposed derivative action "is in the best interests of the company" under s.237(2)(c). Empirical evidence shows that this requirement is most difficult to satisfy. The purpose of this chapter is to explain why s.237(2)(c) is most difficult for an applicant to fulfil, and needs amendment, by putting forward an argument based on qualitative assessment of court cases. It discusses the inconsistencies in the courts' treatment of s.237(2)(c) and the practical problems surrounding the costs/benefits approach, including the uncertainty in the application of s.237(2)(c) to company liquidation. The requirement of an applicant undertaking to pay for the proposed derivative action and to indemnify the company against any adverse costs order as a way of showing the proposed action "is in the best interests of the company" is a serious cause for concern. The idea is that if the company is not required to pay for the action and will not lose anything in the end, then the action will be in the company's best interests. This chapter argues that the costs/benefits approach is flawed in that not all shareholder applicants can financially afford to litigate and the requirement in s.237(2)(c) makes no cross-reference to the costs provision in s.242. In making suggestions for reform, the chapter also considers the legislative provisions and case law from other jurisdictions (Canada, British Columbia and Singapore) and points out that these countries and British Columbia have a far more lenient approach and they all have fewer leave criteria than Australia. The chapter provides some suggestions for amending the provision, in particular by removing the words "is" and "best" and substituting the expression, "appears to be in the interests of the company".

Chapter 6 focuses on the costs provision in s.242. The purpose of this chapter is to explain why the provision in s.242 is overly broad and uncertain and to provide some suggestions for amendment. The chapter sets out to argue that the uncertainty in the recovery of costs by applicants is possibly a major factor for the lack of use of the SDA as a shareholder remedy, contributing to its ineffectiveness as a tool for deterrence of corporate wrongdoings and enhancement of directors' accountability. The chapter draws on the outcomes of the empirical study and discusses the uncertainty in the recovery of costs and how the overlap of s.242 with the "best interests of the company" requirement in s.237(2)(c) is a serious issue. While the chapter highlights some circumstances where it may be appropriate for the applicant to bear the costs of the derivative action, the chapter sets out reasons why, under some other circumstances, the company should pay for the applicants' costs. The chapter also explains the overseas approaches in support of the company funding the derivative actions in some limited circumstances, such as in New Zealand and the United Kingdom to some extent. The chapter considers various other funding models as a possibility, and concludes that the United

States common fund approach and the substantial benefits test coupled with the lodestar method may be appropriate for Australia in resolving the costs issue.

Chapter 7 discusses other key factors that might have affected the use of the SDA, namely, uncertainty in obtaining an order for inspection of company books, availability of oppression/unfair prejudice action and availability of funded class action. The objective of this chapter is to argue that, because of the strict leave requirement in s.237(2), coupled with the uncertainty in the recovery of costs under s.242, and with the difficulty in obtaining an order for inspection of company books and other documents, it is not uncommon for shareholders to rely on an oppression action or a class action as an alternative.

Chapter 8 summarises the book's main empirical findings and the key research arguments, showing how they answer the research questions. The main argument is that in order to provide shareholders with a more effective remedy and better protection against corporate wrongdoings, it is necessary to amend the SDA provisions and adopt a more liberal approach. The book concludes with a summary of suggestions for minor and yet significant amendments to the current SDA. The purpose of this monograph is to inform the world about the uniqueness of the Australian SDA and how other countries can learn from it. The chapter provides some suggestions for future research.

2 The need for statutory derivative action and its current problems

2.1 Introduction

Debate about the need for a statutory derivative action ("SDA") went on for at least ten years in Australia before it came into operation on 13 March 2000. The SDA in Australia was adapted from the Canadian model, and in turn, some countries around the world followed suit, with their local variants. There are still countries that do not have a statutory derivative action, such as Greece, Brazil and Cyprus. For this reason, this book will be of interest to countries that are considering introducing the statutory framework and countries that are considering amending their existing SDA model.

One of the reasons for introducing the SDA in Australia was that the common law derivative action was "inadequate".[1] The other reason for the introduction of the SDA was that the other existing statutory remedies, such as an oppression action and an injunction order, were considered to be equally "inadequate and inappropriate" as a shareholder remedy.[2] It was reported that Australia should have an SDA to rectify these inadequacies. The SDA would provide shareholders with an "effective remedy".[3] The SDA could be a valuable tool for promoting directors' accountability and maintaining good corporate governance by deterring directors from engaging in improper or wrongful conduct in the first place.[4]

The idea was to abolish the common law derivative action and replace it with the statutory provisions. It was anticipated that the statutory model would be a simpler and more efficient way for an individual member of the company to bring an action on behalf of the company where a wrong has

1 Companies and Securities Law Review Committee ("CSLRC"), *Enforcement of the Duties of Directors and Officers of a Company byMeans of a Statutory Derivative Action* (Report No. 12, Nov 1990); at 6.

2 Corporate Law Economic Reform Program Proposal Paper No. 3 ("CLERP Proposal No. 3"), *Proposals for Reform: Directors' Duties and Corporate Governance* (1997), at 30.

3 House of Representatives, *Explanatory Memorandum to the CLERP Bill* 1998 (*"CLERP Bill* 1998"), at 21.

4 Companies and Securities Advisory Committee ("CASAC"), *Statutory Derivative Action* (Report, 1993), at 4; CLERP Proposal Paper No. 3, *Proposals for Reform: Directors' Duties and Corporate Governance* (1997), at 32–33.

DOI: 10.4324/9781003430063-2

been done to the company and where the company is unwilling or unable to do so.

The establishment of the SDA constituted a major development in Australian corporate law. It has been a positive move towards providing shareholders with better protection and better remedy. However, further simplification may be necessary. The SDA, in its current form, has not gone far enough to protect shareholders against breach of directors' duties and abuse of power.

The argument advanced in this chapter is that the current SDA process is still in need of further simplification from the common law position in order to provide shareholders with better protection against managerial misconduct. Some problems previously faced by shareholder plaintiffs under the old common law system have been rectified, while other problems have been brought across in a different form. The statutory provisions have not addressed all the problems seen at common law. There is still much uncertainty in obtaining court permission for the bringing of an SDA; and added to the list is the uncertainty in the recovery of litigation costs – these have not been addressed satisfactorily under Part 2F.1A of the *Corporations Act* 2001 (C'th). It is also debatable whether the SDA, in its current form, is an effective tool for enhancing corporate governance, that is, whether it can be used for ensuring directors and managers are held accountable for their actions.

The purpose of this chapter is to critically compare and examine the old and the current statutory models and explain why the current model has not eliminated the problems previously seen at common law, and how the current model has created other and further problems. This chapter explains in detail the transformation from the common law derivative action to the statutory framework, and provides a setting for further analysis in later chapters as to why the SDA, in its current form, is not working in the way it was originally intended by the legislature, and why there is a need for further legislative reform. This chapter is therefore structured as follows. Part 2 discusses the role of the SDA, including its importance and purposes. Part 3 discusses the historical development of the SDA, focusing on issues surrounding the government's perception that ultimately brought about the abolition of the common law derivative action. Part 4 highlights problem areas that have not been addressed properly in the SDA and provides some comments that will lead to further discussion in later chapters to explore ways of improving the utility of the statutory model. This part will also consider the conceptual difficulty in the distinction between a corporate wrong that leads to a derivative action and a personal wrong that gives rise to only a personal action. Part 5 is the conclusion.

2.2 Statutory derivative action as a shareholder remedy

2.2.1 Overview and justification

Part 2F.1A (ss.236-242) of the *Corporations Act* 2001 (Cth) provides the process for bringing an SDA. For ease of reference, these provisions are reproduced in Appendix A.

There was a consensus from different branches of the Australian government that Australia should have an SDA to rectify the inadequacies in the common law derivative action. The first report was released in 1989,[5] followed by the 1990 discussion paper,[6] which suggested the court be given the statutory power to decide on the grant of leave to bring a derivative action.[7] The 1990 report included draft provisions adopted from the Canadian model,[8] which formed the basis for further discussions in subsequent reports.[9] In the lead up to the introduction, it was perceived that the SDA would provide shareholders with "a more effective avenue for enforcement" than the common law derivative action, and that the statutory model "would make a derivative action more feasible and practical than under the common law".[10]

The justifications for recommending the SDA were that:

(i) the common law derivative action was "inadequate";[11]
(ii) the existing statutory remedies were also "inadequate and inappropriate";[12]
(iii) the SDA would provide shareholders with an "effective remedy";[13] and

5 Senate Standing Committee on Legal and Constitutional Affairs ("SSC on LCA"), *Company Directors' Duties: Report on the Social and Fiduciary Duties and Obligations of Company Directors* (Discussion Paper, 1989).

6 CSLRC, *Enforcement of the Duties of Directors and Officers of a Company by means of a Statutory Derivative Action* (Discussion Paper No 11, 1990).

7 CSLRC, *Enforcement of the Duties of Directors and Officers of a Company by Means of a Statutory Derivative Action* (Report No. 12, Nov 1990); at 65.

8 Canada was the first country that pioneered the statutory derivative action in 1971, followed by New Zealand and Singapore in 1993, then by Australia in 2000. For ease of comparison, the New Zealand provisions are reproduced in Appendix B, Singapore in Appendix C, Canada in Appendix D and Australia in Appendix A.

9 CSLRC, *Enforcement of the Duties of Directors and Officers of a Company by Means of a Statutory Derivative Action* (Report No. 12, Nov 1990); House of Representatives Standing Committee on LCA, *Corporate Practices and the Rights of Shareholders* (Discussion Paper, 1991); House of Representatives Standing Committee on LCA, *Corporate Practice and the Rights of Shareholders* (Report, Nov 1991); CASAC, *Statutory Derivative Action* (Report, 1993); Corporations Law Simplification Task Force ("CLSTF"), *Commentary on Draft Provisions Dealing with Proceedings on Behalf of a Company by Members and Others* (Report, 1995); CLERP Proposal Paper No. 3, *Proposals for Reform: Directors' Duties and Corporate Governance* (1997); House of Representatives, *Explanatory Memorandum to the CLERP Bill* 1998.

10 CLERP Proposal Paper No. 3, *Proposals for Reform: Directors' Duties and Corporate Governance* (1997), at 32 and 34.

11 CSLRC, *Enforcement of the Duties of Directors and Officers of a Company by Means of a Statutory Derivative Action* (Report No. 12, Nov 1990); at 6.

12 CLERP Proposal Paper No. 3 (*"CLERP"*), *Proposals for Reform: Directors' Duties and Corporate Governance* (1997), at page 30, citing report from CASAC, *Statutory Derivative Action* (Report, 1993).

13 House of Representatives, *Explanatory Memorandum to the CLERP Bill* 1998, at 21.

(iv) the SDA could potentially be a valuable tool for enhancing corporate governance by maintaining investor confidence and improving directors' accountability to the company.[14]

These were the reasons for which the Australian government ultimately decided to abolish the common law derivative action and introduce the statutory model.[15] The remaining discussion under this part will be on the role of the SDA, followed by points (iii) and (iv) above. Part 3 of this chapter will then explore the above points (i) and (ii) as inadequacies.

2.2.2 The role of the SDA

The SDA has an important role in corporate law. It is the only mechanism for a shareholder or a minority director to bring an action on behalf of the company for the benefit of all shareholders.[16] Quite often, a derivative action is viewed as an avenue for shareholders to obtain compensation or relief for the injury done to the company. It is generally acknowledged that, in a successful SDA, compensation awarded by the court accrues to the company, and its shareholders, including the applicant, will only be entitled to a *pro rata* amount; so, in real terms, this could only be an insignificant amount for individual shareholders.[17]

It has also been argued that the SDA could be used as a way of promoting directors' accountability and maintaining good corporate governance. The SDA could serve as the primary purpose of deterring corporate wrongdoings by imposing the threat of liability on directors.[18] It could serve to reduce the agency costs inherent in corporate management.[19] It could be used as a "cor-

14 CASAC, *Statutory Derivative Action* (Report, 1993), at page 4; CLERP Proposal Paper No. 3, *Proposals for Reform: Directors' Duties and Corporate Governance* (1997), at 32–33.

15 See, *Corporations Act* 2001 (C'th), s.236(3). See also *Explanatory Memorandum to the CLERP Bill* 1998, at 20.

16 Hereinafter, where reference is made that a derivative action may be brought by a shareholder, it is also possible that a minority director could bring a similar suit.

17 Lang Thai, "How popular are statutory derivative actions in Australian Comparisons with USA, Canada, and New Zealand" (2002) 30 *Australian Business Law Review* 118, at 135; Peter Prince, "Australia's statutory derivative action: Using the New Zealand experience" (2000) 18 *Company and Securities Law Journal* 493, at 508; Roberta Romano, "The shareholder suit: Litigation without foundation" *(1991) 7 Journal of Law, Economics and Organisation* 55, at 84–85.

18 David Gibbs-Kneller and Chidiebere Ogbonnaya, "Empirical analysis of the statutory derivative claim: de facto application and the sine quibus non" (2019) 19 *Journal of Corporate Law Studies* 303, at 323; Pearlie KM Choo, "The statutory derivative action in Singapore: A critical and comparative examination" (2001) 13 *Bond Law Review* 64, at 69.

19 Ian Ramsay, "Corporate governance, shareholder litigation and the prospects for a statutory derivative action" (1992) 15 *University of New South Wales Law Journal* 149, at 156; John C. Coffee Jr and Donald E. Schwartz, "The survival of the derivative suit: An evaluation and a proposal for legislative reform" (1981) 81 *Columbia Law Review* 261, at 302–309.

porate watchdog",[20] as a weapon to deter and punish managerial misconduct if enacted properly,[21] or as "a major policeman of managerial integrity".[22]

However, other scholars have expressed doubts as to whether the SDA could be used to improve corporate governance. One scholar argues that it is "far from obvious" that managerial liability in derivative action will reduce agency costs.[23] The liability rules "play little or no role in creating incentives for beneficial conduct" as other measures of corporate governance already encourage directors to act in shareholders' best interests.[24] Some argue that the SDA cannot be used to measure empirically the benefits of deterrence of corporate wrongdoing because it does not result in a positive outcome.[25] Other scholars argue that it is not possible for the SDA alone to be used as a complete deterrence against managerial misconduct,[26] and that some public enforcement by a corporate regulator is necessary.[27]

Needless to say, the debate over the role of the SDA will continue. The SDA, if utilised properly, can provide an avenue for bona fide shareholders

20 Lynden Griggs, "The statutory derivative action: Lessons that may be learnt from its past" (2002) 6 *University of Western Sydney Law Review* 64, at 65.

21 Andrew Keay, "Assessing and rethinking the statutory scheme for derivative actions under the Companies Act 2006" (2016) 16 *Journal of Corporate Law Studies* 39, at 42; Samantha S. Tang, "Corporate avengers need not be angels: Rethinking good faith in the derivative action" (2016) 16 *Journal of Corporate Law Studies* 471, at 474; Kristina de Vere Stevens, "Should we toss Foss? Toward an Australian statutory derivative action" (1997) 25 *Australian Business Law Review* 127 at 127.

22 M. A. Maloney, "Whither the statutory derivative action?" (1986) 64 *Canadian Bar Review* 309, at 315.

23 Michael J. Whincop, "The role of the shareholder in corporate governance: A theoretical approach" (2001) 25 *Melbourne University Law Review* 418, at 432–438 (contending a litigious model of corporate governance is difficult to support).

24 Daniel R. Fischel and Michael Bradley, "The role of liability rules and the derivative suit in corporate law: A theoretical and empirical analysis" (1983) 71 *Cornell Law Journal* 261, at 262–263.

25 Robert B. Thompson and Randall S. Thomas, "The public and private faces of derivative lawsuits (2004) 57 *Vanderbilt Law Review* 1747, at 1775. See also Arad Reisberg, "Funding derivative action: A re-examination of costs and fees as incentives for commencing litigation" (2004) 4 *Journal of Corporate Law Studies* 345.

26 Matthew Berkahn and Lindsay Trotman, "Public and private enforcement of company law in New Zealand 1986–1990" (2000) 7 *Canterbury Law Review* 516, at 518, where the authors note that "public enforcers may also act as surrogates for company stakeholders".

27 Jasper Hedges, Helen Bird, George Gilligan, Andrew Godwin and Ian Ramsay, "An Empirical Analysis of Public Enforcement of Directors' Duties in Australia: Preliminary Findings" (Working Paper No. 105/2016, Centre for International Finance and Regulation, Melbourne Law School, March 2016), at 7; Michelle Welsh, "Realising the public potential of corporate law: Twenty years of civil penalty enforcement in Australia" (2014) 42 *Federal Law Review* 217 (contending the public regulator's primary role should be to act in the interests of shareholders and the larger community and to encourage greater compliance by directors); John Armour, Bernard Black, Brian Cheffins and Richard Nolan, "Private enforcement of corporate law: An empirical comparison of the United Kingdom and the United States" (2009) 6 *Journal of Empirical Legal Studies* 687.

to be awarded some compensation or relief, as this is the dominant purpose for bringing an SDA. It could also play the role of deterring directors from improper conduct and bad behaviour by making them accountable for the wrong done to the company, thereby improving overall directors' accountability and corporate governance. Successful outcomes in SDAs could bring about some deterrent effect. It is possible for the SDA to serve these two purposes concurrently.[28] SDA provides shareholders with a self-help mechanism for bringing about positive changes in corporate management.

2.2.3 Compensation purpose

It has been reported that the "basic policy objective" of the SDA is to provide shareholders with an "effective remedy".[29] However, there is no further explanation as to how this is to be achieved other than saying that the statutory model would provide shareholders with a "self-help" measure.[30]

In a successful derivative action, any compensation or benefit awarded by the court will accrue to the company, which means that its shareholders individually will only be entitled to an insignificant *pro rata* benefit. Under the current statutory model, a shareholder applicant who applies for permission to bring an SDA and has successfully brought the action will only be entitled to a *pro rata* amount in the compensation awarded by the court, while non-participating shareholders will benefit from the successes. There is currently no provision in the legislation dealing with the free rider problem. No active steps have been taken to rectify this problem.

In a successful derivative action, the amount received may be insignificant for some existing shareholders but may be a bonus for incoming shareholders. Coffee and Schwartz have summed up three key problems with an award of compensation to the company rather than to the individual plaintiff. They note that:[31]

(1) the identity and composition of many shareholders will change between the time of the wrongdoing by corporate fiduciaries and the time of recovery, with the effect that shareholders who have disposed of their

28 William Kaplan and Bruce Elwood, "The derivative action: A shareholder's bleak house" (2003) 36 *University of British Columbia Law Review* 443, at 455 (pointing out the derivative action to have two purposes, "it seeks to provide some level of deterrence against abuses of managerial or directorial authority, and it provides an avenue whereby, through shareholder activism in the absence of action by the board of directors, the corporation can recover damages or property belonging to the corporation".)

29 CLERP Proposal Paper No. 3, *Proposals for Reform: Directors' Duties and Corporate Governance* (1997), at 35.

30 CLERP Proposal Paper No. 3, *Proposals for Reform: Directors' Duties and Corporate Governance* (1997), at 35.

31 Coffee and Schwartz, n 19, at 302–306. See also Ramsay, n 19, at 156.

shares prior to a court ordered recovery will not receive any compensation, while incoming shareholders will receive a windfall gain;

(2) the change in value of the company's shares may differ from the amount either of its loss or of its recovery, and so the injury to the company resulting from, for example, a breach of directors' duties, is not necessarily the same as the injury suffered by shareholders; and

(3) while the total amount of corporate recovery may be significant, individual shareholders may receive only an insignificant amount on a per share basis.

The more concerning issue is that the current statutory model has *not properly* addressed matters relating to litigation costs and funding support. These issues will be explored further in the later part of this chapter and in Chapter 6.

2.2.4 Directors' accountability purpose

Various government reports have provided another purpose for introducing the SDA, namely, directors' accountability purpose. It has been said that the SDA could operate to "provide strong encouragement for company managers to be accountable to shareholders for the decisions they make";[32] it could potentially be used as a tool for enhancing managerial accountability and maintaining good corporate governance;[33] and it could also help to maintain "investor confidence".[34]

Whether this purpose is achievable through legislation is debatable. As explained in the above, there are differences in academic opinion on the role of the SDA. If enacted appropriately, the SDA could serve as an effective pathway for shareholders to sue directors for breach of directors' duties, and thereby enhance the overall corporate governance. This would only be possible if the leave requirement to bring an SDA is not made too onerous on the applicant and if the court can shift its focus and allow some scrutiny to be made on the directors' actions and decisions.[35] The criteria for leave will be explored further in subsequent chapters.[36]

Theoretically in corporate law and according to the separation of control and ownership concept,[37] there is a clear division between directors of a

32 CLERP Proposal Paper No. 3, *Proposals for Reform: Directors' Duties and Corporate Governance* (1997), at 32.

33 CASAC, *Statutory Derivative Action* (Report, 1993), at 32.

34 CASAC, *Statutory Derivative Action* (Report, 1993), at 5.

35 Keay, n 21, at 68, where the author argues that corporate accountability could be achieved by "ensuring that shareholders are not overly deterred from bringing actions and that they have a reasonable avenue for complaining about the wrongs against their company".

36 The leave criteria will be explored in Chapters 3, 4 and 5.

37 Adolf A. Berle and Gardiner C. Means, "Chapter VI: The divergence of interest between ownership and control" in *The Modern Corporation and Private Property* (Harcourt Publishing,

company who have the power to make decisions for the company and shareholders as investors who expect profit maximization. In practice, however, this division can become blurred, particularly in small privately owned companies, such as a family company, where it is common to see majority shareholders who are also company directors. In this scenario where the control/ownership structure is blurred, where there is no clear framework for monitoring directors, there is potential for abuse of power and misuse of company resources by some directors for their own benefit.

2.2.5 SDA as a self-help private enforcement approach

The SDA has been reported as a "self-help measure" for shareholders. The Corporate Law Economic Reform Program Proposal noted the intended purposes of the SDA as:[38]

> "not intended to be regulatory in nature but to facilitate private parties to enforce existing rights attaching to the company – in effect, the action is designed to be a self-help measure. In this regard, a statutory derivative action has the potential to remove some of the regulatory burden from the [public regulator] by making it easier for investors themselves to protect the interests of a company."

This was repeated in the Explanatory Memorandum to the bill introducing the SDA.[39] The report from the Companies and Securities Advisory Committee too stated that "in many respects, private enforcement accomplished via shareholder litigation may be preferable to public enforcement".[40]

It is clear that the SDA is designed as a private enforcement tool for shareholder protection against managerial misconduct. A public regulator, such as ASIC, is not included as an eligible applicant under the SDA procedure. It has been a way of removing some of the regulatory burden from ASIC and providing shareholders with some power to pursue appropriate actions. ASIC has only limited resources and cannot afford to pursue public investigation and prosecution of all alleged breaches of directors' duties.

The effectiveness of this self-help private enforcement approach is dependent on a number of factors. One important factor is the type of company involved. As discussed in Chapter 1, private enforcement of this kind (that is, SDA) by shareholders would be more effective and appropriate in small

---

1932); Margaret M. Blair, "Whose interests should corporations serve?" Chapter 6, in *Ownership and Control: Rethinking Corporate Governance for the Twenty-First Century* (The Brooking Institution, Washington DC, 1995).

38 CLERP Proposal Paper No. 3, *Proposals for Reform: Directors' Duties and Corporate Governance* (1997), at 35.

39 House of Representatives, *Explanatory Memorandum to the CLERP Bill* 1998, at [6.30]. 21.

40 CASAC, *Statutory Derivative Action* (Report, 1993), at 4.

privately owned or closely held companies. In small private companies, an SDA would give shareholders a better chance of recovery from the wrongdoer and a better chance of remedying the wrong done to the company than through public enforcement by a public regulator where its objective may sometimes be different from that of the shareholders. Arguably, a public regulator has little or no motivation in understanding the corporate culture and business conditions in small private companies in which to properly administer and enforce corporate rights and duties.

Professor Bottomley considers the nexus between corporate law and administrative law and notes that:[41]

> "modern public bureaucracies and large-scale business corporations have much in common... Both public and private bureaucracies operate on the basis of a separation between those who manage the enterprise and those who are the intended beneficiaries. This separation results, amongst other things, from the fact that each constituency – the general public and shareholders – is widely dispersed and therefore unable itself to perform the tasks of management effectively. Moreover, these dispersed constituencies face similar difficulties in monitoring the actions of those to whom the power of management is delegated."

For this reason, he then concludes that a shareholder derivative action is more applicable to small private companies than to large companies or corporate groups.[42] Another scholar has noted that the advantage of a shareholder derivative action is that shareholders are more likely to be able to recover assets "belonging to the corporation".[43]

Thus, an SDA is preferable in small private companies. However, the high litigation cost and free riding were the main problems for shareholders seeking to pursue a derivative action at common law. Private enforcement by shareholders *alone* may not always be an effective way of deterring managerial misconduct and enforcing directors' duties. As discussed in Chapter 1, public enforcement on behalf of shareholders is necessary in some instances.[44] For a shareholder derivative action to be truly effective as a compensation tool and as a mechanism for bringing about enforcement of directors' duties, especially in small private or closely held companies where a public

41 Stephen Bottomley, "Shareholder derivative actions and public interests suits: Two versions of the same story" (1992) 15 *University of New South Wales Law Journal* 127, at 130.

42 Bottomley, n 41, at 141–142.

43 Kaplan and Elwood, n 28, at 455.

44 Hedges, Bird, Gilligan, Godwin, and Ramsay, n 27; Jennifer G. Hill, "Images of the shareholder: Shareholder power and shareholder powerlessness" (pp. 53–73) in Jennifer G. Hill and Randall S. Thomas (eds.), *Research Handbook on Shareholder Power* (Edward Elgar, 2015); Michelle Welsh, "Realising the public potential of corporate law: Twenty years of civil penalty enforcement in Australia" (2014) 42 *Federal Law Review* 217.

regulator is unlikely to take an interest, issues relating to high litigation costs coupled with the free rider problem should be addressed appropriately in the statute.

2.3 Reasons for the abolition of the common law derivative action

2.3.1 Limitations in the common law position

The common law derivative action was necessary to prevent a company from being harmed by its directors. Although the right to sue remains with the company, a derivative action was thought to be appropriate to allow an individual shareholder to bring an action on behalf of the company where the company had failed to act; for example, where the board of directors or the majority shareholders had decided not to allow the company to pursue an action against one of its directors for breach of a duty. However, circumstances in which a derivative action might be brought at common law were limited. A minority shareholder had to establish that his or her situation fell into one of the recognised exceptions, but even so, a common law derivative action could still be blocked if majority shareholders had ratified the breach. Below is a further discussion of the common law limitations.

2.3.1.1 The strict "proper plaintiff" rule in *Foss v. Harbottle*

The common law derivative action came about as a consequence of the two strict rules established in *Foss v. Harbottle* in 1843.[45] The first was that if a company has suffered a wrong, it is the company that is the "proper plaintiff" that has the right to sue the defendant for redress.[46] This rule regards the company as the only party with the standing to sue for a wrong done to the company. It is in recognition of the concept that the company is a separate legal entity.[47] The second rule derived from that case relates to the internal management of the company.[48] Where the majority shareholders had made a decision or were in favour of a decision made by the board of directors and that decision was made within the powers conferred by the company, the court would not ordinarily intervene in the company's internal management.[49] Likewise, where the board or majority shareholders decided against a legal action, then under the rule in *Foss v. Harbottle*, that would be "the end

45 *Foss v. Harbottle* (1843) 2 Hare 461.

46 *Foss v. Harbottle* (1843) 2 Hare 461, as cited in *Edwards v. Halliwell* [1950] 2 All ER 1064, at 1066.

47 *Salomon v. Salomon & Co Ltd* [1897] AC 22.

48 *Foss v. Harbottle* (1843) 2 Hare 461, as interpreted in *Edwards v. Halliwell* [1950] 2 All ER 1064, at 1066.

49 *Burland v. Earle* [1902] AC 83. See also, KW Wedderburn, "Shareholders' rights and the rule in *Foss v. Harbottle*" (1957) *Cambridge Law Journal* 194 and (1958) *Cambridge Law Journal* 93.

of the matter".[50] This internal management rule is based on a number of corporate law principles necessary to achieve economically desirable outcomes for shareholders, including the principle relating to the business judgment rule,[51] by allowing directors and managers the freedom to do their job and run the company.[52]

These strict rules in *Foss v. Harbottle* have long been accepted as a significant obstacle to private enforcement of shareholders' rights against directors and majority shareholders.[53] Individual and minority shareholders were unable to sue a director for breach of directors' duties. They were also unable to sue on behalf of the company against the board of directors due to successful shareholder ratification of their own breaches. They were unable to sell or return their shares to the company due to a lack of majority vote. Majority shareholders were, in most cases, directors and controllers of the company, and given that they held the majority voting rights, they could easily pass a resolution to ratify their own breaches and make whatever decision that suited them. As a further example, in a call for a statutory derivative action to be introduced, Professor Baxt concisely described the position at common law as one where the rule in *Foss v. Harbottle* "rears its ugly head".[54] This was how "exceptions" to these rules were developed over time and were considered necessary to prevent these rules from becoming a cover for unreviewable abuses by directors.

2.3.1.2 Limitations in the common law exceptions

Following the analysis of the courts in *Edwards v. Halliwell*[55] and in *Mesenberg v. Cord Industrial Recruiters Pty Ltd*,[56] five exceptions or "situations" were

50 Bottomley, n 41, at 138.

51 Although the US common law business judgment rule was not referred to in Australia prior to March 2000, it was still a relevant consideration, in that, as discussed in Chapter 1, there was a presumption that directors had made a good business decision at the relevant time based on their fiduciary role to the company that they had fulfilled in acting in good faith, diligently and had no personal conflict.

52 Christopher Hale, "What's right with the rule in *Foss v. Harbottle*?" (1997) 2 *Company Financial Insolvency Law Review* 219, at 225.

53 Robert Baxt, "The rule in *Foss v Harbottle* rears its ugly head: The case for a statutory derivative action gathers strength" (1996) 14 *Companies and Securities Law Journal* 174. See also John Kluver, "Derivative actions and the rule in *Foss v Harbottle*: Do we need a statutory remedy?" (1993) 11 *Companies and Securities Law Journal* 7.

54 Baxt, n 53, at 174. See also, Robert Baxt, "A body blow to Section 1324 of the Corporations Law: Will the derivative action get a new lease of life?" (1996) 14 *Company and Securities Law Journal* 312.

55 *Edwards v. Halliwell* [1950] 2 All ER 1064, 1066–1069.

56 *Mesenberg v. Cord Industrial Recruiters Pty Ltd* (1996) 14 ACLC 519, at 523 where Young J affirmed the availability of the "interest of justice" exception in Australia even though the United Kingdom refused to accept recognition of this exception. It has been criticised in the United Kingdom as "too nebulous, vague and infinitely elastic" – see O.A. Osunbor, "A

identified as appropriate for minority shareholder litigation.[57] An individual shareholder could bring an action in court if:

(a) The act of the company was *ultra vires*;[58]
(b) The act of the company required a special majority;[59]
(c) A shareholder's personal rights were infringed;[60]
(d) The majority committed a fraud on the minority;[61] or
(e) The interest of justice required.[62]

The last two from the list, "fraud on the minority" and "interest of justice" have been described as true exceptions to the rule in *Foss v. Harbottle*, where the court might grant a shareholder a right to bring a derivative action on behalf of the company.[63] The other three situations, (a), (b) and (c) above, only allowed a shareholder a right to bring a personal action against the company and/or against the offending directors or other members of the company.[64] The exception in (a) is no longer applicable as the *ultra vires* doctrine has been abolished.[65] The lack of special majority exception in (b) and the infringement of personal rights exception in (c) still exist in some form, either as an oppression/unfair prejudice action provided in the statute or as a breach of contract giving rise to a personal action.

---

critical appraisal of 'The interests of justice' as an exception to the rule in *Foss v. Harbottle*" (1987) 36 *International and Comparative Law Quarterly* 1, at 13.

57 There was a debate as to whether these were best described as exceptions to the rule in *Foss v. Harbottle*, or as "situations" – See discussion in Wedderburn, n 49.

58 E.g., *Hawkesbury Development Co. Ltd v. Landmark Finance Pty Ltd* (1969) 2 NSWLR 782; *Smith v. Croft (No.2)* [1988] Ch 114.

59 E.g., *Baillie v. Oriental Telephone Co Ltd* [1915] 1 Ch 503; *Cotter v. National Union of Seamen* [1929] 2 Ch 58; *Edwards v Halliwell* [1950] 2 All ER 1064.

60 E.g., *Pender v. Lushington* (1877) 6 Ch D 70; *Efstathis v. Greek Orthodox Community of St George* (1988) 6 ACLC 706; *Residue Treatment & Trading Co Ltd v. Southern Resources Ltd (No.4)* (1989) 14 ACLR 569.

61 E.g., *Cook v. Deeks* [1916] 1 AC 554; *Peters' American Delicacy Company Ltd v. Heath* (1939) 61 CLR 457 and *Nicron Resources Ltd v. Catto* (1992) 8 ACSR 219.

62 E.g., *Biala Pty Ltd v. Mallina Holdings Ltd (No.2)* (1993) 11 ACSR 785; *Aloridge Pty Ltd v. West Australian Gem Explorers Pty Ltd* (1995) 127 ALR 410; *Mesenberg v Cord Industrial Recruiters Pty Ltd* (1996) 14 ACLC 519. See also, Robert P. Austin and Ian M. Ramsay, *Ford, Austin and Ramsay's Principles of Corporations Law* (LexisNexis Butterworths, Sydney, 2018) at [10.300.9].

63 Maloney, n 22, at 311. See G.P. Stapleton, "Locus standi of shareholders to enforce the duty of company directors to exercise the share issue power for proper purposes" (1990) 8 *Company and Securities Law Journal* 213.

64 Pamela Hanrahan, "Distinguishing corporate and personal claims in Australian company litigation" (1997) 15 *Company and Securities Law Journal* 21.

65 The introduction of the *CLERP Act* in July 1999 had seen the abolition of the doctrine of ultra vires, with the effect that the company will not be in breach even if the company engages in activities that are outside its objects stated in the constitution or outside the stated restrictions. This abolition is now noted in s.124 of the *Corporations Act 2001* (C'th).

In relation to the "fraud on the minority" exception, it was not always easy for a shareholder to prove fraud to be granted a right to proceed with a derivative action. A shareholder would be given a right to bring an action on behalf of the company against the persons controlling the company only where "directors use their powers, intentionally or unintentionally, fraudulently or negligently, in a manner which *benefits themselves at the expense of the company*".[66] The term "fraud" in this context was in reference to an abuse of power by the majority directors and controlling shareholders in ways where the majority secured an unfair gain at the expense of the company. An example is where a director had misappropriated corporate assets to themselves at the expense of the company.[67] This exception was only applicable in extreme cases involving serious "fraud" or "illegal activities"[68] committed by the persons who controlled the company.[69] A derivative action was rarely granted under this exception, not only because it was difficult to prove fraud, but also because the majority were often able to acquire enough voting power to ratify their conduct or omission that appeared "improper", so as to release them from any personal liability.

The "interest of justice" situation was a more recent exception recognised in Australia for permitting a shareholder to proceed with a derivative action.[70] This exception was opposed in the United Kingdom as being "non-exhaustive" and too vague.[71] This exception was applicable in Australia in circumstances where the shareholder was unable to establish any of the other recognised exceptions and where the court considered that serious injustice would occur if the shareholder was denied the right to bring an action on behalf of the company to remedy the wrong done to it.[72] It was considered necessary because "the complexities and sophistications of modern shareholding" that made it "very difficult" for a derivative claim to fall within the

66 *Daniels v. Daniels* [1978] Ch 406 at 414 (Templeman J).

67 See, for example, in *Cook v. Deeks* [1916] 1 AC 554, at 564 (Lord Buckmaster LC), where the three directors who owned the majority of the shares in the company had improperly transferred assets from an existing company to their newly incorporated company, leaving behind the fourth director/minority shareholder.

68 *Hutton v. West Cock Railway Ltd* (1993) LR 23 Ch D 654.

69 Wedderburn, n 49, at 96; G.R. Sullivan, "Restating the scope of the derivative action" (1985) 44 *Cambridge Law Journal* 236, at 239.

70 *Hawksbury Development Co Ltd v. Landmark Finance Pty Ltd* [1969]2 NSWLR 782, at 789 was one of the earlier cases where the court stated the interest of justice exception as "a useful tool to be left open" for a derivative action to be brought "in some extremely unusual circumstances". See also in *Mesenberg v. Cord Industrial Recruiters Pty Ltd* (1996) 14 ACLC 519 at 523, where Young J affirmed the interest of justice as an exception for a derivative action.

71 *Prudential Assurance Co. Ltd v. Newman Industries Ltd (No.2)* [1982] Ch 204; *Estmanco (Kilner House) Ltd v. Greater London Council* [1982] 1 All ER 437. See also Osunbor, n 56.

72 *Biala Pty Ltd v. Mallina Holdings Ltd (No. 2)* (1993) 11 ACLC 1082, at 1102. See also *Aloridge Pty Ltd v. West Australian gem Explorers Pty Ltd* (1995) 127 ALR 410; *Mesenberg v. Cord Industrial Recruiters Pty Ltd* (1996) 14 ACLC 519, at 523; *Nece Pty Ltd v. Ritek Incorporation* (1997) 15 ACLC 813, 818–819.

other four exceptions.[73] Some scholars supported this flexible approach, noting that the interest of justice exception had enabled the courts to minimise the common law procedural obstacles.[74] It was clear that Australia was more willing to apply this exception than the United Kingdom, in order to circumvent the harshness of the common law rules in respect to shareholder derivative action.

However, despite this flexible application of the interest of justice exception, there were other problems preventing shareholders from obtaining permission of the court to proceed with a derivative action at common law, as discussed in the next segment.

2.3.2 Inadequacies in the common law derivative action

Prior to the introduction of the statutory model in March 2000, there were doubts as to whether the common law derivative action was adequate. The perception from the government law reform reports was that the common law exceptions were "too narrow".[75] In support for a statutory framework, some scholars criticized the common law derivative action as an "accumulation of procedural codswallop",[76] and as "complex and arcane".[77] The common law exceptions had a "leaden impact" on shareholders' ability to litigate.[78] The shareholders had to face "considerable, sometimes insurmountable, barriers... to enforce a cause of action vested in the company".[79] One scholar provided a summary of what a common law derivative action was like:[80]

> "Despite judicial innovations,... there are just too many hurdles to jump before bringing derivative suits. You must identify the wrongdoers, gather sufficient information, show there is fraud, prove the alleged

73 *Biala Pty Ltd v. Mallina Holdings Ltd (No. 2)* (1993) 11 ACLC 1082, at 1102 (Ipp J). In this case, Ipp J found that the wrongdoer controller owned 42.36% of the shares, short of 51%, but decided that, in the "interest of justice" exception, the minority shareholder be allowed to proceed with a derivative action.

74 Len S. Sealy, "The rule in *Foss v. Harbottle*: The Australian experience" (1989) 10 *Company Lawyer* 52, at 57; where Professor Sealy compared both the Australian and the UK approaches on the exceptions. See also Ramsay, n 19, at 158–160 where Professor Ramsay observed the "flexible approach" adopted in Australia to overcome the inadequacies in the common law exceptions.

75 CASAC, *Statutory Derivative Action* (Report, 1993), at 2. See also, CLERP Proposal Paper No. 3, *Proposals for Reform: Directors' Duties and Corporate Governance* (1997), at 30.

76 Len S. Sealy, "Foss v. Harbottle – A marathon where nobody wins" (1981) 40 *Cambridge Law Journal* 29, at 31.

77 S. Watkins, "The common law derivative action: An outmoded relic?" (1999) 30 *Cambrian Law Review* 40, at 40.

78 Bottomley, n 41, at 137.

79 John Kluver, n 53, at 8.

80 James Corkery, *Directors' Powers and Duties* (Longman Professional, 1987), at 172. See also, Kaplan and Elwood, n 28, at 450.

> wrongdoers control the company, and discover whether or not the acts complained of are ratifiable by a majority at a general meeting. Then you must somehow fund the action. In the face of all this and more, genuine grievances go unremedied."

Other scholars opposed the introduction of the SDA. One argument was that the SDA had not had any major impact in Canada and that a similar trend was likely to be seen in Australia.[81] A point was raised that there was no clear evidence demonstrating "any real need" for SDA.[82] Another scholar noted that the push for SDA was simply a political response to a perceived problem, rather than an informed response to a problem.[83] It is worth noting at this point that a study conducted in 1995 revealed that the number of shareholder litigations for breaches of directors' duties, including derivative actions, was relatively small when compared with the number of public prosecutions by the corporate regulator.[84] That study goes to show that Australia traditionally favoured the public prosecution approach rather than creating a strong incentive for private enforcement by shareholders.

Despite the conflicting academic views, the government law reform reports highlighted three key problem areas in the common law position: (a) restrictive shareholder's right to sue; (b) costs of litigation; and (c) ratification. These are explained below.

2.3.2.1 Restriction on shareholder's right to sue and common law limitations

The shareholder's right to sue was too restrictive, in that only current registered shareholders were recognised as legal owner of shares for the purposes of establishing a standing to sue and to put forward a case as to whether they were fit enough to bring a lawsuit on behalf of the company at common law.[85] An equitable owner, for example, someone who had been allotted shares but whose shares had not been registered, could not be accepted as having the same standing as the registered legal owner to bring a derivative action.[86]

81 Brian Cheffins and J Dine, "Shareholder remedies: Lessons from Canada" (1992) 13 *Company Lawyer* 89; Griggs, n 20.

82 Griggs, n 20, at 86.

83 Rob McQueen, "Company law as imperialism" (1995) 5 *Australian Journal of Corporate Law* 187.

84 Ian Ramsay, "Enforcement of corporate rights and duties by shareholders and the Australian Securities Commission: Evidence and analysis" (1995) 23 *Australian Business Law Review*174, where a survey conducted in the period from September 1983 to March 1994 indicated 93 reported judgments in which litigation had been commenced by a shareholder, and of these, 25 related to an oppression action. By comparison, for the year ending 30 June 1994, the corporate regulator had commenced 107 criminal prosecutions for breaches of directors' duties, 184 other criminal prosecutions and 79 civil matters.

85 *Maas v. McIntosh* (1928) 28 SR (NSW) 441; *Hooker Investments Pty Ltd v. Email Ltd* (1986) 10 ACLR 443.

86 *Fulloon v. Radley* (1991) 9 ACLR 1434.

Even if a shareholder was a current registered owner, another complication was that the shareholder must *establish a case* for a derivative action, proving that the nature of their complaint fell either within the "fraud on the minority" exception or within the "interest of justice" exception. These were the only exceptions available for a derivative action. The shareholder had to establish either of these exceptions as a further way of proving standing to sue.

As discussed above, proving "fraud on the minority" was never an easy task, and these preliminary hearings could develop into a long and expensive series of hearings.[87] Proving fraud involved proof of controllers of the company abusing their powers.[88] An example would be "illegal activities" committed by the board of directors,[89] or gross misappropriation of company assets which benefitted the controllers at the expense of the company.[90] Numerous cases had failed to satisfy the court on this exception.[91]

Not only was the "fraud on the minority" exception difficult to establish, but also the possibility of majority shareholders being able to ratify breaches of directors' duties was enough to discourage a shareholder from taking legal action.[92] At common law, when a breach of a director's duty had been ratified, a minority shareholder would be barred from bringing a derivative action.[93] There were numerous instances at common law where directors and controlling shareholders released themselves from personal liability by calling a general meeting and ratifying their breaches or proposed breaches. Almost all kinds of ratification were effective at common law. A "mere *possibility* of ratification was sufficient to deprive a shareholder" from pursuing a derivative action.[94] As observed by one judge, there was "no consistent pattern" set out by the courts in dealing with shareholder ratification.[95] There was no consistency in the way the courts dealt with the "fraud on the minority" exception.

Where the "interest of justice" exception might be seen as relevant, it was still up to the court to decide whether substantial injustice had or would

87 Kaplan and Elwood, n 28, at 448.

88 *Daniels v. Daniels* [1978] Ch 406 at 414 (Templeman J).

89 *Hutton v. West Cock Railway Ltd* (1993) LR 23 Ch D 654.

90 *Cook v. Deeks* [1916] 1 AC 554.

91 For example, see *Biala Pty Ltd v. Mallina Holdings Ltd (No. 2)* (1993) 11 ACLC 1082; *Nece Pty Ltd v. Ritek Incorporation* (1997) 15 ACLC 813. See also Wedderburn, n 49; J Mayanja, "Standing to challenge the implementation of improper defensive measures" (1995) 5 *Australian Journal of Corporate Law* 66.

92 For example, in *Winthrop Investments Ltd v. Winns Ltd* (1975) NSWLR 666; *Residue Treatment & Trading Co Ltd v. Southern Resources Ltd* (1988) 14 ACLR 397; *Biala Pty Ltd v Mallina Holdings Ltd (No. 2)* (1993) 11 ACLC 1082; *Nece Pty Ltd v. Ritek Incorporation* (1997) 15 ACLC 813.

93 This is discussed further under "ratification".

94 Saul Fridman, "Ratification of directors' breaches" (1992) 10 *Company and Securities Law Journal* 252, at 271–273

95 *Winthrop Investments Ltd v. Winns Ltd* [1975] 2 NSWLR 666, at 671 (per Glass JA).

have occurred that warranted a derivative action to be brought. There was no clarity on the actual scope of the interest of justice ground or the circumstances in which the court would exercise its discretion to allow derivative action. Under this exception, the courts had full discretion to decide whether to allow a derivative action to proceed. Some courts had allowed a shareholder to proceed with a derivative action in the interest of justice,[96] while other courts had denied such action.[97] In other cases, the courts were reluctant to intervene in the company's internal management,[98] even where the directors' mistake was obvious.[99] There was no clear approach as to what constituted "interest of justice". This exception was entirely within the power of the court in determining what was just and unjust, but if shareholder ratification had taken place, the courts would not grant a derivative action.

2.3.2.2 Lack of funding support from the company

Another problem often faced by shareholder plaintiffs at common law was the lack of funding support from the company in derivative actions. The question of who bears the costs of litigation is of particular importance to shareholders. Ordinarily, if a derivative action is successful, any compensation awarded by the court will accrue to the company as a whole with the shareholder plaintiff receiving only a small *pro rata* benefit. The fact that other shareholders will have a free ride on the plaintiff's efforts creates a disincentive for the bringing of a derivative action. The problem is further exacerbated by the fact that if the derivative action is unsuccessful, the plaintiff is likely to be ordered to pay the costs of the successful defendant in addition to his or her own costs.

The problem with high litigation costs in derivative action was acknowledged in a number of government law reform reports. One report stated that the issue of costs coupled with the uncertainty in the standing to sue had been a "strong deterrent to shareholders seeking to take common law derivative actions".[100] Another report stated the costs issue as "a formidable barrier to shareholders contemplating an action".[101] Another report stated it as

96 *Cook v. Deeks* [1916] 1 AC 554.

97 *Residue Treatment & Trading Co Ltd v. Southern Resources Ltd (No.4)* (1988) 14 ACLR 396.

98 See, for example, *Moran v. Moranco Enterprises Pty Ltd* (1996) 14 ACLC 1,669, where failure of the founding directors to provide minority shareholders with important information and notice of meeting was considered a matter of technical breach only and that such breach did not warrant the court to intervene.

99 Robert Baxt, "The Unwillingness of courts to Correct Directors' Mistakes – especially where Minorities are Involved" (1997) 15 *Company and Securities Law Journal* 65.

100 CLERP Proposal Paper No. 3, *Proposals for Reform: Directors' Duties and Corporate Governance* (1997), at 32.

101 SSC on LCA, *Company Directors' Duties: Report on the Social and Fiduciary Duties and Obligations of Company Directors* (Report, 1989), at [11.29].

"possibly the greatest inhibitor to shareholder litigation".[102] The uncertainty in the recovery of costs "effectively prevents shareholders from pursuing the legal remedies open to them".[103] Some scholars have expressed a similar view.[104] Professor Ramsay argued that litigation costs coupled with the free ride problem had been "the main impediment" to shareholders' ability to litigate.[105]

At common law, applying for costs indemnity was always a problem for shareholder plaintiffs in the derivative action, regardless of the outcome of the case. For example, in *Farrow v. Registrar of Building Societies*,[106] the Supreme Court of Victoria held that it would only grant a costs order if the shareholder plaintiff was so "destitute" or "financially handicapped" that the case otherwise could not proceed.[107] In that case, the court had originally adopted the English decision in *Wallersteiner v. Moir (No.2)*,[108] and ordered the company to pay for the derivative action. However, the action was later found to have no merits after a discovery was made at trial. The Supreme Court of Victoria subsequently ordered the shareholder plaintiff to discontinue the action and made an order to recall the original costs order, making the shareholder ultimately liable to reimburse the costs of the failed action. In *Parker v. National Roads & Motorists Association*,[109] another Australian case, the court held that an interim costs order should not be made until after the discovery stage and only in circumstances where there was a genuine need.[110]

It was clear that shareholder plaintiffs had no certainty in the recovery of their costs. Funding support was never an automatic right for shareholders seeking to bring a derivative action. The shareholder had to apply to the court for the company to fund the action, and it was not always readily granted.[111] A further problem was that if a derivative action was unsuccessful, the shareholder plaintiff might have to bear not only his or her own costs, but also the costs of the successful defendant(s). These deficiencies undermined the effectiveness of the common law derivative action.

102 CASAC, *Statutory Derivative Action* (Report, 1993), at 8.

103 House of Representatives Standing Committee on LCA, *Corporate Practices and the Rights of Shareholders* (November 1991), at 190.

104 Thai, n 17; Baxt, n 54; Choo, n 18; Kluver, n 53.

105 Ramsay, n 19, at 150.

106 *Farrow v Registrar of Building Societies* [1991] 2 VR 589

107 *Farrow v Registrar of Building Societies* [1991] 2 VR 589, at 595–596

108 In *Wallersteiner v. Moir (No2)* [1975] QB 373, the English Court of Appeal ordered the company to pay the costs of the derivative action at common law, irrespective of the outcome, on the basis that the action was brought on behalf of the company and the company was named as the principal plaintiff.

109 *Parker v. National Roads & Motorists Association* (1993) 11 ACSR 370.

110 *Parker v. National Roads & Motorists Association* (1993) 11 ACSR 370, at 382. See also Smith v Croft (No2) [1988] Ch 114

111 Elizabeth Boros, *Minority Shareholders Remedies* (Oxford University Press, 1995), at 191–192.

2.3.2.3 Issues relating to majority ratification

A shareholder could pursue a derivative action *only* if the director's wrongdoing could *not* be ratified. The fact that majority shareholders who controlled the company could ratify certain breaches of directors' duties (whether or not they had, in fact. done so) was a serious concern under the old common law derivative action. There were at least three issues relating to shareholder ratification. First, any form of shareholder ratification would bar a minority shareholder from pursuing a legal action.[112] The theoretical foundation of this use of the *ability* of shareholders to ratify certain breaches is the idea that the general meeting constitutes a form of internal dispute resolution within the company and the courts should therefore take a hands-off approach to intervention.[113]

The other difficulty was dealing with the types of conduct that were ratifiable by the shareholders in general meeting and those that were non-ratifiable.[114] There were conflicting authorities in this area.[115] Even a serious form of fraud carried out by the majority shareholders and controllers had been seen as ratifiable.[116] In *Winthrop Investments Ltd v. Winns Ltd*, while acknowledging the difficulties in distinguishing a ratifiable breach from a non-ratifiable breach, Glass JA of the NSW Supreme Court concluded that he was not competent in suggesting a reform to the law relating to ratification as there were "too many threads of principle" and too many inconsistencies.[117]

A further problem regarding shareholder ratification was that where a breach of directors' duties had been ratified, the minority shareholder lost not only the right to pursue a derivative action, but also the right to bring a *personal* claim against the company. In other words, a minority shareholder would be barred from bringing any type of court action, including an oppression action, if majority shareholders had ratified breaches of directors' duties. In *Residue Treatment & Trading Co Ltd v. Southern Resources Ltd (No.4)*,[118]

112 *Winthrop Investments Ltd v. Winns Ltd* (1975) NSWLR 666; *Residue Treatment & Trading Co Ltd v. Southern Resources Ltd* (1988) 14 ACLR 397. See also, Baxt, n 99.

113 Kenny Yeung, "Disentangling the Tangled Skein: The Ratification of Directors' Actions" (1992) 66 *Australian Law Journal* 343, at 356–357; Sarah Worthington, "Corporate Governance: Remedying and ratifying directors' breaches" (2000) 116 *Law Quarterly Review* 638, at 642.

114 Lynne Taylor, "Ratification and the statutory derivative action in the Companies Act 1993" (1998) 16 *Company and Securities Law Journal* 221, at 233; Mayanja, n 91, at 69; Fridman, n 94, at 255; BH McPherson, "Duties of directors and the powers of shareholders" (1977) 51 *Australian Law Journal* 460, at 468–469.

115 For example, in *Cook v. Deeks* [1916] 1 AC 554, the court held that the directors who held the majority shares collectively could not ratify their improper conduct when they had already misappropriated company assets to themselves. In contrast in the case of *Regal Hastings Ltd v. Gulliver* [1942] 1 All ER 378, it was held that the directors who pocketed a large sum of money given by a customer "could … have protected themselves" [at 389, Russell LJ) by shareholder ratification in a general meeting, either before or subsequent to the conduct.

116 *Regal Hastings Ltd v. Gulliver* [1942] 1 All ER 378; and *Residue Treatment & Trading Co Ltd v. Southern Resources Ltd (No.4)* (1988) 14 ACLR 396.

117 *Winthrop Investments Ltd v. Winns Ltd* (1975) NSWLR 666, at 671.

118 *Residue Treatment & Trading Co Ltd v. Southern Resources Ltd (No.4)* (1988) 14 ACLR 396.

one of the issues was whether the minority shareholders could sue in their personal capacity for compensation when they had been barred from pursing a derivative action because directors had obtained a shareholder resolution to ratify their breaches. The claim was that the directors had improperly allotted shares originally, which had diluted the voting rights of some of the shareholders. In denying the minority shareholders' right to sue, Parry J stated:[119]

> "[The plaintiffs] attempted to argue that the plaintiffs had standing by reason of an infringement of personal rights in that any allotment of shares for an improper purpose operated as an unlawful dilution of the plaintiffs' shareholding. ... [F]or that exception to the rule in *Foss v Harbottle* to be called into play, the infringement of personal rights must be peculiar to the plaintiffs as opposed to the shareholders as a whole."

The outcome in *Residue Treatment* was harsh. The implication was that shareholder ratification could effectively extinguish the personal right of an individual shareholder to sue.[120]

A large volume of literature can be found criticising the law relating to shareholder ratification. For example, it has been said that ratification was one of the "most debatable" issues in corporate law,[121] an "unclear minefield" that could often lead to unjust outcomes.[122] Another scholar noted that ratification was about the "uncertain boundaries of the majority rule".[123] A government report identified shareholder ratification as "undoubtedly the greatest legal difficulty".[124] It was clear that the law relating to shareholder ratification had a crippling effect on the minority shareholders' ability to take any form of court action.

2.3.3 Inadequacies in other statutory remedies

Another area of concern reported as "inadequate" protection for shareholders was the few existing statutory remedies.[125] Apart from the winding up

119 *Residue Treatment & Trading Co Ltd v. Southern Resources Ltd (No.4)* (1988) 14 ACLR 396, at 405.
120 On appeal in *Residue Treatment & Trading Co Ltd v. Southern Resources Ltd (No.4)* (1989) 14 ACLR 569, at 575, King CJ acknowledged the difficulty in differentiating between a corporate claim and a personal claim and decided to allow the shareholders to proceed with a personal claim under the "personal rights" exception.
121 A.J. Boyle, *Minority Shareholder remedies* (Cambridge University Press, 2002), at 21–22.
122 Fridman, n 94, at 255.
123 S.M. Beck, "The shareholder's derivative action" (1974) 52 *Canadian Bar Review* 159, at 199. See also McPherson, n 114.
124 CASAC, *Statutory Derivative Action* (Report 1993), at 6
125 CASAC, *Statutory Derivative Action* (Report, 1993), at 5–10; CLERP Proposal Paper No. 3, *Proposals for Reform: Directors' Duties and Corporate Governance* (1997), at 29–30.

application, which is drastic,[126] the two other existing statutory remedies were the oppression action[127] and the application for an injunction order.[128] One government report provided an example of the extent of inadequacy in the statutory injunction provision by illustrating the two conflicting judicial decisions.[129] This type of inadequacy was said to be another reason for needing the SDA to come into force.

These perceived inadequacies of the existing statutory remedies have drawn a mixed reaction from scholars. While Bottomley notes that the "oppression provision has not enjoyed great success as a response to *Foss v. Harbottle*",[130] Ramsay, in drawing support from Sealy, asserts that Australian courts "have adopted a flexible approach" to issues relating to standing and "have given new emphasis to the personal rights of shareholders" as well as given "increased importance to statutory remedies; most notably, the oppression remedy".[131] It has also been said that, because of its generous interpretation, the oppression provision "has been used effectively by the courts to combat the rule in *Foss v. Harbottle*".[132] Furthermore, the "liberal approach currently favoured in the interpretation of the oppression remedy has made it a very useful remedial tool for minority shareholders".[133] An empirical study has shown a "significant increase in the use of the oppression remedy".[134]

Putting aside the debate on whether the existing statutory remedies are adequate for shareholders as protection of their rights and interests in the company, it is important to note that a derivative action is distinctly different to the other statutory remedies. A derivative action is an action brought not in the capacity of oneself but on behalf of the entire company, and thus, a derivative action enables the shareholder to enforce a corporate right (as opposed to making a personal claim). The other existing statutory actions, such as an oppression action, continue to play an important role in the protection of shareholders' interests in circumstances where they fail to obtain court permission to bring a derivative action or where a claim is more appropriately categorised as an infringement of one's personal right.

126 *Corporations Act* 2001 (C'th), s.461.

127 *Corporations Act* 2001 (C'th), Part 2F.1 (ss.232–234).

128 *Corporations Act* 2001 (C'th), s.1324.

129 CLERP Proposal Paper No. 3, *Proposals for Reform: Directors' Duties and Corporate Governance* (Report 1997), at 30 in fn 56, referring to *Mesenberg v. Cord Industrial Pty Ltd (No.2)* (1996) 39 NSWLR 128, and comparing with *Airpeak Pty Ltd v. Jetstream Aircraft Ltd* (1997) 23 ACSR 715.

130 Bottomley, n 41, at 142.

131 Ramsay, n 19, at 160, citing support from Sealy, n 74, at 57.

132 Anil Hargovan, "Under judicial and legislative attack: The rule in *Foss v. Harbottle*" (1996) 113 *South African Law Journal* 631, at 637.

133 Matthew Berkahn, "The derivative action in Australia and New Zealand: Will the statutory provisions improve shareholder's enforcement rights? (1998) 10 *Bond Law Review* 74, at 89.

134 Ian M. Ramsay, "Am empirical study of the use of the oppression remedy" (1999) 27 *Australian Business Law Review* 23, at 29.

2.3.4 Other problems and uncertainties

Other problems and uncertainties with the common law derivative action could be summarised as follows.

2.3.4.1 Shareholder must come to court with "clean hands"

In addition to demonstrating an exception to the rule in *Foss v. Harbottle*, some scholars have observed that a shareholder seeking to bring a derivative action must also establish that he or she came to the court with "clean hands"[135], that is, there must be nothing in the shareholder's behaviour that rendered it unjust to allow the derivative action to proceed.[136] Although the courts at common law rarely referred to this equitable maxim in derivative action cases, the courts had tended to apply it to ensure that the shareholder plaintiff was acting in good faith and that the interests of the company had been looked after.[137]

The concept of "clean hands" in equity is associated with the requirement of "good faith" in the SDA, which will be examined in detail in Chapter 4.

2.3.4.2 Company in liquidation

At common law, when a company went into liquidation, an aggrieved shareholder could no longer pursue a derivative action. Instead, the shareholder had to go through the insolvency process and rely on the liquidator for a recovery if there was any surplus.[138]

2.3.4.3 The problem with free riding

The problem with free riding from non-participating shareholders was another reason why derivative action had little use at common law. In a successful derivative action, any compensation or benefit awarded by the court will accrue to the company, and not to the shareholder plaintiff alone. The shareholder plaintiff will only be entitled to a small *pro rata* amount.

135 Jennifer Payne, "Clean hands in derivative actions" (2002) 61(1) *Cambridge Law Journal* 76, at 76; Dennis H. Peterson and Matthew J. Cumming, *Shareholder Remedies in Canada* (Looseleaf services, 2nd ed, LexisNexis, 2009) at [16.39].

136 *Nurcombe v Nurcombe* [1985] 1 WLR 370, at 378 (Brownie-Wilkinson LJ). In this case, the complaining shareholder, who was the wife of the other shareholder, had already benefited from the wrongdoing. When their relationship broke down, she brought a derivative action against the husband. The Court of Appeal held that she was not qualified to bring a derivative action to recover profits for the company.

137 See, Jennifer Payne, n 135.

138 *Zempilas v. J N Taylor Holdings Ltd (in liq.) (No.6)* (1991) 5 ACSR 28; *Aloridge Pty Ltd v. West Australian Gem Exporters Pty Ltd* (1995) 15 ACSR 645.

2.3.5 Summary

In summary, reasons for the abolition of the common law derivative action were numerous. The three main areas of defect in the common law derivative action, as perceived in the various government reports, were:

- the restrictive shareholders' right to sue coupled with the strict common law permission criteria;
- the uncertainty in the recovery of litigation costs; and
- issues relating to majority shareholder ratification of breaches of directors' duties.

It was noted too that the SDA would provide shareholders with an "effective remedy" and could potentially deter corporate misconduct and bring about directors' accountability and good corporate governance.

The objective of this book is to consider whether the SDA has overcome these deficiencies and achieved the intended purposes.

2.4 To what extent has the SDA eliminated the common law problems?

This part provides an overview of the SDA, and at the same time, it addresses the question as to what extent the SDA in Part 2F.1A of the *Corporations Act* 2001 (C'th) has eliminated the common law problems.[139] This part highlights the problem areas that have not been addressed properly or at all in the Act, and provides some comments for further analysis in later chapters. The main conclusion in the book is that the SDA, in its current form, is not working in the way it was originally intended by the legislature.

2.4.1 Areas that have been addressed

2.4.1.1 Standing to sue

Section 236 provides the following persons a right to apply to the court for permission to bring an SDA or to defend an action on behalf of the company:

- a member, former member or person entitled to be registered as a member of the company or of a related body corporate; or
- an officer or former officer of the company.

A former member is included as an eligible applicant as he or she may have been compelled to leave the company in view of the dispute giving rise to an action on behalf of the company; and a director or an officer of the company

139 For ease of reference, the SDA provisions contained in Part 2F.1A of the *Corporations Act* 2001 (C'th) are reproduced in Appendix A.

is also included as they are most likely to be the first to become aware of a right of action that is not being pursued by the company.[140] An empirical study conducted in the first five years of the SDA's operation has, however, shown that most of the SDAs have been brought by current shareholders or directors with shareholding interests,[141] and this is also true in Canada where its SDA has been available since the 1970s.[142]

Section 236 has overcome the common law restrictions on standing by widening the scope of eligible applicants to include a former member, a former officer and any person entitled to be registered as a member of the company (the latter includes an equitable owner of shares). In practice, however, the persons who are allowed to bring a derivative action are, in fact, very limited, as they also need to pass the leave tests provided in s.237(2). There is no automatic entitlement to bring an SDA. The statutory rules on standing are further complicated by the leave tests under s.237(2), under which a complainant is required to apply to the court for leave to bring a derivative action. An eligible applicant must go through a two-step process in bringing an SDA. An applicant must first satisfy the court of the five criteria for leave to bring an SDA; and if successful, only then can the applicant proceed to the next stage and bring the approved SDA with the company being named as the plaintiff.

ASIC is not included as an eligible applicant. As mentioned earlier, ASIC has limited resources and cannot pursue public investigation of all alleged breaches of directors' duties. In some instances, private enforcement by way of a derivative action is preferable, especially in small closely held companies.

2.4.1.2 Ratification no longer a bar to bringing a derivative action

One major transformation and improvement in the derivative action process is that the common law principle relating to shareholder ratification has now been abolished in the context of the SDA. Under s.239, an applicant is not prevented from applying to the court for leave to bring an SDA, even if other members within the company have ratified or approved certain bad behaviour or conduct committed by the directors. Section 239 has clearly abolished the common law position in this regard. Instead, the court may take the ratification or approval into account in deciding what order or judgment to make in relation to the leave application or in the actual derivative proceedings, and in doing so, the court may consider whether the ratification was reasonable and for proper purposes.

140 House of Representatives, *Explanatory Memorandum to the CLERP Bill* 1998, at 20.

141 Ian Ramsay and Ben Saunders, "Litigation by shareholders and directors: An empirical study of the Australian statutory derivative action" (2006) 6 *Journal of Corporate Law Studies* 397, at 26–27.

142 Brian R. Cheffins, "Reforming the derivative action: The Canadian experience and British prospects" (1997) *Company Financial & Insolvency Law Review* 227, at 239.

2.4.2 Areas that have not been properly addressed

2.4.2.1 The leave requirement for bringing statutory derivative action

Section 237(2) sets out five criteria that an applicant must satisfy the court for leave to bring an SDA. The provision states that the court must grant the application if:

(a) it is probable that the company will not itself bring the proceedings, or properly take responsibility for them;
(b) the applicant is acting in good faith;
(c) it is in the best interests of the company that the applicant be granted leave;
(d) there is a serious question to be tried by the court; and
(e) the applicant has given 14 days notice to the company (if practicable) of his or her intention to apply to the court for a derivative action.

The rationale for this provision is that a derivative action is brought on behalf of the company, and so the court is arguably being used as a "filter" to distinguish between vexatious and legitimate actions. The intention was to strike a balance between, on the one hand, allowing shareholders to assert their corporate rights through bringing an SDA, and on the other hand, providing directors with the freedom to make corporate business decisions.[143] It has been said that "tight constraints on the availability" of the SDA are necessary to minimise any abuse by disgruntled shareholders.[144] Clearly, the aim is to screen out any vexatious, frivolous or doubtful action, and allow only applicants who fit into these five preconditions to bring a derivative action.

The five preconditions for leave in s.237(2) were intended to replace the "fraud on the minority" and the "interest of justice" exceptions. Section 237(2) was designed to simplify matters for an applicant seeking to bring an SDA. However, the statutory framework has created a different set of complications for shareholder applicants, particularly in relation to:

- the "good faith" requirement in s.237(2)(b); and
- the need to demonstrate that the proposed SDA "is in the best interests of the company" under s.237(2)(c).

Both "good faith" and "best interests" are not defined in the Act.

(I) "GOOD FAITH" IN S.237(2)(B)

It has been argued that the concept of "good faith" is similar to the "clean hands" approach in derivative actions.[145] Although "good faith" is relevant in

143 House of Representatives, *Explanatory Memorandum to the CLERP Bill* 1998, at 21, [6.33].
144 House of Representatives, *Explanatory Memorandum to the CLERP Bill* 1998, at 5.
145 Payne, n 135.

SDA, its inclusion in the statute is questionable, as will be explained in detail in Chapter 4. Some judges have noted that it is "unwise" to list all categories of "good faith", as there are "different factual circumstances".[146] In *Swansson v. R A Pratt Properties Pty Ltd*, Palmer J states:[147]

> "[I]n my opinion, there are at least two interrelated factors to which the Courts will always have regard in determining whether the good faith requirement of s.237(2)(b) is satisfied. The first is whether the applicant honestly believes that a good cause of action exists and has a reasonable prospect of success. Clearly, whether the applicant honestly holds such a belief would not simply be a matter of bald assertion; the applicant may be disbelieved if no reasonable person in the circumstances could hold that belief. The second factor is whether the applicant is seeking to bring the derivative suit for such a collateral purpose as would amount to an abuse of process."

This statement has been followed in numerous subsequent cases.[148] Although s.237(2) states that the court must grant leave if the criteria have been satisfied, it is possible for the court to deny the grant of leave if the applicant has not met these two further tests in *Swansson v. R A Pratt Properties Pty Ltd;* that is, if the court is not satisfied that the proposed derivative action has strong prospects of success and if the applicant is found to have a collateral purpose in the proposed derivative action. In short, when deciding whether to grant leave, the court will consider a wide range of other relevant factors to decide whether the applicant is acting in "good faith", effectively this means that the court can deny the grant of leave on other grounds. For example, if an applicant cannot afford to pay for the derivative action, then the applicant is unlikely to succeed in establishing "good faith" and "best interests".[149]

(II) "BEST INTERESTS" IN S.237(2)(C)

The more concerning issue relates to the criterion that the applicant must demonstrate to the court that the proposed action "is in the best interests of the company". There is much uncertainty in the interpretation of this provision. Australia is one of the exceptionally few countries that use this expression.[150]

146 *Swansson v. R A Pratt Properties Pty Ltd* (2002) 42 ACSR 313, at [35] (Palmer J); approved unanimously by the NSW Court of Appeal in *Chahwan v. Euphoric Pty Ltd* (2008) 65 ACSR 661, at [83].

147 *Swansson v. R A Pratt Properties Pty Ltd* (2002) 42 ACSR 313, [36].

148 *Huang v. Wang* [2016] NSWCA 164; *Fiduciary Ltd v. Morningstar Research Pty Ltd* [2005] NSWSC 442.

149 *Cooper v. Myrtace Consulting Pty Ltd* [2014] FCA 480; *Re Fishinthenet Investments Pty Ltd and Coastal Waters Seafood Pty Ltd* [2014] NSWSC 260.

150 The South African SDA, introduced in July 2012, has its provision identical to the Australian counterpart. Many other developed jurisdictions (such as Canada, Singapore, New Zealand,

The decisions of the courts have been varied in Australia. There are several problems with this phrasing. First, it is *phrased in absolute terms* that the applicant must demonstrate that the proposed derivative action *is* in the best interests of the company,[151] which is quite difficult to fulfill. Obviously, it is not possible to predict the outcome of a court case. Litigation involves risks and there is no certainty of a successful outcome even where the plaintiff has strong evidence to support the arguments. For an applicant to prove in absolute terms that the proposed action will have a successful outcome is almost impossible.

Second, the "best interests" test is rather subjective. There is no legal definition of that term and no way of quantifying "best". There will often be uncertainty in determining what is "in the best interests of the company" from the applicant's perspective and from the perspective of the presiding court. A successful derivative action may lead to a number of possible outcomes, and not all outcomes can be considered as "in the best interests of the company". For example, if a company is awarded a large amount of compensation, this may be seen as beneficial to the company; however, if a company is awarded only a non-monetary relief (for example, an order requiring directors to comply with their duties to the company), this may or may not be regarded as beneficial to the company. Defining what is "best" is a matter of opinion, and is based very much on an individual's perception of the outcome. As will be canvassed in chapter 5, there is no clarity in the judicial interpretation of the term "best interests".

Paragraphs (a), (d) and (e) of s.237(2) does not seem to cause any major issue.

2.4.2.2 Derivative action against a third party and the business judgment rule

A vexing problem with the statutory model is whether it is possible for an applicant to apply for leave to bring an SDA against a *former director of the company*. Whether it is harder for an applicant to bring a derivative action is dependent on when that former director has departed from the company. If the former director has left the company more than six months ago, the former director is no longer categorised as a "related party", but rather as a "third party",[152] which means that the applicant must establish to the court's

United Kingdom, Hong Kong, Malaysia) have a much more lenient provision in favour of shareholder litigation, as will be discussed further in Chapter 5.

151 See, *Swansson v. RA Pratt Properties Pty Ltd* (2002) 42 ACSR 313; [2002] NSWSC 583, at [55] (Palmer J); *Drew v. Lynch* [2019] FCA 632, at [108]; *Re Dynamic Industries Pty Ltd* [2014] VSC 101, at [96].

152 Section 237(4) of the *Corporations Act* 2001 (C'th) defines a person to be a "third party" if the person is *not* a related party; and related party is, in turn, defined in s.228 to include current directors and relatives. A former director is included as a "related party" under s.228(5), but only if he or she was a director within the first six months.

satisfaction not only the leave criteria under s.237(2) but must also overcome the hurdle in s.237(3).

This scenario could occur in cases involving alleged breaches of directors' duties for the proposed defendant to become a former director. Section 237(3) refers to a "third party", and there is a rebuttable presumption that granting leave to bring a derivative action may not be in the best interests of the company if:

- the derivative proceedings are by the company against a third party or by a third party against the company; and
- the company has decided not to bring any proceedings or not to defend the proceedings or to discontinue, settle or compromise the proceedings; and
- all of the directors who participated in that decision acted in good faith for a proper purpose; did not have a material personal interest in the decision; informed themselves about the subject matter of the decision to the extent they reasonable believed to be appropriate; and rationally believed that the decision was in the best interests of the company. (A director's belief to that effect will be deemed to be a rational one unless no reasonable person in the director's position would hold that belief.)

This third point in s.237(3) is equivalent to the BJR referred to in s.180(2) whereby this rule (or the presumption in favour of the directors) makes it harder for an applicant to succeed in obtaining leave to bring an SDA against a former director on the basis that the board of directors has made a good business decision not to sue at the time.

Section 237(3) could be a significant hurdle for some applicants. If an applicant wishes to bring a derivative action against a former director, the applicant may need to apply to bring an SDA preferably within the first six months of the director's departure from the company. If an application for leave is made after six months, the applicant will be faced with the rebuttable presumption under s.237(3) that granting leave is not in the best interests of the company because the proceeding is by the company against a third party.

Even if a former director has resigned from the company less than six months before the leave application is brought, it may still be difficult for an applicant to rebut the presumption in s.237(3) referred to in the third point, equivalent to the BJR.[153] The underlying purpose of this rule is to provide

153 This third point in s.237(3) is phrased in identical terms to the business judgment rule in s.180(2) of the *Corporations Act* 2001 (C'th). Some scholars have argued that the business judgment rules is "unnecessary": See Paul Redmond, "Safe Harbours or Sleepy Hollows? Does Australia need the Statutory Business Judgment Rule?" in Ian Ramsay (ed.), *Corporate Governance and Duties of Company Directors*, Centre for Corporate Law and Securities Regulations, University of Melbourne, 1997, where Redmond argued that it was "unnecessary" for Australia to introduce the BJR given the nature of court cases we had on the duty

greater protection to directors in the exercise of their duty of care and diligence to the company. The rule confirms the common law position that the court will not review *bona fide* business decisions.[154]

It is difficult to understand how the strict leave criteria for an SDA under s.237(2) against the operation of the statutory BJR in favour of the directors would achieve a balance between the need to allow shareholder litigation to enforce directors' duties and the need to provide directors with the freedom to manage the company and discharge their duties. It seems that s.237(3) leans too much towards the protection of company directors in the sense that the board of directors could easily hide behind the business judgment rule in s.237(3).[155]

2.4.2.3 The costs provision

Section 242 is the only provision dealing with litigation costs in SDA. Under the current wording, there is no certainty that an applicant's costs will be indemnified out of company funds. This is one of the main obstacles to shareholder litigation. Section 242 reads:

> The Court may at any time make any orders it considers appropriate about the costs of [the applicant, the company or any other party] ... in relation to proceedings brought or intervened in with leave under section 237....

Further, the Explanatory Memorandum explains the intent of s.242 as follows:[156]

> "The Court's discretion regarding the allocation of costs is aimed at providing an additional safeguard in respect of use of company funds. In particular, the court would be able to protect a bona fide shareholder against liability for costs indemnifying them out of company funds while at the same time allowing the Court a further means of discouraging unmeritorious or doubtful action."

---

of care and diligence. See Jason Harris and Anil Hargovan, "Still a sleepy hollow? Directors' liability and the business judgment rule" (2016) 31 *Australian Journal of Corporate Law* 319, at 324; W. Bainbridge and T. Connor, "Another way forward? The scope for an appellate court to reinterpret the statutory business judgment rule" (2016) 34 *Company and Securities Law Journal* 415, at 419–421.

154 House of Representatives, *Explanatory Memorandum to the CLERP Bill* 1998, at 17, [6.3–6.4].

155 The statutory business judgment rule has been described to mean offering directors "a *safe harbour* from personal liability in relation to honest, informed and rational business judgments" which is reflected in s.237(3) of the *Corporations Act* 2001 (C'th). See also CLERP Proposal Paper No. 3, *Proposals for Reform: Directors' Duties and Corporate Governance* (Report 1997), at 21.

156 House of Representatives, *Explanatory Memorandum to the CLERP Bill* 1998, at 26.

Clearly, the provision is broad enough to the point where it gives the court a complete discretion to decide when, how and against whom costs are to be awarded. The court can make a costs order against the applicant, the company or any other party irrespective of the outcome of the leave application or the derivative proceedings.

Although the above explanatory statement is clear in providing support to shareholders by allowing them an indemnity out of company funds, it is, however, not clear as to when exactly the court will make that indemnity costs order. The drafting of s.242 was not a mistake.[157]

It has been stated in government law reform reports that the costs issue was "the greatest inhibitor" to shareholders seeking to bring a derivative action at common law.[158] However, s.242 has not properly addressed the costs issue.

As will be explained in Chapter 6, the current position is that the courts have often linked the "best interests of the company" criterion in s.237(2)(c) with the costs provision in s.242 and made a conditional order that leave be granted *subject to* the applicant paying costs of the proceedings.[159] It is the view of the author that, if an applicant has satisfied the court with the leave requirement, then the successful applicant ought to be entitled to a costs indemnity order payable by the company.

2.4.3 Areas that have not been addressed

2.4.3.1 Company in liquidation

There is no provision in Part 2F.1A that refers to insolvency. It is therefore unclear whether the SDA provisions would apply to cases where a company has gone into liquidation. Section 237(2)(c) states that the proposed derivative action has to be in the best interests of the "company", without mentioning "in liquidation". Some courts have made it clear that Part 2F.1A does not apply to a company in liquidation, while other courts have exercised their inherent jurisdiction under the insolvency provisions to allow shareholder derivative action.[160]

157 Keith L Fletcher, "CLERP and minority shareholder rights" (2001) 13 *Australian Journal of Corporate Law* 290, at 299, where the author noted s.242 to have been "deliberately drafted in a manner that denies the successful applicant the assurance that court recognition will result in the company becoming liable for the reasonable costs of litigating on its behalf".

158 CASAC, *Statutory Derivative Action* (Report, 1993), at 8. See also, SSC on LCA, *Company Directors' Duties: Report on the Social and Fiduciary Duties and Obligations of Company Directors* (1989), [11.29]; House of Representatives Standing Committee on LCA, *Corporate Practices and the Rights of Shareholders* (November 1991), at 190; CLERP Proposal Paper No. 3, *Proposals for Reform: Directors' Duties and Corporate Governance* (1997), at 32.

159 *Power v. Ekstein* [2010] NSWSC 137; *Huang v. Wang* [2016] NSWCA 164.

160 This will be canvassed in Chapter 5, Part 4.

2.4.3.2 The free riding problem

There is no provision in the Act dealing with the free riding problem. One possible solution could be to allow a successful shareholder applicant to recover some of their costs and to require non-participating shareholders who are to benefit from the successful action to make some contribution towards indemnifying the plaintiff. This may be achieved by way of the non-participating shareholders receiving less of the benefit and giving the plaintiff that extra bit more as an incentive for bringing the action on behalf of the company.

The other possibility in minimising the free riding problem could be to allow only the shareholder applicant and other affected shareholders to receive compensation. For example, in Canada, the court has the power to award a remedy only to the shareholder complainant in the derivative action.[161]

2.4.4 Provisions in the SDA that were not previously available

Provisions added to the SDA that were not previously available under common law are these:

2.4.4.1 Leave requirement for discontinuing, compromising or settling the approved action

Just as there is a requirement for leave to bring an SDA, there is a corresponding requirement for leave to discontinue or compromise or settle the approved action under s.240. This is to ensure that there is no collusion between the applicant and the defendant in ways that would benefit only the applicant and not the company as a whole. This requirement is reasonable given that a derivative action is an action brought on behalf of the company.

Section 240 is clear to the extent that where an applicant has commenced the approved derivative action but later wishes to discontinue the action or to compromise or settle with the defendant that they must return to the court for approval. However, it is not clear whether the applicant has to return to the court to explain "why" if the applicant decides *not* to proceed to the next stage and bring the approved action. There appears to be no obligation for a successful applicant to commence the approved derivative action. Some applicants might not be able to afford bringing the derivative action due to a lack of litigation funding support, while other applicants might have used the successful leave application as a threat of liability on the proposed defendant to try to resolve their internal disputes. This lack of clarity in s.240 is not a major issue and will not be considered further in the book.

161 *Canada Business Corporations Act* 1985, s.240(c); and *Ontario Business Corporations Act* 1990, s.247(c).

2.4.4.2 Leave requirement for a substituted applicant

Where leave has been granted to an applicant to bring the proposed derivative action, it is possible under s.238 for another person to be substituted to take over the running of that action, provided that the person is an eligible applicant under s.236 and is acting in good faith with a view to continuing the derivative action in the company's best interests as per the requirement in s.237(2). In essence, the substituted applicant may have to go through the same process as the previous applicant and demonstrate his or her suitability to continue that action.

2.4.4.3 Power of the court to appoint an independent investigator

Section 241 provides the court with a wide power to make various other orders in relation to the derivative action and the conduct of the action, including the power to appoint "an independent person to investigate and report to the court" on:

- the financial affairs of the company;
- the facts or circumstances that gave rise to the cause of action; or
- the costs incurred in the proceedings by all relevant parties.

In effect, the investigator appointed will have access to all company books and information for determining whether the application for a derivative action be granted, and whether the intention to bring the proposed action is one that is legitimate and not vexatious or frivolous.

Regrettably, this provision is rarely used. Instead, the courts appear to have relied mainly on the evidence presented by the applicants to decide whether to grant leave. One possible explanation could be that the courts are being cautious not to add further unnecessary costs to the proceedings.

2.5 Conclusion

As noted earlier, the introduction of the SDA was a major development in Australian corporate law. The transformation from the common law derivative action to a statutory model has been a worthwhile exercise. However, whether the legislation has achieved a balance between the need to allow shareholders to bring an SDA to enforce directors' duties and obtain a remedy on behalf of the company where the company is unable or unwilling to do so, and the need to allow directors the autonomy in exercising their power and discharging their duties is questionable.

On the one hand, the strict leave requirement contained in the SDA under s.237(2) is intended to prevent unmeritorious or frivolous action on the part of the shareholder applicant. On the other hand, the simultaneous introduction of the statutory business judgment rule in s.237(3) was intended to provide directors with protection against any personal liability to the company. In other words, s.237(3) provides directors with a "safe harbour" from being sued by a shareholder by way of allowing directors the presumption that they have made a good corporate business decision in every case and that a shareholder who wishes to challenge that decision would have the onus of rebutting it. In reality, a shareholder applicant who wishes to bring a derivative action must satisfy the court of the five leave criteria in s.237(2), and if a director to be sued for breach of directors' duties happens to be a former director (or has become a "third party" as described earlier), the situation for a shareholder to apply for leave and bring a derivative action appears even more gloomy, in the sense that the shareholder applicant must also rebut the presumption under s.237(3).

It is the view of the author that the balance is tilted too far towards the protection of directors. To correct this, the objective of this book, as noted in Chapter 1, is to suggest modification to the existing SDA by making slight adjustments or amendments to the SDA provisions.[162] In reading the provisions closely, it appears that some problem areas previously surfaced in the common law derivative action have not been addressed properly in the statutory framework; and by removing the common law exceptions and replacing them with a very strict leave requirement, this has essentially created new problem areas instead, as noted in the discussions above.

More importantly, although the costs provision in s.242 was added to the legislation, that costs provision has done no more than reinvent the original common law problem relating to costs, that is, the court has a broad power to decide when, how and against whom a costs order will be made. The broad phrasing of the costs provision is unhelpful. There remains an uncertainty for shareholder applicants as to the recovery of their costs for bringing a derivative action. In short, there is no incentive for shareholders to seek to bring a derivative action due to the uncertainty in the recovery of their costs.

A second concerning factor is the strict leave requirement in s.237(2). In particular, for a court to consider granting leave, an applicant must show "good faith" and must show that the proposed derivative action "is in the best interests of the company". Both of these criteria are onerous and have no clear measure. These are new problem areas under the SDA. They are a further obstacle for shareholders seeking to bring an SDA.

As noted above, the book aims to correct the imbalance by making suggestions for changes to the SDA provisions. To strengthen the utility of the SDA, and to encourage genuine shareholders to monitor directors' duties and to bring appropriate actions on behalf of the company when necessary to remedy a wrong done to the company and to assist in bringing about corporate accountability, changes to the legislative provisions are necessary. Broadly,

162 This book is not about proposed amendment to the Business Judgment Rule, as this area has been covered extensively over the years by other scholars.

the subsequent chapters will provide suggestions for changes in relation to the "good faith" and "in the best interests of the company" tests and in relation to the costs provision. To do this, the next chapter, Chapter 3, will first present the findings of an empirical study of the SDA in Australia to substantiate and add to the reasons as to why the SDA, in particular the provisions in s.237(2)(b) and (c) and the costs provision in s.242, is in need of reform.

3 An empirical study of the statutory derivative action in Australia

3.1 Introduction

The purpose of this chapter is to conduct an empirical study of the statutory derivative action ("SDA") under Part 2F.1A (sections 236-242) of the Australian *Corporations Act* 2001 (C'th) ("CA"). As noted in the earlier chapters, the outcomes of this empirical study will be of interest to not only countries that already have the statutory framework that are considering amending their local variants but also to countries that do not yet have the statutory framework that may find this book helpful and relevant when considering introducing their own local variants. This chapter provides the first comprehensive empirical study into the statutory derivative action in Australia. The study assesses the utility of the SDA in the 20 year period from 13 March 2000 to 28 December 2019.[1] In particular, the study aims to address the following research questions:

(1) What is the proportion of successful and unsuccessful leave applications over the period of 20 years?
(2) On the successful leave applications – Was the applicant successful in obtaining costs indemnity for the leave application, and was the company required to fund the approved derivative action?
(3) On the unsuccessful leave applications – Which of the five criteria in s.237(2) have been most difficult for an applicant to satisfy the court for leave to bring an SDA?

The first question measures the success and failure rate in obtaining leave of the court to bring an SDA, which will provide some indication of the criteria that shareholders have found most difficult in establishing a case for leave to bring an SDA. The second question is relevant insofar as analysing the courts' treatment of the costs provision in s.242. The empirical data collated in this

1 Since that period and with the outbreak of COVID-19 pandemic in 2020, there has been no substantial increase in the number of court decisions relating to the statutory derivative action. A slight increase in case number would not have changed the outcomes of this study. 13 March 2000 was the date the statutory derivative action came into operation in Australia.

DOI: 10.4324/9781003430063-3

study will form a further discussion in Chapter 6 for the purposes of assessing whether the costs provision needs changing. The third question relates to identifying which of the criteria in s.237(2) that the applicant has found most challenging in satisfying the court for leave. The datasets collated will then be used to further analyse in later chapters as to whether and to what extent the leave criteria are in need of amendment in order to improve the utility of the SDA process.

Overall, there are two purposes in this study: (i) to understand which of the parties is liable to pay costs in the leave application and the substantive derivative action under s.242; and (ii) to identify which of the criteria in s.237(2) that the applicants have difficulty in satisfying the court for leave to bring an SDA.

As stated in Chapter 2, the introduction of the SDA has been a major development in Australian corporate law. The main reason for introducing the SDA was that the common law derivative action was perceived to be "inadequate" as shareholder protection of their rights in the company.[2] The intention of the legislation was twofold: First, to provide shareholders with a more "effective remedy" by enabling them to bring the necessary court action on behalf of the company;[3] and second, SDA could be used as a private enforcement tool to bring about enhancement of shareholder protection by deterring corporate misconduct and making directors accountable for their actions.[4] This empirical study serves to partly address the first intended purpose, that is, whether SDA in its current form has provided an "effective remedy" for shareholders. This study is not a measure of directors' accountability. It is not possible to empirically assess whether the SDA framework has achieved the purpose of enforcing directors' duties or deterring corporate misconduct. A successful outcome in an SDA may *indirectly* bring about some directors' accountability, but there is no guarantee that a successful outcome will deter breach of directors' duties, as discussed in the preceding chapters.

To present the empirical data in a meaningful way, Part 2 begins with an outline of the key provisions applied in the SDA as a point of reference, and provides a brief overview of other available shareholder remedies so that the SDA is understood in both its legal and empirical contexts. Part 3 sets out the study's objectives, describes the research methodology and presents results relating to leave applications for SDAs. Part 4 analyses the results and

2 Companies and Securities Law Review Committee ("CSLRC"), *Enforcement of the Duties of Directors and Officers of a Company by Means of a Statutory Derivative Action* (Report No. 12, Nov 1990); at [6].

3 House of Representatives, *Explanatory Memorandum to the Corporate Law Economic Reform Program ("CLERP") Bill* 1998, at 21.

4 Companies and Securities Advisory Committee ("CASAC"), *Statutory Derivative Action* (Report, 1993), at 4; Corporate Law Economic Reform Program Proposal Paper No. 3 ("CLERP Proposal Paper No. 3"), *Proposals for Reform: Directors' Duties and Corporate Governance* (1997), at 32–33.

provides some observations. Part 5 summarises the findings and provides an overview for subsequent chapters.

This chapter focuses on the quantitative aspects of the study by presenting results and forming a conclusion as to which of the leave criteria in s.237(2) need further consideration in subsequent chapters and whether the costs provision in s.242 needs amendment. Extensive case law analysis and discussions will be reserved for later chapters.

3.2 Background

3.2.1 Key provisions in Part 2F.1A of the Corporations Act

Chapter 2 discussed the differences between SDA and common law derivative action and the reasons for the abolition of the common law position. That chapter also considered the role of the SDA. For this chapter, this part provides only a brief overview of the key provisions relevant for this study.

There is a two-step process for bringing a derivative action under Part 2F.1A of the *Corporations Act* 2001 ("CA"), comprising sections 236–242. These provisions are reproduced in Appendix A. This two-step process has been "well-accepted".[5] The first is that an applicant must obtain leave of the court to bring an SDA, and if granted leave, only then can the applicant proceed to the next stage and bring the substantive derivative action, in which case the company will be named as the plaintiff, with the successful applicant facilitating the action. The approved action will proceed in the usual process similar to other civil litigation cases, with discovery and interrogatory conducted as part of the proceedings. If an applicant is unsuccessful in the leave application and there is no appeal or the court dismisses the appeal, the case ends there and no derivative action has taken place.

Section 236 sets out the rights of certain persons to apply to bring a derivative action. The person who is said to have standing to bring such action would have to be a shareholder, a former shareholder or a person entitled to be registered as a member of the company or a related body corporate, or an officer or former officer of the company. The word "officer" is defined to include company director. The term "company" is defined narrowly to apply only to a "company" registered under the CA.[6] Further, leave of the court must be obtained.

Section 237(2) sets out five criteria that an applicant must satisfy the court for leave, namely:

(a) It is probable that the company will not itself bring the proceedings, or properly take responsibility for them;

5 *Akierman Holdings Pty Limited v Akerman (No 3)* [2021] NSWSC 869, at [150] (Parker J); see also *Huang v. Wang* [2016] NSWCA 164, at [85] (Barrett AJA).

6 The terms "officer" and "company" are defined in s.9 of the CA.

(b) The applicant is acting in "good faith";
(c) It "is in the best interests of the company" that the applicant be granted permission to bring the proposed derivative action;
(d) There is a serious question to be tried; and
(e) The applicant has given a 14-day notice to the company (if practicable) of his or her intention to apply to the court for a derivative action.

The Explanatory Memorandum accompanying the introduction of the SDA notes that the requirements in s.237(2) are intended to strike a balance between the need to encourage shareholders to seek redress on behalf of the company where it is unable to do so and the need to prevent proceedings that are unlikely to succeed in court.[7]

An application for leave can be made to a Supreme Court of a State or Territory or to the Federal Court.[8] If an applicant has satisfied all five criteria, the court must grant the application for leave to bring a derivative action.[9] However, as will be canvassed in later chapters, there are other ways for a court to deny leave, for example, if an applicant is unable to fund the proposed derivative action.[10] An applicant for leave under s.237(2) has the burden of establishing the grounds for leave on the balance of probabilities.[11] If a matter relevant to the s.237 leave application is in contest, the court may permit limited cross-examination.[12]

It is worth noting that if a wrong done to the company or certain conduct of directors has been approved or ratified by shareholders at a general meeting, such ratification or approval will not bar a minority shareholder from applying to bring a derivative action; instead, the court may take the ratification or approval into account when making judgment regarding the derivative proceedings. This is provided for under s.239 and has overturned the common law position, where previously ratification was a potential barrier to the bringing of a common law derivative action.

Section 242 provides the court with a broad power to make any order it "considers appropriate" *at any time* about the costs of the applicant, the company or any other party in relation to the leave application or the proceedings brought or intervened in on behalf of the company. The provision also allows the court to make an order for "indemnification for costs".

7 House of Representatives, *Explanatory Memorandum to the CLERP Bill* 1998, at [6.33]
8 The term "Court" is defined in s.58AA of the CA, as comprising these courts.
9 *Connective Services Pty Ltd v. Slea Pty Ltd* [2018] VSCA 229, at [2] (Ferguson CJ, Whelan and McLeish JJA); *Fiduciary Ltd v. Morningstar Research Pty Ltd* [2005] NSWSC 442, (2005) 53 ACSR 732, at 735 (Austin J).
10 See, for example, *Hughes v. Robba* [2021] NSWSC 1414; *Cooper v. Myrtace Consulting Pty Ltd* [2014] FCA 480; *Robash Pty Ltd v. Gladstone Pacific Nickel Pty Ltd* [2011] NSWSC 1235.
11 *Slea Pty Ltd v. Connective Services Pty Ltd* [2017] VSC 609, at [51] (Robson J) (Appeal dismissed: *Connective Services Pty Ltd v. Slea Pty Ltd* [2018] VSCA 229; *Swansson v. RA Pratt* [2002] NSWSC 583, at [54].
12 *Swansson v. RA Pratt Properties Pty Ltd* (2002) 42 ACSR 313; [2002] NSWSC 583, at [26].

In addition to s.242, the court has a wide power to make a range of other orders under s.241, including power to appoint "an independent person to investigate and report to the court" on matters relating to the proceedings and the conduct of the proceedings,[13] including on matters relating to the financial affairs of the company, the facts or circumstances that gave rise to the cause of the action and the costs incurred in the proceedings. In effect, s.241 allows the court to have access to company information so as to determine whether an application for a derivative action be granted, whether the intention to bring a derivative action is one that is legitimate and not vexatious, unmeritorious or frivolous. This provision, however, is rarely used by the court.

3.2.2 Brief summary of alternative shareholder remedies[14]

SDA is not the only type of remedy available to shareholders. It may be the only type available for them to enforce their corporate rights and bring an action on behalf of the company as a corporate entity. However, if the criteria for leave in s.237(2) are too onerous for an applicant to satisfy the court, or if there is uncertainty in the recovery of the applicant's costs in bringing the derivative proceedings, some aggrieved shareholders may turn to other alternatives in seeking relief instead.

A statutory oppression action is one example. A minority shareholder can make a personal claim for an oppression remedy if the conduct of the company's affairs or the actual or proposed act of the company or a resolution or proposed resolution of members in the company is contrary to the interests of the members as a whole or is oppressive or unfair to a member.[15] Permission is not required to commence an oppression action. It is available to all types of shareholders in all types of companies, but it is most used in private or closely held companies where a minority shareholder cannot satisfactorily deal with the other shareholders and may be restricted in some way from transferring their shares to others. A shareholder may also bring an oppression action to remedy a corporate wrong under some circumstances,[16] and the remedy granted by the court will be personal to the plaintiff. Section 233 provides a range of remedies that an oppressed shareholder can request from the court, including an order regulating the conduct of the company's affairs in the future or an order requiring the company to purchase the oppressed member's shares or even an order for the company to institute or defend in specified actions. An oppression remedy is only available to members of the company or who have shareholding interests in the company.[17]

13 *Corporations Act* 2001 (C'th), s.241(1)(d) and (2).

14 These will be discussed in detail in Chapter 7.

15 *Corporations Act* 2001 (C'th), s.232.

16 Elizabeth Boros, "Remedies for oppression cases for derivative wrongs" (2014) 32 *Company and Securities Law Journal* 151.

17 *Corporations Act* 2001 (C'th), s.234.

A class action is another example, though this tends to be relied upon by shareholders in large and public companies. A class action is a type of representative or group action brought, *not* on behalf of the company, but against the company, on the grounds that the company has been involved in, for example, misleading or deceptive conduct or has failed to provide full disclosure in relation to a share value or share price.[18] Where there is a large pool of shareholders, a litigation funder is more willing to fund a class action with the arrangement that these shareholders would agree to give a percentage of their recoveries to the litigation funder at the conclusion of the case.[19] In Australia, the class action procedure is regulated under Part IVA of the *Federal Court of Australia Act* 1974 (C'th). It is possible for shareholders in small private companies to bring a class action against the company provided there are at least seven members affected by the same, similar or related circumstances.[20] The advantage of bringing a class action is that court approval is not required to commence such action.[21]

3.3 Empirical study of the Australian SDA

3.3.1 Objectives of this study

The two main objectives in this study are (i) to identify which of the criteria in s.237(2) are most difficult for an applicant to demonstrate to the court for leave, and (ii) to assess how the courts have treated the costs provision in s.242 in terms of the number of costs orders made in favour of the applicants. To this end, this study aims to answer the following **research questions**:

(1) What is the ratio of successful and unsuccessful leave applications over the entire 20 years?
(2) For those successful leave applications – Was the applicant successful in obtaining a costs indemnity order for the application and was the company required to fund the approved derivative action?
(3) For those unsuccessful leave applications – Which of the criteria in s.237(2) have been most difficult for the applicant to satisfy the court for leave to bring an SDA?

18 See for example, *Caason Investments Pty Limited v. Cao* (No.2) [2018] FCA 527; *Clarke v. Sandhurst Trustees Limited (No.2)* [2018] FCA 511; *Perera v. Getswift Limited* [2018] FCA 732.
19 For further discussion on commercial litigation funding, see Lang Thai, "Commercial litigation funding: The need to impose regulations to improve the outcome of the shareholder class actions" (2011) 4 *Journal of the Australasian Law Teachers Association* 1. For discussion relating to shareholder class action, see Lang Thai, "Class action procedure in Australia – Issues and challenges" in Colin Picker and Guy Seidman (eds.), *The Dynamism of Civil Procedure: Global Trends and Developments* (Ius Gentium: Comparative Perspectives on Law and Justice series, Springer, 2016), at 215–236; Michael Legg and Samuel J. Hickey, "Finality and fairness in Australian shareholder class action settlements" (2019) 41 *Sydney Law Review*, 185.
20 *Federal Court of Australia Act* 1974 (C'th), s.33C.
21 Class action and commercial litigation funding will be discussed further in Chapter 7.

In answering the above research questions, this empirical study will take the approach of answering the following twelve **design questions** first:[22]

(1) When was the case decided?
(2) What was the name of the court that decided the case?
(3) Was the case at first instance or on appeal?
(4) What type of company was it – private or public?
(5) Was the company solvent or under some form of external administration?
(6) Who was the applicant?
(7) Who opposed the leave application?
(8) What were the allegations pleaded?
(9) What was the outcome in the leave application?
(10) For unsuccessful leave applications – what types of reason were given by the court?
(11) For successful leave applications – was the applicant successful in obtaining costs indemnity for the application?
(12) Was the company required to fund the applicant in relation to the approved derivative action?

These design questions have been adapted from a 2006 study where Ramsay and Saunders compared the first five years of operation of the SDA with the previous five years under the common law position and found that there was no significant increase in the use of SDA. Their empirical data shows only 31 leave applications for an SDA during the period 2000–2005 and 30 common law cases for a derivative action during 1995–2000.[23]

This current study extends the entire period of 20 years, and therefore statistically, a larger sample of data over an extended period is likely to yield a more accurate and more reliable picture of the patterns of use of the SDA. This study provides a comprehensive update of empirical data of all leave application cases decided from 13 March 2000 to 28 December 2019 in order to assess which areas of the law within SDA require further consideration and closer analysis of cases in subsequent chapters.

3.3.2 Research methodology

The study begins by searching through cases from two electronic databases in the period 13 March 2000 to 28 December 2019. The Australian Legal Information Institute's website ("AustLII") was used as a preliminary search, followed by the LexisNexis AU database to confirm search results, collect datasets and download all relevant court judgments. These databases are

22 Some of these questions have been adapted from an article by Ian M. Ramsay and Ben Saunders, "Litigation by shareholders and directors: An empirical study of the Australian statutory derivative action" (2006) 6 *Journal of Corporate Law Studies* 397.

23 Ramsay and Saunders, n 22, at 425.

chosen as they are regarded as reputable and reliable by legal academics and practitioners. Searches were carried out using the following terms: "Corporations Act 2001 Part 2F.1A"; "Corporations Act 2001 Pt 2F.1A"; "Corporations Act 2001 section 237"; "Corporations Act 2001 s237"; "Corporations Act 2001 section 236"; "Corporations Act 2001 s236"; "statutory derivative action"; "derivative action"; "statutory derivative litigation"; "derivative litigation"; "Corporations Act 2001 section 242"; "Corporations Act 2001 s242"; "Corporations Act 2001 section 241"; "Corporations Act 2001 s241". The purpose of using these search terms was to look for all relevant court judgments relating to applications for leave filed in all court jurisdictions in Australia and the relevant costs indemnity orders. A vast majority of cases consider only s.237 (the leave criteria), and a few consider s.236 (applicant's right to apply) and the costs issue under s.242. Judges in many of the cases did not consider other provisions in Part 2F.1A.

Some judges considered the costs issue in the leave application without referring to s.242, which is not unusual given the flexibility in the wording of the provision. In some of the earlier cases, Barrett J of the New South Wales Supreme Court, a leading corporate law scholar and practitioner, has noted that "costs could be dealt with in a general way",[24] and the court is "free to approach matters … unconfined by statutory prescriptions".[25]

The research found 449 reported court judgments. These were read and analysed, and narrowed down to 168 *relevant* leave application cases based on the above 12 design questions. Some judgments involve appeal against the original first instance decision, in which case, both the appeal and the first instance decisions were combined and counted as one leave application. The other judgments not counted as relevant were about other matters other than an application for leave to bring a derivative action. For example, there were cases about an oppression remedy, a winding up application, an injunction order or an application for inspection of company documents – these have not been included in the count of 168. Other cases not included in the 168 leave applications were those where the applicants had filed a separate application for costs, in which case, these were counted as relating to the costs question.

Where an application for leave was successful, further searches were carried out using the name of the proposed company plaintiff and the proposed defendant(s) in order to try to assess whether there was any derivative action resulting from the successful leave application. Surprisingly, only three derivative actions have gone through to final judgment.[26]

24 *Charlton v. Baber* [2003] NSWSC 745, at [73].

25 *Foyster v. Foyster Holdings* [2003] NSWSC 135, at [12]. See also *In the Matter of Wan Jia (Australia) International Development Pty Ltd* [2012] NSWSC 1007, at [13] (Black J); *McLaughlin v. Dungowan Manly Pty Limited* [2010] NSWSC 306, at [8–9] (Ward J).

26 *Reale v Duncan Reale* [2006] NSWSC 227; *Maher v. Honeysett & Maher Electrical Contractors Pty Ltd* [2005] NSWSC 859; *Wood v. Links Golf Tasmania Pty Ltd* [2010] FCA 570. These cases will be canvassed further in Chapter 6.

As in all other empirical studies, the data collected are inevitably subject to the issue of selection bias. In other words, the datasets and judgments collected in the current study may not be a representative sample for a number of reasons. First, the study is limited to reported judgments only and does not include cases where the applicants have withdrawn the application before court hearing. Second, although the electronic databases used for this research are reputable, they are subject to some inaccuracy (for example, issues relating to duplication due to cases with different citations given). Third, some leave application cases may have been settled or rejected by the court and may not have been publicly reported. Finally, the datasets collected for this study are limited to the selection of 12 design questions identified as relevant for the intended purposes in the analysis. While these limitations may affect some conclusions drawn in this research, they are not significant enough to prevent meaningful use of the data. This is because this empirical study will be further supported by a qualitative assessment in later chapters.

This next part answers the above 12 design questions by way of presenting the results.

3.3.3 Results and interpretations

(i) When was the case decided?

Figure 3.1 shows the number of leave applications filed per year in all court jurisdictions over the entire 20 years. There is a year-to-year variation, with no more than 10 cases in an annual total in 2000–2005, then with a slight increase between 11 and 14 cases per year in 2006–2012, before returning to the low annual total in 2013–2019.

The few leave applications in the first five years could be explained by the fact that the SDA procedure was still new at the time, which might have prompted prospective litigants to approach it with caution and not to apply for leave unless there was no better choice. As for the slight increase in the leave applications in 2006–2012, there is no clear explanation, other than to say that within this period, there were three derivative actions that went through to final judgment. The first started towards the end of 2005 and the third case ended about the end of 2012.[27] It could be that other applicants at the time felt a little more confident in following the same path and choosing to apply for leave to bring an SDA. However, as it turned out, the applicants in all three cases were ultimately ordered to contribute to the costs of the

27 *Reale v. Duncan Reale* [2006] NSWSC 227; *Duncan Reale v. Cameda Investments* [2006] NSWSC 1099; *Maher v. Honeysett & Maher Electrical Contractors Pty Ltd* [2005] NSWSC 859; *Maher v. Honeysett and Maher Electrical Contractors Pty Ltd* [2009] NSWSC 445; *Wood v. Links Golf Tasmania Pty Ltd* [2010] FCA 570; *Wood v. Links Golf Tasmania (No.2)* [2013] FCA 143.

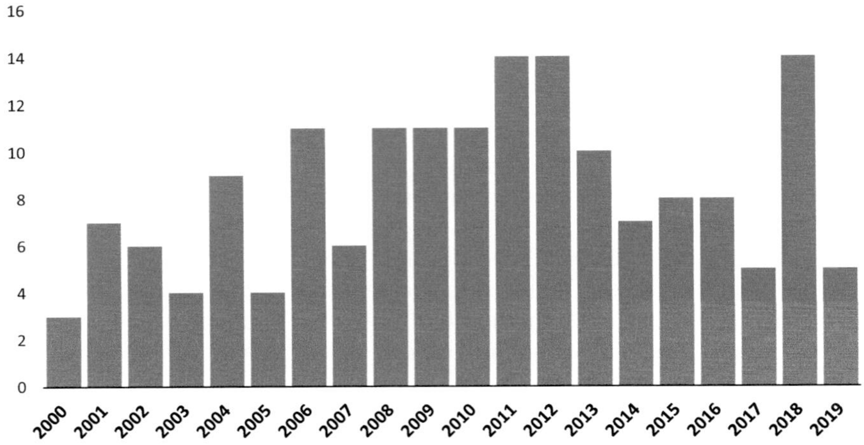

Figure 3.1 When Was the Case Decided?

derivative proceedings, *regardless* of the outcome in the final judgment.[28] For example, in *Maher v. Honeysett and Maher Electrical Contractors Pty Ltd*, the successful applicant was unable to recover his costs even though he had a successful outcome in the substantive derivative action.[29] The unfavourable outcomes in these cases in relation to costs might have discouraged other prospective applicants from pursuing an SDA, which could be a plausible explanation for why there has been a decrease in the leave applications since 2012. Instead, as mentioned above, some aggrieved shareholders might have chosen to make a claim for an oppression remedy as an alternative.

(ii) What court decided the leave application?

Figure 3.2 provides a distribution of cases according to the court jurisdiction in which the leave application was heard. New South Wales received the highest number of leave applications (72 out of 168 or 42.9%), followed by Victoria (29 out of 168 or 17.3%) and the Federal Court of Australia (17.3%). The remaining smaller proportions are from other court jurisdictions across Australia. Given the volume of businesses and financial activities in Sydney, it does not come as a surprise that the NSW Supreme Court has received more leave applications than any other states.

28 The costs provision and the three derivative action cases will be analysed in detail in Chapter 6.

29 *Maher v. Honeysett and Maher Electrical Contractors Pty Ltd* [2009] NSWSC 445. Instead, in this case, the court combined the costs incurred by both parties and split into 50/50, with the resultant effect that no company funds were to be used.

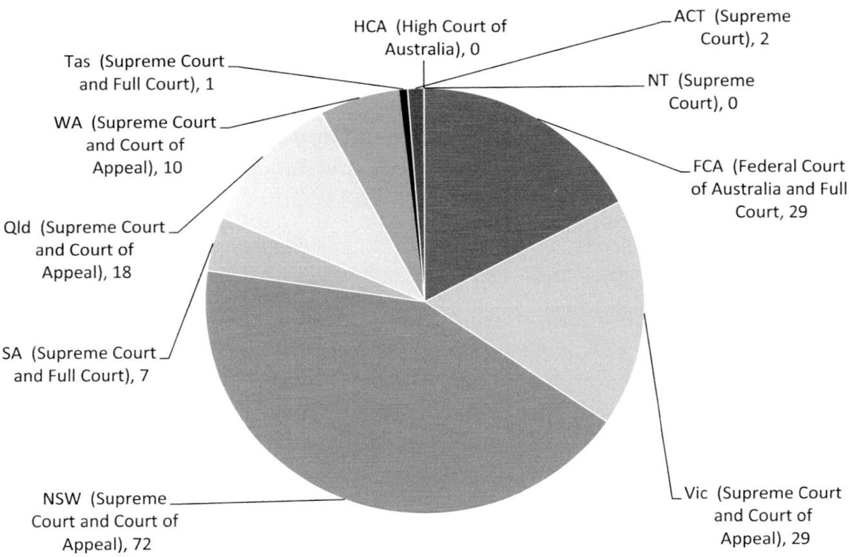

Figure 3.2 Court Jurisdiction

(iii) Was the case at first instance or on appeal?

Table 3.1 provides a breakdown of first instance decisions (single judge) and appeal decisions (three judges). Most cases have been at first instance, with only 13.1% (22 out of 168) being appeal cases. As shown in Figure 3.2, there is no reported judgment in the High Court of Australia, and this is not surprising given the high costs of litigation and the uncertainty in the recovery of costs.[30] One explanation for the low number of appeal cases could be due to the high cost of litigation, and because s.242 is expressed in unclear terms,

Table 3.1 Was the case at first instance or on appeal?

Nature of case	*Number of cases*	*Percentage (%) of leave application cases*
First instance	146	86.9
Appeal	22	13.1
TOTAL	168	168 = 100%

30 Furthermore, special leave of the HCA is required for an appeal, and in most cases, an applicant for appeal to the HCA is expected to pay the costs of that application: see Kieran Pender, "The 'price' of justice? Costs-conditional special leave in the High Court" (2018) 42 *Melbourne University Law Review* 149, where the author conducted an empirical study of HCA decisions relating to special leave for appeal granted with costs.

there is no certainty that an applicant can recover their costs if they appeal to a higher court.

The data shown in Table 3.1 are based on the 168 *leave applications*, and if there was an appeal against the original decision, this is counted as an appeal decision, with no repeat in the count on cases where the first instance decision has been appealed. That is, where an appeal has been made to the Full Court or the Court of Appeal, both the first instance and the appeal decisions are counted as one leave application and counted as an appeal.

(iv) What type of company was it – private or public?

Table 3.2 provides information about the type of company involved in the proposed SDA, whether it is a private or a public company. Table 3.2 shows that privately owned companies, with less than 10 shareholders in the company, make up 89.9% as the proposed plaintiff. Most of these privately owned companies are closely held by family members or have been set up as joint ventures or quasi-partnerships.

It is common to see a leave application being made for an SDA to settle a dispute between two equal shareholders and directors in a privately owned company, in particular to resolve a deadlock. For example, one spouse may be applying for leave to bring an SDA to sue the other spouse for breach of directors' duties or for misappropriation of company funds.[31] It is also common to see a leave application for an SDA for resolving deadlock between siblings,[32] business partners,[33] or for settling a long-running family dispute,[34] or a joint-venture dispute,[35] or a dispute between minority shareholders and company directors who were also majority shareholders.[36]

Table 3.2 What type of company was it – private or public?

Type of company	*Number of cases*	*Percentage (%) of leave application cases*
Private	150	89.9
Public	18	10.1
TOTAL	168	168 = 100%

31 *Duncan Reale v. Cameda Investments* [2006] NSWSC 1099; *Swansson v. RA Pratt Properties Pty Ltd* [2002] NSWSC 583.

32 *Vlahos v. Vlahos* [2016] VSC 824; *Blakeney v. Blakeney* [2016] WASCA 76.

33 *Li v. Dao* [2018] VSC 530; *MG Corrosion Consultants Pty Ltd v. Vinciguerra* [2011] FCAFC 31.

34 *Vicad Pty Ltd – Pottie v. Dunkley* [2011] NSWSC 166; *Cassegrain v. Gerard Cassegrain and Co Pty Ltd* [2012] NSWSC 403.

35 *Zhu v. Orico Australia Pty Ltd Zhu* [2019] VSC 313; *True Value Solar Holdings Pty Ltd v. Fernandez* [2013] VSCA 27; *Vinciguerra. MG Corrosion Consultants Pty Ltd v. Vinciguerra* [2011] FCAFC 31.

36 *Connective Services Pty Ltd v. Slea Pty Ltd* [2018] VSCA 229.

(v) Was the company solvent or under some form of administration?

This question relates to whether an SDA is available where a company has become insolvent or under some form of administration. As shown in Table 3.3, a vast majority of companies were solvent at the time the court decided on the leave application (72.6%). In these cases, the court found no problem in applying the SDA provisions under Part 2F.1A of the CA.

However, where a company had become insolvent or in some form of administration (i.e., liquidation, administration or receivership), there was a period of uncertainty as to whether *shareholder* derivative action was possible under Part 2F.1A.[37] Part 2F.1A of the CA does not refer to whether the provisions apply to insolvency cases. It was not until 2008 in *Ragless v. IPA Holdings Pty Ltd (in liq)* that the full Supreme Court in South Australia held that Part 2F.1A would not be applicable to company liquidation cases.[38] Instead, the court in *Ragless* decided to exercise its *inherent discretion* and granted the shareholder applicant a discretionary leave to bring the necessary derivative action on behalf of the company in liquidation, only if the shareholder applicant was prepared to pay for the court proceedings.[39]

The term "company in liquidation" means a "general body of [the company's] creditors", and does not include shareholders unless they can be categorised as creditors.[40] When a company is in liquidation, a shareholder can only

Table 3.3 Was the company solvent or under some form of administration?

Financial status of company	*Number of leave application cases*	*Percentage (%) of leave application cases*
Solvent	122	72.6
Under some form of administration (liquidation, administration, receivership)	46	27.4
TOTAL	168	168 = 100%

37 For example, in *HPM Pty Ltd v. Fear* (2002) 171 FLR 12; [2002] WASCA 24, Steytler J (at [18–19]) was unsure whether Part 2F.1A would have any application to a company in liquidation. In *BL & GY International Co Ltd v. Hypec Electronics Pty Ltd* (2001) 164 FLR 268; [2001] NSWSC 705, Einstein J in the NSW Supreme Court said that Part 2F.1A would not be applicable to a company in liquidation, but later changed his opinion in *Kamper v. Applied Soil Technology Pty Ltd* (2004) 211 ALR 337.

38 *Ragless v. IPA Holdings Pty Ltd (in liq)* (2008) 65 ACSR 700, [2008] SASC 90. See also *Chahwan v. Euphoric Pty Ltd* (2008) 65 ACSR 661, [2008] NSWCA 52 where the NSW Court of Appeal provided arguments against shareholder derivative action in liquidation.

39 The court's inherent discretion comes from the insolvency provisions, in particular ss.477(6) and s.511(1) of the *Corporations Act* 2001 (C'th), where the shareholder may be treated as a "creditor" or "contributor".

40 *Charlton v. Baber* [2003] NSWSC 745, at [53] (Barrett J). See also, *Re DH International Pty Ltd (in liq)* [2017] NSWSC 870 and *Sons of Gwalia Ltd (admin appt'd) v. Margaretic* (2007) 231 CLR 160; [2007] HCA 1.

bring a derivative action on behalf of the company's creditors, which could be a problem for the shareholder litigant, as will be canvassed further in Chapter 5.

While the courts in some cases have exercised their inherent discretion to grant leave,[41] there were other cases where the court has refused to exercise its discretion, such as in cases where the applicant's offer to indemnify the company in liquidation was inadequate.[42] Generally, the courts appear to have granted leave for an applicant to bring a shareholder derivative action in liquidation where the company was only marginally insolvent (i.e., the company had paid off most of the debts to the creditors) and there was a possibility that the shareholder could obtain further recoveries from directors for breach of directors' duties.[43]

(vi) Who was the applicant?

Section 236 provides standing for a current or former shareholder or current or former officer of the company to apply to the court for leave to bring an SDA. However, Table 3.4 shows that nearly all applicants were *current* shareholders (92.9% or 156 out of 168 cases), with a small percentage whose status was either unknown or unspecified.

The fact that most of the applicants were current shareholders could indicate that many of them were acutely aware that proof of "good faith" under s.237(2)(b) would not be easy if they were a former shareholder. In *App Shop Pty Ltd v. Jalal Bros Pty Ltd*, the court stated that the "good faith" element would be "relatively easy" to establish where an applicant is a "current

Table 3.4 Who was the applicant?

Type of Applicant	*Number of leave application cases*	*Percentage (%) of leave application cases*
Current shareholder who is also current director	51	30.4
Current shareholder who is former director	46	27.4
Current shareholder who is not current or former director	59	35.1
Not specified / Unknown	12	7.1
TOTAL	168	168 = 100%

41 *Re Colorado Products Pty Ltd* [2014] NSWSC 64; *Re Sundara Pty Ltd* [2015] NSWSC 1694. In these cases, the applicant's offer of indemnity to cover the legal costs of the company in liquidation was held to be adequate.

42 *Cooper v. Myrtace Consulting Pty Ltd* [2014] FCA 480.

43 For example, in *Freshstart Australia Pty Ltd v. Lofthouse* [2006] VSC 317, the creditors had all been paid in full and the only creditors remaining were the shareholders who wished to sue directors for breach of duties.

shareholder who has more than a token shareholding".[44] Conversely, in *Zhu v. Orico Australia Pty Ltd*, the court stated that where an applicant is a former shareholder or officer with nothing obvious to gain directly from the SDA, the court will scrutinise the applicant's ulterior purpose.[45] In *South Johnston Mill Ltd v. Dennis and Scales*, the court found there were "31 applicants properly identified as current shareholders" who collectively held "more than a token shareholding" in the company, and because of this, the court concluded that there was some "positive evidence" of good faith from all the applicants.[46] Thus, it comes as no surprise that almost all of the applicants were current shareholders. In these instances, the status of the applicant appears to be an important factor for establishing "good faith" under s.237(2)(b).

Another possible reason why a former shareholder did not want to apply for leave to bring an SDA could be because any compensation or remedy awarded by the court in a successful derivative action would go only to the company, and only the current shareholders would benefit from the success. Under the current model, there is no incentive for a former shareholder to bring an SDA.

It should be noted that some leave applications had more than one applicant; and where all applicants shared a similar feature (for example, they were all shareholders) or where a key applicant was a shareholder (or director if applicable), then for ease of presentation of results and discussion, they are treated as one applicant in the dataset shown in Table 3.4.

(vii) Who opposed the leave application?

Table 3.5 provides the spread of respondents opposing the leave applications.[47] It is worth noting that an application for leave is not an *ex parte* application. Most of the respondents opposing the leave application have been current directors (70.2% of the cases, or 110 out of 168). The remaining respondents were former directors, majority shareholders, third parties (such as creditors and former directors)[48] and liquidators. Only a few applications were unopposed.[49]

44 *App Shop Pty Ltd v. Jalal Bros Pty Ltd* [2019] NSWSC 490, at [16] (Black J). See also *Swansson v Pratt Properties Pty Ltd* (2002) 42 ACSR 313, [2002] NSWSC 583, at [38] (Palmer J).

45 *Zhu v. Orico Australia Pty Ltd* [2019] VSC 313, at [46] (Connock J). See also *Swansson v. RA Pratt Properties Pty Ltd* (2002) 42 ACSR 313, [2002] NSWSC 583, at [39] (Palmer J).

46 *South Johnston Mill Ltd v. Dennis and Scales* [2007] FCA 1448, at [68–69] (Middleton J).

47 Various terms have been used in case law to describe the person opposing the leave application, including calling them "defendant". For the purpose of this chapter, the terms "respondent" or "prospective defendant" will be used.

48 Under ss.237(4) and 228(5), a former director is someone who has resigned from the company six months earlier or longer when an applicant applies for leave to bring an SDA to sue the former director. In this situation, the applicant has the onus of rebutting the presumption in s.237(3) that the proposed SDA against a third party is not in the best interests of the company.

49 For example, in *Re Referral Marketing Services Pty Ltd (in liq)* [2012] NSWSC 1291, the liquidator had exhausted his task and there was no money left in the company for him to bring

Table 3.5 Who opposed the leave application?

Type of respondent (opposing leave application)	*Number of leave application cases*	*Percentage (%) of leave application cases*
Current director(s) who are also shareholder(s)	110	70.2
Former director (with no shareholding or shareholding unknown)	11	6.5
Majority shareholders who are not current or former directors	9	5.4
Liquidator	4	2.4
Third party	17	10.1
Not specified	17	10.1
TOTAL	168	168 = 100%

There is no information contained in the SDA provisions about who can oppose the leave application. However, given that the applicant has the burden of satisfying the court for leave under s.237(2) and the decision of the court on the leave application tends to be final, proposed defendants whose names appear in the leave application and are known as the "normal decision-makers of the corporation" and who are usually those within s.236, have some rights in presenting their case as to why such application should not be granted.[50] Their rights in opposing the application are, however, limited to the extent permitted by the court.[51] This is to prevent the leave application from turning into a trial of the proposed action.[52]

Given the high volume of respondents being directors, and if an applicant can successfully carry through the derivative action to final judgment, then arguably, the SDA framework could have some use in deterring future misconduct. However, as discussed in the preceding chapters, such private enforcement alone would not be enough to bring about complete directors' accountability and enhancement of corporate governance. Some form of public enforcement of directors' duties by a corporate regulator may be necessary to achieve the full effect.

It is common for an applicant to name more than one proposed defendant in the leave application. Table 3.5 counts only one main proposed defendant opposing the application in each case.

---

proceedings against anyone else, so instead of opposing the leave application, the liquidator allowed the shareholder applicant to sue the wrongdoing directors.

50 *Hislop v. Paltar Petroleum Ltd (No 2)* [2017] FCA 1213, at [42-51]; *Hislop v. Paltar Petroleum Ltd (No 3)* [2017] FCA 1253, at [24–29].

51 *Swansson v. RA Pratt Properties Pty Ltd* (2002) 42 ACSR 313; [2002] NSWSC 583, at [26].

52 *Blakeney v. Blakeney* [2016] WASCA 76, at [58]; *MG Corrosion Consultants Pty Ltd v. Vinciguerra* [2011] FCAFC 31, at [59]; *Metyor Inc (formerly Talisman Technologies Inc) v. Queensland Electronic Switching Pty Ltd* (2002) 42 ACSR 398; [2002] QCA 269, at [19]; *Li v. Dao* [2018] VSC 530.

(viii) What was the nature of the claims against the proposed defendant(s)?

Figure 3.3 shows a breakdown of the nature of claims made against the proposed defendant(s). Most cases were about breaches of directors' duties (57.7% or 97 out of 168 cases); this consists of breaches of directors' duties alone (44%) and breaches of directors' duties and of contracts (13.7%). Other claims made in the leave application were breaches of contracts (4.8%), oppressive conduct committed by majority shareholders including abuse of power by controllers (4.2%), debt recoveries (6.0%) and setting aside default judgments and statutory demands (5.3%) against third parties. In the remaining 22%, the claims were either unclear or unspecified.[53]

Based on the empirical data shown in Table 3.5 (that is, majority of respondents being named in the leave application as directors) and in Figure 3.3 (most of the alleged claims being about breaches of directors' duties), one may be inclined to argue that SDA has some use in promoting directors' accountability and corporate governance. SDA has provided some protection for some shareholders by enabling them to exert their corporate rights and take action on behalf of the company against directors, making them accountable for

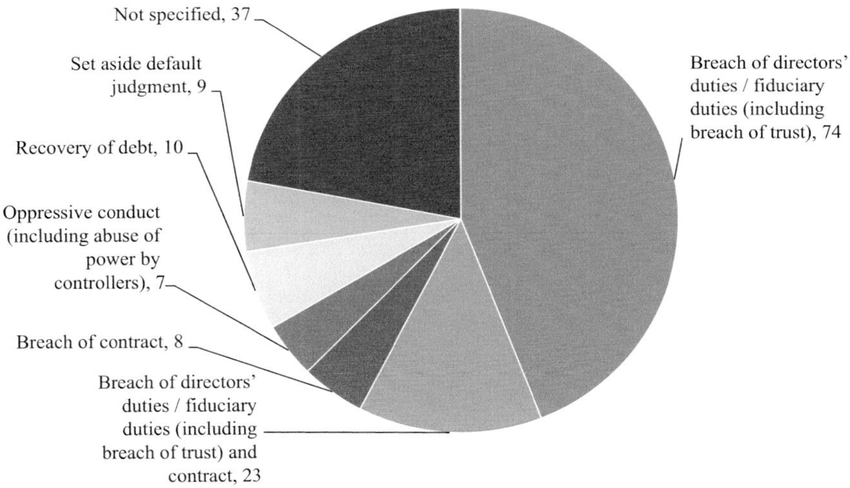

Figure 3.3 Nature of Claims (Allegations)

53 For example, in *Fehring v. Brighter Directions Pty Ltd* [2010] VSC 287, because the limitation period for making a claim was about to expire, an ex parte conditional interim leave was made by Davies J in the Victorian Supreme Court even though the applicant had not filed a statement of claims. It is possible for the court to revoke the grant of leave later when more or opposing evidence becomes available, such as seen in *Fehring v. Brighter Directions Pty Ltd* [2010] VSC 287 and in *Ragless v. IPA Holdings Pty Ltd (in liq)* [2012] SASC 203.

their inappropriate behaviour.[54] In *Slea Pty Ltd v. Connective Services Pty Ltd*, a shareholder applicant initiated the leave application against directors for breach of directors' duties when they restructured the company without consultation with the relevant shareholders. The directors gave 25% interest in the business to a third party financier and reduced the applicant's business interests from about 33% to 25% in order to prevent the applicant from exercising their pre-emptive rights under the company's constitution.[55] The applicant was successful in obtaining leave of the court to bring an SDA. In *Henry v. Western Downs Group Ltd*, a group of native title claimants initiated the leave application to bring an SDA against the board of directors for breaches of their fiduciary duty to the company by failing to pass on the charitable benefits to the native title claimants, including the applicants, under the Indigenous Land Use Agreement. Instead, the directors misappropriated the trust funds by paying the funds to themselves as remuneration.[56] The claimants in this case were also successful in obtaining leave of the court to bring an SDA. Thus, the SDA framework could be used as a threat of liability against directors and in turn, promote directors' accountability. However, there is no conclusive evidence that this is in fact working. In both cases, there was no further report as to whether the successful applicants had proceeded to bringing the approved derivative action; the applicants might have settled their dispute through other means.

Overall, the empirical data shown in Table 3.5 and Figure 3.3 are still useful in terms of providing information confirming who the majority of proposed defendants are and the type of claims against them. These data provide some information that SDA could have some use in regulating corporate governance.

(ix) What is the proportion of successful and unsuccessful leave applications?

The results in Table 3.6 answer the first research question. Table 3.6 provides data on the proportion of successful and unsuccessful leave applications. It shows that in 55.4% of the cases, the applicant was successful in satisfying the court of the leave requirement under s.237(2); that is, in obtaining leave of the court to bring an SDA, while in 44.6% of the cases, the applicant was unsuccessful. This information assists in understanding the patterns of use of the SDA in terms of assessing the level of difficulty experienced by

54 Chapter 2 discusses directors' accountability and corporate governance as one of the government's intended purposes: see, for example, CASAC, *Statutory Derivative Action* (Report, 1993), at 4; CLERP Proposal Paper No. 3, *Proposals for Reform: Directors' Duties and Corporate Governance* (1997), at 32–33.

55 *Slea Pty Ltd v. Connective Services Pty Ltd* [2017] VSC 609; and in *Connective Services Pty Ltd v. Slea Pty Ltd* [2018] VSCA 229.

56 *Henry v. Western Downs Group Ltd* [2018] FCA 1168.

Table 3.6 Outcome in the leave applications

Decision of court	*Number of leave application cases*	*Percentage (%)*
Leave granted	93	55.4
Leave denied	75	44.6
Total	168	168 = 100%

shareholders in applying for leave. A "successful" leave application means that the applicant can proceed to the next stage, which is the derivative action stage.[57]

It is important to understand what constitutes a "successful" leave application. Just because an applicant has obtained leave to bring an SDA, this does not necessarily mean they have satisfied the court on the five leave criteria under s.237(2).

There are other instances where an applicant can successfully obtain leave of the court to bring an SDA and these instances are included in the counts in Table 3.6. For example, the Table 3.6 result showing the number of "successful" leave applications includes cases where a company has become insolvent and the court grants leave to bring a shareholder derivative action based on its inherent jurisdiction under the insolvency provisions.

An applicant may be successful in "satisfying" the court of the leave requirement under s.237(2) by undertaking to pay for the derivative action and to indemnify the company against all adverse costs associated with the SDA. Undertaking to pay for the action appears to be the most common way for an applicant to show "good faith" under s.237(2)(b) and to show that the proposed derivative action "is in the best interests of the company" under s.237(2)(c). It has been noted that an undertaking by an applicant to bear all costs and expenses in bringing the proposed action can be seen as a "consideration *material* to the satisfaction of the good faith and best interests of the company requirements".[58] The idea is that if a company is not required to pay for the action and the company will not lose anything regardless of the outcome, then this factor would be an important indication that the proposed action "is in the best interests of the company".

Thus, the success rate shown in Table 3.6 includes cases where the court has granted leave *on terms* that the applicant undertakes to pay for the SDA

57 There have been instances where the court has allowed an application for leave to be heard at the same time as the proposed derivative action. For example, in *Rinfort Pty Ltd v. Arianna Holdings Pty Ltd* [2016] NSWSC 251, at [17], where an application for leave and an application to set aside the statutory demand were filed at the same time.

58 *Li v. Dao* [2018] VSC 530, at [183] (Connock J) (Emphasis added). See also in *Re Woodbine Project Pty Ltd* [2021] VSC 617, at [60] (Button J) and in *Stanisis v. Trace Pty Ltd* [2022] WASC 281.

and to indemnify the company against all adverse costs orders.[59] Table 3.6 also includes cases where the court has granted leave because the applicant has *offered* to bear all costs and charges in bringing the SDA.[60] In these instances, the court did not consider too closely the leave criteria under s.237(2). Other cases included in the count of "successful" leave applications are those where the court had granted a conditional leave to bring an SDA on urgent matters without discussing the leave criteria; for example, the limitation period for bringing a court action was about to expire.[61]

There are problems when an applicant is required to pay for the proposed derivative action as a way of satisfying the court of the leave requirement in s.237(2). Chapters 4, 5 and 6 will cover these and other grounds in more detail, where there will be further analysis of court cases.

(x) Why was the leave application not successful?

The results shown in Table 3.7 are relevant for answering the third research question, that is, which of the five criteria under s.237(2) have been most difficult for applicants to satisfy the court for leave to bring an SDA? The purpose in this study is to *identify* the problematic criteria for further consideration and discussion in subsequent chapters, in order to put forward a case as to why and how the provisions need to be amended. The goal is to provide shareholders with greater protection and a more effective remedy.

Table 3.7 provides a detailed breakdown of the different reasons given by the courts as to why the leave applications were unsuccessful under s.237(2). There are five criteria that an applicant must satisfy the court for leave. As shown in Table 3.6, unsuccessful leave applications amount to 44.6% (or 75 out of 168); and in Table 3.7, a vast majority of unsuccessful applicants have difficulties satisfying the court of the leave requirement, amounting to 74.7% of the cases. On closer analysis of the empirical evidence, the majority of unsuccessful applicants failed to establish the "good faith" and/or "in the best interests of the company" requirements under s.237(2)(b) and s.237(2)(c), totalling 65.3% of the unsuccessful cases. These have been the two most difficult criteria for applicants to satisfy the court for leave, and these will receive further consideration in Chapters 4 and 5.

Very briefly on the other three criteria, in relation to s.237(2)(a), the courts in many cases did not find it necessary to consider this criterion. In *Li v. Dao*,

59 *App Shop Pty Ltd v. Jalal Bros Pty Ltd* [2019] NSWSC 490; *Suh v. Cho* [2013] VSC 491.

60 For example, in *Re Poly Pacific Pty Ltd* [2013] VSC 670, at [60], the applicant submitted, at the start of the court hearing, a draft consent order signed by the proposed defendant, with the applicant undertaking to bear all costs and to indemnify the company.

61 *Fehring v. Brighter Directions Pty Ltd* [2010] VSC 287 (ex parte conditional interim leave was granted, even though the applicant had not filed a statement of claims). In *Vlahos v. Vlahos* [2016] VSC 824, urgent leave application was granted to allow the applicant to appeal against a decision of the County Court of Victoria on a matter involving the company.

Table 3.7 Reasons for unsuccessful leave application

Types of reason given for unsuccessful leave application – section 237(2)	*Number of unsuccessful leave applications*	*Percentage (%) of unsuccessful leave applications based on reason*
(a) Not proven that company will not bring proceedings	2	2.7
(b) Not in good faith	2	2.7
(c) Not in the company's best interests	17	22.6
(d) No serious question to be tried	5	6.7
(b) and (c) Not in good faith and not in the company's best interests	17	22.7
(c) and (d) Not in company's best interests and no serious question to be tried	6	8.0
(b), (c) and (d) Not in good faith, not in the company's best interests and no serious question to be tried	7	9.3
* **Total number of leave applications in which criteria were not met**	56	74.7
Other reasons: * Barred by s.236(3), no standing * Application premature N/A, oppression instead * Company already in liquidation * Claim not in company's name	19	25.3
TOTAL	75	75 = 100%

the court observes that "in many cases, it will be readily apparent whether it is probable that the company will not itself bring the proceedings".[62] In *Henry v. Western Downs Group Ltd*, the beneficiary claimants were applying for leave to bring an SDA against the entire board of company directors for breach of directors' duties, and thus the fact was clear that the company had refused to bring any court action.[63] In a case where there is a deadlock, it would be "readily apparent" from the facts that neither of the directors would want the company to bring proceedings against himself or herself.[64]

In relation to s.237(2)(d), the court in most cases seemed to have no issue finding that there was "a serious question to be tried". This criterion has a "low threshold".[65] The applicant only needs to show that there is "sufficient likeli-

62 *Li v. Dao* [2018] VSC 530, at [57] (Connock J). In this case, both the applicant and the respondent were 50% shareholders of the company and its only directors.

63 *Henry v. Western Downs Group Ltd* [2018] FCA 1168. See also *Slea Pty Ltd v. Connective Services Pty Ltd* [2017] VSC 609 and on appeal, *Connective Services Pty Ltd v. Slea Pty Ltd* [2018] VSCA 229.

64 *Zhu v. Orico Australia Pty Ltd* [2019] VSC 313, at [38] (Connock J).

65 *Swansson v. RA Pratt Properties Pty Ltd* [2002] NSWSC 583, at [25] (Palmer J); *Li v. Dao* [2018] VSC 530, at [115] (Connock J).

hood of success" to justify the claim going to trial.[66] The leave application is not a trial within a trial;[67] the court only has to satisfy the existence of a substantive claim, and "there is no requirement for the court to make factual determination about contested issues".[68] Given its low threshold requirement, there were some cases where the courts made no mention of s.237(2)(d) and still granted leave based on the satisfaction of the other criteria.[69]

Section 237(2)(e) is about an applicant needing to show that a 14-day notice has been given to the company before making the leave application. This has not been a major problem in practice. In many cases, the court did not refer to s.237(2)(e). Even if an applicant has not given the required notice to the company, there is a presumption that where "both parties have been aware of the issue for a considerable period", the court may displace the need for a written notice.[70]

(xi) Results on costs

Tables 3.8 and 3.9 provide empirical findings relating to the award of costs under s.242. In nearly all successful leave cases, the courts did not order the *company* to indemnify the applicant. The results in these two tables answer the second research question, which has two components. First, was the applicant successful in obtaining a costs indemnity order for the leave application? Second, was the company required to fund the approved derivative action? Some scholars have asserted that the uncertainty in the recovery of costs under s.242 has prevented bona fide shareholders from pursuing an SDA.[71] This study helps to understand the courts' treatment of the costs provision.

In relation to the first sub-question, Table 3.8 shows that a great majority of applicants who were successful in the leave application were *not* entitled

66 *Ragless v. IPA Holdings Pty Ltd (in liq)* (2008) 65 ACSR 700; [2008] SASC 90, at [40] (Debelle J, Sulan and Vanstone JJ agreeing); *Daiwa Can Company v. Barokes Pty Ltd* [2016] VSC 296 (Sifris J).

67 *MG Corrosion Consultants Pty Ltd v. Vinciguerra* [2011] FCAFC 31, at [67] (North, McKerracher, Jagot JJ).

68 *South Johnston Mill Ltd v. Dennis* [2007] FCA 1448, at [80] (Middleton J). See also in *Slea Pty Ltd v. Connective Services Pty Ltd* [2017] VSC 609, at [175] (Robson J), which s.237(2)(d) issue was not raised again on appeal in *Connective Services Pty Ltd v. Slea Pty Ltd* [2018] VSCA 229.

69 For example, in *Fehring v. Brighter Directions Pty Ltd* [2010] VSC 287, urgent leave was granted by the court without the applicant having filed a statement of claims.

70 *Li v. Dao* [2018] VSC 530, at [179] (Connock J).

71 Lang Thai, "How popular are statutory derivative actions in Australia? Comparisons with USA, Canada, and New Zealand", (2002) 30 *Australian Business Law Review* 118; Albert Monichino, "Costs in statutory derivative actions: The lingering ghost of *Wallersteiner*" (2015) 33 *Company and Securities Law Journal* 104; Peter Prince, "Australia's statutory derivative action: Using the New Zealand experience" (2000) 18 *Company and Securities Law Journal* 493; Keith Fletcher, "CLERP and minority shareholder rights" (2001) 13 *Australian Journal of Corporate Law* 290.

Table 3.8 Was the successful applicant granted costs for the leave application?

Were costs granted?	*Number of successful leave applications*	*Percentage (%)*
Yes	7	7.5
Yes in part	7	7.5
No (in some cases, applicants prepared to pay)	33	35.5
Costs not discussed / Costs reserved	46	49.5
TOTAL	93	93 = 100%

to a costs indemnity order on the leave application. In some successful leave cases, the courts reserved their power to consider all questions relating to costs at a later date, subject to the outcome of the derivative proceedings (14% or 13 out of 93 successful leave cases); and in other successful leave cases, the courts did not discuss the costs question (35.5%). In these two instances, the applicants paid their own costs in the interim. In other words, if no order is made by the court on costs, the company is not liable to pay.[72] In about a third of the successful leave cases, the court granted a conditional leave, requiring the applicant to pay all costs and charges in relation to the bringing of a derivative action and that the applicant could not apply for an indemnity from the company.

Interestingly, only 15% of the successful applicants were able to obtain some recovery of their costs from the proposed defendant or from a third party not named in the leave application.[73] It is rare to see a court making an order requiring the company to pay for the derivative action.[74]

Table 3.9 relates to the costs of the substantive derivative proceedings. Table 3.9 answers the second sub-question, whether the company is required to fund the approved derivative action. In most leave cases, the courts did not discuss the prospective costs of bringing the approved action (74.2%). The other common approach has been that the court expressly ordered the applicant to bear all of the costs (23.6%). To date, *Wood v. Links Golf Tasmania Pty Ltd* is the only case where the *company* was required to fund the applicant for the substantive derivative proceedings.[75] In that case,

72 *Steinier v. Sunlea Enterprises Pty Ltd* [2016] WASC 81, at [64] (Martino J). See also *Swansson v. RA Pratt Properties Pty Ltd* (2002) 42 ACSR 313; [2002] NSWSC 583, at [75–76] (Palmer J).

73 *MG Corrosion Consultants Pty Ltd v. Vinciguerra (No 2)* [2011] FCAFC 48.

74 In *Steinier v. Sunlea Enterprises Pty Ltd* [2016] WASC 81, at [73], Martino J ordered the trustee company to reimburse the applicant's costs of the leave application, saying that this was part of the "domestic arrangement". In this case, the tribunal decided the dispute and the parties subsequently settled their differences. Generally, both parties in a tribunal case are expected to pay their own costs.

75 *Wood v. Links Golf Tasmania Pty Ltd* [2010] FCA 570.

Table 3.9 Was the company required to fund the applicant for the substantive derivative action?

Was the company required to fund the derivative action?	*Number of successful leave applications*	*Percentage (%)*
Yes	1	1.1
No (in some cases, applicants prepared and consented to pay and indemnify)	23	24.7
Not discussed	69	74.2
Total	93	93 = 100%

Finkelstein J in the Federal Court of Australia ordered the company to pay the applicant's costs of the leave application and the approved derivative proceedings, subject to a recall order if the applicant failed in the derivative proceedings.[76]

Although it has been said that it may be possible for an applicant to be relieved from costs obligations at a later stage if the company succeeds in the SDA,[77] in practice, this has not been the case. For example, in *Maher v. Honeysett and Maher Electrical Contractors Pty Ltd*,[78] the applicant was successful in the final judgment in the SDA, but because only a modest compensation was awarded in favour of the company. The court subsequently issued an order requiring the losing defendant to pay only half of the applicant's costs, and the applicant bore the other half. The overall effect was that the company had not lost anything.

It is common to see inconsistencies in the judicial treatment of the costs provision under s.242. For example, in *In the matter of Jimmy's Recipe Pty Limited*, Brereton J of the NSW Supreme Court discussed the pros and cons in making a costs order when the SDA was still pending,[79] and concluded that, because the decision in the leave application was in itself final and not interlocutory, a costs order should be made at that point.[80] In that case, the successful applicant was entitled to costs indemnity from the responding directors who lost in the leave application.[81] An interesting contrast is in *White (Trustee) v. MWL Financial Group Pty Ltd (No.2)*.[82] In agreeing with Brereton J that a decision in the leave application was final and not

76 Unfortunately, however, that order was subsequently recalled because the applicant failed in the substantive derivative proceedings: see *Wood v. Links Golf Tasmania* (No.2) [2013] FCA 143. This approach has not been repeated since.

77 *Hannon v. Doyle* [2011] NSWSC 10, at [121].

78 *Maher v. Honeysett and Maher Electrical Contractors Pty Ltd* [2009] NSWSC 445.

79 *In the matter of Jimmy's Recipe Pty Limited* [2018] NSWSC 1331, at [22–34].

80 *In the matter of Jimmy's Recipe Pty Limited* [2018] NSWSC 1331, at [35].

81 *In the matter of Jimmy's Recipe Pty Limited* [2018] NSWSC 1331, at [37].

82 *White (Trustee) v. MWL Financial Group Pty Ltd (No.2)* [2019] FCA 364.

interlocutory, Davies J nonetheless considered it more appropriate to follow the "weight of authority" from other earlier decisions and followed a similar pattern that costs should be subject to the outcome of the final derivative proceedings.[83] In the latter case, it means that the applicant was required to pay costs in the interim.

Chapter 6 will consider further the law relating to costs in SDA, in particular whether the costs provision in s.242 is in need of reform.

3.4 Brief analysis of the results

This part provides a brief analysis of the outcomes, with detailed discussions to follow in later chapters.

3.4.1 The costs provision in s.242

This part answers the second research question referred to earlier in this chapter. Two important issues have been identified in this study in relation to costs: (i) the courts are generally reluctant to allow the company to fund SDAs or to indemnify the applicant for the costs of the leave application; and (ii) there is diversity in the judicial approaches to costs. To illustrate diversity and inconsistency in the court decisions, these are some examples:

(a) In many of the successful leave cases, the approach of the courts has been that the grant of leave is subject to the applicant undertaking to pay for the application and the derivative proceedings and that they are not to seek contribution or indemnity from the company;[84]
(b) In numerous other successful leave cases, the courts have reserved their power to consider costs at a later date pending the outcome of the final judgment, or they have simply decided not to discuss matters relating to costs. This means that the applicant would have to pay costs in the interim.[85] In other words, if no court order as to costs is made, the company is not liable to pay.[86]
(c) In a few cases, the courts have ordered the unsuccessful opposing party to indemnify the applicant on the costs of the leave application.[87]

83 *White (Trustee) v. MWL Financial Group Pty Ltd (No.2)* [2019] FCA 364, at [2 and 5]. See also, *In the matter of Imperium Projects Pty Limited* [2015] NSWSC 123; *Fiduciary Ltd v. Morningstar Research Pty Ltd* (2005) 53 ACSR 732; [2005] NSWSC 442.

84 *Vicad Pty Ltd – Pottie v. Dunkley* [2011] NSWSC 166: *Fiduciary Ltd v. Morningstar Research Pty Ltd* (2005) 53 ACSR 732; [2005] NSWSC 442.

85 *Maher v. Honeysett & Maher Electrical Contractors Pty Ltd* [2005] NSWSC 859; *Hannon v. Doyle* [2011] NSWSC 10.

86 *Steinier v. Sunlea Enterprises Pty Ltd* [2016] WASC 81, at [64] (Martino J).

87 *In the matter of Jimmy's Recipe Pty Limited* [2018] NSWSC 1331; *Hannon v. Doyle* [2011] NSWSC 10.

(d) Given the broad discretion of the court on costs, it is not unusual for the court to award costs against a third party not already named in the leave application.[88]
(e) On one occasion, the court has ordered the company to indemnify the applicant on the costs of the leave application.[89]
(f) In one instance, the court has required the company to bear the costs of both the leave application and the substantive derivative proceedings.[90]

These different approaches are the product of the broad power conferred on the court under s.242, where the court has the power to decide on how, when and against whom costs are to be awarded. The need for the court to protect the company's assets is another possible explanation for the diverse approaches. It is rare for a court to order the company to pay costs. The general approach is that the proposed action would be in the company's best interests if the company does not have to pay, even where the company is prosperous,[91] and even where the applicant has a successful outcome in the derivative proceedings.[92] These will be analysed further in Chapter 6 (costs).

Unlike in New Zealand, there is no requirement in Australia for an applicant to make a separate application for costs. The costs question, if discussed by the court, is considered together in the leave application. There are numerous cases where the court did not refer to s.242 when deciding on costs. It has been stated that the court can deal with the costs question "in a general way".[93]

3.4.2 Two most difficult criteria to satisfy the court

This part answers the third research question referred to earlier in this chapter. The findings in Table 3.7 have identified "good faith" and "in the best interests of the company" as the two most difficult criteria for an applicant to satisfy the court for leave. Between them, the "in the best interests of the company" criterion appears to be most onerous. Chapters 4 and 5 will explore these two tests in detail, but for now, a brief overview of the challenges faced by shareholder applicants is given below.

88 *MG Corrosion Consultants Pty Ltd v. Vinciguerra (No 2)* [2011] FCAFC 48.
89 *Steinier v. Sunlea Enterprises Pty Ltd* [2016] WASC 81, at [64], where Martino J held that it was appropriate for the trustee company to pay costs as this was part of the trustee's "domestic arrangement".
90 *Wood v. Links Golf Tasmania Pty Ltd* [2010] FCA 570.
91 *Ehsman v. Nutectime International* [2006] NSWSC 887.
92 *Maher v. Honeysett and Maher Electrical Contractors Pty Ltd* [2009] NSWSC 445.
93 *Charlton v. Baber* [2003] NSWSC 745, at [73] (Barrett J).

3.4.2.1 In the best interests of the company in s.237(2)(c)

Section 237(2)(c) requires an applicant to demonstrate that the proposed derivative action "is in the best interests of the company". The failure rate for this test is 62.6%.[94] Similar to the "good faith" element, there is no definition given in the Act for the term "best interests". The difficulty relates to the burden of proof. In *Swansson v. RA Pratt Properties Pty Ltd,* Palmer J construes this test as one that the court must be satisfied "not that the proposed derivative action *may be, appears to be, or is likely to be,* in the best interests of the company, but ... that it *is* in its best interests".[95] Subsequent cases have confirmed this statement to be the correct construction of the law on s.237(2)(c).[96] In *Carpenter v. Pioneer Part Pty Ltd (in liq),* the court has added that s.237(2)(c) is "not an inquiry into possibility or potential", but rather the proposed action must be shown to be in the company's best interests.[97] In *Vinciguerra v. MG Corrosion Consultants Pty Ltd,* Gilmour J has noted that this criterion has "no fixed test".[98] As is commonly known, it is almost impossible for anyone to predict the exact outcome of any court action. It is challenging to satisfy this test in absolute terms.

Owing to the wording in s.237(2)(c) and the high threshold requirement, the courts have approached this test by focusing more on the position of the applicant rather than the company. In most cases, the court has taken into account the financial position of the applicant as a significant factor for determining the company's "best interests".[99] Other factors are important as well such as the company's business and its operation,[100] but the financial position of the applicant appears to be the main hurdle.[101] If an applicant is poor, then the proposed derivative action would not be seen as in the company's best interests.[102] In most cases, the court has imposed costs on the applicant as a condition for the grant of leave even though the provision in s.237(2)(c) does not refer to costs. This type of entanglement between the leave requirement and the costs provision in s.242 has been said to be necessary as a way of

94 See Table 7 – The breakdown of this percentage is: on s.237(2)(c) alone making up 22.6%, in combination with s.237(2)(b) making up 22.7%, in combination with s.237(2)(d) making up 8.0% and in combination with both s.237(2)(b) and (c) making up 9.3%.

95 *Swansson v. RA Pratt Properties Pty Ltd* (2002) 42 ACSR 313; [2002] NSWSC 583, at [55] (Palmer J).

96 See, for example, *Drew v. Lynch* [2019] FCA 632, at [108]; *Re Dynamic Industries Pty Ltd* [2014] VSC 101, at [96].

97 *Carpenter v. Pioneer Part Pty Ltd (in liq)* [2004] NSWSC 1007, at [19].

98 *Vinciguerra v. MG Corrosion Consultants Pty Ltd* [2010] FCA 763, at [119].

99 *Robash Pty Ltd v. Gladstone Pacific Nickel Pty Ltd* [2011] NSWSC 1235, *Re Fishinthenet Investments Pty Ltd and Coastal Waters Seafood Pty Ltd* [2014] NSWSC 260.

100 *Swansson v. RA Pratt Properties Pty Ltd* (2002) 42 ACSR 313; [2002] NSWSC 583, where Palmer J provides a list of factors.

101 *Ragless v. IPA Holdings Pty Ltd (in liq)* (2008) 65 ACSR 700; [2008] SASC 90 (Full Court); *Robash Pty Ltd v. Gladstone Pacific Nickel Pty Ltd* [2011] NSWSC 1235.

102 *Cooper v. Myrtace Consulting Pty Ltd* [2014] FCA 480.

protecting the company's interests (by protecting its assets).[103] Still, neither s.237(2)(c) nor the Explanatory Memorandum accompanying the introduction of the SDA makes reference to the linkage between s.242 and the company's best interests element in s.237(2)(c).

While it is important for the court to strike a balance between the need to filter out frivolous or unmeritorious actions and the need to allow other actions to proceed so that the company can obtain relief against the wrongdoer, it is the view of the author that the costs question should not be part of the test for leave. It is possible that the current judicial approaches may have prevented some bona fide shareholders from seeking leave of the court to bring an SDA due to the courts' narrow interpretation of s.237(2)(c). Even those who can afford to litigate may feel less inclined to do so. The added problem to this is the uncertainty in the recovery of legal costs, and that any benefit or compensation awarded by the court in a successful derivative action will go to the company and not to the derivative litigant/applicant.

3.4.2.2 Good faith in s.237(2)(b)

Section 237(2)(b) is judicially recognised as comprising two interrelated tests: (i) whether the applicant has an "honest belief" that the company has a good cause of action with a "reasonable prospect of success"; and (ii) whether the applicant has any "collateral purpose" in bringing the proposed action that would constitute an abuse of process.[104] As shown in Table 3.7, the failure rate for this test is 34.7%.[105] Good faith focuses on the applicant's state of mind.[106] There is no definition given in the Act for the term "good faith". Some scholars have criticised this test as too vague.[107] The courts have tended to interpret this criterion by considering the negative aspect, that is, bad faith.

While the first limb of the test requires the applicant to make an assessment on the likelihood of success in the proposed action, which, in some cases,

103 *Steinier v. Sunlea Enterprises Pty Ltd* [2016] WASC 81, at [73] (Martino J); *Fiduciary Ltd v. Morningstar Research Pty Ltd* (2005) 53 ACSR 732; [2005] NSWSC 442, at [56] (Austin J).

104 *Swansson v. RA Pratt Properties Pty Ltd* (2002) 42 ACSR 313; [2002] NSWSC 583, at [36] (Palmer J). See also in *Connective Services Pty Ltd v. Slea Pty Ltd* [2018] VSCA 229, at [55], where the Victorian Court of Appeal has endorsed these two tests.

105 This comprises 2.7% failing to satisfy s.237(2)(b) good faith alone plus failing on other combined criteria, such as on s.237(2)(c) best interests of the company and/or s.237(2)(d) serious question to be tried, i.e., 22.7%, and 9.3%.

106 *Maher v. Honeysett & Maher Electrical Contractors Pty Ltd* [2005] NSWSC 859, at [33].

107 Andrew Keay and Joan Louhrey, "Something old, something new, something borrowed: An analysis of the new derivative active action under the Companies Act 2006" (2008) 124 *Law Quarterly Review* 469 at 485; Pearlie Koh, "Of links and legal merits – Good faith in the statutory derivative action in Singapore" (2014) 14 *Oxford University Commonwealth Law Journal* 225, at 229.

may overlap with the costs provision,[108] the second limb has become less problematic as there is now some judicial recognition that not all collateral purposes would constitute bad faith. For example, an applicant who has a desire to restore the value of her shares, which also benefits other shareholders in the company, has been held to be acting in good faith.[109] However, in other instances, there seems to be some disparity in the judicial reasoning as to whether personal animosity and malice would constitute bad faith. In *Re 383 Latrobe Street Development Pty Ltd*, the court held that considerable animosity between two shareholders is not enough to be considered as a ground for providing bad faith; the level of animosity needs to be "far from unusual" to say lacking good faith.[110] In another case, the court held that having personal animosity or malice towards the proposed defendant is not a clear indication of the applicant acting in bad faith, as this is considered normal and reasonable in litigious matters.[111] It has also been held that an applicant having a long history of grievances with her brother was not acting in bad faith in bringing the proposed action in an attempt to settle their late father's estate.[112] Yet, in another case, the court held that an applicant may be acting in bad faith where she has a "long history of grievances and private vendetta" towards her former husband/proposed defendant.[113] Overall, there is uncertainty in the interpretation and application of the "good faith" element.

3.4.3 Other observations

3.4.3.1 How popular is SDA as a shareholder remedy?

When considering a sample size of 168 leave applications over a period of 20 years, it seems that SDA has not been a popular choice as a shareholder remedy when compared with an oppression claim. On average, there has been only eight leave applications per year, and to date, only three SDA cases have gone all the way to final judgment.[114] These numbers are comparatively low.

In the 2006 study, Ramsay and Saunders found 30 common law cases on derivative action in the last five years prior to the introduction of the SDA and

108 For example, in *Re Dynamic Industries Pty Ltd* [2014] VSC 101, at [95], the court has held that the applicant may be able to satisfy the good faith requirement by undertaking to indemnify the company and meet the costs of the proceedings.

109 *In the Matter Vicad – Pottie v Dunkley* [2011] NSWSC 166 at [43]; *Vinciguerra v. MG Corrosion Consultants Pty Ltd* [2010] FCA 763 (21 July 2010), at [84].

110 *Re 383 Latrobe Street Development Pty Ltd* [2021] VSC 655, at [40] (Connock J).

111 *Vinciguerra v. MG Corrosion Consultants Pty Ltd* [2010] FCA 763. See also *Power v. Ekstein* [2010] NSWSC 137.

112 *In the Matter Vicad – Pottie v. Dunkley* [2011] NSWSC 166.

113 *Swansson v. Pratt* [2002] NSWSC 583, at [41].

114 *Duncan Reale v. Cameda Investments Pty Ltd* [2006] NSWSC 1099; *Maher v. Honeysett and Maher Electrical Contractors Pty Ltd* [2009] NSWSC 445: *Wood v. Links Golf Tasmania Pty Ltd* [2010] FCA 570.

31 leave applications filed in the first five years of its operation.[115] On average, there were six cases per year relating to derivative actions regardless of whether it was operated under the common law system or under the statutory framework. There was no change in the pattern. In the 1999 study, Professor Ramsay found a steady "increase in the use of the oppression remedy" over a period from the 1960s through to 1997.[116] He found that there were four oppression judgments in the 1960s; 25 judgments in the 1980s; a further 27 judgments in 1990–1994; and another 25 judgments in 1995–1997.[117] These findings support the argument that, twenty years on in this current empirical study, SDA in Australia has not been very popular, in that the average number of leave applications per year remains the same as when the common law derivative action was in use. Further, the number of oppression claims appears to be far greater than the number of SDA cases and leave applications. A similar trend is also seen in class actions where empirical evidence has revealed that class action cases are steadily increasing in Australia.[118]

In New Zealand, in the 2006 study of the SDA over a 12-year period, Taylor found that, by comparison, the oppression action is moderately more popular than the SDA.[119] As for other countries, some scholars have reported that shareholder litigation is "rare" in the United Kingdom[120] and in other parts of Europe.[121] In the 2019 study of the SDA in the United Kingdom, Gibbs and Ogbonnaya found that only 21 leave applications were filed in court in the first ten years of its operation (2006–2016) and 27 cases relating to common law derivative action in the previous ten years.[122]

Overall, SDA appears to have no significant influence on incentivising shareholders to litigate. The oppression action is the preferred choice for

115 Ramsay and Saunders, n 22, at 417.

116 Ian Ramsay, "An empirical study of the use of the oppression remedy" (1999) 27 *Australian Business Law Review* 23, at 26.

117 Ramsay, n 115, at 26, Table 1 at 31.

118 Vince Morabito, "An Empirical Study of Australia's Class Action Regimes: The First Twenty-Five Years of Class Actions in Australia" (Fifth Report, July 2017), available at https://papers.ssrn.com/sol3/papers.cfm?abstract_id=3005901 (viewed 16 August 2020)

119 Lynne Taylor, "The derivative action in the Companies Act 1993: An empirical study" (2006) 22 *New Zealand Universities Law Review* 337, at 361.

120 John Armour, Bernard Black, Brian Cheffins and Richard Nolan, "Private enforcement of corporate law: An empirical comparison of the United Kingdom and the United States" (2009) 6(4) *Journal of Empirical Legal Studies* 687, at 714–715. See also Andrew Keay, "Assessing and rethinking the statutory scheme for derivative actions under the Companies Act 2006" (2016) 16 *Journal of Corporate Law Studies* 39, at 43.

121 See Martin Gelter, "Why do shareholder derivative suits remain rare in continental Europe?" (2012) 37 *Brooklyn Journal of International Law* 843 (explaining the scarcity of shareholder derivative actions in Austria, Belgium, the Netherlands, Spain, Germany, France and Switzerland).

122 David Gibbs-Kneller and Chidiebere Ogbonnaya, "Empirical analysis of the statutory derivative claim: De facto application and the sine quibus non" (2019) 19(2) *Journal of Corporate Law Studies* 303, at 319–320.

shareholders. One would argue that the uncertainty in the recovery of legal costs and the difficulties in obtaining leave of the court to bring an SDA are the likely contributing factors that explain the lack of use of the SDA. SDA and comparisons with the oppression remedy will be canvassed further in Chapter 7.

3.4.3.2 SDA is more widely used in private companies than in public companies

In 168 leave applications, nearly all cases involve small privately owned or closely held companies, as opposed to large public companies (see Table 3.2). Further, most of the applicants in those companies were current shareholders (see Table 3.4). This is not surprising given that compensation or benefit awarded by the court in a successful action accrues only to the company. This means that only the current shareholders will benefit from success in the SDA. These findings are consistent with the outcomes reported in a similar study in New Zealand,[123] where Taylor reported that in 91.3% of the cases, the proposed plaintiff company was "closely held" with each having "five or fewer shareholders"; and in 92.6% out of the 27 leave applications, the applicant was a shareholder.

The government has noted that SDA could be used as a "valuable tool" for maintaining "investor confidence".[124] This implies that the primary role of the SDA was intended for use in large public companies, where shareholders could monitor the conduct of the management and bring about director's accountability. Instead, empirical evidence indicates that SDA is more common in small and closely held companies to resolve internal disputes between shareholders and between shareholders and directors. One possible explanation is that in a public company where shareholdings are diverse and scattered, there is very little incentive for individual shareholders to litigate on behalf of other people in the company. Shareholders in large public companies can easily sell their shares back to the company rather than pursue litigation on behalf of the company that may have very little benefit to them individually.

Institutional shareholders that own a large percentage of shares generally do not want to deal with issues relating to, for example, breach of directors' duties. They would rather sell their shares and move on. It is very rare to see a public company involved in a derivative action. In *Henry v. Western Downs Group Ltd*,[125] the claimants were beneficiaries under a charitable trust with the public company appointed as corporate trustee, and because it was not ideal for the claimants to leave the trust, they decided to apply for leave to bring an SDA and deal with issues relating to breaches of directors' duties.

123 Taylor, n 118, at 351–352.

124 House of Representatives, CLERP Proposal Paper No. 3, *Proposals for Reform: Directors' Duties and Corporate Governance: Facilitating innovation and protecting investors* (Paper No.3, 1997), at 33. See also CASAC, *Statutory Derivative Action* (Report, July 1993), at 4 and 32.

125 *Henry v. Western Downs Group Ltd* [2018] FCA 1168.

3.4.3.3 Leave requirement generally

Section 237(2) states that the court must grant the application if an applicant has satisfied all five criteria.[126] However, this has not always been the case. In some cases, the court has granted leave without having considered the hurdle requirement. For example, in *Vlahos v. Vlahos*, the Supreme Court of Victoria granted leave to allow the applicant to appeal against a decision of the County Court of Victoria on a matter involving the company, even though the applicant had not filed a statement of claims and this was because the limitation period for appeal was about to expire.[127] In another case, leave was granted on the basis that the applicant had submitted a signed draft consent order to pay all costs in bringing the proposed action and there was very little discussion by the court on the criteria in s.237(2).[128]

The threshold in proving "there is a serious question to be tried" under s.237(2)(d) is very low. An applicant is not required to provide complete evidence to substantiate the claims made in the leave application stage, only enough to satisfy the court under s.237(2)(d) that there is "sufficient likelihood of success" in the claims to justify it going to trial.[129] The court only has to be satisfied of the existence of a substantive claim, and is not required to make any factual determination about contested issues in the leave stage.[130] The only difficulty for an applicant is to establish "good faith" and to show that the proposed action "is in the best interests of the company".

3.4.4 Bringing about directors' accountability

An interesting point to note from this study is that many of the proposed defendants opposing the leave application were directors (65.5%) and many of them were alleged to have breached their duties (57.7%). This suggests that the SDA may have some use in deterring corporate wrongdoings and thereby promoting directors' accountability and maintaining corporate governance, not in large public entities but in small privately owned companies.

However, it is questionable whether this form of private enforcement can, in practice, bring about directors' accountability. A successful leave application may be used as a threat of further litigation and possible liability if, for

126 For example, *Connective Services Pty Ltd v. Slea Pty Ltd* [2018] VSCA 229, at [2] (Ferguson CJ, Whelan and McLeish JJA).

127 *Vlahos v. Vlahos* [2016] VSC 824. See also *Fehring v. Brighter Directions Pty Ltd* [2010] VSC 287 in relation to another urgent leave application.

128 *Re Poly Pacific Pty Ltd* [2013] VSC 670, at [60].

129 *South Johnston Mill Ltd v. Dennis* [2007] FCA 1448, at [79] (Middleton J).

130 *Slea Pty Ltd v. Connective Services Pty Ltd* [2017] VSC 609, at [175] (Robson J). This point was not raised again in the Court of Appeal decision, which means there was no issue with s.237(2)(d): *Connective Services Pty Ltd v. Slea Pty Ltd* [2018] VSCA 229. See also, *South Johnston Mill Ltd v. Dennis* [2007] FCA 1448, at [80] (Middleton J); *Ehsman v. Nutectim International Pty Ltd* (2006) 58 ACSR 705; [2006] NSWSC 887, at [6].

example, a director fails to settle a dispute. If a successful leave application is all that an applicant desires to have, to use it as a threat of litigation against the proposed defendant in an attempt to settle a dispute without taking the matter further, then, arguably, the SDA may have some benefit to the applicant. A successful leave application may be enough to compel a party to settle the dispute. However, if an alleged wrongdoer does not react in the way the applicant expects, then the successful leave application alone would have no use to the applicant if they cannot financially afford to take the matter to the next level and bring the approved action. Some scholars have argued that there is no easy way to empirically assess behavioural changes in the directors or the improvement of corporate governance.[131]

3.5 Conclusion

This empirical study has provided answers to the three research questions referred to in the introduction. In summary, some interesting findings are these:

(1) Most applicants were shareholders (87.5%);
(2) Nearly all companies involved in the SDA were small privately owned or closely held companies (89.9%);
(3) Most of the proposed defendants opposing the leave application were company directors (65.5%), and the majority of claims against them relate to breaches of directors' duties (57.7%);
(4) In the total 168 leave applications filed in all court jurisdictions in the 20-year period from 13 March 2000 to 28 December 2019, 93 cases had a successful outcome on the application and 75 had an unsuccessful outcome;
(5) In those 93 successful leave cases, many of the applicants were unsuccessful in obtaining an indemnity for the leave application or an order for the company to fund the approved derivative action. Instead, the practice of the courts is to grant leave on terms that the applicant undertakes to bear all costs and charges in relation to the SDA or to grant leave but reserve their power to decide on the costs question at a later date. The overall effect is that the applicant pays costs in the interim and there is no certainty that they can recover their costs. The rationale for this approach is to protect the company's assets, and it is an easy way for an applicant to show "good faith" as required under s.237(2)(b) and to show that the proposed action "is in the best interests of the company" as required under s.237(2)(c).

131 Robert B. Thompson and Randall S. Thomas, "The public and private faces of derivative lawsuits" (2004) 57 *Vanderbilt Law Review* 1747, at 1775.

(6) In those 75 unsuccessful leave cases, the majority of applicants failed to demonstrate "good faith" in s.237(2)(b) and/or failed to demonstrate that the proposed derivative action "is in the best interests of the company" in s.237(2)(c). The combined failure rate on these criteria was 65.3%.
(7) There is a considerable overlap amongst the criteria in s.237(2) and the costs provision in s.242.

It is questionable whether Part 2F.1A has achieved the SDA purposes. The legislative intent was for the SDA to be used as an "effective" shareholder remedy. However, empirical evidence shows that the proportion of successful and unsuccessful leave applications is 55.4% and 44.6% respectively; and many of the applicants were successful on their leave application because they had undertaken to pay costs, which is not a clear sign that SDA has provided an effective remedy as such.

It is not clear what happens to those successful leave applications. There are two possibilities. First, the successful applicants may have settled their dispute with the proposed defendant, using the successful leave application as a bargaining chip or as a threat of further litigation to negotiate a settlement (in which case, the SDA may have some positive use). Alternatively, they may have abandoned their litigious pursuit due to a combination of factors; for example, funding constraint, uncertainty in the recovery of costs, difficulty with information/evidence gathering, problem with the presence of free riding, cheaper alternative dispute resolution available such as an oppression action or the expiry of the limitation period. Despite a lack of further reported information, there is sufficient empirical evidence to suggest that costs and uncertainty in the recovery of costs are likely to have been the main obstacle to shareholder litigation. So far, only three successful applications have proceeded in bringing the SDA and in these cases, none was successful in obtaining an order for the company to indemnify them, regardless of the outcome in the final judgment. This may have discouraged some applicants from commencing the approved action.

A qualitative evaluation is necessary to understand how the courts have treated the costs provision in s.242 and how they have decided certain applicants to have or not have met the "good faith" and "in the best interests of the company" requirements under s.237(2)(b) and (c), and to consider whether these have aligned squarely with the legislative intent. These issues are explored further in subsequent chapters, with a view to making suggestions for law reform in this important area in order to provide greater clarity and certainty and to provide shareholders with better protection. The outcomes in this study may also give some indication for other countries to consider how best in moving forward with their own reforms in respect to derivative litigation.

4 Rethinking the "good faith" requirement in statutory derivative action

4.1 Introduction

This chapter provides a critical analysis of the "good faith" requirement in statutory derivative action ("SDA"). The chapter considers the relevance of "good faith" and queries whether "good faith" should be a necessary precondition for an SDA.

For a court to grant leave, s.237(2)(b) requires an applicant to show that he or she is acting in "good faith". This is problematic in practice due to the subjective nature of the term "good faith" and the uncertainty in its application. The applicant has the onus in establishing "good faith".[1] Neither the Parliament nor the courts have provided any clarity to its meaning. Although the task of the court in considering applications under s.237 is evaluative, rather than discretionary, each case is determined on its own facts.[2] This adds to the difficulty in predetermining what "good faith" involves. As the courts remind us, the decision whether to grant leave under s.237 is an "evaluative task involving questions upon which reasonable minds can differ".[3]

The empirical study in Chapter 3 has identified "good faith" as the second difficult criterion for an applicant to satisfy the court for leave. The study reveals that in 44.6% of the unsuccessful leave applications, the reason for this failure rate was due to the applicant failing to establish "good faith" in 34.7% of the cases (or 26 out of 75 unsuccessful leave applications). Although, this may qualify the assertion that good faith is "relatively easy" to prove,[4] the reality is that on close examination and in many cases, the appli-

1 *Bzezinski v. Shaw* [2022] VSCA 173, at [67] (Kyrou, Mcleish and Walker JJA), confirming decision in *Bzezinski v. Shaw* [2021] VSC 654 (First instance); *Zhu v. Orico Australia Pty Ltd* [2019] VSC 313, at [26] (Connock J); *Chahwan v. Euphoric Pty Ltd* [2008] NSWCA 52, at [83] (Tobias JA, with Beazley and Bell JJA agreeing).

2 *Urban v. Junior Academy ELC Pty Ltd* [2019] VSCA 247, applying *Huang v. Wang* [2016] NSWCA 614, at [61] (Bathurst CJ, with McColl JA agreeing) and [79] (Barrett AJA). See also *Re 383 Latrobe Street Development Pty Ltd* [2021] VSC 655, at [6] (Connock J).

3 *Urban v. Junior Academy ELC Pty Ltd* [2019] VSCA 247, at [12] (Whelan JA, Emerton JA, and Kennedy AJA).

4 *Mount Gilead Pty Ltd & Hobhouse v. MacArthur-Onslow & Others* [2021] NSWSC 948, at [55] (Black J); *Connective Services Pty Ltd v. Slea Pty Ltd* [2018] VSCA 229, [55] (Ferguson CJ,

DOI: 10.4324/9781003430063-4

cant succeeded in showing "good faith" by means of undertaking to pay for the derivative action and indemnify the company against any adverse costs orders, including providing security for costs if necessary. Where an applicant undertakes to pay and the company does not have to pay for anything, this goes to show, in technical terms, that the applicant has fulfilled two requirements: (i) the applicant "is acting in good faith" under s.237(2)(b); and (ii) the applicant has demonstrated that the proposed action "is in the best interests of the company" under s.237(2)(c).[5] In other words, if other means of proving good faith fails or is impossible, then an applicant undertaking to pay for the proposed action would be able to justify his or her good faith. It is indeed an easier option if an applicant is financially capable.

One would ask the questions: If a wealthier applicant can afford to pay for the SDA and is willing to pay for it, does it really mean that he or she is acting in good faith? Does it really mean that the proposed derivative action is in the best interests of the company? Could there be a possibility that the applicant may be abusing the SDA process by means of applying for leave but having no intention of commencing or bringing the action but only having the intention of using the successful leave outcome to put pressure on the management to settle on terms less favourable to the company?

This chapter sets out to address these questions and explain why "good faith" should not be a precondition for granting leave to bring an SDA. It sets out to argue that the "good faith" requirement is difficult to fulfil in the "pure" sense. Indeed, "good faith" is a relevant consideration for determining whether an applicant is a suitable person to bring the proposed action, but the author queries whether it is necessary as a prerequisite in the *Corporations Act* 2001 (C'th). By including it as a prerequisite, there is a possibility that some shareholders may feel intimidated by it and not want to apply for leave. The SDA was "designed to improve rather than to place obstacles" to shareholder litigation.[6] The intention was for the SDA to be used as a tool for deterring corporate misconduct and for enhancement of corporate governance.[7] It is worth noting that New Zealand and Hong Kong have chosen not to include "good faith" as a requirement in their SDA, and the United Kingdom has included it not as a prerequisite but as one of several discretionary factors for the court to take into account when determining whether to grant leave. Although Singapore has good faith as a prerequisite, the interpretation of

Whelan and McLeish JJA). See also *App Shop Pty Ltd v. Jalal Bros Pty Ltd* [2019] NSWSC 490, [16] (Black J).

5 The "best interests of the company" criterion is discussed in Chapter 5, and the costs provision in Chapter 6.

6 *Zhu v. Orico Australia Pty Ltd* [2019] VSC 313, at [34] (Connock J).

7 Companies and Securities Advisory Committee ("CASAC"), *Statutory Derivative Action* (Report, 1993), at 4; Corporate Law Economic Reform Program Proposal Paper No. 3 ("CLERP Proposal Paper No. 3"), *Proposals for Reform: Directors' Duties and Corporate Governance* (1997), at 32–33.

that requirement has been thrown into disarray since the Singapore Court of Appeal[8] recently overturned its earlier approach, as discussed in Part 5 below.

This chapter proceeds as follows. Part 2 explains the meaning of "good faith" and its role in the SDA. Part 3 examines how the courts determine whether an applicant has met the good faith requirement. It is important to bear in mind that, in many cases, the applicant has satisfied the court of the good faith requirement by undertaking to bear all costs associated with bringing an SDA. Part 4 considers whether the inclusion of good faith is necessary, explaining that good faith already overlaps with other prerequisites in the SDA framework. Part 5 compares "good faith" from other jurisdictions, such as from New Zealand, Hong Kong, the United Kingdom, Canada and Singapore. Part 6 concludes with a note of recommendation.

4.2 Meaning of "good faith"

4.2.1 What is "good faith"?

Section 237(2)(b) provides that an applicant seeking leave to bring an SDA is required to satisfy the court that they are acting in "good faith". The term "good faith" is easily understood, and yet it cannot be defined with precision simply because there is no clear meaning.[9] Its scope is infinite and fluid. The CA does not attempt to define "good faith", nor does it provide any example of "bad faith" to illustrate the opposite effect. The Explanatory Memorandum provides some guidance on how to approach the "good faith" provision:[10]

> "In assessing whether an applicant is acting in good faith, the Court could be expected to have regard to whether:
>
> - there was any complicity by the applicant in the matters complained of; and
> - the application is being made in pursuit of an interest other than that of the company."

Indeed, as for the first point, if an applicant does have "complicity" as described, it would be obvious that the applicant would not be acting in good faith.[11] As for the second point, the Explanatory Memorandum states further that: "The good faith requirement is designed to prevent proceedings being used to further the purposes of the applicant, rather than the company as a

8 This is the highest court in the hierarchy in Singapore.
9 This point is discussed further in the next part below.
10 House of Representatives, *Explanatory Memorandum to the CLERP Bill* 1998 (C'th), at [6.36].
11 According to the Oxford English Dictionary, "complicity" means "the act of taking part with another person in a crime".

whole".[12] This statement is unhelpful, in that it does not provide any clarity to understanding the meaning of good faith other than to say that the criterion is necessary to discourage potential applicants from applying for a derivative action if the purpose was to further the applicant's own personal interests, as opposed to the interests of the company as a whole. Before moving on to consider case law for circumstances that are relevant in proving good faith, it is worth noting what other scholars have said about good faith.

It is generally agreed that good faith cannot be defined. Some scholars argue that the term "good faith" is "replete with uncertainty in conception and highly unworkable in practice",[13] and that it is "not susceptible of positive proof".[14] The term is "nebulous",[15] "elusive",[16] and somewhat "indirect".[17] The term is "irrelevant",[18] "meaningless",[19] and "unworkable".[20] It has also been said that good faith makes no difference as to whether an applicant's motives are "pure or not" since other prerequisites "already deal adequately" with malicious or unmeritorious actions.[21] In the context of contract law, good faith has also been criticised as a term arousing "confusion and uncertainty",[22] and that "Australian case law and academic commentary also divide on the meaning of good faith".[23] One scholar has summed up good faith as:[24]

12 House of Representatives, *Explanatory Memorandum to the CLERP Bill* 1998 (C'th), at [6.37].

13 Andrew Keay and Joan Louhrey, "Something old, something new, something borrowed: An analysis of the new derivative active action under the Companies Act 2006" (2008) 124 *Law Quarterly Review* 469 at 485.

14 Pearlie Koh, "Of links and legal merits – Good faith in the statutory derivative action in Singapore" (2014) 14 *Oxford University Commonwealth Law Journal* 225, at 229.

15 Dan W. Puchniak and Tan Cheng Han SC, "Company Law" (2015) 16 *Singapore Academy of Law Annual Review*, at 270. See also Alan K. Koh, "Searching for good faith in Singapore's derivative action: Much ado about something? *Wong Kai Wah v Wong Kai Yuan, Ang Thiam Swee v Low Hian Chor*" (2015) 36 *Company Lawyer* 207.

16 Margaret Chew, *Minority Shareholders' Rights and Remedies* (2nd edition, LexisNexis, 2007) at 301.

17 Arad Reisberg, "Theoretical reflections on derivative actions in English law: The representative problem" (2006) 3 *European Company and Financial Law Review* 69, at 102.

18 Dennis H. Peterson and Matthew J. Cumming, *Shareholder Remedies in Canada* (Looseleaf services, 2nd ed, LexisNexis, 2009), at 16.39.

19 Bruce Welling, *Corporate Law in Canada: The Governing Principles* (3rd edition, Scribblers, 2006) at 511 and 528 (contending that good faith is "meaningless", and that "I have no idea what this means, and I get the sense that no one else does either").

20 Andrew Keay and Joan Loughrey, "An assessment of the present state of statutory derivative proceedings" in Joan Loughrey (ed.), *Directors' Duties and Shareholder Litigation in the Wake of the Financial Crisis* (Edward Elgar, 2012), at 207.

21 M. A. Maloney, "Whither the statutory derivative action?" (1986) 64 *Canadian Bar Review* 309, at 320.

22 Lara Jane Piercy, "Comparison of the law concerning implied terms of good faith in Australia and in England" (2017) 6 *Journal of Civil Law and Practice* 163, at 163.

23 Anthony Gray, "Good faith in Australian contract law after Barker" (2015) 43 *Australian Business Law Review* 358, at 365.

24 Robert Summers, "'Good faith' in general contract law and the sales provisions of the Uniform Commercial Code" (1968) 54 *Virginia Law Review* 195, at 201.

"an excluder. It is a phrase without general meaning (or meanings) of its own and serves to exclude a wide range of heterogeneous forms of bad faith. In a particular context the phrase takes on specific meaning, but usually this is only by way of contrast with the specific form of bad faith actually or hypothetically excluded."

4.2.2 Purpose of "good faith"

The concept of "good faith" is relevant and important for two reasons. First, the purpose of the good faith element is to ensure that the person who is given the power to represent the company and act on behalf of the company will be acting for a proper purpose. This power is pointed out succinctly by Dixon J in the High Court of Australia in *Mills v. Mills* in the context of director's duty, where he refers to "a person having a power, must execute it *bona fide* for the end designed, otherwise it is corrupt and void".[25] Thus, the importance of good faith relates to preventing any misuse of power by an applicant bringing the SDA. Another way of saying the same thing is that, because a derivative action is an action brought on behalf of the company, its relevance is to ensure that the approved applicant, representing the company's interests, will not be misusing his or her power and bringing the action purely for personal gain.[26]

Clearly, as explained in the Explanatory Memorandum, the inclusion of the good faith requirement in s.237(2)(b) is intended to prevent the applicant from taking out personal vengeance or malicious action.[27] It is intended as a further screening mechanism to filter out cases that have no merit. Its objective is to ensure that the company's interests and its resources are protected for the benefits of all shareholders.[28] One would expect an applicant to have a personal interest or purpose in bringing a derivative action, but provided that the applicant's purpose aligns with the purpose of the company, this would be seen as acceptable and would not constitute an abuse of power.[29]

The second purpose relates to assessing the suitability of an applicant to bring an SDA. The test should be that the person is fit and proper, in the sense that the person is of good standing and character. However, in many leave

25 *Mills v. Mills* (1938) 60 CLR 150, at 185.

26 *Chahwan v. Euphoric Pty Ltd* [2008] NSWCA 52, at [67-69] (Tobias JA, with whom Beazley and Bell JJA agreed).

27 House of Representatives, *Explanatory Memorandum to the CLERP Bill* 1998, at [2.5] (making reference to the need for "tight constraints on the availability" of the SDA).

28 *Charlton v. Baber* [2003] NSWSC 745, at [43]; *Carpenter v. Pioneer Park Pty Ltd* [2004] NSWSC 1007, at [29]; *Fiduciary Ltd v. Morningstar Research Pty Ltd* [2005] NSWSC 442, at [56].

29 *Connective Services Pty Ltd v. Slea Pty Ltd* [2018] VSCA 229, at [105–110] (Ferguson CJ, Whelan and McLeish JJA); *Swansson v. RA Pratt Properties Pty Ltd* [2002] NSWSC 583, at [36].

applications, the court has tended to focus on the financial position of the applicant and their capability in financing the proposed action as a measure of whether the applicant is suitable for bringing the action, as discussed in the latter part of this chapter. A possible explanation for this approach by the courts is that the phrasing of the leave criteria in s.237(2), in particular in paragraph (c), requires the applicant to demonstrate to the court that the proposed derivative action "is in the best interests of the company". In other words, the threshold is so high that the only way for the court to be satisfied that the applicant has met this particular criterion is to require the applicant to pay for the proposed action. There is considerable overlap between the good faith requirement and other criteria, as discussed later.

It is submitted that in determining the applicant's suitability, the focus on the applicant's good faith should be on the applicant's character and standing, and their motive for desiring to bring a derivative action, not on the purpose of the company or on how much money the applicant has or whether they can afford to pay for the action. The good faith concept is about the applicant. Good faith should be considered independently to the "in the best interests of the company" criterion and unencumbered by costs consideration. If an applicant has an ulterior purpose, then clearly, he would not be of good standing.[30] If an applicant has a personal purpose, then provided there is no conflict with the company's interests, that is, the applicant's purpose coincides or aligns with the company's interests, the applicant should be assessed as suitable and be given the standing to bring the action. These points are explained further in the rest of this chapter.

4.2.3 Comparison with the directors' duty of good faith

There is a stark difference in the treatment of the director's duty to act in good faith in the management of the company and the requirement of good faith on the part of the applicant when seeking leave to bring an SDA. In both instances, good faith is required, but the difference is that an applicant has the onus of proof of good faith for bringing an SDA, while directors are presumed to be acting in good faith in discharging their duty unless proven otherwise. Section 181 of the CA, in part, requires directors to act in good faith in the management of the company.[31] The onus is not on a director to prove that he or she has acted in good faith; rather, it is on the person (or the company) bringing the action to prove that the director has breached the good faith duty. In other words, a director, having the role as manager of the company

30 See for example, *Pentridge Village Pty Ltd (in liq.) v. Capital Finance Australia Ltd* [2018] VSC 633, [239] (where the applicant was found to have given inaccurate, incomplete and out of date financial information and other company information).

31 *Corporations Act* 2001 (C'th), s.181 of the states that a director or an officer of the company "must exercise their power and discharge their duties ... in good faith".

and making corporate decisions, is not required to show that he has acted in good faith in making corporate decisions, as his power is conferred by the majority shareholder votes. An applicant seeking leave to bring an SDA, on the other hand, has the burden of proving that a director has (for example, acted in bad faith), which is a more demanding task for the applicant.

Comparing with the SDA, an applicant is required to demonstrate good faith when seeking leave,[32] which is opposite to the director's duty of good faith scenario. That is, directors are not required to prove good faith in managing the company in the way that shareholders have to prove good faith in bringing a derivative action. Even where, for example, a director has acted in bad faith and for an improper purpose and has clearly breached his duty, the onus is still on the shareholder litigant (or the other director who is not in breach) to demonstrate their own good faith in order to be given leave to bring the necessary derivative action. It has been said that an applicant is required to demonstrate good faith to the court for leave, because he or she "is assuming a role of the company's directors",[33] and is representing the company's interests.

In summary, an applicant seeking leave to pursue a derivative action against a director for breach of a duty is likely to face two separate challenges: proving their own good faith for leave to be granted to bring an action on behalf of the company under s.237(2)(b) and proving the director's lack of good faith in discharging the duty under s.181. The situation is even more challenging if an applicant is not already a company director and has limited inside knowledge and evidence to prove such a breach.

4.3 Judicial approaches to good faith

4.3.1 Proof of good faith

Proving good faith is often difficult. The courts have made it clear that proof of good faith is the task of the applicant seeking a derivative action.[34] There is no standard test. *Swansson v. RA Pratt Properties Pty Ltd* was the first significant case in Australia's statutory derivative action, where Palmer J provides two interrelated tests for determining whether the shareholder applicant was acting in good faith:[35]

> "[I]n my opinion, there are at least two interrelated factors to which the Courts will always have regard in determining whether the good faith

32 *Chahwan v. Euphoric Pty Ltd* [2008] NSWCA 52, at [83] (Tobias JA, with whom Beazley and Bell JJA agreed); *Zhu v. Orico Australia Pty Ltd* [2019] VSC 313, at [26] (Connock J).

33 *Cannon Street Pty Ltd v. Karedis* [2004] Qld SC 104, at [176] (Muir J).

34 *Bzezinski v. Shaw* [2022] VSCA 173, at [67] (Kyrou, Mcleish and Walker JJA); *Chahwan v. Euphoric Pty Ltd* [2008] NSWCA 52, at [83] (Tobias JA, with whom Beazley and Bell JJA agreed); *Zhu v. Orico Australia Pty Ltd* [2019] VSC 313, at [26] (Connock J).

35 *Swansson v. RA Pratt Properties Pty Ltd* (2002) 42 ACSR 313, [2002] NSWSC 583, at [36].

requirement of s.237(2)(b) is satisfied. The first is whether the applicant honestly believes that a good cause of action exists and has a reasonable prospect of success. ... The second factor is whether the applicant is seeking to bring the derivative suit for such a collateral purpose as would amount to an abuse of process."

The first is whether the applicant *honestly believes* that the proposed action has a reasonable prospect of success, and the second is whether the applicant has any *collateral purpose* that would constitute an abuse of process. Palmer J also states that these factors are not intended to be comprehensive or exhaustive, but rather the law on good faith will continue to "develop incrementally".[36] In this case, it was held that the applicant had not acted in good faith.[37] She attempted to use SDA to obtain a further recovery for her own benefit when she had already received a large settlement sum in her divorce proceedings against her former husband.

In a most recent decision in *Bzezinski v. Shaw*, the Victorian Court of Appeal opined with the "good faith" approach adopted in *Swansson v. RA Pratt Properties Pty Ltd*, stating:[38]

"We doubt that Palmer J was intending to say... that a failure to approach good faith question by reference to these two specific criteria [ie the two inter-related factors] would amount to an error of law. Rather, they are features of the good faith inquiry in this context that may be expected to routinely present themselves for consideration."

In *Bzezinski v. Shaw*, the Full Court unanimously upheld the trial judge's decision that a delay of two years before the applicant sought leave to bring a derivative action without any explanation given for the delay was considered not to have acted in good faith.[39] This was a case where the director applicant had used the derivative action application as an attempt to cause further delay in the court proceedings against him for non-payment under loan agreements and guarantees.

In another important case, *Connective Services Pty Ltd v. Slea Pty Ltd*, the Victorian Court of Appeal unanimously agreed with the trial judge that the applicant had successfully proven the leave criteria. On the point of good faith, it was held that the trial judge had not erred in applying the principles set out in *Swansson*.[40] Slea Pty Ltd, which owned 33.33% of the shares in

36 *Swansson v. RA Pratt Properties Pty Ltd* (2002) 42 ACSR 313, [2002] NSWSC 583, [35].

37 The applicant did not appear in court to give evidence: *Swansson* (2002) 42 ACSR 313; [2002] NSWSC 583, [46].

38 *Bzezinski v. Shaw* [2022] VSCA 173, at [65] (Kyrou, Mcleish and Walker JJA).

39 *Bzezinski v. Shaw* [2022] VSCA 173, at [74] (Kyrou, Mcleish and Walker JJA), upholding the first instance decision in *Bzezinski v. Shaw* [2021] VSC 654 (Osborne J).

40 *Connective Services Pty Ltd v. Slea Pty Ltd* [2018] VSCA 229, at [108] (Ferguson CJ, Whelan and McLeish JJA).

Connective Services Pty Ltd, was not informed about the corporate restructure carried out by the two directors of Connective Services. When it was discovered later that the directors had transferred 25% of the business interests to a third party financier, resulting in the reduction of the existing shareholder's interests from 33.33% to 25%, the applicant (Slea Pty Ltd), through its sole director, applied for leave to bring a derivative action on behalf of Connective Services against the two directors in an attempt to restore its shareholding and the overall share value in the company. In needing funding to assist with litigation, the applicant engaged a commercial funder. Robson J in the trial court held that the applicant was acting in good faith:[41]

> "There is no collateral purpose in Slea bringing the application in order to restore full value to its shareholding in the Connective companies, enabling it at some future point in time to realise the value, as well as increasing through dividends, a higher share of the profits."

On the point of litigation funding, Robson J considered prior cases and further stated that there was nothing inappropriate about the applicant engaging a commercial funder to assist with litigation. His statement was repeated and approved by the Full Court on appeal:[42]

> "It is difficult to categorise the rights and obligations under the... agreement as a collateral purpose as defined by the cases discussed. ... The fact that Liberty [a commercial funder] believes it is in its own interests to fund Slea to pursue the proposed claim does not mean that Slea does not have legitimate grounds for pursuing the claim...
>
> ... Liberty's interest in Slea pursuing those grounds does not convert what is otherwise a legitimate claim by Slea into an improper claim for a collateral purpose. The issue is to characterise Slea's purpose and objective."

The importance of this case is twofold. First, the court continues to show support for the principle that an application for leave to bring a derivative action to restore the applicant's share value in the company cannot be taken to mean that the applicant's collateral purpose constitutes an abuse of process or that the applicant is acting in bad faith, because such application would also benefit other shareholders in the company.[43] Second, having a

41 *Slea Pty Ltd v. Connective Services Pty Ltd* [2017] VSC 609, at [108].

42 *Slea Pty Ltd v. Connective Services Pty Ltd* [2017] VSC 609, at [112–113] (Robson J) (Trial court decision); *Connective Services Pty Ltd v. Slea Pty Ltd* [2018] VSCA 229, at [63] (Ferguson CJ, Whelan and McLeish JJA) (Victorian Court of Appeal decision).

43 For other prior cases that have taken a similar approach, see *MG Corrosion Consultants Pty Ltd v. Vinciguerra* [2011] FCAFC 31, at [54] (North, McKerracher and Jagot JJ); *In the matter of Vicad Pty Ltd – Pottie v. Dunkley* [2011] NSWSC 166, at [43].

commercial funder involved in the SDA is no longer construed as an abuse of the court's process, provided that the making of an application for leave is for a legitimate reason, in this case for restoring the applicant's shareholding and share value in the company which also aligns with the interests of other shareholders in the company. This is one of the very few reported cases of a commercial funder being used in SDAs.[44]

It is clear from the above discussion that it was not difficult for the court to find the absence or presence of good faith. However, in some cases, it can be quite difficult for an applicant to show good faith. In *Chahwan v. Euphoric Pty Ltd*, in dismissing the application for leave, the NSW Court of Appeal found that the applicant had not successfully demonstrated good faith. The applicant was the only shareholder and director of the company that had been placed into liquidation. His leave application was seen as an attempt to restrain a creditor from selling off a piece of mortgaged property of which he claimed to be the owner, and not the company, as he had provided his own money to the company to purchase that property. His other claim was that the mortgage was created by the previous director of the same company who breached her duty to the company by failing to repay the loan and that he had no part in that breach. It was held that the applicant was merely thinking about himself as the beneficial owner of the property and not about the legal interests of the company and that his collateral (or more to the point, ultimate) purpose was to obtain the entire benefits for himself, which amounted to lacking good faith. The difficulty in this case is that because the applicant was the only shareholder in the company and the company had gone into insolvency, it seems almost impossible for the applicant to succeed on the argument that he was acting in good faith for the company.

Rather interesting is the case of *Vinciguerra v. MG Corrosion Consultants Pty Ltd*, where the court seems to have been less strict on the applicant needing to show good faith and focuses more on examining the conduct of both parties as a way of getting to understand the applicant's motive.[45] In this case, while the shareholder applicant was focusing on breaches of directors' duties as a ground for pleading for leave to bring a derivative action,[46] the directors, on the other hand, provided the court with a list of factors as to why the applicant had not acted in good faith in making that application for leave. They argued, amongst other things, that the applicant had rejected an offer to buy back his shares, had declined to engage in discussions, and that the applicant (holder of 30% of the shares in the company) had threatened to wind up the company.[47] Gilmour J in the Federal Court of Australia rejected all of the

44 The reasons for the rarity in the use of a commercial funder in SDAs is explained in Chapter 7.

45 *Vinciguerra v. MG Corrosion Consultants Pty Ltd* [2010] FCA 763.

46 *Vinciguerra v. MG Corrosion Consultants Pty Ltd* [2010] FCA 763, at [75], [128], [152], [153].

47 *Vinciguerra v. MG Corrosion Consultants Pty Ltd* [2010] FCA 763, at [30], [47], [70], [76], [98].

opponents' arguments and, in allowing a derivative action, concluded that the applicant was acting in good faith and had satisfied the court of all five criteria under s 237(2). His Honour formed the view that "the conduct of both parties... [was] less than mutually co-operative",[48] and while agreeing with the tests laid down by Palmer J in *Swansson*,[49] Gilmour J nonetheless took a broader approach and decided on the applicant's good faith by "assessing the nature of the allegations and the circumstances out of which [those allegations] arose".[50] The court found that the applicant had spent much time and effort in preparing the leave application, including applying to access relevant company documents. It was clear from the facts that the applicant showed intense animosity towards the opposing directors, but this was held to be normal in matters of litigation.[51] The court in this case did not insist on the strict legalistic approach that the applicant must prove that he was acting in good faith; rather, the opposing directors argued that the applicant was not acting in good faith but failed in their argument.

In summary, while the courts have generally adopted the view that the two factors described in *Swansson* are regarded as the proper test for good faith, the courts are not restricted to those factors.[52] The court "may draw inferences as to the applicant's good faith by assessing the nature of the allegations and the circumstances out of which they arose",[53] and may take into account "the diligence with which the applicant asserts" good faith.[54] Consideration of good faith is therefore based entirely on the facts of each case and the evidence presented, but on the whole, the onus is still on the applicant to prove good faith.[55]

It should be noted too that in the more recent published decision, *De Tocqueville, in the matter of Pacific Current Group Limited v. Pacific Current Group Limited*,[56] the court seems to suggest that one should not be too quick to conclude an absence of good faith on the part of the applicant. In this

48 *Vinciguerra v. MG Corrosion Consultants Pty Ltd* [2010] FCA 763, at [64].

49 *Vinciguerra v. MG Corrosion Consultants Pty Ltd* [2010] FCA 763, at [84].

50 *Vinciguerra v. MG Corrosion Consultants Pty Ltd* [2010] FCA 763, at [54–56].

51 *Vinciguerra v. MG Corrosion Consultants Pty Ltd* [2010] FCA 763, at [81–85].

52 *Chahwan v. Euphoric Pty Ltd* [2008] NSWCA 52, at [69], [81] (Tobias JA, with Beazley and Bell JJA agreeing); *Connective Services Pty Ltd v. Slea Pty Ltd* [2018] VSCA 229, at [105–110] (Ferguson CJ, Whelan and McLeish JJA).

53 *Vinciguerra v. MG Corrosion Consultants Pty Ltd* [2010] FCA 763, at [56] (Appeal dismissed in *MG Corrosion Consultants Pty Ltd v. Vinciguerra* [2011] FCAFC 31, at [22]). See also *Re Wan Ze Property Development (Aust.) Pty Ltd* (2012) 90 ACSR 593; [2012] NSWSC 722, at [13].

54 *Hannon v. Doyle* [2011] NSWSC 10, at [107].

55 *Bzezinski v Shaw* [2022] VSCA 173, at [67] (Kyrou, Mcleish and Walker JJA); *Chahwan v. Euphoric Pty Ltd* [2008] NSWCA 52, at [83] (Tobias JA, with whom Beazley and Bell JJA agreed).

56 *De Tocqueville, in the matter of Pacific Current Group Limited v. Pacific Current Group Limited* [2020] FCA 172.

case, Moshinsky J of the Federal Court of Australia noted that a degree of anger shown towards the board and management is not sufficient to indicate absence of good faith; a shareholder persisting with his s.237 application despite the considered opinion of Counsel that the claim has low prospects of success is not sufficient to suggest an absence of good faith.[57] The approach taken in this case and in *Connective Services Pty Ltd v. Slea Pty Ltd* seems to be illustrative of the point Professor Bob Baxt made in 2013 that the courts are "becoming more comfortable" with the idea of shareholders taking derivative action against a company and its directors.[58]

4.3.2 What circumstances would be relevant to show good faith?

4.3.2.1 Definition and scope of collateral purpose

The term "collateral purpose" was mentioned in *Swansson* for determining when an "abuse of process" occurs. Much can be said about these terms, but this chapter will not discuss abuse of process in the general sense.[59] The discussion will be confined to instances of collateral purpose that go to prove or disprove the applicant's good faith. Indeed, if an applicant has "complicity" in the derivative action, or an ulterior motive or ulterior purpose, then without more to say, the applicant would be acting in bad faith.

A "collateral" purpose is simply another purpose that is personal to the applicant and is to be decided by the court as to whether an applicant is or is not acting in good faith in seeking leave to bring an SDA. The focus is on the applicant's purpose, which is different from the purpose of the derivative action. In the latter, a derivative action is brought for the purpose of benefiting and protecting the interests of all shareholders in the company, including the applicant if they are a shareholder,[60] provided that the applicant has not committed any wrongdoing.[61] An applicant may have a collateral or personal purpose or interest in bringing a derivative action, but that collateral purpose

57 *De Tocqueville, in the matter of Pacific Current Group Limited v. Pacific Current Group Limited* [2020] FCA 172, at [65].

58 Professor Bob Baxt, "Enhancing the rights of shareholders" (2013) Australian Institute of Company Directors: https://www.aicd.com.au/leadership/types/thought/enhancing-the-rights-of-shareholders.html (viewed 22 October 2022)

59 The nexus between collateral purpose and abuse of process and improper purpose is discussed in the High Court decision in *Williams v. Spautz* (1992) 174 CLR 509 and in the Victorian Court of Appeal decision in *Melbourne City Investments Pty Ltd v. Myer Holdings Ltd* [2017] VSCA 187 and in other cases referred to by Robson J in *Slea Pty Ltd v. Connective Services Pty Ltd* [2017] VSC 609, at [108–111]. The first two mentioned cases are unrelated to derivative action.

60 *Steinier v. Sunlea Enterprises Pty Ltd* [2016] WASC 81, at [73] (Martino J); *Fiduciary Ltd v. Morningstar Research Pty Ltd* (2005) 53 ACSR 732; [2005] NSWSC 442, at [56] (Austin J).

61 *Swansson v. RA Pratt Properties Pty Ltd* (2002) 42 ACSR 313, [2002] NSWSC 583, at [37], [43]. See also CLERP Proposal Paper No 3, *Proposals for Reform: Directors' Duties and Corporate Governance: Facilitating Innovation and Protecting Investors* (1997), at 36, [5.3.3].

must align with the company's purpose, which is to protect the interests of the company and its resources.[62] In other words, the applicant's collateral purpose can only be one that also serves the company's purpose and only indirectly benefits the applicant.[63] Case authorities have shown that it is possible for an applicant to have a collateral or personal purpose or interest in pursuing a derivative action, and for a conclusion to be drawn that the applicant is acting in good faith, that collateral purpose must coincide or align with the company's interests.

If good faith is construed in the way described in the Explanatory Memorandum,[64] then it would be virtually impossible for any applicant to satisfy the court of the good faith requirement.[65] The expression "good faith" should not be restrictively construed.[66] In the world of business, it is unlikely that an applicant would want to take on a derivative action as a charity case. An applicant must have some collateral purpose in the derivative action for them to take an interest in pursuing the proposed action. The fact that an applicant has a collateral purpose should not be an indication that the applicant is acting in bad faith in every case.[67]

The question to be addressed now is: What circumstances are relevant to show good faith? The short answer is there is "no fixed test".[68] The following are some examples, and the list is, and will remain, incomplete.

4.3.2.2 Personal animosity and malice

Where there is personal animosity or malice towards other shareholders, this would not necessarily be construed as lacking good faith in the first instance. In *Re 383 Latrobe Street Development Pty Ltd*, the court has made a point that animosity shown by a shareholder towards the proposed director defendants in the context of a derivative leave application has to be "far from unusual" to be considered as not acting in good faith.[69] A rather interesting case is in *Vinciguerra v. MG Corrosion Consultants Pty Ltd*, where the court

62 *Carpenter v. Pioneer Park Pty Ltd* [2004] NSWSC 1007, at [29]; *Charlton v. Baber* [2003] NSWSC 745, at [43].

63 *Li v. Dao* [2018] VSC 530, at [92].

64 As referred to in the above under Part 2 of the discussion.

65 This fear was put forward in the beginning when the SDA came into operation: see Peter Prince, "Australia's statutory derivative action: Using the New Zealand experience" (2000) 18 *Company and Securities Law Journal* 493, at 506–508.

66 *Chahwan v. Euphoric Pty Ltd* (2008) 65 ACSR 661; [2008] NSWCA 52, at [69] (Tobias JA, Beazley and Bell JJA agreeing).

67 When comparing with the directors' duty to act for a "proper purpose", the courts have allowed directors to act for mixed personal and corporate purposes without finding a breach of that duty. The same principle should apply in the case of SDA: see example in *Carpenter v. Pioneer Park Pty Ltd* [2004] NSWSC 1007.

68 *Vinciguerra v. MG Corrosion Consultants Pty Ltd* [2010] FCA 763, at [119] (Gilmour J).

69 *Re 383 Latrobe Street Development Pty Ltd* [2021] VSC 655, at [40] (Connock J).

ruled that having intense personal animosity or malice towards the proposed defendant is not a clear indication of the applicant acting in bad faith, as this is "reasonable" and normal behaviour in matters of litigation.[70] In this case, an applicant who owned 30% of the shares in the company alleged breaches of director's duties and sought to restore the value of his shares in the company. The sole director of the company owned the remaining 70% of the shares. The applicant admitted that he was "upset" and "angry" when he previously told a former employee that he was "really looking forward to destroying the company".[71] Gilmour J in the Federal Court of Australia held that the applicant's intense animosity towards the opponent was "understandable" and "reasonable", that there was "no reason why a proposal to wind up a company by a party seeking leave to pursue a derivative action ... must be demonstrative of bad faith".[72] Gilmour J noted further that it is not the law that only an applicant who feels goodwill towards a defendant is entitled to sue.[73]

Similarly, in *In the matter of Vicad Pty Ltd – Pottie v. Dunkley*,[74] the applicant sought leave to bring an SDA in an attempt to settle her late father's estate and for a range of remedies, including for restoring the share value in the company. The court found that there was a long history of grievances between the applicant and her brother, and held that despite "some personal animosity" towards her brother, the applicant was acting in good faith in trying to settle their longstanding family dispute.[75]

In contrast, in the case of *Swansson*, the court ruled that an applicant who had a "history of grievances" and "private vendetta" towards her former husband/proposed defendant was not acting in good faith.[76] Perhaps one way of reconciling these cases is that in *Pottie v. Dunkley* and in *Vinciguerra*, the applicants were current shareholders while in *Swansson*, the applicant was a former shareholder, which means that, logically, a current shareholder has a better chance of proving good faith than a former shareholder.

70 *Vinciguerra v. MG Corrosion Consultants Pty Ltd* [2010] FCA 763, at [85]; *MG Corrosion Consultants Pty Ltd v. Vinciguerra* [2011] FCAFC 31 (where appeal against the grant of leave was dismissed).

71 *Vinciguerra v. MG Corrosion Consultants Pty Ltd* [2010] FCA 763 (21 July 2010) at [81].

72 *Vinciguerra v. MG Corrosion Consultants Pty Ltd* [2010] FCA 763 (21 July 2010) at [82–85]; see also *Power v. Ekstein* [2010] NSWSC 137; (2010) 77 ACSR 302 at [101] (Austin J).

73 *Vinciguerra v. MG Corrosion Consultants Pty Ltd* [2010] FCA 763, at [84]. It is worth noting that an appeal by the opponent against the grant of leave was dismissed with costs: *MG Corrosion Consultants Pty Ltd v. Vinciguerra* [2011] FCAFC 31. Further, a separate application for leave to bring a derivative action to pursue a cross-claim against the original applicant was denied on the grounds that the cross-claim was vexatious and unmeritorious: *MG Corrosion Consultants Pty Ltd v. Gilmour* [2012] FCA 461.

74 *Pottie v. Dunkley* [2011] NSWSC 166.

75 *Pottie v. Dunkley* [2011] NSWSC 166, at [58].

76 *Swansson v. RA Pratt Properties Pty Ltd* (2002) 42 ACSR 313, [2002] NSWSC 583, at [41].

4.3.2.3 Interaction between "good faith" and "in the best interests of the company"

Another way for an applicant to show good faith is by way of proof that the proposed derivative action "is in the best interests of the company",[77] which is another requirement in s.237(2)(c). The courts have pointed out that these requirements are "not mutually exclusive".[78] The overlap is "common".[79] There are cases where the courts have only considered the "best interests" criterion and paid no or very little attention to the good faith requirement. For example, in *Re Sovereign Lawyers Pty Ltd*, after referring to the leave criteria in s.237(2), Black J stated that he "will assume" the presence of good faith based on the information contained in the applicant's affidavit and went straight to considering whether the proposed action would be in the company's interests and held that it would not be so.[80] In *Blakeney v. Blakeney*, the "best interests of the company" requirement was regarded as more "critical" than the good faith requirement,[81] and given that the applicant had not demonstrated the proposed action to be in the company's interests, the Court of Appeal in Western Australia did not consider it necessary to consider the good faith element.[82] In *Russell v. Lee Holdings Pty Ltd*, Martin J noted "some overlap between the criteria",[83] and felt it only necessary to consider the "best interests" criterion in determining the leave application.[84] These cases suggest that "good faith", as a prerequisite, may be redundant.

There are other cases where the courts have considered these two conditions together as if they are one composite element. For example, in *Catalano v. Managing Australian Destinations Pty Ltd*, Yates J discussed in detail the allegations that the directors had breached their duties, referred to the criteria in s.237 briefly and concluded that the applicant had satisfied all five criteria for leave.[85] In *Re Karinya Haulage Pty Ltd*, Brereton J noted that these two

77 *Robash Pty Ltd v. Gladstone Pacific Nickel Pty Ltd* [2011] NSWSC 1235, at [58], where Ball J stated, "In my opinion, the applicant must also honestly believe that it is in the best interests of the company that the action be brought". See also *Drew v. Lynch* [2019] FCA 632, at [105] (Gleeson J).

78 *Chahwan v. Euphoric Pty Ltd* (2008) 65 ACSR 661; [2008] NSWCA 52, at [68] (Tobias JA, Beazley and Bell JJA agreeing)

79 *Li v. Dao* [2018] VSC 530, at [60].

80 *Re Sovereign Lawyers Pty Ltd* [2018] NSWSC 695, at para 5 (this case is only three pages in length or 12 paragraphs.)

81 *Blakeney v. Blakeney* [2016] WASCA 76, at [51] (Buss and Murphy JJA and Beech J).

82 *Blakeney v. Blakeney* [2016] WASCA 76, at [90] (Buss and Murphy JJA and Beech J), refusing leave by overturning the trial court's decision in *Blakeney v. Blakeney* [2015] WASC 73.

83 *Russell v. Lee Holdings Pty Ltd* [2018] WASC 275, at [13].

84 *Russell v. Lee Holdings Pty Ltd* [2018] WASC 275, at [15–16].

85 *Catalano v. Managing Australian Destinations Pty Ltd* [2012] FCA 632 (Yates J); see also *Catalano v. Managing Australian Destinations Pty Ltd* [2014] FCAFC 55.

conditions were "related" and went on to consider them together and concluded that the applicant had satisfied these criteria for leave.[86]

It seems that either the courts have given more attention to the "best interests" requirement and less to good faith, or they have considered them as one composite element. One view for this is that the test of good faith is redundant if an applicant is unable to demonstrate the proposed action to be in the company's interests. The other view is that good faith will be "relatively easy" to demonstrate if an applicant has passed the test "in the best interests of the company" and proven that there are legitimate grounds for bringing the proposed action.[87] In other words, good faith does not need to be stated explicitly in the statute, in the sense that whether an applicant is acting in good faith will become apparent from the way they present the case in demonstrating the merits of the proposed action and the nature of claims. A determination of the applicant's good faith and suitability for bringing a derivative action is relevant only when the applicant has established the proposed action to be in the company's interests.[88]

4.3.2.4 Applicant undertaking to pay for the derivative action

Another way of showing the applicants' good faith is by undertaking to indemnify the company and pay for the proposed action and any adverse liability.[89] This seems to be the most direct way to satisfy the court of the good faith requirement.[90] It is also a means of satisfying the court of the requirement in s.237(2)(c) that the proposed derivative action "is in the best interests of the company", considering that the company does not have to pay for anything. This approach overlaps with the costs provision in s.242. Empirical evidence in Chapter 3 shows that in 55.4% of the cases, the applicant was successful in obtaining leave of the court to bring an SDA. This is because in many of those successful leave applications, a conditional grant of leave was made, in the sense that leave was granted on the condition that the applicant bore the costs of the leave application and the derivative proceedings.

In *App Shop Pty Ltd v. Jalal Bros Pty Ltd*, the court found that the applicant had spent considerable time in showing how they were not impecunious, that they were able to indemnify the company and bear the costs of the derivative proceedings and that they were willing to undertake to meet any adverse liability made against the company;[91] and these, according to Black J, supported

86 *Re Karinya Haulage Pty Ltd* [2017] NSWSC 888, at [5].
87 *Connective Services Pty Ltd v. Slea Pty Ltd* [2018] VSCA 229, at [55] (Ferguson CJ, Whelan and McLeish JJA).
88 Chapter 5 will further discuss the "best interests of the company" criterion.
89 *Re Dynamic Industries Pty Ltd* [2014] VSC 101, at [95].
90 *Zhu v. Orico Australia Pty Ltd* [2019] VSC 313; *Connective Services Pty Ltd v. Slea Pty Ltd* [2018] VSCA 229; *Re Dynamic Industries Pty Ltd* [2014] VSC 101.
91 *App Shop Pty Ltd v. Jalal Bros Pty Ltd* [2019] NSWSC 490, at [5–8].

the finding of good faith.[92] Another clear example is in *Re Poly Pacific Pty Ltd*, where, at the onset of the court hearing, the applicant submitted a draft consent order signed by both the applicant and the proposed defendant indicating that the applicant was willing and prepared to bear all costs and charges in relation to the bringing of the derivative action and that no company funds were to be used,[93] and the court granted leave on those terms without much consideration of the leave criteria.[94] In other words, leave was granted on the assumption that, having offered to pay, the applicant had proven good faith.

Even where good faith is obvious, the courts have generally required the applicant to pay costs as further proof of good faith, especially in cases where a derivative action also involves an oppression claim.[95] For example in *Li v. Dao*,[96] the applicant and defendant were both equal shareholders, the company was no longer in business, there were no major creditors and the only reason that the applicant sought to bring a derivative action was to settle her dispute over the failed property development venture. The court held that an undertaking to pay the company's costs of the derivative action was a "consideration material to the satisfaction of the good faith … requirement".[97]

This author has issues with an applicant undertaking to pay as a way of showing good faith. First, the leave criteria in s.237(2) is separate from the costs provision in s.242, that the leave criteria operate independently from the costs provision. There is nothing in s.237(2) that refers to costs consideration. If proof of good faith is dependent on the applicant's ability to pay costs, then where is the sincerity in the applicant in the desire to protect the interests of the company when the focus is on money?[98]

It is worth noting that just because a wealthier applicant is successful in the leave application because of an undertaking made to bear all costs related to the bringing of the SDA does not mean that the applicant will go through with it and bring the approved action. The applicant may well use that success as a means of pressuring the proposed defendant to settle on less favourable terms. This could be argued as a form of an abuse of the SDA process, which is not readily recognised as such. There is support for this view. Professors Keay and Loughrey assert that an "abuse of process may also be established where the shareholder has little intention of pursuing the claim to conclusion, but rather is bringing it to harass the company's management, and to force them to purchase his shares at a higher price".[99] *Pentridge Village Pty Ltd*

92 *App Shop Pty Ltd v. Jalal Bros Pty Ltd* [2019] NSWSC 490, at [16].

93 *Re Poly Pacific Pty Ltd* [2013] VSC 670, at [60–61].

94 The reported judgment was only 12 pages in length, and only the last 4 pages referring to the leave criteria.

95 *Li v. Dao* [2018] VSC 530, at [182-183]; *Slea Pty Ltd v. Connective Services Pty Ltd* [2017] VSC 609.

96 *Li v. Dao* [2018] VSC 530, at [63–80].

97 *Li v. Dao* [2018] VSC 530, at [183].

98 Apologies for want of a better term.

99 Keay and Loughrey, n 21, at 221.

(in liq.) v. Capital Finance Australia Ltd is a good illustration.[100] In that case, the applicant was found to have acted in bad faith for lying about having arranged for litigation funding and that he would indemnify the company, but evidence showed that no external funding had been obtained, and the information provided was out of date, incomplete and inaccurate.

The second point to make is that the idea that an applicant's good faith is measured by their ability to pay would appear to be inconsistent with the objectives of the legislation. This current approach leans heavily towards favouring the wealthier applicants who can afford to litigate, leaving out those poorer bona fide shareholders who cannot prove good faith because of their financial situation. This is seen in *Cooper v. Myrtace Consulting Pty Ltd*, where there was no issue with the applicant's good faith,[101] except that the court was concerned that the inability of the applicant to indemnify the company in relation to costs posed "a significant difficulty".[102] In another case, *Knights Quest Pty Ltd v. Barokes Pty Ltd*,[103] the court did not consider good faith but instead focused on the applicant's ongoing issues relating to whether a third party would be funding the proposed action, resulting in an unsuccessful outcome in the leave application. These cases illustrate that the applicant's inability to pay will go against their proof of good faith.

It is worth noting too that s.238 permits substitution of an applicant to take over the running of the derivative action, which implies that the leave prerequisites in s.237(2) and the grant of leave are not subject to costs consideration, but rather subject to proof of the applicant's good standing and suitability, free from issues relating to wealth. In short, a poor person can possess as much of the good faith characteristics as a wealthy person can; the only difference between them is that one is poorer than the other, but that should not stand in the way of allowing a poorer bona fide shareholder a chance to bring a derivative action. If given a proper chance, and if absolutely necessary to pursue a derivative action, a poor applicant may find a way to fund the approved action.

4.3.2.5 Other means of showing good faith or the absence of it

(A) RESTORING THE APPLICANT'S SHARE VALUE

Where the purpose for leave is to bring an SDA to restore the applicant's share value or shareholding, then the court is likely to find that the applicant

100 *Pentridge Village Pty Ltd (in liq.) v. Capital Finance Australia Ltd* [2018] VSC 633, at [239] (Connock J).

101 *Cooper v. Myrtace Consulting Pty Ltd* [2014] FCA 480, at [18] (Davies J).

102 *Cooper v. Myrtace Consulting Pty Ltd* [2014] FCA 480, at [32] (Davies J). See also, *Re Fishinthenet Investments Pty Ltd and Coastal Waters Seafood Pty Ltd* [2014] NSWSC 260, where the applicant's offer of indemnity was inadequate.

103 *Knights Quest Pty Ltd v. Barokes Pty Ltd* (2016) 113 ACSR 505, [2016] VSC 296.

is acting in good faith,[104] as these purposes would benefit not only the applicant but also other shareholders in the company.[105] This would not be an abuse of process as such, even where there is a deadlock between equal shareholders,[106] provided that the applicant has no ulterior purpose.[107]

(B) CURRENT SHAREHOLDER

Good faith has been said to be "relatively easy" to establish where an applicant is a "current shareholder who has more than a token shareholding".[108] An applicant with a small shareholding in the company could still be acting in good faith, provided that there is no ulterior motive in bringing the derivative action.[109] Conversely, where an applicant is a former shareholder or officer with nothing obvious to gain directly by the success of the derivative action, the court will scrutinise the applicant's ulterior purpose.[110] In contrast, a current shareholder has been held to be not acting in good faith if information provided in court seems out of date, incomplete or inaccurate.[111]

(C) SIGNIFICANT EFFORTS SHOWN IN PREPARING THE LEAVE APPLICATION

Where an applicant has put significant efforts into preparing the leave application, the court is likely to support the finding of good faith.[112] In *Re Dynamic Industries Pty Ltd*, the applicant was found to have incurred expenses in obtaining access to company documents to assess the strength of the case

104 *Connective Services Pty Ltd v. Slea Pty Ltd* [2018] VSCA 229, at [105–111] (Ferguson CJ, Whelan and McLeish JJA); *Russell v. Lee Holdings Pty Ltd* [2018] WASC 275, at [25–36]; *MG Corrosion Consultants Pty Ltd v. Vinciguerra* [2011] FCAFC 31, at [54] (North, McKerracher and Jagot JJ).

105 *Re Sirrah Pty Ltd* [2018] NSWSC 1802, at [18] (Black J); *Pottie v. Dunkley* [2011] NSWSC 166, at [43].

106 *Zhu v. Orico Australia Pty Ltd* [2019] VSC 313, at [47]; *Li v. Dao* [2018] VSC 530, at [108].

107 *Vinciguerra v. MG Corrosion Consultants Pty Ltd* [2010] FCA 763 (21 July 2010) at [68–69].

108 *App Shop Pty Ltd v. Jalal Bros Pty Ltd* [2019] NSWSC 490, at [16] (Black J); *Swansson v Pratt Properties Pty Ltd* (2002) 42 ACSR 313, [2002] NSWSC 583, at [38] (Palmer J).

109 Interestingly, in *Carpenter v. Pioneer Park Pty Limited* (2004) 51 ACSR 299; [2004] NSWSC 1007, the applicant had only one share out of two million shares in the company and was held to be acting in good faith, even though his motive in bringing the proposed SDA against a third party, ANZ Bank, was to ultimately have himself removed as a guarantor; this was seen by the court as a separate matter. In contrast, in *Chahwan v. Euphoric Pty Ltd* [2008] NSWCA 52, the NSW Court of Appeal held that the applicant's motive for bringing an SDA against a third party creditor was an attempt to obtain a declaration later in the SDA to discharge the mortgage and have the property reverted to him as the original owner was held to be not acting in good faith.

110 *Zhu v. Orico Australia Pty Ltd* [2019] VSC 313, [46] (Connock J); *Swansson v. RA Pratt Properties Pty Ltd* (2002) 42 ACSR 313, [2002] NSWSC 583, at [39] (Palmer J).

111 *Pentridge Village Pty Ltd (in liq.) v. Capital Finance Australia Ltd* [2018] VSC 633, at [239].

112 *Re Dynamic Industries Pty Ltd* [2014] VSC 101, at [95]; *Re Akierman Holdings Pty Ltd* [2015] NSWSC 1395.

and had undertaken to indemnify the company in respect to the costs in bringing the proposed action.[113] However, where there is a long delay in filing an application for leave to bring a derivative action, the applicant would be construed as not acting in good faith.[114] In *Bzezinski v. Shaw*, the applicant delayed for two years from seeking leave to bring a derivative action until the company had gone into receivership. The Court of Appeal in the Supreme Court of Victoria agreed with the trial court in dismissing the leave application on the ground that the applicant had not provided a valid reason for the long delay, and further the other director had objected. The Court opined that to permit the leave application would only cause further delay in the receivership proceedings.[115]

(D) OPPRESSION ACTION

An applicant may still be acting in good faith in seeking leave to bring an SDA, even if they have a separate action running concurrently, such as for an oppression remedy,[116] or a winding up order.[117] Section 236 (in Note 3) makes it clear that an applicant may bring a separate action "on their own behalf in respect of a personal right". The court may hear both actions at the same time.

4.3.2.6 Is sworn evidence necessary to show good faith?

It is unclear whether a sworn statement of the applicant's honest belief that there is a good cause of action is essential for the finding of good faith. Some courts have stated that the lack of a sworn statement would not be a major problem,[118] as the applicant's good faith could still be established through other means.[119] Other courts have noted that it may have some importance as it goes to show the "state of mind" of the applicant;[120] however, sworn statements alone will not be sufficient to demonstrate good faith, as these

113 *Re Dynamic Industries Pty Ltd* [2014] VSC 101. In contrast, in *RQYS Marina Ltd* [2014] QSC 243, at [140], the court found that the applicant had a history of allegations of dishonesty against the defendant, many of which were unsubstantiated, which led the court to question whether the applicant was acting in good faith.

114 *Bzezinski v. Shaw* [2022] VSCA 173, at [57], [74] (Kyrou, Mcleish and Walker JJA)

115 *Bzezinski v. Shaw* [2022] VSCA 173 (Kyrou, Mcleish and Walker JJA) and the first instance decision, *Re Kalimpa Park Pty Ltd* [2021] VSC 654 (Osborne J).

116 *Drew v. Lynch* [2019] FCA 632; *Pottie v. Dunkley* [2011] NSWSC 166.

117 *Power v. Ekstein* (2010) 77 ACSR 302; [2010] NSWSC 137.

118 *Maher v. Honeysett & Maher Electrical Contractors Pty Ltd* [2005] NSWSC 859, at [33] (Brereton J) (explaining that a sworn statement would just be "unqualified opinion founded on hearsay").

119 *Maher v. Honeysett & Maher Electrical Contractors Pty Ltd* [2005] NSWSC 859, at [33] (Brereton J); *Zhu v. Orico Australia Pty Ltd* [2019] VSC 313, at [43] (Connock J).

120 *Fiduciary Ltd v. Morningstar Research* [2005] NSWSC 442 at [21] (Austin J).

will be of "limited weight and utility" unless supported by objective facts and circumstances.[121] In another case, the court held that the applicant lacked good faith without a sworn statement, even though he had submitted a large volume of documents detailing the sequence of events that took place.[122]

In *South Johnston Mill Ltd v. Dennis and Scales*, the court held that there was "some positive evidence" that the 31 shareholders, who came together to apply for leave and who were willing to indemnify the company and pay for the derivative proceedings, were acting in good faith without the need for a sworn statement.[123] In contrast, in *Coeur De Lion Investments Pty Ltd v. Kelly*,[124] despite having a sworn statement, the court found the applicant lacking good faith because: (i) the interests between the applicant and other shareholders in the company were incompatible; (ii) the applicant appeared not to be interested in resolving the claims by other means other than by litigation; and (iii) none of the 325 other shareholders supported the proposed action. The outcome in an earlier case in *Chapman v. E-Sports Club Worldwide Limited*, decided in 2000, was rather unfortunate and not representative of the general approach of the courts, as much emphasis was placed on the applicant's lack of sworn evidence as a ground for denying leave to bring the proposed action.[125]

4.3.3 Summary

The purpose of the above discussion was to illustrate the variables in the interpretation of the term "good faith" and the uncertainty in the test itself. The Explanatory Memorandum intended the term to be construed narrowly as a way of preventing a flood of shareholder litigation and unmeritorious and malicious actions, while the courts, on the other hand, seem to interpret this test more broadly and yet in a circular way. There is no clarity in the meaning of good faith. Much is dependent on the interpretation of the courts and their judicial opinions based on the evidence presented, both objectively and subjectively. In most cases, the good faith criterion is satisfied by means of the applicant undertaking to indemnify the company and pay the costs of the proposed derivative proceedings. There is no hard and fast rule for deciding on the applicant's good faith.

121 *Zhu v. Orico Australia Pty Ltd* [2019] VSC 313, at [43] (Connock J).

122 *Chapman v. E-Sports Club Worldwide Limited* (2000) 35 ACSR 462; [2000] VSC 403.

123 *South Johnston Mill Ltd v. Dennis and Scales* [2007] FCA 1448, at [68]. *Henry v. Western Downs Group Ltd* [2018] FCA 1168 is another similar case where the applicants had proven good faith by joining together as a large group of beneficiary claimants under the charitable trust to seek leave to bring the proposed action against the entire board of directors of the trustee company for misappropriating trust funds.

124 *Coeur De Lion Investments Pty Ltd v. Kelly* (2013) 95 ACSR 43; [2013] QCA 160, at [61], [65], [66].

125 *Chapman v. E-Sports Club Worldwide Limited*, [2000] VSC 403; (2000) 35 ACSR 462.

It is clear that good faith is a relevant consideration for determining whether an applicant is a suitable person to be given leave to bring a derivative action. The question to be addressed next is: Is the inclusion of good faith necessary as a prerequisite in an SDA? Indeed, if a court decides that the proposed action is likely to be in the company's interests, then the question of good faith would become relevant for determining the suitability of the applicant. However, if the court considers the proposed action not to be meritorious, then there is no point in considering the applicant's good faith. It is the view of the author that consideration of "good faith" is relevant, but it should not be a necessary precondition for an SDA. The next part explains further.

4.4 Is inclusion of good faith necessary in the statutory derivative action?

"Good faith" is a relevant consideration. However, there are several ways in explaining why its inclusion as a requirement is redundant in the SDA. This chapter offers two further reasons.

4.4.1 Why good faith should not be a precondition

It is not surprising to see a range of approaches adopted by the courts in dealing with the good faith requirement, as seen in the above discussion. This is partly because of the considerable overlap between good faith and the other prerequisites. Empirical evidence in Chapter 3 also shows the overlapping effect, in that where an applicant fails to satisfy the court on one leave criterion, the applicant is likely to fail on the other criterion.

One way of explaining why good faith is redundant in the statute is to consider why it is a problem when there are too many prerequisites and they overlap. Indeed, one may argue that the inclusion of good faith is necessary in the statute as a way to cause the applicant to think twice before applying for leave, and to ensure that the leave application is meritorious. This was the intent of the legislature at the time when the good faith requirement was introduced into the Act.[126] However, an opposing argument is that by insisting an applicant satisfies the court of the good faith requirement, the problem is that some bona fide shareholders may shy away from applying for leave, simply because there would just be too much to lose and very little to gain. The mere thought of having to prove one's good faith, in addition to proving all the other prerequisites, is not only exhausting, considering the concept of good faith is vague and subjective, but also daunting and unjust for some applicants who cannot afford to pay for the action. Not all applicants would be willing to bear the costs of the derivative action that has very little benefit

126 House of Representatives, *Explanatory Memorandum to the CLERP Bill* 1998, at 17, [6.3–6.4], (introducing the business judgment rule at the same time as found in s.180(2) and s.237(3) to give directors some protection against being sued by disgruntled shareholders).

to them, and for those who do undertake to pay for the proposed action, it does not mean that they will, in fact, commence or bring the approved action. As explained above, if an applicant undertakes to pay for the proposed action, it does not always mean they are acting in good faith. It may help to expedite a settlement with the proposed defendant without taking the matter further to a derivative action stage, but it is not a measure of the applicant's purity of mind.

One scholar argues that in cases where a shareholder applicant is an outsider (such as a passive investor rather than an active participant), proving one's good faith may be a problem where there is limited access to company information.[127] Conversely, an insider applicant, such as a director, who is able to obtain the necessary evidence through their involvement in the company's operation, may be construed as participating in the wrongdoing and therefore would not be qualified to bring the action.[128] In Hong Kong, where good faith is not found in its legislation, one scholar notes that, by adding good faith into the legislation as a prerequisite, this may "give an impression to potential applicants" that the SDA is "more onerous" than under the previous procedure at common law.[129] One would agree to this comment given that the concept of good faith is no different from the "clean hands" doctrine[130] as previously applied in *Nurcombe v. Nurcombe*.[131]

When putting all these together, a bona fide shareholder with very little to gain would be less inclined to go through those troubles and expose themselves to unfair comments and criticisms about their character and disposition just for the sake of obtaining leave to bring a derivative action. It would take a lot more than just the person's strength and courage to overcome those hurdles and bring the necessary action, and having good faith included as a mandatory requirement in the SDA is not really helping to make the situation better to achieve the objectives aimed for by the legislation. The inclusion of good faith as a requirement is possibly doing more harm than good; it simply frightens away those sincere potential applicants and does little in the improvement of the derivative action as a tool for enhancing directors' accountability and maintaining corporate governance.

127 Samantha S. Tang, "Corporate avengers need not be angels: Rethinking good faith in the derivative action" (2016) 16 *Journal of Corporate Law Studies* 471, at 472 and 477–480.

128 Tang, n 128, at 472 and 477–480.

129 Daniel T. L. Lam, "Statutory derivative action in Hong Kong: So far so good?" (2009) 23 *Australian Journal of Corporate Law* 26, at 43.

130 For consideration of the "clean hands" doctrine as applied in common law derivative actions, see Jennifer Payne, "Clean hands in derivative actions" (2002) 61 *Cambridge Law Journal* 76.

131 *Nurcombe v. Nurcombe* [1985] 1 WLR 370, at 378 yields the principle that a shareholder would not be allowed to take advantage of the derivative action if there was evidence of "behaviour by the minority shareholder, which, in the eyes of equity, would render it unjust to allow a claim brought by the company at his instance to succeed".

4.4.2 Other prerequisites for leave are already adequate

Another argument why the inclusion of good faith is redundant in the SDA may be explained by pointing out that other prerequisites are already adequate for ruling out any potentially unmeritorious or frivolous actions. These other prerequisites are already sufficient for the protection of the company's interests and its resources, and bona fide shareholders should not be overly burdened with additional tests and uncertainties, on terms that are subjective and broad in scope. As correctly pointed out by Barrett J in *Carpenter v. Pioneer Park Pty Limited*:[132]

> "There is a degree of overlap between [the good faith condition in s.237(2)(b)] and not only the third condition (that is, that it is in the best interests of the company that the applicant be granted leave: s.237(2)(c), but also the fourth condition (that there is a serious question to be tried: s.237(2)(d)). I say this because the strength of the case, at a prima facie level, will have a bearing in the question whether it is in the best interests of the company that the case be run and this, in turn, will reflect on matters of motive and purpose that are relevant to the good faith question. It is therefore appropriate, at this point, to consider more closely the proposed proceeding."

In granting leave, Barrett J applied these prerequisites to the facts of the case in the reverse order, putting the good faith test in the last priority, which suggests that the applicant's good faith can ultimately be established through the tests in paragraphs (c) and (d). In the end, his Honour considered the applicant's good faith based on whether he was a suitable person to bring the proposed action, that is, whether his collateral purpose would be contrary to the company's interests. The court found that the applicant proposed to bring the derivative action not for his own financial benefit (because his shareholding in the company was insignificant)[133] but for the benefit of his other family members who were major shareholders. If the derivative action yielded a successful outcome against a third party, the bank, it would mean that, potentially and indirectly, the applicant would be relieved as a guarantor, but this was a separate matter.[134] This decision suggests that good faith can still be established even where an applicant has "mixed" personal and corporate purposes for bringing an SDA.

132 *Carpenter v. Pioneer Park Pty Limited* (2004) 51 ACSR 299; [2004] NSWSC 1007, at [10].
133 *Carpenter v. Pioneer Park Pty Limited* (2004) 51 ACSR 299; [2004] NSWSC 1007, at [25] (showing the applicant having only one ordinary share out of two million shares in the company).
134 *Carpenter v. Pioneer Park Pty Limited* (2004) 51 ACSR 299; [2004] NSWSC 1007, at [23–26]; *Carpenter v. Pioneer Park Pty Limited* (2008) 66 ACSR 564; [2008] NSWSC 551.

It is clear from *Carpenter v. Pioneer Park Pty Limited* and from other cases discussed earlier,[135] that it is impractical at times to consider the different prerequisites in isolation from one another from a given set of facts, particularly the interaction between the "good faith" requirement and the "in the best interests of the company" requirement. This view is further supported by other scholars in Canada and Singapore,[136] where proof of good faith is also a mandatory requirement in their legislation, alongside other prerequisites similar to those in Australia. In Canada, in supporting the removal of good faith in its statute, one scholar argues that good faith is irrelevant,[137] while another argues that the term is "meaningless" and if required, good faith is likely to be present in any event.[138] Maloney is critical of whether good faith is an independent prerequisite for leave:[139]

> "If a wrong has been committed and the other prerequisites fulfilled, it should make little, if any difference whether a plaintiff's motives are pure or not. This is all the more the case if the main reason for allowing statutory derivative action is to ensure some watchdog role over corporate management which society cannot do or does not wish to undertake for administrative and expense reasons. The other procedural devices already deal adequately with malicious or unmeritorious actions."

There is also support for the view that good faith should not be used as a filter to disqualify an applicant from pursuing a derivative action, where the applicant has demonstrated the proposed action to be in the company's interests.[140] One scholar observes that there is no issue in Hong Kong where the term "good faith" is absent in its legislation.[141] Given that it is not possible to consider the different prerequisites in isolation and in the interest of giving bona fide applicants a fair go in bringing the necessary action, perhaps a pre-

135 *Re Sovereign Lawyers Pty Ltd* [2018] NSWSC 695; *Catalano v. Managing Australian Destinations Pty Ltd* [2014] FCAFC 55; *Russell v. Lee Holdings Pty Ltd* [2018] WASC 275.

136 Maloney, n 22, at 320; Meng Seng Wee and Dan W. Puchniak, "Derivative Action in Singapore: Mundanely non-Asian, Intriguingly Non-American and at the Forefront of the Commonwealth" in (Chapter 8) in Dan Puchniak, Harald Baum and Michael Ewing-Chow (eds.), *The Derivative Action in Asia: A Comparative and Functional Approach* (Cambridge University Press, 2012), at 344–347.

137 Peterson and Cumming, n19, at [16.39].

138 Welling, n 20, at 511–528 (contending good faith is "meaningless", and saying "I have no idea what this means, and I get the sense that no one else does either": 528).

139 Maloney, n 22, at 320.

140 Lang Thai and Matthew Berkahn, "Statutory derivative actions in Australia and New Zealand: What can we learn from each other?" (2012) 25 *New Zealand Universities Law Review* 370, at 376-379; Keay and Loughrey, n 21, at 207–208; Peterson and Cumming, n 19, at [16.39]; Koh, Alan, n 16, at 208.

141 Lam, n 130, at 40–44.

ferred approach for Australia could be to leave the question of the applicant's good faith (or for want of a better term, the applicant's suitability) to the court to decide, not as a mandatory term, but as a relevant consideration if it finds that the proposed action is in the company's interests.

4.5 Good faith in other jurisdictions

In understanding further why good faith is redundant in the SDA, it may be useful to compare the situation in Australia briefly with overseas counterparts. New Zealand[142] and Hong Kong[143] have chosen not to include good faith as an express requirement in their SDAs, and both appear to be functioning without any issue of major abuse.[144] The United Kingdom refers to good faith only as a suggestion for the court to take into account.[145] Singapore and Canada have the good faith requirement in their legislation,[146] but while the courts in Canada have taken a more lenient approach, the Singapore Court of Appeal has recently overturned its original approach, which suggests that the law of good faith in SDA is unworkable.

4.5.1 New Zealand and Hong Kong

The SDA in New Zealand, introduced in 1993, does not refer to good faith.[147] The condition for the grant of leave is divided into two categories: those on which the court must be satisfied[148] and those to which the court must merely have regard.[149] Of particular relevance is the second category, where s.165(2) provides a list of matters that the court is required to consider before deciding whether to grant leave,[150] and good faith is not included in the list. Instead, it

142 *Companies Act* 1993 (NZ), ss.165–168.

143 *Laws of Hong Kong Special Administration Region* (or HKSAR), Chapter 32 (Companies Ordinance), Part IVAA, ss.168BA-168BJ.

144 Felix E. Mezzanotte, "The unconvincing rise of the statutory derivative action in Hong Kong: Evidence from its first 10 years of enforcement" (2017) 17 *Journal of Corporate Law Studies* 469; Lynne Taylor, "The derivative action in the Companies Act 1993: An empirical study" (2006) 22 *New Zealand Universities Law Review* 337; David C. Donald, *A Financial Centre for Two Empires: Hong Kong's Corporate, Securities and Tax Laws in its Transition from Britain to China* (CUP, 2014), at 202–203, cited in Puchniak and Tan, n 16, at 255–269.

145 *Companies Act 2006* (UK), ss.260-264 (England, Wales and Northern Ireland) and ss.265–269 (Scotland).

146 *Companies Act* (Singapore, Chapter 50, 2006, revised ed), ss.216A-216B; and *Canada Business Corporations Act* (RSC 1985), ss.238–242.

147 *Companies Act* 1993 (NZ), ss.165–168.

148 *Companies Act* 1993 (NZ), s.165(3). As for this first category, the court may grant leave if under s.165(3), it is satisfied that either (a) the company does not intend to bring or continue proceedings itself or (b) it is not in the company's interests to leave the conduct of the proceedings to the directors or the shareholders as a whole.

149 *Companies Act* 1993 (NZ), s.165(2).

150 Section 165(2) provides that the court "shall have regard to": (a) the likelihood of the proceedings succeeding; (b) the costs of the proceedings in relation to the likely relief; (c) any

has been said that the provision provides the court with a "broad discretion" to decide whether to grant leave.[151]

Taylor has suggested that s.165(2) may be used to deny leave in circumstances where the applicant is not acting in good faith, despite the fact that this factor is not included in the legislation.[152] She makes this point, citing *Torrice v. Hayhow*.[153] In that case, the New Zealand High Court denied leave to bring derivative proceedings on the basis that the applicant had "ulterior motives" stemming from his feeling that the defendant directors had "deeply ... wronged him and [the company]", and described the motives of the applicant as a "matter of relevance".[154] In *Vrij v. Boyle*,[155] Fisher J accepted an argument from the director opposing the leave application that there was an incompatibility in allowing the applicant to pursue an action on behalf of the company concurrently with a personal oppression action against the same proposed defendant director in the proposed derivative action. Fisher J stated:[156]

> "One can well understand that if a shareholder tried to recover both personal damages for indirect losses caused by a reduction in the value of the shareholder's shares due to a wrong done to the shareholder's company and a derivative action with respect to the same wrong, there would be duplication and the risk of double recovery."

In exercising its broad discretion, the court in *Vrij v. Boyle* decided that both actions be brought together to be determined at the same hearing so as to avoid the risk of double recovery by the applicant. It was clear that the element of good faith was in the court's mind when this decision was reached. Subsequent cases appear to have followed a similar trend, where although the applicant has no burden of proof of their good faith, the court may take into account their motives for seeking leave to bring a derivative action.[157]

---

action already taken by the company to obtain relief; and (d) the "interests of the company" in commencing or continuing the proceedings.

151 *Vrij v. Boyle* [1995] NZLR 763, at 767, where Fisher J stated that s.165(1) "confers a broad discretion [on the court] undiminished by the particular considerations referred to in later subsections". This view is supported by *Needham v. EBT Worldwide Ltd* (2006) 3 NZCCLR 57; [2006] NZHC 509, at [19]; and *Re Irving Baker Ltd* HC Whangarei, CIV-2003-488-00042, 29 July 2004 at [4].

152 Lynne Taylor, "Derivative Action", in John Farrar (ed) *Company and Securities Law in New Zealand* (Brookers, Wellington, 2008), at 551.

153 *Torrice v. Hayhow* HC Auckland, CIV-2004-404-1453, 14 May 2004 at [31].

154 *Torrice v. Hayhow* CIV-2004-404-1453 (NZHC), at [31]. See also *Cameron v. Coleman* [2011] NZHC 1190, at [24], [57]; and *Needham v. EBT Worldwide Ltd* (2006) 3 NZCCLR 57; [2006] NZHC 509, at [62], [65]; *Tweedle v. Packsys Ltd* (2005) 2 NZCCLR 584 (NZHC).

155 *Vrij v. Boyle* [1995] 3 NZLR 763.

156 In *Vrij v. Boyle* [1995] 3 NZLR 763, at 767.

157 See for example, *Nobilo v Nobilo* [2015] NZCA 54 where the Court of Appeal upheld the original decision in *Nobilo v. Nobilo* [2014] NZHC 401 (NZHC); *Cameron v. Coleman*

Although not referred to in the Act, the applicant's motive is still an important factor for the court to determine whether to grant leave.[158]

Similarly, Hong Kong has chosen not to include good faith as a requirement in its SDA. Prior to introducing its SDA in July 2005, some members of the law reform body queried whether good faith was necessary for inclusion.[159] It has been noted that the non-inclusion of good faith in the SDA is to avoid a trial within a trial at the leave stage.[160]

4.5.2 The United Kingdom

Good faith is not a requirement in the United Kingdom, but only one of the several non-exhaustive factors that the court must take into account when considering whether to grant leave.[161] Good faith is included as a discretionary factor for the court to consider (that is, without putting the burden of proof on the applicant), but no definition is given in the legislation as it was suggested that the term is "generally readily recognisable".[162] Prior to introducing its SDA in 2007, there were fears that the broad approach conferred on the court would be equivalent to the "clean hands" approach used at common law.[163] However, case law subsequently shows that the issue of good faith has been raised in most, but not all, leave applications.[164] The courts have generally adopted the broad approach similar to New Zealand.

In *Iesini v. Westrip Holdings Ltd*, in denying leave, the UK High Court held that the applicants were not acting in good faith because of their involvement in the wrongdoing.[165] Lewison J said that "a person may be prevented from bringing a derivative claim if he participated in the wrong ... it will count

---

[2011] NZHC 1190, at [24]; *Needham v. EBT Worldwide Ltd* [2006] NZHC 509 (NZHC), at [19], [62], [65]; *Torrice v Hayhow* (2004) CIV-2004-404-1453 (NZHC) at [31]. *Re Irving Baker Ltd* HC Whangarei (2003) CIV-2003-488-00042, 29 July 2004, at [4].

158 Christopher Hare, "Shareholder Remedies: Personal Rights, Corporate Rights and the Derivative Action", in Peter Watts, Neil Campbell and Christopher Hare, *Company Law in New Zealand* (LexisNexis, Wellington, 2011) at 750–751; Taylor, n 153, at 551.

159 Hong Kong Legislative Council, *Report of the Bills Committee on Companies (Amendment) Bill 2003*, 30 June 2004, LC Paper No.: CB(1) 2264/03-04, at [124]. For discussion of the historical development of the Hong Kong SDA, see Paul von Nessen, Say H. Goo and Chee Keong Low, "The statutory derivative action: Now showing near you" (2007) 7 *Journal of Business Law* 627.

160 Lam, n 130, at 41. See also the comments in *Re Lucky Money Ltd* [2007] 4 HKC 598.

161 *Companies Act 2006* (UK), s.263(3).

162 Law Commission, *Shareholder Remedies: Report on a Reference under section 31(e) of the Law Commissions Act* 1965 (Law Commission Report No. 246, 1997), at [6.76].

163 See Payne, n 131, at 80. See also Andrew Keay and Joan Loughrey, "Derivative proceedings in a brave new world for company management and shareholders" (2010) *Journal of Business Law* 151, at 168. See also examples in *Towers v. African Tug Co* [1904] 1 Ch 558 and *Nurcombe v. Nurcombe* [1985] 1 WLR 370.

164 Keay and Loughrey, n 21, at 207.

165 *Iesini v. Westrip Holdings Ltd* [2009] EWHC 2526 (Ch), [2010] All ER 108.

against a claimant if the action is brought to escape the consequences of his own misdeeds".[166] This was an earlier case and the decision appears similar to the application of the "clean hands" approach. The case was about leave to bring a derivative action to restore the share value in the company. In *Stimpson v. Southern Private Landlords Ltd*, a broader approach was adopted, in that the court noted the legislative provision had provided it with a broad discretion and that included the discretion to consider the conduct of the applicant in relation to the company and matters giving rise to the claim in assessing the applicant's good faith.[167] In *Hook v. Summer*, it was held that although the applicant was the only person to benefit from the claim, this could not mean that he was acting in bad faith and the conclusion that the applicant was acting for a proper motive on behalf of the company meant that he must be considered to be acting in good faith.[168] It has also been said that, where a court is unable to conclude that the applicant lacks good faith, then the case will generally proceed on the assumption that the applicant is proceeding in good faith.[169] In *Kiani v. Cooper*, the court held that transfer of money from the company's bank account to the applicant's personal account was insufficient evidence to conclude that he was acting in bad faith as some of that money was used to pay the company's creditors and some was still available.[170] Overall, it appears that the courts in the United Kingdom accept the fact that whether or not an applicant is acting in good faith may be difficult to determine in the early stage of the proceedings, such as in the leave application.

4.5.3 Singapore

As noted earlier, the Singapore Court of Appeal has, in recent years, overturned its original approach, by now shifting the burden of proof of good faith onto the applicant. Its latest approach is unhelpful for Australia in terms of suggesting removal of the good faith requirement. However, the purpose of considering it briefly here is to illustrate the unworkability of the requirement of good faith in the SDA due to its subjective nature and its variability.

Singapore introduced its SDA in 1993, and until 2013, the good faith test was not a major issue as the courts tended to apply the test by assuming that an applicant who sought leave to bring an SDA and who had a legitimate

166 *Iesini v. Westrip Holdings Ltd [2009] EWHC 2526* (Ch), [2010] All ER 108, at [122] (Lewison J).

167 *Stimpson v. Southern Private Landlords* Ltd [2009] EWHC 2072 (Ch), [2010] BCC 387, at [44]. See *Stainer v. Lee* [2010] EWHC 1539 (Ch).

168 *Hook v. Summer* [2015] EWHC 3820, [2016] BCC 220, at [126].

169 Andrew Charman and Johan du Toit SC, *Shareholder Actions* (Bloomsbury Publisher, 2nd edition, 2018), at [6.37], citing *McAskill v. Fulton* (Unreported, England and Wales High Court, Chancery Division, Norris J, (2014) WL 8106597, 31 October 2014), at [40].

170 *Kiani v. Cooper* [2010] EWHC 577 (Ch).

or arguable case would be acting in good faith.[171] The onus was on the person opposing the leave application to prove that the applicant was not acting in good faith in seeking leave.[172] In one case, the court stated that it would "*assume* that every party who comes to court with a reasonable and legitimate claim is acting in good faith – unless proven otherwise".[173] This approach was upheld by the Singapore Court of Appeal in 2004,[174] and it was applied in subsequent cases without difficulty.[175] The requirement then was that an applicant only had to prove a legitimate or arguable claim in the leave application as a way of demonstrating good faith.[176] The threshold was low, in the sense that the onus of proof was not on the applicant.

Section 216A(3) of the Singapore Act states that a derivative action cannot be brought unless the Court is satisfied that: (a) the applicant has given "14 days' notice" to the directors of the company of his or her intention to apply for leave; (b) the applicant "is acting in good faith"; and (c) the proposed action "appears to be prima facie in the interests of the company".[177]

It was not until in 2013 that the Singapore Court of Appeal decided to overturn its original approach. The onus is now on the applicant to prove good faith,[178] and this is similar to the Australian position.[179] In *Ang Thiam Swee v. Low Hian Chor,*[180] Rajah JA, on behalf of the Full Court, states that:[181]

> "[T]he court ought to assess the motivations of the applicant in order to determine whether he is acting in good faith. ... [A]n applicant whose judgment is clouded by purely personal considerations may not honestly *intend* to serve the company's interests, and also may not be the proper party to *represent* the company's interests."

171 *Companies Act* (Singapore, Chapter 50, 2006, Revised Edition), s.216A(3)(b) simply states that the court is required to be "satisfied that … the complainant is acting in good faith".

172 *Agus Irawan v. Toh Teck Chye* [2002] SGHC 49 (SGHC), at [471].

173 *Agus Irawan v. Toh Teck Chye* [2002] SGHC 49 (SGHC) 471, at [9].

174 *Pang Yong Hock v. PKS Contracts Services Pte Ltd* [2004] SGCA 18 (SGCA) at [19]. The Singapore Court of Appeal is the highest court in the hierarchy.

175 See for example, *Fong Wai Lyn Carolyn v. Airtrust (Singapore) Pte Ltd* [2011] SGHC 88; [2011] 3 SLR 980; *Poondy Radhakrishnan v. Sivapiragasam s/o Veerasingam* [2009] SGHC 228 (SGHC).

176 *Pang Yong Hock v. PKS Contracts Services Pte Ltd* [2004] SGCA 18 (SGCA) at [20], where the Singapore Court of Appeal added that "the best way of demonstrating good faith is to show a legitimate claim which the directors are unreasonably reluctant to pursue with the appropriate vigour or at all".

177 *Companies Act* (Singapore, Chapter 50, 2006, revised ed) s.216A(3)(a), (b) and (c).

178 *Ang Thiam Swee v. Low Hian Chor* [2013] SGCA 11, at [23].

179 *Ang Thiam Swee v. Low Hian Chor* [2013] SGCA 11, at [13], where Rajah JA notes that the approach is "neatly encapsulated in Palmer J's judgment in *Swansson v. RA Pratt Properties Pty Ltd*".

180 *Ang Thiam Swee v. Low Hian Chor* [2013] SGCA 11.

181 *Ang Thiam Swee v. Low Hian Chor* [2013] SGCA 11, at [21–23].

It is clear that Singapore has changed its position, making it more difficult for potential applicants to succeed in the leave application. The court further states that whether an applicant has a legitimate or arguable claim is a matter that is more appropriate under the test of "in the interests of the company",[182] which is a separate criterion from the good faith element. In *Ang Thiam Swee v. Low Hian Chor*, both the applicant and the defendant each held 10% of the shares in the company with the remaining shares held by a third party, who was declared bankrupt as a consequence of misappropriating company funds. The applicant alleged that the defendant too had misappropriated company funds. On appeal, the court found that the applicant's intent was to secure sole control of the company and because of this ulterior motive, he was not acting in good faith and would not be the proper person to represent the company's interests.

In subsequent cases, remarks were made that the new test requires the applicant to prove "utmost candour and honesty".[183] In another case, the court inferred that the applicant was not acting in good faith due to the reason that the applicant had targeted particular persons to sue based on limited inaccurate information available to the applicant and without knowing that there were other wrongdoers involved.[184] In another case, the court found the applicant lacked good faith because the applicant had participated in the alleged wrongdoing even though evidence showed that the applicant was less blameworthy than the opponent was.[185] These cases illustrate that when proof of good faith is forced upon the applicant, the outcome is that the applicant must show absolute purity in their good intention to pursue the action in the company's interests, and this concept, the requirement of proof and of high threshold, is unworkable. It is impossible to achieve absolute purity in the show of good faith.

Pearlie Koh argues that this shift in the law is "unfortunate" as the current test "does little to give effect to" the applicant's role in the derivative action.[186] Tang argues that the requirement of high threshold puts many shareholder applicants in a "no-win situation".[187] She notes further that "this requirement of good faith has evolved into a serious obstacle for claimants by imposing impossible demands on them".[188] These criticisms are just as relevant for suggesting a possible removal of good faith in the Australian SDA. Hypothetically, if these cases were decided in Australia, it is likely that Australian courts would grant leave on the condition that the applicant bears the costs of the derivative proceedings as a way of showing good faith; however, the costs/benefit approach has a different problem, as discussed above.

182 *Ang Thiam Swee v. Low Hian Chor* [2013] SGCA 11, at [58]. The relevant provision for "in the interests of the company" is contained in s.216A(3)(c) of the Singapore Act.

183 *Wong Kai Wah v. Wong Kai Yuan* [2014] SGHC 147 [66–67].

184 *Chua Swee Kheng v. E3 Holdings* [2015] SGHC 22 [47–48].

185 *Petroship Investments Pte Ltd v. Wealthplus Pte Ltd* [2016] SGCA 17.

186 Koh, Pearlie, n 15, at 234.

187 Tang, n 128, at 472. See also Koh, Alan, n 16, at 209.

188 Tang, n 128, at 471.

It is not clear why it was considered necessary to change the law with the effect of raising the threshold to such high level. There appears to be no meaningful impact in the use of the SDA (or other personal shareholder actions) in Singapore; one possible explanation could be that the Asian culture favours the "familial bonds and face-saving settlements" approach,[189] not wanting personal disputes to end up in court.

4.5.4 Canada

Canada is the birthplace of the SDA that came into effect in the 1970s.[190] There is not much to say about the good faith requirement in that jurisdiction other than to point out that the general reasoning process laid down by the courts in Canada, in respect to good faith, is less strict than that in Australia. Yet, there is still support for its removal from the legislation. Professors Cheffins and Dine argue that the SDA has had "no dramatic impact" in Canada and one of the reasons is due to the uncertainty in the scope and interpretation of the good faith requirement.[191] Another scholar describes good faith as "irrelevant".[192] Another argues that the good faith requirement is unnecessary as "other procedural devices already deal adequately with malicious or unmeritorious actions".[193]

Similar to Australia, the courts in Canada generally agree that the onus is on the applicant to establish good faith,[194] However, in Canada, there are differences in the judicial opinions on what should be an appropriate threshold for good faith. Maisonville J in *Arkansas Teacher Retirement System v. Lions Gate Entertainment Corp* opined that the onus of proving good faith is "substantial",[195] while in *Bertram v. Fundy Tidal Inc.*, Hood J stated that when determining whether good faith has been established, the threshold is a "low" threshold.[196] In a most recent decision in *Barrett v. Ballott*, Marshall J preferred

189 Dan Puchniak, "The complexity of derivative actions in Asia: An inconvenient truth" in Puchniak, Baum and Ewing-Chow (eds.), n 137, Ch 2, at 118.

190 *Canada Business Corporations Act*, RSC 1985 (formerly *Canada Business Corporations Act*, RSC 1975); *Ontario Business Corporations Act*, RSC 1990 (formerly *Ontario Business Corporations Act*, RSC 1970).

191 Brian Cheffins and J Dine, "Shareholder remedies: Lessons from Canada" (1992) 13 *Company Lawyer* 89, at 94.

192 Peterson and Cumming, n 19, at [16.39].

193 Maloney, n 22, at 320.

194 *Jordan Enterprises Ltd v. Barker* 2015, BCSC, at [27]; *Luft v. Ball* 2013, BCSC 574, at [46]; *Discovery Enterprises Inc v. Ebco Industries Ltd* [1998] 50 BCLR (3d) 195, at [5].

195 *Arkansas Teacher Retirement System v. Lions Gate Entertainment Corp* 2016, BCSC 432, at [157]. See also *Tremblett v. SCB Fisheries Limited* (1993) 16 Nfld & P.E.I.R. 139, at [82-83] (Puddester J).

196 *Bertram v. Fundy Tidal Inc.*, 2018 NSSC 165, at [29]. This first instance decision was upheld by the Court of Appeal in Nova Scotia in *Budd v. Bertram* 2018, NSCA 95, but good faith was not the issue raised on appeal.

not to characterise the threshold as "low" or "substantial", but instead stated that "cogent evidence" is required to establish good faith,[197] meaning:[198]

> "the Court must assess all the evidence and circumstances ... to determine whether there is any bad faith" and this includes "whether ... the claim has merit (i.e. the subjective element of good faith); and whether there is an arguable case for trial, which is neither frivolous nor vexatious (i.e. the objective element of good faith)."

Overall, it seems that there is also no clarity in the judicial approach to good faith in Canada. However, it has been indicated that the subjective and objective elements are important for assessing good faith,[199] and without categorising the threshold as "low" or "substantial", their approach seems less strict than the one from Australia. For example, on the subjective element, an applicant in Canada is only required to show "reasonable belief" that the proposed action has "some chance of success" (as opposed to "honest belief" in Australia).[200] In other words, an applicant only has to show a "legitimate or arguable" claim that the proposed action has merit.[201]

On the objective element, the courts in Canada prefer to look, not for "collateral purpose" but rather for "ulterior" purpose as the more extreme point for considering whether an applicant lacks good faith so as to declare the leave application to be frivolous or vexatious.[202] Examples are cases involving malice[203] or a history of personal vendetta.[204] In Australia, a derivative action would be frivolous or unmeritorious if the applicant's "collateral" purpose does not align with the company's interest.

4.6 Conclusion

This chapter has explained the fundamental problems with the operation of the good faith requirement in the SDA. The chapter has pointed out the

197 *Barrett v. Ballott* 2019 NLSC 82, at [67].

198 *Barrett v. Ballott* 2019 NLSC 82, at [68].

199 *Bertram v. Fundy Tidal Inc*, 2018 NSSC 165, at [29]; *Valgardson v. Valgardson* (2012) 98 BLR 223; [2012] BCBC 124, at [20]; *Discovery Enterprises Inc. v. Ebco Industries Ltd* [1998] 50 BCLR (3d) 195, at [105–106].

200 *L & B Electric Ltd v. Oickle* 2006 NSCA 41 (CA), at [59-60]. See also *Valgardson v. Valgardson* (2012) 98 BLR 223; [2012] BCBC 124, at [27]; *Mackenzie v. Craig* (1997) 205 AR 363, 2 WWR 106, at [36–40]; *Primex Investments Ltd v. Northwest Sports Enterprises Ltd and 453333 BC Ltd* [1996] 4 WWR 54, at [39–41].

201 *Discovery Enterprises Inc. v. Ebco Industries Ltd* [1998] 50 BCLR (3d) 195, at [105]; *Richardson Greenshields of Canada Limited v. Kalmacoff et al* (1995) 22 OR (3d) 577, at 585.

202 *Luft v. Ball* 2013, BCSC 574, para 46; *Bennett v. Rudek* 2008 BCSC 1278, at [46]; *Discovery Enterprises Inc. v. Ebco Industries Ltd* [1998] 50 BCLR (3d) 195, at [117].

203 *Tremblett v. SCB Fisheries Ltd* (1993) 116 Nfld & P.E.I.R. 139.

204 *Jennings v. Bernstein* (2000) Carswell Ont 4039; *Primex Investments Ltd v. Northwest Sports Enterprises Ltd and 453333 BC Ltd* [1996] 4 WWR 54.

considerable overlap inherent in the good faith requirement, the "in the best interests of the company" requirement and the costs provision in s.242 and because of these overlaps, this chapter submits that it is not necessary to include good faith as a prerequisite in the SDA. In many cases, the courts have tended to consider good faith based on whether an applicant has undertaken to indemnify the company and pay for the proposed action and for any adverse liability made against the company. By undertaking to cover all costs and charges, the applicant shows good faith and demonstrates that the proposed action is in the company's interests.

Some critics may dislike the idea of having the term "good faith" removed from the SDA; this could be because the concept of good faith has a long history in corporate law, for example, in the context of directors' duty, as well as in other areas of the law. However, it is important to remember that good faith is difficult to define in practice. Its lack of clarity and uncertainty in SDA has resulted in circularity in the courts' reasoning, and at times, has produced conflicting decisions.

Both New Zealand and Hong Kong have chosen not to include good faith as a prerequisite in their SDA, and their approach seems to be functioning well without any issues of abuse. This chapter has suggested that to be the preferred approach. The phrasing of their legislative provision (that is, by not including the term "good faith" but leaving the matter for the court to decide) appears to be less intimidating for bona fide potential applicants. The other prerequisites are already adequate for the court to make a determination of the applicant's good faith and the suitability of the applicant to bring the derivative action. When they are not threatened with the need to prove their good faith and to put their character and disposition to the test, potential applicants are more inclined to bring appropriate actions against wrongdoers. Removing the term "good faith" would be likely to have the effect of bringing about some deterrence of improper behaviour in those who are in positions of power, and in turn, enhance directors' accountability and corporate governance as originally intended by the legislation. The term "good faith" has been in the Australian SDA for over the past twenty years; it may be time for reform.

5 The "best interests of the company" requirement in statutory derivative action: Is there a need for amendment?

5.1 Introduction

One of the criteria that an applicant must satisfy the court for leave to bring a statutory derivative action in Australia is that the applicant must demonstrate that the proposed derivative action "is in the best interests of the company" under s.237(2)(c) of the *Corporations Act* 2001 (C'th).[1] The discussion in this chapter may provide some insights for countries that consider adopting the statutory framework,[2] and that require some guidance on how best to phrase their leave criteria in order to achieve a balance between providing shareholders with better protection, on the one hand, and deterring directors' misconduct, on the other hand, through encouraging corporate compliance. The discussion will also be of interest to countries that have a similar provision in their corporate law legislation and may wish to compare it with the Australian counterpart.[3] This chapter aims to provide a critical analysis of s.237(2)(c). One of the purposes is to consider whether s.237(2)(c) should be amended to reflect the true intention of the legislature that the statutory derivative action ("SDA") framework is designed to provide shareholders with a more "effective" remedy, as explained in the Explanatory Memorandum.[4] The argument put forward in this chapter is that the provision in s.237(2)(c) is too onerous,

1 Hereinafter, references to a provision are to the *Corporations Act* 2001 (C'th), unless stated otherwise.

2 For example, statutory derivative action is currently not available in Brazil, Cyprus and Greece. For further discussion, see Organisation for Economic Co-operation and Development, *Private Enforcement of Shareholder Rights: A Comparison of Selected Jurisdictions and Policy Alternatives for Brazil* (2020 Report) – https://www.oecd.org/corporate/shareholder-rights-brazil.htm (viewed 21 May 2022)

3 For example, in Singapore, s.216A(3)(c) of its *Companies Act* states that leave of the court must not be granted unless the proposed derivative action "appears to be prima facie in the interests of the company". Similarly, s.239(2)(c) of the Canada *Business Corporations Act RSC* says that a derivative action must not be brought "unless the court is satisfied that ... it appears to be in the interests of the corporation". In the United Kingdom, s.263(3)(b) of its *Companies Act* states that for a derivative claim to be brought, "the court must take into account, in particular... the importance that a person [meaning the applicant] acting in accordance with section 172 (duty to promote the success of the company)".

4 See Chapter 2.

DOI: 10.4324/9781003430063-5

in that it is not possible for an applicant to fulfil this criterion to the complete satisfaction of the court. It is not possible for an applicant or anyone to make a prediction of the outcome of a derivative action or any other court proceedings.

The other purpose of this chapter is that if the argument put forward as noted in the above is accepted, then the next logical step is to provide suggestions for law reform, with a view to providing shareholders with better protection by further simplifying the SDA process in order to encourage bona fide shareholders to apply for leave to bring an action on behalf of the company to remedy a wrong done to it. The goal is to improve the utility of the SDA as a private enforcement tool that would enable shareholders to enforce their corporate rights against directors for breach of directors' duties.

Empirical evidence in Chapter 3 shows that of all unsuccessful leave applications (44.6%), most of the applicants who failed in obtaining leave of the court to bring an SDA have, in fact, failed on satisfying the court of the requirement in paragraph (c) of s.237(2) or failed on satisfying that requirement in combination with two other requirements,[5] which makes up 62.6% of all fail cases. That is, the main reason for their unsuccessful leave applications was due to their failing to show the court (in 62.6% of all fail cases) that the proposed derivative action "is in the best interests of the company" under s.237(2)(c). This high percentage of failure under this category indicates that a further investigation is necessary to understand why s.237(2)(c) has been the most difficult hurdle for applicants to pass. The empirical data in Chapter 3 also indicate that when an applicant failed on the requirement in s.237(2)(c), many of them also failed on one or two other requirements.[6]

It is worth noting at this point that in those other successful leave applications, the applicants were granted leave to bring a derivative action largely on terms that they would bear all or nearly all legal costs associated with the leave application and with the bringing of the SDA; in addition, they would undertake to indemnify the company against any adverse costs orders made. This is a way of working around the complexity in the wording in s.237(2)(c). As the courts have reminded us, there is considerable overlap amongst the leave criteria in s.237(2) and the costs provision in s.242. In *Re Woodbine Project Pty Ltd*, Button J noted that:[7]

> "[t]he question of how the costs of the company… are to be met may be approached from a number of angles, which overlap… the willingness

5 The two other associated criteria are s.237(2)(b) (proof of "good faith", as discussed in Chapter 4) and s.237(2)(d) (proof that the case is arguable, that is "there is a serious question to be tried").

6 See Table 7, Chapter 3.

7 *Re Woodbine Project Pty Ltd* [2021] VSC 617, at [60]. See also *Li v. Dao* [2018] VSC 530, at [60] (Connock J) and *Carpenter v. Pioneer Park Pty Limited* [2004] NSWSC 1007, at [10] (BarrettJ), *Carpenter v. Pioneer Park Pty Limited* (2008) 66 ACSR 564; [2008] NSWSC 551.

> of those seeking leave to intervene to bear those costs, has been considered relevant both to the assessment of the good faith of the applicants for leave, and to the assessment of the best interests of the company pursuant to s 237(2)(c)."

The effect is that if a company is not required to pay costs and has very little to lose, then the proposed derivative action is deemed to be "in the best interests of the company" as per the requirement under s.237(2)(c).

This chapter is therefore structured as follows. Part 2 explains the ambiguity in s.237(2)(c), including terms such as "best interests" and "company", and the uncertainty in the amount of evidence required to show the proposed action "is in the best interests of the company". Part 3 provides further examples and variations of the courts' interpretation of s.237(2)(c) and the overlapping effect with s.237(2)(d).[8] The main point is to illustrate why the wording in s.237(2)(c) is unworkable insofar as requiring the applicant to show the proposed action "is" in the best interests of the company. Part 4 considers the uncertainty in the application of s.237(2)(c) to company liquidation cases, the difficulty in bringing proceedings against related third parties pursuant to s.237(3) and the overlapping problem with the s.237(2)(d) criterion. Part 5 provides some suggestions for law reform, and by doing so, this part also considers the SDA provisions from Canada, British Columbia and Singapore as an example to illustrate how their approaches are arguably more effective in terms of providing shareholder protection and relief. In these countries and this province, there is no sign of abuse to their SDA procedure. There are many good reasons why their provisions are appropriate for Australia. Part 6 is the conclusion.

As noted in Chapter 1, literature on the Australian SDA is very limited. There is no academic publication on only s.237(2)(c). This chapter will be the first on the provision.

5.2 Ambiguity in section 237(2)(c)

5.2.1 Meaning and scope of s.237(2)(c)

This part of the discussion begins by explaining why s.237(2)(c) is ambiguous and unworkable. For ease of reference, s.237(2)(c) states, amongst other things, that "[t]he Court must grant the application if it is satisfied that... it is in the best interests of the company that the applicant be granted leave".

The wording in s.237(2)(c) appears simple and yet it is full of confusion and uncertainty. There is no clarification in the CA as to the scope of its application or what is meant by "best interests" or who the "company" is exactly or how much evidence is required to satisfy the court of this requirement.

8 Section 237(2)(d) states that the applicant is also required to establish "there is a serious question to be tried".

Palmer J in *Swansson v. RA Pratt Pty Ltd* has interpreted this provision to read that the court must be satisfied "not that the proposed derivative action *may be, appears to be,* or *is likely to be,* in the best interests of the company but, rather, that it *is* in its best interests".[9] His Honour further states that the provision is to be considered "in a prima facie way",[10] and that it can only be determined by taking into account all relevant circumstances.[11] In support of that interpretation, Barrett J in *Carpenter v. Pioneer Part Pty Ltd (in liq)* makes a similar comment that s.237(2)(c) is "not an inquiry into possibility or potential", but rather the proposed action must be shown to "positively serve the best interests of the company".[12] These are the earlier cases and the courts in subsequent cases have routinely endorsed these interpretations.[13]

The Explanatory Memorandum that accompanied the introduction of the SDA explains s.237(2)(c) as follows:[14]

> "This criterion would allow the Court to focus on the true nature and purpose of the proceedings. It would recognise that a company might have sound business reasons for not pursuing a cause of action open to it and that its management might legitimately have decided that the best interests of the company would be served by not taking action. For example, a decision may be taken in a case where, *although it may be clear that there has been a breach of duty by a director, the loss to the company may only be nominal. In this case, the costs of taking proceedings may outweigh any benefit to the company.*
>
> The inclusion of this criterion would allow the Court to refuse to grant leave in these circumstances because the applicant for leave would not be able to show that to do so would be in the best interests of the company."

In short, the above statement simply provides the court with complete discretion to decide on the matter and whether the proposed derivative action is or is not in the company's best interests depends on the extent of a breach of duty by a director. The statement does not appear to reflect the intended purposes of the SDA.[15] There are two observations. First and as discussed in Chapter 2, much emphasis has been given in the Explanatory Memorandum

9 *Swansson v. RA Pratt* [2002] NSWSC 583, at [55].
10 *Swansson v. RA Pratt* [2002] NSWSC 583, at [55].
11 *Swansson v. RA Pratt* [2002] NSWSC 583, at [56].
12 *Carpenter v. Pioneer Part Pty Ltd (in liq)* [2004] NSWSC 1007, at [19] (Barrett J).
13 *App Shop Pty Ltd v. Jalal Bros Pty Ltd* [2019] NSWSC 490, at [17] (Black J); *Zhu v. Orico Australia Pty Ltd* [2019] VSC 313, at [61] (Connock J); *Drew v. Lynch* [2019] FCA 632, at [108] (Gleeson J).
14 House of Representatives, *Explanatory Memorandum to the Corporate Law Economic Reform Program ("CLERP") Bill* 1998 (C'th), at [6.38], [6.39] at 22. (Emphasis added).
15 As discussed in Chapter 2.

for the need to provide shareholders with an "effective remedy" and to overcome the difficulties seen at common law. The SDA was intended to make the process "easier for investors themselves to protect the interests of a company" and to "provide a real avenue for applicants to seek redress on behalf of a company where it fails to do so".[16] Another earlier report stated:[17]

> "More importantly, a statutory form of derivative action could potentially be a valuable tool to enhance corporate governance and to maintain investor confidence. ... A direct accountability mechanism that can be used by shareholders in an efficient and effective manner provides an added incentive for directors to ensure that they always act in the interests of the company."

Overall, there is a sense of strong encouragement for SDA to be used as a private enforcement tool to enhance directors' accountability by deterring improper conduct. However, the above explanatory statement seems to have restricted shareholders' access to SDA by noting that a certain "breach of duty by a director" is acceptable. In one case, in reference to that explanatory statement, Austin J notes that s.237(2)(c) deserves a "broader enquiry".[18]

The other point raised in the Explanatory Memorandum is the costs/benefits approach. It implies that if the cost of a proposed action appears to outweigh the benefit to the company, then it would not be in the best interests of the company, and the court should turn away such application for leave. The Explanatory Memorandum has not been helpful in explaining the scope of s.237(2)(c); in fact, it has, as will be discussed later in this chapter, severely restricted shareholders' access to SDA in the way the courts have narrowly applied the provision. The reality is that litigation is generally expensive, and if a shareholder is refused leave because the proposed action is too expensive, then where is the justification for introducing the SDA? Further problems with s.237(2)(c) are discussed below.

5.2.2 Uncertainty in the word "company"

The question to ask is *who* is "the company"? It is not clear from the CA whether "the company" comprises only the shareholders as members of the company or whether the term includes other stakeholders such as employees, customers, suppliers and other creditors, in the sense that a company has a general corporate social responsibility ("CSR") to the community at large. The

16 *Explanatory Memorandum to the CLERP Bill* 1998, at [2.5], [6.11], [6.17], [6.33], [6.30].

17 CLERP Proposal Paper No. 3, *Proposals for Reform: Directors' Duties and Corporate Governance* (1997), at 33. See also Companies and Securities Advisory Committee ("CASAC"), *Statutory Derivative Action* (Report, 1993), at 4.

18 *Fiduciary Ltd v. Morningstar Research Pty Ltd* (2005) 53 ACSR 732, [2005] NSWSC 442, at [44–45].

conundrum for a shareholder applicant is whether they also need to satisfy the court regarding the interests of other stakeholder groups. There are two schools of thought.

First, a narrow view is that shareholders are "owners" of a company.[19] The courts have rarely found the need to define what a "company" is other than referring to a "company as a whole",[20] or "company as a separate and independent welfare".[21] In *Huang v. Wang*, it was held that "best interests of the company" means best interests in the sense of "its separate and independent welfare", and provided the company is solvent, this would "predominantly reflect the interests of [its] shareholders in that capacity".[22] Where a company has become insolvent, the company would be the representative of "a general body of its creditors".[23] These interpretations are the same as in directors' duties, where the general understanding (and acceptance) is that directors' duties to the company are to the "shareholders as a general body",[24] and in circumstances where a company is insolvent, its best interests may turn to reflect its creditors.[25]

However, the related problem is whether "company" includes "company in liquidation". It is clear that when a company becomes insolvent, the "interests of the company" reflects the "interests of its creditors". What is not clear is whether an applicant can still use s.237(2)(c) to show that the proposed derivative action is in the best interests of the *company in liquidation* and whether the applicant is entitled to a claim of benefit through that process.[26]

19 Adolf A. Berle and Gardiner C. Means, *The Modern Corporation and Private Property* (Transaction Publishers, 1932), at 352–353 (where "separation of ownership and control" was referred to as illustration of shareholders being collective owners).

20 *Maher v. Honeysett & Maher Electrical Contractors Pty Ltd* [2005] NSWSC 859, at [44] (Brereton J); Re *Gladstone Pacific Nickel Limited* [2011] NSWSC 1235, at [57] (Ball J); *True Value Solar Holdings Pty Ltd v. Fernandez* [2013] VSCA 27, at [13] (Full Court); *Daiwa Can Company v. Barokes Pty Ltd* [2016] VSC 296, at [60] (Sifris J).

21 *Charlton v. Baber* (2003) 47 ACSR 31; [2003] NSWSC 745, at [52]; *Huang v. Wang* [2016] NSWCA 164, at [59].

22 *Huang v. Wang* [2016] NSWCA 164, at [59] (Bathurst CJ, McColl JA and Barrett AJA), citing *Chahwan v. Euphoric Pty Ltd* (2008) 65 ACSR 661; [2008] NSWCA 52, at [88] and *Charlton v. Baber* (2003) 47 ACSR 31; [2003] NSWSC 745, at [52]. See also *Bzezinski v. Shaw* [2022] VSCA 173, at [92] (Kyrou, Meleish and Walker JJA).

23 *Charlton v. Baber* (2003) 47 ACSR 31; [2003] NSWSC 745, at [53] (Barrett J), citing the High Court of Australia decisions in *Walker v. Wimborne* (1976) 137 CLR 1, [1976] HCA 7 and *Spies v. The Queen* [2000] HCA 43; (2000) 201 CLR 603 (non-SDA cases relating to duties of directors in the company). See also SDA cases in *Robash Pty Ltd v. Gladstone Pacific Nickel Pty Ltd* [2011] NSWSC 1235, at [57]; *Carpenter v. Pioneer Park Pty Ltd (in liq)* [2004] NSWSC 1007.

24 *Greenhalgh v. Arderne Cinemas Ltd* [1951] Ch 286, at 291; *Parke v. Daily News* [1962] Ch 927, at 963. See also *Ngurli Ltd v. McCann* (1953) 90 CLR 425, at 438; *Pilmer v. Duke Group Ltd (in liq)* (2001) 207 CLR 165, at 178–179; *Percival v. Wright* [1902] 2 Ch 421.

25 *Charlton v. Baber* (2003) 47 ACSR 31; [2003] NSWSC 745, at [53] (Barrett J).

26 Part 4 of this chapter explains further on this point.

The other school of thought is that "company" could be construed as including other stakeholder groups, in the sense that the company needs to consider and respond to socioeconomic and political pressures as well, not just shareholders and directors.[27] This view has received considerable debate in the past decades, and given that it is rapidly gaining public acceptance,[28] it is important that the legislation clarifies the scope of "company" in s.237(2)(c). In *Bell Group Ltd (in liq) v. Westpac Banking Corporation (No. 9)*, in the context of directors' duties, Owen J of the WA Supreme Court states that "directors' fiduciary duties are owed to the company, not to the shareholders (or to creditors)",[29] which suggests that a broader approach should be adopted. Keay asserts that the phrase "best interests of the company" could mean "the maximization of the value of the corporation".[30] Greenfield takes an even broader view and asserts that a company represents the interests of all stakeholders.[31] Du Plessis argues that it is a "myth" to think of shareholders as "owners" of the company. and cites several cases to support his view that a company is a separate legal entity in the broader sense to include other stakeholders.[32] The modern trend in favouring a stakeholder approach is rapidly gaining momentum. It may be necessary to clarify the scope of "company" in the CA to avoid confusion.

5.2.3 Lack of clarity in the term "best interests"

Another problem with s.237(2)(c) is in relation to the term "best interests". The word "best" is a comparative word, and without qualification, it can lead to confusion and ambiguity, in the sense that what is "best" for one person may not be good enough for another person. In *Charlton v. Baber*, Barrett J criticises the term "best interests", saying that it is "apt to create a

27 For example, see Kent Greenfield, *Corporations are People Too (And They Should Act Like It)* (Yale University Press, 2018), at 215–216; Lynn Stout, *The Shareholder Value Myth: How Putting Shareholders First Harms Investors, Corporations and the Public* (Berrett-Koehler Publishers, 2012); Margaret M. Blair, *Ownership and Control: Rethinking Corporate Governance for the Twenty-first Century* (Brookings Institution Washington DC,, 1995), Ch 6.

28 See for example, Corporations and Markets Advisory Committee, *Report on the Social Responsibility of Corporations* (2006); Parliamentary Joint Committee on Corporations and Financial Services, *Corporate Responsibility: Managing Risks and Creating Value* (2006).

29 *Bell Group Ltd (in liq) v. Westpac Banking Corporation (No. 9)* (2008) 39 WAR 1, at 533 [4,389] (Owen J). See also *Australian Securities Investments Commission v. Cassimatis (No.8)* (2016) 336 ALR 209, at 299 (Edelman J). See also the New Zealand position, *Coleman v. Myers* [1977] 2 NZLR 225.

30 Andrew Keay, "Ascertaining the Corporate Objective: An Entity Maximisation and Sustainability Model" (2008) 71 *Modern Law Review* 663, at 678–691, citing a Canadian decision in *Peoples Department Stores Inc v. Wise* [2004] 3 SCR 461, at 481.

31 Kent Greenfield, *Corporations are People Too (And They Should Act Like It)* (Yale University Press, 2018), at 215–216.

32 Jean J. du Plessis, "Directors' duty to act in the best interests of the corporation: 'Hard cases make bad law'" (2019) 34 *Australian Journal of Corporate Law* 3, at 17–22.

false impression that some absolute or superlative is in contemplation".[33] In *Fiduciary Ltd v. Morningstar Research Pty Ltd*, Austin J notes that the best interests of the company criterion is "difficult to assess" given that an application for leave is not a trial case.[34] Much is dependent on what a court views as an acceptable standard and this could lead to inconsistent and unfair outcomes when applied rigidly.

If one were to try to understand what "best interests" means, it would be an impossible task. In practice, one cannot expect an applicant to have no financial interests at all in the proposed derivative action. Section 236 provides only a shareholder or director to apply to bring an SDA, and from this, one would assume that these applicants would have some form of financial interest in the company. There has to be a strong reason for them to take an initiative to pursue an action on behalf of the company and this could be a desire to protect the value of their own shares.[35] There either has to be a clear definition of "best interests" if possible or the alternative would be to remove the word "best" from the provision.

The expression "in the best interests of the company" is not alien in corporate law. In the context of directors' duties, s.181(1) requires a director to act "in the best interests of the company", and in that context, both judges and scholars have criticised this expression as one of the "most problematic" areas in corporate law.[36] There is voluminous case law on this statutory requirement and yet the case law has not really advanced the discussion. In *Bell Group Ltd (in liq) v. Westpac Banking Corporation (No. 9)*, an issue was raised as to whether directors had breached their duty to act in the best interests of the company.[37] Owen J in that case did not deal with the differences in the expressions in detail, but of particular relevance for this chapter, his Honour stated, in the context of directors' duties:[38]

> "In so far as I can see, there is no material difference, for present purposes, between the phrases 'benefit of the company', 'best interests of the company' and 'interests of the company. ... In the authorities, they are often used interchangeably and, in my view, are all to the same broad effect."

Austin and Ramsay also argue that there is no significant difference between acting "in the best interests of the company" and acting "in the interests of

33 *Charlton v. Baber* [2003] NSWSC 745, at [46].

34 *Fiduciary Ltd v. Morningstar Research Pty Ltd* (2005) 53 ACSR 732, [2005] NSWSC 442, at [40].

35 It is common for a director to own shares in the same company.

36 Justice K. M. Hayne, "Directors' Duties and a Company's Creditors" (2014) 38 *Melbourne University Law Review* 795, 808–809, citing Dan D. Prentice, "Creditors' interests and director's duties" (1990) 10 *Oxford Journal of Legal Studies* 265, at 273; du Plessis, n 32, at 7.

37 *Bell Group Ltd (in liq) v. Westpac Banking Corporation (No. 9)* (2008) 39 WAR 1 (Owen J).

38 *Bell Group Ltd (in liq) v. Westpac Banking Corporation (No. 9)* (2008) 39 WAR 1, at 532, [4,384] (Owen J), citing as an example, *Mills v. Mills* (1938) 60 CLR 150, at 175 (Starke J).

the company".[39] They observe that "within the one case, it is possible to come across some judgments that refer to directors acting in the interests of the company while other judgments in the same case refer to directors acting in the best interests of the company", citing as an example *Whitehouse v. Carlton Hotel Pty Ltd*.[40]

5.2.4 Uncertainty in the amount of proof required

A further difficulty with s.237(2)(c) relates to the uncertainty in the amount of proof required. Under s.237(2)(c), an applicant seeking leave must show that the proposed derivative action "is [in absolute terms] in the best interests of the company". It has been repeated by the Courts on multiple occasions that the emphasis should be on the word "is". In a more recent case, *Bzezinski v. Shaw*, the Court of Appeal in the Supreme Court of Victoria unanimously agreed that "[t]he applicant for derivative leave must persuade the Court that the proposed proceeding 'is' in the best interests of the company, not that it merely may be, appears to be or is likely to be in its best interests".[41]

However, despite the reminder, there is still a lack of clarity in the scope of s.237(2)(c). It has been said many times that there is "no fixed test" and there is "no special standard of proof",[42] except that it is clear from the provision and from case law that the applicant has the burden of proof.[43] There is a sense that the applicant must demonstrate with absolute certainty that the proposed action will have a successful outcome and that the outcome will be in the company's best interests.

39 Robert P. Austin and Ian M. Ramsay, *Ford, Austin and Ramsay's Principles of Corporations Law* (LexisNexis Butterworths, 17th ed, 2018,), at 475, [8.070.6].

40 Austin and Ramsay, n 39, at [8.070.6], citing *Whitehouse v. Carlton Hotel Pty Ltd* (1987) 162 CLR 285 at 293.

41 *Bzezinski v. Shaw* [2022] VSCA 173, at [92] (Kyrou, Meleish and Walker JJA), citing *Blakeney v. Blakeney* [2016] WASCA 76; (2016) 113 ACSR 398, 409, at [52–53] (Buss and Murphy JJA and Beech J). See also *Swansson v. RA Pratt* [2002] NSWSC 583, at [55] (Palmer); *Carpenter v. Pioneer Part Pty Ltd (in liq)* [2004] NSWSC 1007, at [19] (Barrett J); *App Shop Pty Ltd v. Jalal Bros Pty Ltd* [2019] NSWSC 490, at [17] (Black J); *Zhu v. Orico Australia Pty Ltd* [2019] VSC 313, at [61] (Connock J); *Drew v. Lynch* [2019] FCA 632, at [108] (Gleeson J).

42 *Vinciguerra v. MG Corrosion Consultants Pty Ltd* [2010] FCA 763, at [119] (Gilmour J) (Appeal dismissed: *MG Corrosion Consultants Pty Ltd v. Vinciguerra* [2011] FCAFC 31). (North, McKerracher and Jagot JJ). See also *Daiwa Can Company v. Barokes Pty Ltd* [2016] VSC 296, at [61] (Sifris J), citing *True Value Solar Holdings Pty Ltd v. Fernandez* [2013] VSCA 27, at [13] (Osborn JA, Neave JA and Priest JJA agreeing); *Zhu v. Orico Australia Pty Ltd* [2019] VSC 313, at [65] (Connock J); *Oats v. Consolidated Capital Services Ltd* [2009] 76 NSWLR 69, 93 at [119] (Campbell JA, Spigelman CJ and Allsop P agreeing).

43 *Townshend as Legal Representative for the Estate of Mervyn Townshend v. Fendall Farms Pty Ltd* [2022] FCA 848, at [36] (McEvoy J); *Slea Pty Ltd v. Connective Services Pty Ltd* [2017] VSC 609, at [51] (Robson J) (Appeal dismissed: *Connective Services Pty Ltd v. Slea Pty Ltd* [2018] VSCA 229; *Swansson v. RA Pratt* [2002] NSWSC 583, at [54] (Palmer J).

There are two main issues with the wording in s.237(2)(c). First, it is not possible for anyone to predict what the outcome of a court action will be. One cannot make a definitive assessment about events that have not occurred. Second, a successful outcome in a court action does not always equate to it being in the best interests of the company. For example, a successful outcome could be in the form of a non-monetary relief where the court issues an injunction order to restrain a director from committing further breaches of directors' duties when the applicant might have expected a compensation order instead. Conversely, a large compensation awarded to the company will not always lead to an enhancement of directors' accountability; it may help to ensure some degree of accountability, but compensation alone will not deter all forms of misconduct.

Nonetheless, to show that the proposed derivative action "is in the best interests of the company" as required under s.237(2)(c), the courts have formulated a number of non-exhaustive factors that are considered relevant; but even so, there are some inconsistencies in the judicial treatment of s.237(2)(c), as further explained in the next two parts below.

5.3 Factors relevant for considering what is "in the best interests of the company"

5.3.1 Non-exhaustive list of factors

Factors or circumstances relevant for deciding whether a proposed derivative action "is in the best interests of the company" are these. In *Swansson v. RA Pratt Pty Ltd,* Palmer J provides four that are considered relevant,[44] as summarised by the Full Court of the Supreme Court of South Australia in *Ragless v. IPA Holdings Pty Ltd (in liq)*:[45]

- the character of the company and the nature of its operations;
- the company's business so as to understand the effects of the proposed litigation;
- whether alternative relief is available so as not to bring the company into litigation against its will; and
- the ability of the defendant to meet at least a substantial part of any judgment in favour of the company so that the court may ascertain whether the action would be of practical benefit to the company.

In *Robash Pty Ltd v. Gladstone Pacific Nickel Pty Ltd,* Ball J provides additional factors focusing largely on the costs/benefits analysis, including an

44 *Swansson v. RA Pratt Pty Ltd* [2002] NSWSC 583, at [55–60].

45 *Ragless v. IPA Holdings Pty Ltd (in liq)* (2008) 65 ACSR 700; [2008] SASC 90 (Full Court), at [35] (Debelle, Sulan and Vanstone JJ).

applicant's ability to indemnify the company against any adverse costs order:[46]

> "In considering what is in the best interests of the company, it is necessary to consider the prospects of success of the action, the likely costs and likely recovery if the action is successful and likely consequences if it is not. One relevant matter in considering these issues is the nature of any indemnity the applicant has offered to the company if the action is brought and the likelihood that the company will recover under that indemnity. It is also necessary to consider the resources the company will be required to devote to the action and the resources it has available."

5.3.2 The costs/benefits approach and its problem

The costs/benefits analysis, as described in *Robash*, has become the dominant focus for resolving the question of whether the proposed derivative action "is in the best interests of the company".[47] This has been the position even where an applicant has established all the other factors referred to in *Swansson* and *Ragless*.[48] One approach has been to compare the likely costs of bringing the proposed derivative action and the benefit that the company would acquire from that action;[49] it is often difficult for an applicant to fulfil this process to the court's satisfaction.

The other approach has been to require the applicant seeking leave to bring a derivative action to show that they have the ability to pay for the proposed action and to undertake to indemnify the company against any adverse costs order. It has therefore become common practice for the court to adopt the latter approach and grant leave on terms that the applicant undertakes to pay costs associated with the SDA and to indemnify the company against any adverse costs liability. This is to ensure that the interests and resources of the company are protected,[50] and that the company would not be worse

46 *Robash Pty Ltd v. Gladstone Pacific Nickel Pty Ltd* [2011] NSWSC 1235, at [57] (Ball J); *Fiduciary Ltd v. Morningstar Research Pty Ltd* (2005) 53 ACSR 732, 92005] NSWSC 442; *Suh v. Cho* [2013] VSC 491, at [49].

47 See, for example, *Jensen v. RQYS Marina Ltd* [2015] QCA 153, at [42] (Gotterson JA, Boddice and Flanagan JJ agreeing); *Huang v. Wang* [2016] NSWCA 164, at [38], [67] (Bathurst CJ, with McColl AJ and Barrett AJA agreeing); *Suh v. Cho* [2013] VSC 491, at [49] (Derham J).

48 See for example, *Zhu v. Orico Australia Pty Ltd* [2019] VSC 313; *Li v. Dao* [2018] VSC 530.

49 *Robash Pty Ltd v. Gladstone Pacific Nickel Pty Ltd* [2011] NSWSC 1235.

50 *Drew v. Lynch* [2019] FCA 632, at [146], [164] (Gleeson J); *Slea Pty Ltd v. Connective Services Pty Ltd* [2017] VSC 609, at [159]; *Vinciguerra v. MG Corrosion Consultants Pty Ltd* [2010] FCA 763, at [138–139] (Gilmour J), (appeal against grant of leave dismissed: *MG Corrosion Consultants Pty Ltd v. Vinciguerra* [2011] FCAFC 31; *Fiduciary Ltd v. Morningstar Research Pty Ltd* (2005) 53 ACSR 732; [2005] NSWSC 442, at [56] (Austin J).

off financially at the end of a court case;[51] and the approach is said to reflect the notion that the proposed action "is in the best interests of the company" as per s.237(2)(c). The thinking is that if an applicant undertakes to fund the proposed action and the company is not required to spend any money on the case, the proposed action would be deemed to be in the company's best interests.[52]

The author has issues with this approach for two reasons. First, if an applicant must pay for a derivative action as a way of showing that the proposed action "*is*" in the company's interests, then s.237(2)(c) would inevitably deter some bona fide shareholders from pursing the necessary action because of their financial constraints. For example, in *Cooper v. Myrtace Consulting Pty Ltd*, there was no issue with the applicant's good faith,[53] except that the fact that the applicant was unable to offer adequate indemnity was noted by the court as posing "a significant difficulty", which led the court not to grant leave.[54]

Second, it is impractical for the parties and the court in the leave application to spend time and money on assessing costs and benefits. It is not cost effective. In *Blakeney v. Blakeney*, the Court of Appeal of Western Australia cautions against a detailed costs/benefits analysis,[55] saying that such analysis:[56]

> "would be almost impossible for [the court] to undertake with any degree of confidence or accuracy. The court should not permit an application for leave to become a trial of the proposed action."

It is worth noting that the costs provision is covered in s.242. Section 237(2)(c) makes no cross-reference to s.242. These two provisions are entirely separate matters and should remain so.[57] The leave criterion in s.237(2)(c) should not hinge on the costs provision in s.242; rather, the costs question should be decided on after a determination has been made on the leave application, not during or before such determination.

An example of a case where an applicant has satisfied the court of all the other factors, and yet is still required to bear the costs of bringing the proposed

51 *Vlahos v. Vlahos* [2016] VSC 824, at [52].

52 *In the Matter of Jimmy's Recipe Pty Ltd* [2018] NSWSC 1331, at [75] (Brereton J); *Zhu v. Orico Australia Pty Ltd* [2019] VSC 313, at [72–86] (Connock J); Cf *White (Trustee) v. MWL Financial Group Pty Ltd (No.2)* [2019] FCA 364, at [3–5] (Davies J).

53 *Cooper v. Myrtace Consulting Pty Ltd* [2014] FCA 480, at [18] (Davies J).

54 *Cooper v. Myrtace Consulting Pty Ltd* [2014] FCA 480, at [32] (Davies J). See also, *Re Fishinthenet Investments Pty Ltd and Coastal Waters Seafood Pty Ltd* [2014] NSWSC 260, where the applicant's indemnity offer was also inadequate.

55 *Blakeney v. Blakeney* [2016] WASCA 76, at [52–58] (Buss and Murphy JJA and Beech J).

56 *Blakeney v. Blakeney* [2016] WASCA 76, at [58] (Buss, Murphy JJA and Beech J), citing *Metyor Inc (formerly Talisman Technologies Inc) v. Queensland Electronic Switching Pty Ltd* (2002) 42 ACSR 398; [2002] QCA 269, at [19] and *MG Corrosion Consultants Pty Ltd v. Vinciguerra* [2011] FCAFC 31, at [59].

57 Chapter 6 considers the issue of costs.

derivative action is seen in *Li v. Dao*.[58] The applicant and defendant were equal shareholders, the company was no longer trading, there were no major creditors, and the only reason that the applicant sought to bring a derivative action was to settle her bitter dispute over the failed property development venture. In deciding the proposed action to be in the best interests of the company, the court found the following as relevant consideration:[59]

- the financial position of the company would likely be improved in a successful outcome;
- the company was no longer in business, and so the proposed action would not occupy physical, human or other resources of the company;
- the derivative action would help to break down the deadlock between the two shareholders;
- as shareholder of 50%, the defendant would also benefit from any successful outcome flowing through to the two shareholders; and
- more importantly, the applicant had undertaken to pay the costs of the derivative action and indemnify the company against adverse costs orders, which meant that the financial risk to the company was limited.

However, in conclusion, the court stated that the fact that the applicant had undertaken to bear all costs in bringing the proposed action that this was a "consideration *material* to the satisfaction of the good faith and best interests of the company requirements".[60] This was the main reason for the court granting leave, that the financial risk to the company was minimal.

5.3.3 Shareholder deadlock in joint-venture companies

Another important factor where there is inconsistency in the judicial approaches is in matters relating to shareholder deadlock in joint-venture companies, a deadlock between two equal shareholders or two groups of shareholders. In most instances, the court has ruled that an SDA is appropriate, but only if the applicant undertakes to pay costs of the proposed action;[61] while in other cases, the court has been less supportive of this idea.[62]

58 *Li v. Dao* [2018] VSC 530.

59 *Li v. Dao* [2018] VSC 530, at para 93–102. Similar reasoning was provided in another case where the company was no longer in business: *Zhu v. Orico Australia Pty Ltd* [2019] VSC 313, at [72–86] (Connock J).

60 *Li v. Dao* [2018] VSC 530, at [183] (Connock J) (Emphasis added).

61 See, for example, *Zhu v. Orico Australia Pty Ltd* [2019] VSC 313; *Li v. Dao* [2018] VSC 530; *Knights Quest Pty Ltd v. Barokes Pty Ltd* (2016) 113 ACSR 505, [2016] VSC 296; *Vlahos v. Vlahos* [2016] VSC 824.

62 *Blakeney v. Blakeney* [2016] WASCA 76; *Huang v. Wang* [2016] NSWCA 164; *Transmetro Corporation Ltd v. Kol Tov Pty Ltd* [2009] NSWSC 350 (Barrett J), (Appeal against grant of leave dismissed: *McEvoy v. Caplan* [2010] NSWCA 115 (Allsop P, Beazley and MacFarlan JJA)).

In *Talisman Technologies Inc. v. Queensland Electronic Switching Pty Ltd*,[63] the court in the first instance decided that an SDA would not be in the best interests of the company. The Queensland Court of Appeal reversed the decision, and in allowing the applicant to bring the necessary action, McPherson JA noted:[64]

> "It is because one group of members are in control of the management or affairs of the company and refuse to permit it to take proceedings that there is a dispute between the two groups of shareholders or members here. It is only by permitting proceedings to be taken on behalf of the company that the dispute in question can be resolved at all and that the complaint of one set of members against the others can be remedied."

The South Australian Court of Appeal in *Ragless* agreed with McPherson J and added that:

> "Joint venture companies in which no one shareholder has a controlling interest have a real potential to become bogged down in a stalemate because the shareholders cannot agree how to conduct the business of the company. The decisions in *Metyor Inc* and in *Fiduciary* establish that a grant of leave is a suitable means by which to resolve deadlocks of that kind."

A clear example of two conflicting decisions in this area may be illustrated in *Vlahos v. Vlahos* and *Blakeney v. Blakeney*.[65] In *Vlahos v. Vlahos*, the case involved an urgent application that the applicant, Andrew, needed to apply for an appeal to the Court of Appeal on behalf of the company on a matter relating to an order made by the County Court granting his brother, James, an entitlement to 22.57% in the value of the property purchased by the company some years previously. In the County Court, a declaration order was made that the company held the property on a resulting trust in favour of James the plaintiff who argued that he contributed 22.57% of the purchase price. Andrew and James were two equal shareholders and the only directors in the trustee company, which was established by their late father. One of the arguments put forward by the applicant seeking leave to bring a derivative action was that the trustee company had a duty to recover trust property belonging to the trust.[66] In granting leave, Digby J agreed with that submission, saying that

63 *Talisman Technologies Inc. v. Queensland Electronic Switching Pty Ltd* [2001] QSC 324.

64 *Metyor Inc (formerly Talisman Technologies Inc) v. Queensland Electronic Switching Pty Ltd* [2002] QCA 269, at [10] and 11 (McPherson JA, Williams and Wilson JJA agreeing). See also *Knights Quest Pty Ltd v. Barokes Pty Ltd* [2016] VSC 296, at [60] (Sifris J).

65 *Vlahos v. Vlahos* [2016] VSC 824; Cf *Blakeney v. Blakeney* [2016] WASCA 76 (Full Court) and *Blakeney v. Blakeney* [2015] WASC 73 (First instance).

66 *Vlahos v. Vlahos* [2016] VSC 824, at [39]

"the trustee's obligation to maintain the trust assets against misappropriation or erroneous alienation is ... action taken in the best interests or welfare of a trustee company".[67]

In contrast, in *Blakeney v. Blakeney*, two brothers came together as business partners and both were equal shareholders and the only directors in the trustee company. This case also involved a trust property held in trust, and the two brothers were the only beneficiaries. One of them sought leave to bring an SDA to settle their differences in relation to the ownership of the trust property. The trial judge found that it was in the best interests of the company that a derivative action be allowed in order to resolve a deadlock between two business partners. However, the Court of Appeal in Western Australia reversed the decision on the basis that:[68]

- as trustee, the company would have no beneficial entitlement in the proposed action;
- as beneficiary in the trust, the applicant's participation in the proposed action would result in a conflict of duties with the trustee company; and
- there were at least three other options available to the applicant, namely applying for appointment of a new trustee, commencing an action on behalf of the trust or commencing an action in his own name seeking a declaration against the other director for breach of contract.

It is difficult to see how the decision *Blakeney v. Blakeney* can be reconciled with cases such as *Henry v. Western Downs Group Ltd*[69] and *Vlahos v. Vlahos*. In *Blakeney*, the WA Court of Appeal took into account the fact that the applicant was a beneficiary was a ground for deciding that an SDA would not be suitable. In *Henry v. Western Downs Group Ltd*, the applicant being a beneficiary was not an issue. The company was incorporated as a charitable trustee to distribute benefits to the native title claimants under the indigenous land use agreement. The applicant was one of the many beneficiary claimants seeking leave to bring a derivative action against the board of directors for breach of their duties. Barrett J of the Federal Court of Australia granted leave and there was no issue raised in relation to a perceived conflict of duties or the corporate trustee not having any beneficial entitlement in the SDA. Perhaps the distinguishable fact in *Henry* is that the leave application involved a large pool of beneficiary claimants, which could possibly indicate that the proposed action was in the best interests of the company.

67 *Vlahos v. Vlahos* [2016] VSC 824, at [46] (Digby J).

68 *Blakeney v. Blakeney* [2016] WASCA 76, at [79–84]. See also *Blakeney v. Blakeney* [2015] WASC 73 (first instance).

69 *Henry v. Western Downs Group Ltd* [2018] FCA 1168.

5.3.4 Availability of other or alternative remedies

A factor tended to take into account by the courts in deciding whether the proposed action "is in the best interests of the company" is whether other or alternative remedies are available to the applicant. However, there is no consistency in the way the courts have treated s.237(2)(c) in this area. In some cases, the court has tended to disallow a statutory derivative action.[70] For example, an applicant has commenced an oppression action[71] or some other form of personal action[72] or has applied for a winding up order,[73] or an alternative action has been identified as more suitable.[74] In *Zong v. Lin*, the plaintiff initiated three separate actions – an oppression claim, an application for a derivative action and a personal claim for breach of the shareholder agreement. In dismissing the appeal filed by the defendant, the New South Wales Court of Appeal approved the trial court's reasoning and rejected the personal claim and upheld the oppression action as being most appropriate and "least intrusive" to the company than the derivative action.[75]

In other cases, the court has no issue in bringing both the oppression claim and the leave application together and dealing with them at the same time, if possible.[76] It has been said that the court can determine the two cases together to decide whether the applicant's grievances should be categorised as one that is personal to the applicant and thus an oppression action is more appropriate,[77] or one in which only the company should have the right to bring an action.

There are also instances where the court has granted leave to bring a derivative action dealing with oppression issues subject to the applicant

70 *Jensen v. RQYS Marina Ltd* [2014] QSC 243, at [129] (appeal dismissed: *Jensen v. RQYS Marina Ltd* [2015] QCA 153, at [14] (Gotterson JA, Boddice and Flanagan JJ agreeing); *Ragless v. IPA Holdings Pty Ltd (in liq)* (2008) 65 ACSR 700; [2008] SASC 90 (Full Court), at para 35 (Debelle, Sulan and Vanstone JJ); *Swansson v. RA Pratt Pty Ltd* [2002] NSWSC 583, at [55–60].

71 *Victory Projects Pty Ltd v. AAA Self Storage Pty Ltd* [2016] NSWSC 1758.

72 See for example, *Swansson v. RA Pratt Pty Ltd* [2002] NSWSC 583 (claim already made in the Family Court for property settlement).

73 *In the Matter of Innovateq Pty Ltd* [2018] VSC 124, at [95–98] (the opposition filed a separate application for a winding up order on the "just and equitable" ground). See also *Galanopoulos v. Ali Moustafa* [2010] VSC 380.

74 *Blakeney v. Blakeney* [2016] WASCA 76 (three other options identified as available to the applicant as per earlier discussion). See also *Jensen v. RQYS Marina Ltd* [2015] QCA 153 (suggesting the applicants bring an oppression action because the 93-page pleadings were mostly about allegations of oppressive conduct).

75 *Zong v. Lin* [2022] NSWCA 136, at [79] (Gleeson JA, with Leeming JA and Kirk JA concurring).

76 *In the Matter of Jimmy's Recipe Pty Ltd* [2018] NSWSC 1331, at [20] (Brereton J), citing *Gerard Cassegrain & Co Pty Ltd v. Cassegrain* [2010] NSWSC 91, at [124]; *Connective Services Pty Ltd v. Slea Pty Ltd* [2018] VSCA 229, at [118–119]; *True Value Solar Holdings Pty Ltd v. Fernandez* [2013] VSCA 27, at 19–20], [29]; *MG Corrosion Consultants Pty Ltd v. Vinciguerra* [2011] FCAFC 31, at [60] (North, McKerracher and Jagot JJ).

77 *Vadori v. AAV Plumbing Pty Ltd* [2010] NSWSC 274.

undertaking to bear all costs incurred by the company, in effect making the case look more like an oppression action rather than a derivative action.[78] In short, it is not always clear-cut that a particular proposed action is or is not in the best interests of the company.

Two cases may be used to illustrate the differences in the judicial approach in this area, *In the Matter of Innovateq Pty Ltd* (2018) and *Suh v. Cho* (2013).[79] In both cases, both business partners were in a deadlock for a considerable period, and they had both more or less abandoned the company. In the 2018 case, both shareholders were effectively competing in the same line of business against each other. One of them later sought leave to bring an SDA to sort out their differences. The other shareholder who opposed the leave application had, in turn, filed a separate application for a winding up order on the "just and equitable" ground under s.246(1)(k). The court held that in "a situation of ongoing unresolvable deadlock", a more appropriate solution would be to make an order for winding up the company,[80] in essence agreeing with the opposition that the applicant had not established the leave application for an SDA to be in the company's interests.[81] In contrast, in *Suh v. Cho*, the main difference was that there was no other concurrent action running alongside the leave application. The court noted that an application for a winding up order would have been more appropriate where the company had become deadlocked,[82] but decided that an SDA was still in the best interests of the company and granted leave subject to the applicant paying costs.[83]

Another example of the differences in the outcome may be seen in *Jensen v. RQYS Marina Ltd* and *Victory Projects Pty Ltd v. AAA Self Storage Pty Ltd*.[84] In both cases, a draft statement of claims filed in support of the leave application for an SDA was mostly about oppression. In *Jensen v. RQYS Marina Ltd*, the concern the court had was that none of the five applicants had offered to indemnify the company in their leave application to bring an SDA, and this was pivotal to the court's decision that the proposed action was not in the company's best interests.[85] The lower court suggested, and the Queensland Court of Appeal approved, that the applicants should consider bringing an oppression action instead, given their extensive allega-

78 *In the Matter of Jimmy's Recipe Pty Ltd* [2018] NSWSC 1331, at [27] (Brereton J). See also *True Value Solar Holdings Pty Ltd v. Fernandez* [2013] VSCA 27.

79 *In the Matter of Innovateq Pty Ltd* [2018] VSC 124; cf *Suh v. Cho* [2013] VSC 491.

80 *In the Matter of Innovateq Pty Ltd* [2018] VSC 124, at [96–98] (Kennedy J), citing *Galanopoulos v. Ali Moustafa* [2010] VSC 380, at [34].

81 *In the Matter of Innovateq Pty Ltd* [2018] VSC 124, at [88–90] (Kennedy J).

82 *Suh v. Cho* [2013] VSC 491, at [53].

83 *Suh v. Cho* [2013] VSC 491, at [55] (Derham AJ).

84 *Jensen v. RQYS Marina Ltd* [2015] QCA 153; Cf *Victory Projects Pty Ltd v. AAA Self Storage Pty Ltd* [2016] NSWSC 1758.

85 *Jensen v. RQYS Marina Ltd* [2014] QSC 243, at [121–123] (appeal dismissed: *Jensen v. RQYS Marina Ltd* [2015] QCA 153, at [14] (Gotterson JA, Boddice and Flanagan JJ agreeing).

tions of oppressive conduct in their pleadings.[86] In *Victory Projects Pty Ltd v. AAA Self Storage Pty Ltd*, the applicant had earlier commenced a separate personal action,[87] and relied on the same statement of claims for use in the leave application. The court went through those claims individually to assess whether there was an arguable case for relief under an oppression action and found that the applicant had not provided sufficient evidence to substantiate many of those oppression claims.[88] The court concluded that because it would be unlikely for the applicant to succeed in an oppression action that the proposed derivative action too would not be in the company's best interest.[89]

Vadori v. AAV Plumbing Pty Ltd[90] yields a different outcome to that in *Victory Projects Pty Ltd v. AAA Self Storage Pty Ltd.* All three shareholders were also directors. Following a dispute, two of them diverted company assets to their new entity. The third shareholder commenced an oppression action and applied for leave to bring an SDA. Wade J decided that an SDA would not be in the best interests of the company, even though there was strong evidence that the two directors had breached their duties to the company. Instead, the court granted an oppression remedy by ordering a compulsory buy-out of the other shareholders' interests.

One may contend that leave to bring an SDA may not be appropriate where a personal action is available because there is no need to bring a company into litigation against its will and disrupt its business. However, a counter argument may be seen in *MG Corrosion Consultants Pty Ltd v. Vinciguerra* where the Full Court of the Federal Court of Australia has stated:[91]

> "It is not a requirement under s.237(2) CA that oppression proceedings be unavailable to a shareholder. There would be no basis to conclude that an oppression action (as an alternative approach) would have less impact on [the company's] affairs than a statutory derivative action. It is no more in the interests of the company as a whole that an oppression action be brought rather than a derivative action be pursued."

86 *Jensen v. RQYS Marina Ltd* [2014] QSC 243, at [2], [129] (appeal dismissed: *Jensen v. RQYS Marina Ltd* [2015] QCA 153, at [14] (Gotterson JA, Boddice and Flanagan JJ agreeing).

87 *Victory Projects Pty Ltd v. AAA Self Storage Pty Ltd* [2016] NSWSC 1758.

88 *Victory Projects Pty Ltd v. AAA Self Storage Pty Ltd* [2016] NSWSC 1758, at [59–64] (Black J). The oppression provision is explained in Chapter 7.

89 *Victory Projects Pty Ltd v. AAA Self Storage Pty Ltd* [2016] NSWSC 1758, at [110], [145] (Black J). For a similar outcome, see *Mio Art Pty Ltd v. Macequest Pty Ltd* [2013] QSC 211, at [234–245]. In contrast, see *Re Legal Practice Management Group Pty Ltd* [2018] NSWSC 527, at [61].

90 *Vadori v. AAV Plumbing Pty Ltd* [2010] NSWSC 274.

91 *MG Corrosion Consultants Pty Ltd v. Vinciguerra* [2011] FCAFC 31, at [60] (North, McKerracher and Jagot JJ). See also *White (Trustee) v. MWL Financial Group Pty Ltd* [2018] FCA 2018, at [31] (Davies J).

It should be noted that s.236 in Note 3 permits an applicant to bring an SDA as well as any other proceedings on their own behalf in respect of a personal right.[92]

5.4 Further reasons for supporting amendment to s.237(2)(c)

This part explains three other problems with s.237(2)(c).

5.4.1 Overlapping effect with the criterion in s.237(2)(d)

Section 237(2)(d) is another criterion that an applicant must satisfy the court for leave to be granted to bring an SDA, that the applicant is required to establish "there is a serious question to be tried". The test has a low threshold of proof. It essentially means that the applicant is required to show that there is an "arguable case",[93] or a case that has "sufficient likelihood of success to justify a grant of leave".[94] In a leave application, the court is not required to go into "any great degree" in determining the merits of the proposed action.[95]

As reported in the empirical study in Chapter 3, s.237(2)(d) does not seem to cause any major issue for the applicant. The courts only need to know what the claims are and whether those claims have merit for the case to be brought to trial. These is "no requirement for the court to make factual determinations about contested issues".[96]

There is a considerable overlap between demonstrating the proposed action "is in the best interests of the company" under s.237(2)(c) and showing there is an arguable case under s.237(2)(d),[97] and this poses a serious con-

92 Section 236 Note 3 states that the section "does not prevent a person bringing, or intervening in, proceedings on their own behalf in respect of a personal right". The oppression remedy is considered further in Chapter 7.

93 *Re Gladstone Pacific Nickel Limited* [2011] NSWSC 1235, at [57] (Ball J); *Fiduciary Ltd v. Morningstar Research Pty Ltd* [2005] NSWSC 442, at [40] (Austin J).

94 *Ragless v. IPA Holdings Pty Ltd (in liq)* (2008) 65 ACSR 700; [2008] SASC 90, at [40] (Debelle J, Sulan and Vanstone JJ agreeing), citing a High Court of Australia decision in *Australian Broadcasting Corporation v. O'Neill* (2006) 227 CLR 57 in the context of an interlocutory injunction application. See also Li *v. Dao* [2018] VSC 530, at [119] (Connock J); *In the Matter of Innovateq Pty Ltd* [2018] VSC 124, at [79] (Kennedy J), citing *South Johnston Mill Ltd v. Dennis* (2007) FCR 343; [2007] FCA 1448, at [80] (Middleton J); *Slea Pty Ltd v. Connective Services Pty Ltd* [2017] VSC 609, at [175] (Robson J).

95 *Li v. Dao* [2018] VSC 530, at [115] (Robson J), citing *Swansson v. RA Pratt* [2002] NSWSC 583, at [25] (Palmer J); *Ehsman v. Nutectim International Pty Ltd* (2006) 58 ACSR 705; [2006] NSWSC 887, at [58] (Austin J); *Maher v. Honeysett & Maher Electrical Contractors Pty Ltd* [2005] NSWSC 859, at [19] (Brereton J).

96 *South Johnston Mill Ltd v. Dennis* (2007) FCR 343; [2007] FCA 1448, at [80] (Middleton J). See also *Slea Pty Ltd v. Connective Services Pty Ltd* [2017] VSC 609, at [175] (Robson J); *In the Matter of Innovateq Pty Ltd* [2018] VSC 124, at [79] (Kennedy J).

97 *Vinciguerra v. MG Corrosion Consultants Pty Ltd* [2010] FCA 763, at [114] (Gilmour J); *Carpenter v. Pioneer Park Pty Limited* (2004) 51 ACSR 299; [2004] NSWSC 1007; at [10] (Barrett J).

cern, in that the former has a very high threshold of proof while the latter has a low threshold. Furthermore, the courts have repeatedly stated that a leave application is not a trial within a trial.[98] In *MG Corrosion Consultants Pty Ltd v. Vinciguerra*, the Full Federal Court of Australia has stated:[99]

> "there would be no point in conducting the derivative action if all the facts needed to be established in the derivative action had already been proven in the leave application. It would turn the leave application into a trial. There is no basis for thinking that this was the legislative intention when the amendments were introduced in 2000."

Similarly, in *Zhu v. Orico Australia Pty Ltd*, Connock J has added:[100]

> "When addressing the criterion of serious question to be tried in s.237(2)(d) of the Act, care must be taken not to allow the task to descend into a forensic exercise of the kind that would occur at trial rather than on an application for leave to proceed. Although sufficient evidence is required for an applicant to discharge the onus regarding the existence of a serious question to be tried, it does not follow that an applicant is required to bring forward all of the evidence that might be presented on the issue at trial."

The problem revolves around the amount of evidence that an applicant is permitted to present a case for leave to bring an SDA; more importantly, to satisfy the court of the requirement in s.237(2)(c). At one end of the spectrum, an applicant is advised to provide only enough evidence to establish there is an arguable case under s.237(2)(d); and at the other end of the spectrum, an applicant is severely restricted in the presentation of full evidence to show the proposed action "is in the best interests of the company" under s.237(2)(c). A better approach would be that if an applicant has proven there is "sufficient likelihood of success" under s.237(2)(d), this should be enough to show that the proposed action is meritorious and not frivolous or vexatious, and that the proposed action is in the company's interests for the purposes of granting leave.

It is important to remember that an application for leave is not about apportioning liabilities or making a judgment on the alleged wrong. An application for leave is at a preliminary stage, and at this stage, not everyone, even the applicant, has the ability to gather enough evidence to prove that the

98 *MG Corrosion Consultants Pty Ltd v. Vinciguerra* [2011] FCAFC 31, at [59] (North, McKerracher and Jagot JJ). See also *Blakeney v. Blakeney* [2016] WASCA 76, at 58] (Buss and Murphy JJA and Beech J).

99 *MG Corrosion Consultants Pty Ltd v. Vinciguerra* [2011] FCAFC 31, at [67] (North, McKerracher and Jagot JJ).

100 *Zhu v. Orico Australia Pty Ltd* [2019] VSC 313, at [99] (Connock J).

proposed action is in the company's best interests. Shareholders who have no direct role in the management of the company have an even harder battle in gathering precise evidence to mount a leave application.

It is worth noting briefly that in Canada and Singapore, their SDAs do not require an applicant to establish "there is a serious question to be tried"; but rather, their corresponding provision, relating to the "interests of the company", is more about whether there is an arguable case for leave to be granted to bring an SDA, as will be explained further in Part 5 below.

5.4.2 Uncertainty in the application of s.237(2)(c) in company liquidation

A further concern is the uncertainty in the application of s.237(2)(c) where a company is already in liquidation. It is not clear whether, and to what extent, a shareholder derivative action is possible under s.237(2)(c) in this situation. When a company has become insolvent and a liquidator has been appointed to wind up the company, and when leave is granted to bring an SDA under s.237(2)(c), this could, in effect, turn the matter into a situation where the shareholder applicant will be competing with creditors for recoveries. The SDA provisions have not addressed the issue of insolvency.

Some courts have decided that s.237(2)(c) is not applicable to shareholders where a company has been placed into liquidation,[101] other courts have held that s.237(2)(c) was applicable,[102] and one court was unsure of the position.[103] The NSW Court of Appeal in *Chahwan v. Euphoric Pty Ltd* provides its view as to why s.237(2)(c) cannot be used in company liquidation:[104]

> "As the court has no discretion to refuse leave where the requirements of s.237(2) are satisfied, there is a significant potential for conflict with the established notion recognised in the Act of the overriding control by the court under Ch 5 over the whole of the winding up process of an insolvent company, including the conduct of the liquidator. That control would be lost or at least diminished given the mandatory terms of ... s.237(2) if it were to apply to such a company."

101 *Chahwan v Euphoric Pty Ltd* [2008] NSWCA 52; (2008) 65 ACSR 661; *Ragless v. IPA Holdings Pty Ltd (in liq)* (2008) 65 ACSR 700; [2008] SASC 90 (Court of Appeal decision); *BL & GY International Co Ltd v. Hypec Electronics Pty Ltd* (2001) 164 FLR 268; [2001] NSWSC 705; *Promaco Conventions Pty Ltd v. Dedline Printing Pty Ltd* (2007) 159 FLR 486; *Re Sundara Pty Ltd* [2015] NSWSC 1694.

102 *Roach v. Winnote Pty Ltd (in liq)* [2001] NSWSC 822; *Brightwell v. RFB Holdings Pty Ltd (in liq)* (2003) 44 ACSR 186; *Charlton v. Baber* (2003) 47 ACSR 31; [2003] NSWSC 745; *Kamper v. Applied Soil Technology Pty Ltd* (2004) 211 ALR 337; [2004] NSWSC 891.

103 *HPM Pty Ltd v. Fear* (2002) 171 FLR 12; [2002] WASCA 249, at [18] (Steytler J, with Malcolm CJ and Murray J agreeing).

104 *Chahwan v. Euphoric Pty Ltd* [2008] NSWCA 52, at [121] (Tobias JA, with whom Beazley and Bell JJA agreed).

One reason why s.237(2)(c) is unworkable in matters relating to a company in liquidation stems from the ambiguity in the interpretation of the provision discussed earlier; namely lack of clarity in the terms "company" and "best interests". Section 237(2)(c) has no reference to the company "in liquidation", so it is not clear whether the provision can be used in such cases. The other possible explanation is that by requiring an applicant to demonstrate the proposed action to be in the best interests of the company, it means that the applicant must demonstrate that they are willing and prepared to act wholeheartedly on behalf of the creditors and that they will push aside their own personal interests. This is not possible, in practice, to expect an applicant to sacrifice their own interests and act only in the interests of creditors, unless the company is only marginally insolvent and there is still a chance for shareholders to obtain some recovery through that process.[105]

To overcome this difficulty, the courts have exercised their *inherent discretion* under the insolvency provisions[106] to grant the applicant leave to bring a shareholder derivative action,[107] but this is only possible if:[108]

(a) there is no or only minimal outstanding debt owing to the creditors;
(b) there is a possibility that the applicant can obtain a better recovery for the company in the shareholder derivative action than the liquidator can;
(c) the liquidator has approved the proposed derivative action or at least indicated that it will not oppose the leave application; and
(d) more importantly, the applicant has undertaken to bear all costs and expenses incurred in bringing the shareholder derivative action and to indemnify the company against any adverse costs liability.

105 For discussion on the extent in which the courts have granted leave for shareholders derivative action in company liquidation, see Lang Thai, "Calling for reform to the statutory derivative action in Australia: Critical analysis and suggestions for reform" (2013) 21 *Insolvency Law Journal* 242, at 255–258; Geoffrey Egert, Colin Anderson and Scott Kiel-Chisholm, "The application of the statutory derivative action in Pt 2F.1A of the Corporations Act to companies in liquidation under Ch 5: Well oiled machine or is Pt 2F.1A in need of a tune up?" (2011) 25 *Australian Journal of Corporate Law* 318, at 328–344.

106 Section 477(6) of the *Corporations Act* 2001 (C'th) provides the court with the power to authorise "any creditor or contributor" or ASIC to bring legal proceedings in the name of the company in liquidation, and s.511(1) states that "any creditor or contributor" is entitled to apply to the court to "determine any question arising in the winding up of a company".

107 *Manny v. David Lardner Lawyers* (No 2) [2022] ACTCA 13; *Challis v. Hoffman* [2017] NSWSC 870; 121 ACSR 585, at [28–29]; *Re Wan Ze Property Development (Australia) Pty Ltd* [2013] NSWSC 1977; *Ragless v. IPA Holdings Pty Ltd (in liq)* (2008) 65 ACSR 700; [2008] SASC 90 (Court of Appeal decision); *Pearl Coast Divers Pty Ltd v. Cossack Pearls Pty Ltd* (2008) 249 ALR 591; [2008] FCA 927.

108 *Re Colorado Products Pty Ltd* [2014] NSWSC 64, at [9]; *Re Sundara Pty Ltd* [2015] NSWSC 1694, at [77–79]; *Re Staway Pty Ltd (in liq.)* [2013] NSWSC 819, at [24–25]; *Carpenter v. Pioneer Park Pty Ltd* [2008] NSWSC 551, at [23–36].

Currently, s.237(2)(c) has limited use when a company goes into insolvency. Amendment to s.237(2)(c) is necessary to clarify its operation with insolvency law. Just because the courts have exercised their inherent jurisdiction to permit shareholder derivative action, this has not resolved the underlying problems with regard to competing interests between the shareholder applicant and the creditors. The courts are seen to allow shareholder derivative action in liquidation under strict conditions.

5.4.3 Problem suing a related third party under s.237(3)

Section 237(3) provides a rebuttable presumption that granting leave is not in the best interests of the company if the proposed action involves a "third party" and the directors' decision not to litigate meets the criteria in s.237(3)(c). For the presumption to arise, the directors must: (i) act in good faith; (ii) not have a material personal interest in the decision; (iii) properly inform themselves about the subject matter in which the decision is made; and (iv) rationally believe that not initiating an action is in the best interests of the company.

The presumption does not apply where a third party is someone related to the directors or a third party is a related party. The difficulty arises where a third party is a former director against whom an applicant wishes to take a derivative action (for example, for breach of directors' duties).

A "third party" is defined in s.237(4) as someone who is not a related party, and in turn, s.228(5) defines "related party" to include a former director within the first six months of his or her departure from the company. This means that if a former director has departed from the company more than six months ago, the presumption is that an application for leave to bring an SDA against the former director is not in the best interests of the company, unless the applicant can rebut the presumption under s.237(3)(c). In short, it is harder for an applicant to bring an SDA against a former director/third party (for example, for breach of director's duties) if the board of directors in the company has decided not to initiate an action against a former fellow director. This could be a significant hurdle for an applicant. For example, a non-director shareholder who suspects a breach of directors' duties may need to act quickly in gathering evidence and applying for leave within the first six months of the director's resignation from the company, otherwise the applicant will be faced with the need to rebut the presumption in s.237(3).

It has been said that s.237(3) is necessary to prevent shareholder interference in the directors' management and to prevent unmeritorious and frivolous actions.[109] However, it is difficult to see how s.237(3) could be viewed as such. If the facts are clear and the proposed derivative action is in

109 House of Representatives, *Explanatory Memorandum to the CLERP Bill* 1998 (C'th), at 22, [6.41].

the best interests of the company, then it is irrelevant whether an applicant applies for leave before or after the six-month period; the core facts of the case and the nature of claims will not change. There may be times when an applicant needs extra time to gather evidence, for example, applying for an inspection of company documents under s.247A to determine the strength of the case.

The author's submission is that s.237(3) seems to further limit a shareholder's opportunity to pursue a derivative action. A former director may have resigned from the company with a golden handshake approved by the board of directors, and there may be very little that a non-director shareholder can do about it, especially in a situation where they suspect a breach of directors' duties by the former director, and they have difficulty obtaining company information to confirm that suspicion.

Case law in this area is scarce, and this is not surprising given the extra layer of difficulty that a minority shareholder has to go through in order to get the case up and running. Empirical research in Chapter 3 shows only 6.5% of leave applications involved a former director as the proposed defendant. The court has indicated some uncertainty in the application of s.237(3) when a related third party is involved.[110] In *Pentridge Village Pty Ltd (in liq) v. Capital Finance Australia Ltd*, suggestion was made that the onus is not on the applicant to rebut the presumption but held that s.237(3) was not relevant in the present case as the liquidator had initiated the action.[111] It is also not clear whether the presumption in s.237(3) is applicable in a situation where a company has two equal shareholders who are also the only directors in the company. For example, in *In the Matter of Innovateq Pty Ltd*, due to a deadlock, one of the two directors sought employment elsewhere and effectively abandoned the company. After an extended period, the remaining director sought leave of the court to bring an SDA. In opposition, the proposed defendant filed an application for a winding up order. There was no mention of s.237(3); instead, the court applied s.237(2)(c) in the usual way and held that the proposed action would not be in the best interests of the company as a winding up application had commenced.[112]

110 See, for example, *Chahwan v. Euphoric Pty Ltd* (2008) 65 ACSR 661; [2008] NSWCA 52, at [107–122] (Tobias JA, Beazley and Bell JJA agreeing) (discussing the difficulties whether s.237(3) applies only where the company is a going concern or whether it is also applicable to a company in liquidation, citing *Roach v. Winnote Pty Ltd (in liq)* [2001] NSWSC 822 at [20], (Santow J) and contrasting it with *Kamper v. Applied Soil Technology Pty Ltd* (2004) 211 ALR 337; [2004] NSWSC 891, at [11] (Einstein J).

111 *Pentridge Village Pty Ltd (in liq.) v. Capital Finance Australia Ltd* [2018] VSC 633, at [282] (Connock J). Also in *Chahwan v. Euphoric Pty Ltd* (2008) 65 ACSR 661; [2008] NSWCA 52, at [121] (Tobias JA, Beazley and Bell JJA agreeing), it was said that s.237(3) presumption cannot be used as protection for directors where a company is in the control of the liquidator.

112 *In the Matter of Innovateq Pty Ltd* [2018] VSC 124; *Cf Suh v. Cho* [2013] VSC 491.

The criteria in s.237(3)(c) are almost an exact replica of the four requirements of the business judgment rule in s.180(2) of the CA,[113] which operates as a defence mechanism for directors to protect themselves against an alleged breach of duty of care and diligence.[114] In other words, if directors rationally believe they have discharged their duty of care and diligence when making a business decision, in the sense that they have met the four requirements under s.180(2), the presumption will apply to protect their position; and so a minority shareholder has the burden of rebutting that presumption.[115] Similarly, in the context of s.237(3), if the board of directors has decided not to initiate proceedings against a former director who has become known as a "third party", then their decision is final and is not easily challengeable in most cases. This is a problem faced by a shareholder applicant when attempting to seek leave to bring an SDA against a former director.

5.5 Where to from here?

5.5.1 Preliminary

This part puts forward some suggestions for law reform in an attempt to provide shareholders with better protection under the SDA framework, and more importantly, to achieve its intended purposes, which are to bring directors to account for their improper conduct in the company and thereby to improve and maintain corporate governance. To this end, it may be helpful to briefly examine the corresponding provisions from Canada, British Columbia (a province in Canada) and Singapore to see how Australia may be able to learn from these jurisdictions.

These jurisdictions are chosen because their provisions are different from one another, and they all have a much lower threshold in terms of requiring an applicant to only show that the proposed action appears to be in the interests of the company. Furthermore, their courts have also given effect to that low threshold. In addition, there appears to be no sign of systemic abuse of the SDA in these regions.

113 Section 180(2) provides a presumption that a director has made a good business judgment if they: (a) act in good faith for a proper purpose; (b) have no material personal interest in the subject matter; (c) have informed themselves about the subject matter to the extent they reasonably believe to be appropriate; and (d) rationally believe the judgment is in the company's best interests. Basically, this "business judgment rule" protects a director against an alleged breach of a duty of care and diligence under s.180(1).

114 Section 180(1) refers to directors' duty of care and diligence.

115 For further discussion on s.180(2), see, for example, Justice Geoffrey Nettle, "The changing position and duties of company directors" (2018) 41 *Melbourne University Law Review* 1402; Wesley Bainbridge and Tim Connor, "Another way forward? The scope for an appellate court to reinterpret the statutory business judgment rule" (2016) 34 *Company and Securities Law Journal* 415; Jason Harris and Anil Hargovan, "Still a sleepy hollow? Directors' liability and the business judgment rule" (2016) 31 *Australian Journal of Corporate Law* 319.

It is worth noting that prior to the introduction of the SDA, the Canadian provision was put forward as recommendation for Australia.[116] It is not clear why that provision was rejected in favour of the current strict requirement. There was no explanation given.

5.5.2 Other jurisdictions with "interests of the company" test

5.5.2.1 Canada and British Columbia[117]

The examples from Canada and British Columbia are particularly important for Australia for two reasons. First, although Canada is a country, many of its provinces have adopted the federal *Canada Business Corporations Act* 1985 in respect to the SDA,[118] while British Columbia has chosen to have different provisions in its legislation; of particular relevance is in relation to "in the interests of the company" (Canada) and "in the best interests of the company" (British Columbia). Second, even though there is a slight difference in the legislative provisions between British Columbia and the rest of the other provinces in Canada, the courts in British Columbia appear to have borrowed the judicial interpretation from other provinces and apply it as part of their interpretation of their legislative provision. In other words, there is no real difference in the judicial interpretation regardless of whether the legislation says the proposed action "appears to be in the interests of the company" (Canada) or whether it says the proposed action "appears to be in the *best* interests of the company" (British Columbia). For ease of reference, these provisions are reproduced in Appendix D and Appendix E.

Under the Canadian model, for a court to grant leave to commence an SDA, a complainant is only required to satisfy the court of three requirements, one of which is that the proposed derivative action "appears to be in the interests of the corporation".[119] In Canada, the question of whether the proposed derivation action "appears to be in the interests of the company" also encompasses the Australian fourth criterion "there is a serious question is be tried" in s.237(2)(d). This is essentially about whether there is "an arguable case" for it to go to trial.

In *Jahnke v. Johnson*,[120] the Saskatchewan Court of Appeal observes, with approval, that different courts have used different phrases to explain how

116 CSLRC, *Enforcement of the Duties of Directors and Officers of a Company by means of a Statutory Derivative Action* (Discussion Paper No 11, 1990).

117 British Columbia is a province in Canada.

118 For example, Ontario, Alberta, Saskatchewan and Newfoundland.

119 *Canada Business Corporations Act* RSC 1985 Chapter C-44, s.239(2)(c). The other two requirements are that the complainant has given fourteen days' notice to the company directors before applying for leave in s.239(2)(a) and the complainant "is acting in good faith" in s.239(2)(b). The applicant in Canada also has the onus of proof in the leave application: *Re Bellman and Western Approaches Ltd* (1981) 130 DLR (3d) 193.

120 *Jahnke v. Johnson*, 2018 SKCA 59.

a judge should determine whether a proposed action "appears to be in the interests of the company":[121]

> "Numerous cases have attempted to explain how a judge should determine whether a proposed action 'appears to be in the interests of the company' by framing the relevant test in terms of the apparent strength or merit of the proposed action. In this regards, courts have used terminology such as 'an arguable issue worthy of trial' ..., 'a reasonable argument which would not be dismissed out of hand' ... 'a claim that does not appear frivolous or vexatious or is bound to be unsuccessful' ... , and 'whether the proposed action has a reasonable prospect of success or is bound to fail'."

The court goes on to provide some examples of when a proposed action would not be in the interests of the company:[122]

> "I have in mind ... situations such as those where an action will cost far more to prosecute than it can possibly yield in damages, where pursuing a claim will harm important and ongoing business relationships, or where going to court will general problematic publicity for the corporation. ... This is not a new idea. ... while the strength of the proposed action is the central consideration ... Thus, it is not the only, consideration or, necessarily, the deciding consideration."

The leave application in this case involves breaches of directors' duties and unjust enrichment. The company, Sask Corp, purchased property for development but then encountered financial problems and was unable to continue with the project. The complainant agreed with the other directors to sell back his shares to Sask Corp at a nominal price so that those shares could be used to secure a third party loan, with an understanding that in return he would receive 30% profit once the property development had completed. The profit sharing agreement was not in writing. Instead, Sask Corp continued to experience financial problems and was dissolved about a year later. The main issue was whether the proposed derivative action would be in the interests of the company. In refusing to grant leave, the court held that the complainant's motivating concern was not protecting the interests of the company but attempting to enforce the bargain he claimed to have made verbally with one of the directors for the sale of his shares.[123]

121 *Jahnke v. Johnson*, 2018 SKCA 59, at [64] (Richards CJ, with Caldwell and Whitmore JJA agreeing).
122 *Jahnke v. Johnson*, 2018 SKCA 59, at [68].
123 *Jahnke v. Johnson*, 2018 SKCA 59, at [18], [22] (Richards CJ, with Caldwell and Whitmore JJA agreeing).

Budd v. Bertram is about whether the court was required to conduct a costs/benefits analysis in determining whether the proposed action "appears to be in the interests of the company".[124] The complainants, with 25% shares in the energy company, were successful in obtaining leave of the court to bring an SDA. They claimed that the directors had breached their fiduciary duties when they failed to consider business proposals from two reputable energy developers and considered Spray Energy's proposal instead without adequate information. The proposed defendants, all of whom were directors, appealed against that decision on the ground that the court at first instance had failed to conduct a costs/benefits analysis as part of a test that the proposed action "appears to be in the interests of the company". In dismissing the appeal, the Nova Scotia Court of Appeal considered a long list of case law in this area,[125] and ruled that the costs/benefits analysis in not necessary in all cases:[126]

> "another consideration should be the financial effect on the company of the proposed action proceeding or not proceeding. ... earning a profit is in the company's interest. However, there may be cases where a consideration of costs and benefits will be less important, for instance where the issue is whether directors are in breach of their fiduciary duties due to being in a conflict of interest position."

This approach was applied recently in *Barrett v. Ballott*. In granting leave to bring an SDA and awarding costs in favour of the applicant, the court in Newfoundland states that a "consideration of costs and benefits is not as important where, as in the case before me, there is an arguable case for breach of fiduciary duty due to a conflict of interests position".[127]

To sum up, the two important propositions from these three Canadian cases are:

- Their test for whether the proposed derivative action "appears to be in the interests of the company" is the same as asking whether there is "an arguable case" or "a reasonable prospect of success", which indicates that the threshold is low; and
- The costs/benefits analysis of a proposed action is not necessary in all cases, especially where claims in the proposed action are about breaches of directors' duties.

124 *Budd v. Bertram*, 2018, NSCA 95.
125 *Budd v. Bertram*, 2018, NSCA 95, at [34–45] (Hamilton JA, with Derrick and Scanlan JJA agreeing).
126 *Budd v. Bertram*, 2018, NSCA 95, at [46], citing *Richardson Greenfields of Canada Ltd v. Kalmacoff*, ONCA, 1995 OJ 941, at [32].
127 *Barrett v. Ballott*, 2019, NLSC 82, at [117] (Marshall J).

Turning now to the law in British Columbia ("BC"), a complainant applying for leave to bring an SDA is required to satisfy the court of four requirements, one of which is that the proposed derivative action "appears to the court that it is in the best interests of the company".[128] Unlike in Australia, the courts in BC have treated "in the best interests of the company" to be the same as "in the interests of the corporation". This low threshold of proof is indicated by the word "appears" in the provision. Abrioux J in the Supreme Court of BC in *Jordan Enterprises Ltd v. Barker*,[129] and citing a Court of Appeal decision from the same jurisdiction in *Gartenberg v. Consolidated Stone Industries Inc*,[130] states the law in the following terms:[131]

> "When embarking on an analysis of the principles pertaining to 'the best interests of the company', the threshold for the applicant to meet is that there is an *arguable case* that the derivative action is in the interest of the corporation."

This statement implies that there is no real difference between "appears to the court that it is in the best interests of the company" in the BC provision and "appears to be in the interests of the corporation" in the Canada provision. The term "appears to the court" indicates "whether the proposed action has a reasonable prospect of success", which is the same as asking whether a case is "arguable",[132] which in effect, means the onus on the applicant to satisfy this requirement is low. In relation to "best interest", Abrioux J has described it as "a more rigid consideration of what is good for the corporation than what would be required under "interest"; an example could be maximising the company's value.[133] In short, the courts in Canada treat these SDA provisions in a similar way.

In *Jordan Enterprises Ltd v. Barker*, Bickerstaff ("complainant") filed an application for leave to bring an SDA against Barker for alleged breaches of directors' duties, misappropriation of company funds and breach of contract. The company founded by Jordan was a property developer and had been operating for many years. Barker later became 50% shareholder in the company, with Jordan holding the other 50%. Agreement was in place that Barker would have control of daily management and Jordan would provide financial backing for the company to undertake development projects. The complainant, a new director appointed to the company in place of Jordan who retired

128 *Business Corporations Act*, SBC 2002, Chapter 57 (British Columbia), s.233(1)(d).

129 *Jordan Enterprises Ltd v. Barker* 2015, BCSC 559.

130 *Gartenberg v. Consolidated Stone Industries Inc*. 2005 BCCA 462, at [26].

131 *Jordan Enterprises Ltd v. Barker* 2015, BCSC 559 at [33] (Abrioux J) (emphasis added). See also *Gill v. Kalgidhar Darbar Sahib Society*, 2018 BCSC 813, at [46].

132 *Jordan Enterprises Ltd v. Barker* 2015, BCSC 559 at [35–36]; *Luft v. Ball* 2013, BCSC 574 at [54]; *Holdyk v. Adolph* 2012, BCCA 37 at [19]; *Carr v. Cheng* 2005 BCSC 445, at [21].

133 *Jordan Enterprises Ltd v. Barker* 2015, BCSC 559 at [38].

in his eighties, became concerned when he discovered some discrepancies in the financial documents, which led him to raise the matter and pursue an SDA. Jordan also commenced an oppression action. One of the issues was whether the proposed derivative action "appears to the court to be in the best interests of the company". The court found that Barker had no explanation for the missing funds or the other allegations made in the complaint.[134] Abrioux J in the BC Supreme Court ordered that a derivative action would be in the best interests of the company in the circumstances and concluded that the proposed action be set for trial at the same time as Jordan's personal action and that the complainant's costs of the leave application be awarded.

In summary, despite the slight variation in the legislative provisions ("best interests of the company" in British Columbia and "interests of the company" in other parts of Canada), the courts in British Columbia seem to have adopted a similar approach to the rest of Canada, treating both provisions to be the same. Thus, whether a proposed action "appears to be in the interests of the company" is treated the same as asking whether there is an arguable case or a reasonable prospect of success as to amount to being meritorious and non-vexatious. Their approaches are different to the Australian counterpart and less strict on the applicant.

5.5.2.2 Singapore

Singapore has approached this area of law similarly to Canada. For a court to grant leave in Singapore, a complainant is only required to satisfy the court of three requirements,[135] and for the purpose of this chapter, s.216A(3)(c) provides that the complainant is to show that the proposed derivative action "appears to be prima facie in the interests of the company".[136] Similar to Canada, there is no separate provision relating to "there is a serious question to be tried" as there is in Australia. The standard of proof for the requirement that the proposed derivative action "appears to be prima facie in the interests of the company" is equivalent to showing that the company's claim is "legitimate and arguable" and that it must not be frivolous, vexatious or bound to be unsuccessful.[137] Similar to Canada, it has been said that this standard is "low and only the most obviously unmeritorious claims will be culled".[138]

134 *Jordan Enterprises Ltd v. Barker* 2015, BCSC 559 at [53–59].

135 *Companies Act* (Singapore, chapter 50, 2006, revised ed), s.216A(3). This and other provisions relevant to the Singapore SDA are reproduced in Appendix C.

136 *Companies Act* (Singapore, chapter 50, 2006, revised ed), s.216A(3)(c). Similar wording is seen in Hong Kong: *Companies Ordinance* (chapter 32) (Hong Kong), Part IVAA, s.168BC(3)(a).

137 *Ang Thiam Swee v. Low Hian Chor* [2013] 2 SLR 340; [2013] SGCA 11, at [53–54] (the main issue in this case was about "good faith" and since the applicant was unable to demonstrate good faith, the Singapore Court of Appeal did not consider necessary to examine s.216A(3)(c) in detail.)

138 *Ang Thiam Swee v. Low Hian Chor* [2013] 2 SLR 340; [2013] SGCA 11, at [55]. See also *Ganesh Paulraj v. A & T Offshore Pte Ltd* [2019] SGHC 180, at [36].

Since only affidavits are available to the court in the leave application, the court is "not required to make an extensive enquiry into the merits of the claim and should not be drawn into an adjudication on the disputed facts".[139]

For example, in *Ganesh Paulraj v. A & T Offshore Pte Ltd*,[140] the court granted leave on the basis that there was some evidence of substantial unpaid debts owing to the company. The fact that the applicant had proven good faith in making the leave application led the court to conclude that the proposed action was "*prima facie* in the interests of the [company] as it was not so unmeritorious that it should be rejected out of hand at this point".[141]

Chan Tong Fan v. Chiam Heng Luan Realty Pte Ltd was about alleged breaches of directors' duties.[142] The court dealt with the "interests of the company" requirement first, stating that the applicant had a "two-fold burden of proving" (i) there is a reasonable basis for the complaint and a legitimate or arguable action against the proposed defendants; and (ii) the proposed action appears to be in the interests of the company.[143] It was held that of the six proposed actions, only one was of sufficient objective merit, and this fact alone was sufficient to satisfy the interests of the company requirement, and hence leave was granted.[144]

It is worth noting that the courts in Hong Kong have approached their SDA in the same way as the Singapore counterpart, that the threshold for an SDA is for an applicant to establish the proposed action "appears to be prima facie in the interests of the company",[145] which is low. The courts will only consider whether there is an arguable case,[146] and whether the company will suffer any prejudice from the proposed action.[147] It is also worth noting that since 2008, an applicant who is successful in obtaining leave of the court to bring an SDA is permitted to also bring multiple derivative actions against the same wrongdoer(s) who had control in other subsidiary companies.[148]

139 *Ganesh Paulraj v. A & T Offshore Pte Ltd* [2019] SGHC 180, at [36] (Acdit Abdullah J), citing *Urs Meisterhans v. GIP Pte Ltd* [2011] 1 SLR 552, at [25].
140 *Ganesh Paulraj v. A & T Offshore Pte Ltd* [2019] SGHC 180.
141 *Ganesh Paulraj v. A & T Offshore Pte Ltd* [2019] SGHC 180, at [8] (Acdit Abdullah J).
142 *Chan Tong Fan v. Chiam Heng Luan Realty Pte Ltd* [2013] SGHC 192.
143 *Chan Tong Fan v. Chiam Heng Luan Realty Pte Ltd* [2013] SGHC 192, at [33].
144 *Chan Tong Fan v. Chiam Heng Luan Realty Pte Ltd* [2013] SGHC 192, at [73]. This case was decided after the Singapore Court of Appeal decided in *Ang Thiam Swee v. Low Hian Chor* [2013] SGCA 11, effectively overturning its earlier approach on the "good faith" requirement as discussed in Chapter 4.
145 *Companies Ordinance* (Cap. 32) (Hong Kong), Part IVAA, s.168BC(3)(a)
146 *Re F & S Express Ltd* [2005] 4 HKLRD 743; *Re Grand Field Group Holdings Ltd* [2009] 3 HKC 81; *Re Li Chung Shing Tong (Holdings) Ltd* [2011] 5 HKC 531.
147 *Re Lucky Money Ltd* [2007] 4 HKC 598; *Re Li Chung Shing Tong (Holdings) Ltd* [2011] 5 HKC 531.
148 *Waddington Ltd v Chan Chun Hoo & Others* [2006] 2 HKLRD 896 (HKCA) and *Waddington Ltd v Chan Chun Hoo & Others* (2008) 11 HKCFAR 370 (HK Final CA), where both the Hong Kong Court of Appeal and the Hong Kong Court of Final Appeal ruled that a successful applicant for leave could pursue multiple derivative actions.

5.5.3 What is good about the provisions in Canada and Singapore?

The provisions in Canada and Singapore seem to make more sense in many ways. Their significance may be summarised as follows, with comparison to the Australian counterpart.

5.5.3.1 Applicants in Canada and Singapore only need to fulfil three requirements

First, one significant difference is that in Canada and Singapore, there are only three requirements that an applicant needs to satisfy the court for an SDA, which means that the costs of the leave application, and the time spent on the case by both parties and the court, can be kept to a minimum at the preliminary stage. In Australia, an applicant has five requirements to establish for leave, and this could be expensive in both costs and time.

5.5.3.2 Canada and Singapore do not have "serious question to be tried" as a separate test

Second, an Australian applicant is required to prove "best interests of the company" and "serious question to be tried" as two separate requirements and both have two different standards of proof, which is where the problem lies. While the "serious question to be tried" in s.237(2)(d) has a relatively low threshold, requiring only proof of an arguable case or that the case has merit, the other requirement in s.237(2)(c) has an unusually high burden of proof. Section 237(2)(c) in Australia requires the applicant to demonstrate with absolute certainty (which is impossible in most cases) that the proposed action "is in the best interests of the company". The way around this problem has been for the Australian courts to grant leave subject to the applicant undertaking to pay all costs and charges in bringing the proposed action and not seeking indemnity or contribution from the company.

Canada and Singapore do not have these as two separate requirements. Rather, they have only the "in the interests of the company" test and within this test, the requirement is that the applicant shows the proposed derivative action to be in the interests of the company by showing that there is "an arguable case" or there is "a reasonable prospect of success" in the proposed action. This seems to be more logical in the sense that the focus is on the company and the test is whether those claims made by the applicant are of interests to the company, and not on the test of whether an applicant can financially afford to pay for the action.

5.5.3.3 Canada and Singapore have a far lower threshold

A third important difference is that in Canada and Singapore, their legislation uses the word "appears", which indicates that their test has a lower threshold. In showing that the proposed derivative action "appears to be in the interests of the company", the applicant is only required to show that the proposed action has a reasonable chance of success or has an arguable case. These are the same as asking the question whether "there is a serious question to be tried", with a low threshold. In Australia, the position with regard to proof is switched; it is far more difficult for an applicant to demonstrate that the proposed action "is" in the best interests of the company than for an applicant in Canada or Singapore to prove that the proposed action "appears to be in the interests of the company". The onus of proof in Australia is unusually high.

5.5.3.4 Costs/benefits analysis is not that important in Canada

A fourth and final important difference is that in Canada, the costs/benefits analysis of the proposed action is not so important for considering whether the proposed action appears in the interests of the company where the claim involves a breach of directors' duties due to their conflict of interests position. This is a stark contrast to the Australian approach where the focus has been on the applicant paying costs and indemnifying the company. In Canada, by not putting significance on the costs/benefits analysis, some courts have given formal recognition to the role of the SDA. For example, in *Budd v. Bertram*, the Nova Scotia Court of Appeal has expressly referred to the purpose of the SDA by saying that it serves not only to ensure that a shareholder has a right to a recovery and appropriate relief, but also to help ensuring "some degree of [directors'] accountability" and corporate governance.[149]

The author has not been able to find any case law in Australia that has reported favourably on the practical purpose of the SDA. Due to the strict language used in the legislative provisions, Australian courts seem to have no other option than to apply the law, and this includes requiring the applicant to bear the costs of the proposed derivative action as a way of showing the proposed action "is in the best interest of the company". The closest statement where Australian courts have expressed support for the SDA's purpose is saying that the SDA "should be approached as measures of reform designed to improve rather than to place obstacles" to shareholder litigation.[150] Interestingly, in *Vlahos v. Vlahos*, in granting leave, Digby J of the Victorian Supreme Court seems to have adopted a more lenient approach, saying, "Section 237(2)(c) will be satisfied if it is established the proposed application is likely to be in the best interests of the company".[151] The point

149 *Budd v. Bertram*, 2018, NSCA 95, at [33], [35] (Hamilton JA, with Derrick and Scanlan JJA agreeing). See also *Chen v. Sumwa Trading Co Ltd* 2018, ABQB 269, at [34]; *Richardson Greenfields of Canada Ltd v. Kalmacoff*, ONCA, 1995 OJ 941, at [21].

150 *Zhu v. Orico Australia Pty Ltd* [2019] VSC 313, at [34] (Connock J). Similar phrasing is seen in *Metyor Inc (formerly Talisman Technologies Inc) v. Queensland Electronic Switching Pty Ltd* [2002] QCA 269, at [10] (McPherson JA, Williams and Wilson JJA agreeing).

151 *Vlahos v. Vlahos* [2016] VSC 824, at [36] (Digby J).

of the author is that s.237(2)(c), in its current form, is far too restrictive to have any meaningful impact on the use of the SDA.

5.5.4 Suggestions for law reform

In order to give proper meaning to the Australian SDA and to support its intended purposes, the suggested changes are these.

5.5.4.1 Amending to "appears to be in the interests of the company"

By removing the words "best" and "is" from the requirement and replacing with the word "appears", making the new proposed provision similar to the Canadian approach, this would help to bring about some improvement in the deterrence of improper conduct and maintenance of corporate governance. This would also give recognition that an application for leave is only at the preliminary stage and available evidence may be limited that it may not be possible to determine what is in the interests of the company in all cases until during the trial proceedings.

5.5.4.2 Clarifying the scope of "company"

It is important to clarify the word "company" in order to remove any crossover ambiguity associated with the concept of CSR and various other stakeholders. Given there is still considerable debate on the CSR concept and the uncertainties relating to strategies for regulating and policing, the preferred definition for "company", for the time being, may be confined to the conservative approach. Suggestion would be to define "company" as "shareholders as a whole" in a company that is still a going concern and "a general body of creditors" in cases where the company has entered into insolvency.

5.5.4.3 The "serious question to be tried" in s.237(2)(d) is unnecessary

The criterion on "there is a serious question to be tried" in s.237(2)(d) seems unnecessary, because proof of whether the leave application has merit and whether there is an arguable case would flow directly from the test that the proposed action "appears to be in the interests of the company". In other words, satisfaction of the provision in s.237(2)(d) would become clear when an applicant has successfully shown the proposed action to be "in the interests of the company" (as seen in the examples from Canada and Singapore). By removing s.237(2)(d), this would mean that there will be lower costs and less time incurred in proving a case for an SDA, which may also make it less intimidating for potential applicants. Having too many preconditions contained in s.237(2) only hinders, rather than promotes, shareholder litigation.

5.5.4.4 Clarifying the use of statutory derivative action in company liquidation

If the intention of the Parliament is to allow the SDA provisions to apply to a company in liquidation, then this should be made clear in the CA, by including the term "in liquidation" as in "company in liquidation". In addition, one way of eliminating the confusion and uncertainty in s.237(2)(c) and in the whole of Part 2F.1A would be to incorporate some guidelines addressing its relationship with the insolvency provisions. The main objective is to ensure that shareholders in the SDA must not be permitted to compete with or to adversely affect the interests of the creditors and employees when a company has become insolvent or is on the verge of insolvency. Examples of guidelines to be included could be:

- Leave of the court may only be granted under s.237(2) only after the court is satisfied that the liquidator has completed the task of paying out employees and creditors. The only item left to be done would be to grant leave under s.237(2) for a shareholder to seek recoveries from persons who have committed wrongs to the company;
- Grant of leave should only be possible if the liquidator is unable to pursue any legal actions because of financial constraint or there is some other valid reason that prevents the liquidator from pursing legal actions;
- if a company is heavily in debt, then with permission of the liquidator, it may be possible for a shareholder to step in under s.237(2) to bring a derivative action in liquidation, with the court giving directions under s.241, provided that any compensation awarded will first be distributed to the employees and creditors ahead of the shareholders, with the exception that the applicant's costs be reimbursed first.

5.5.4.5 Removing related/third party provision in s.237(3)

The provisions in s.237(3) and (4), in relation to the time limit and the restriction imposed on the applicant to seek leave to pursue against a related third party, should be removed entirely because the existence of these provisions serves as a defence mechanism for directors, which hinders the effective use of the SDA procedure. These provisions make it harder, not easier, for a shareholder applicant to pursue against former directors. Currently, there is much debate on the functionality of the business judgment rule in s.180(2) and its uncertainty in the context of directors' duties, and it has often been described as providing directors with a "safe harbour" against alleged breaches of duty of care and diligence.[152] In the context of SDA, s.237(3) is an equivalent of

152 Paul Redmond, "Safe Harbour or Sleepy Hollows? Does Australia need the Statutory Business Judgment Rule?" in Ian Ramsay (ed.), *Corporate Governance and Duties of Company Directors* (Centre for Corporate Law and Securities Regulations, University of Melbourne, 1997); Bainbridge and Connor, n 115. See also Jenifer Varzaly, "Protecting the authority of

s.180(2); and because of its uncertainty in the use under s.180(2), this could be a reason why the courts in the leave application cases in respect to SDA have tended not to refer to s.237(3). In some cases, the court has simply referred to s.237(3) as irrelevant in the case at hand. It is worth noting that many jurisdictions (Canada, New Zealand, Singapore, United Kingdom, Hong Kong) do not have the Australian s.237(3) equivalent.

5.5.5 "Best interests" in directors' duties and in statutory derivative action

A brief mention of the important differences between directors' duties and the role of an applicant in SDA may be necessary.

Some critics (especially those who are not researchers of corporate law) may not like the idea of change and may be fixated on the idea that because the "best interests of the company" expression is familiar and used in directors' duties that the same expression should be used in SDAs, and that there is no need for any change. However, it is worth noting that Canada, Singapore, Hong Kong (and to some extent, New Zealand and the United Kingdom) do not seem to have any problem having two dissimilar expressions used in two different contexts.[153] In Canada, in the context of directors' duties, the law requires directors to act in "the best interests of the corporation",[154] and in SDAs, the law only requires the applicant to show that the proposed derivative action "appears to be in the interests of the corporation".[155] Similarly, in Singapore and Hong Kong, and in respect to SDAs, one of the three preconditions for leave to be granted is to demonstrate that the proposed action "appears to be prima facie in the interests of [the company]".[156] The threshold for an applicant in these jurisdictions to prove a case for an SDA is far lower than in the case of directors requiring "to act in the best interests of the company" in discharging their duty.

---

directors: An empirical analysis of the statutory business judgment rule" (2012) 12 *Journal of Corporate Law Studies* 429.

153 For example, in *Canada Business Corporations Act* RSC 1985 Chapter C-44, s.122 requires a director to act "with a view to the best interests of the corporation" and s.239(2)(c) in the context of SDA requires a complainant to show that the proposed action "appears to be in the interests of the corporation". See also New Zealand *Companies Act* 1993, s.131(1) requires a director to act in the "best interests of the company" and in the context of the SDA, s.165(2) states that the court shall have regard to "the interests of the company".

154 *Canada Business Corporations Act* RSC 1985 Chapter C-44, s.122. Similar wording is seen in many other jurisdictions in the context of directors' duties.

155 *Canada Business Corporations Act* RSC 1985 Chapter C-44, s.239(2)(c).

156 *Companies Act* 1993 (Chapter 50, 2006, revised ed), s.216A(3)(c) (Singapore); *Companies Ordinance* (Chapter 32, as amended in March 2014), Part IVAA, s.168BC(3)(a) (Hong Kong). Based on the empirical findings, one scholar has concluded that there is no observable abuse of the SDA processes in Hong Kong: Felix E. Mezzanotte, "The unconvincing rise of the statutory derivative action in Hong Kong: Evidence from its first 10 years of enforcement" (2017) 17 *Journal of Corporate Law Studies* 469.

As seen from the above discussion, this chapter has provided a number of reasons why the Australian provision is in need of reform. The author offers two further explanations as to why an applicant for leave to bring a derivative action should not be subjected to the same treatment as the directors in fulfilling their duties to the company:

(a) An applicant as shareholder seeking leave to bring an SDA to obtain compensation or relief will be acting not only for the company, but also for himself or herself. An applicant as shareholder would naturally have some level of personal financial interests in the outcome of the proposed action and cannot be expected to sacrifice their own interests and act solely in the best interests of the company in a derivative action. This notion of a shareholder needing to act in the best interests of the company (or needing to demonstrate that the proposed derivative action is in the best interests of the company) is simply impractical.

 In the context of directors' duties, directors are appointed and employed to manage the company, and thus, it is understandable that the law in Canada (as in most other jurisdictions) requires directors "to act in the best interests of the company".[157] It is also understandable why the law in Canada does not insist on the applicant fulfilling the same high threshold in the leave application for an SDA. In essence, the role of an applicant is different from the role of a director, and the legislation in Canada, Singapore, Hong Kong and New Zealand has accounted for these differences.

(b) By not putting such a high threshold on the applicant in SDAs, it could be in recognition in Canada and in most other jurisdictions that not all applicants have readily available evidence in the early stage to formulate an argument that the proposed action "is" in the interests of the company. A director, as manager of the company, is expected to have all relevant information and documents about the company and therefore it is reasonable for the law to impose a higher standard of duty on directors (to act in the "best" interests of the company). It is important to remember that an application for leave is at a preliminary stage. A shareholder applicant for an SDA, not being a director of the company, may not have all the relevant evidence at this stage. An applicant at this stage has no right to a pre-trial discovery or interrogatory until leave of the court is granted to bring the proposed action to trial. Given these differences and in recognition that an applicant may lack evidence at the initial stage, it would be appropriate and adequate, at the application stage, to only require the applicant to show that the proposed action "appears to be in the interests of the company".

157 See, for example, *Howard Smith Ltd v. Ampol Petroleum Ltd* [1974] AC 82.

5.6 Conclusion

This chapter has critically analysed why it is not possible for an applicant to demonstrate that the proposed derivative action "is in the best interests of the company" under s.237(2)(c). The arguments that have been put forward are that the provision in itself is ambiguous, filled with uncertainties and confusions over what is meant by "best interests", "company" and the amount of evidence required to be shown in the leave application to satisfy the court of this requirement. The chapter has provided numerous examples to illustrate the various inconsistencies in the courts' treatment of s.237(2)(c), and to illustrate that, in most cases, the courts have tended to require the applicant to bear the costs of bringing the proposed action on behalf of the company as a way of complying with this strict requirement.

In calling for an amendment to the provision in s.237(2)(c), the author has suggested considering the legislative provisions from Canada, British Columbia and Singapore, and their judicial approaches, to understand how their corresponding provisions have been operating effectively without any systemic abuse of the SDA. Furthermore, their SDAs have fewer preconditions for an applicant to satisfy the court for leave, which means that their procedure for bringing an SDA is cheaper and less cumbersome, as the applicant in these jurisdictions does not have to spend as much time and money in proving those preconditions. One clear example is that the element where an applicant is required to show that "there is a serious question to be tried" in Australia is, in fact, embedded in their provisions that the applicant only needs to show that the proposed action "appears to be in the interests of the company". In other words, under the Canada and Singapore models, proof that the proposed derivative action is arguable and has merit or that there is a reasonable prospect of success in the action is sufficient to satisfy the court that the proposed action appears to be in the interests of the company.

To give meaningful effect to the Australian SDA and in support of the idea that the SDA can be utilised as a tool for deterring managerial misconduct, improving directors' accountability and maintaining corporate governance, the author suggests that the equivalent of the Canada or Singapore provision could be more appropriate for Australia. It is hoped that the analysis and the ideas presented in this chapter will be useful for the re-write of the law in this area.

6 Uncertainty in the recovery of costs

6.1 Introduction

This chapter focuses on the issue of costs relating to the statutory derivative action. It discusses the current uncertainty in the recovery of legal and court costs by applicants who have been given leave to bring the approved action. The purpose of this chapter is to explain why the costs provision is in need of amendment in Australia and to suggest some ideas for reform.

In matters relating to civil litigation, costs will always be an important consideration for parties in the assessment of whether to commence or continue a court action. The general rule in Australia is that costs follow the event, that an unsuccessful party will pay his or her own costs and the costs of the successful party.[1] The court has a general power to decide when to make a costs order; and typically the two types broadly reflected in the legislation that the court will make in favour of the successful party are the party/party costs and the indemnity costs.[2] However, these general costs rules that apply to most civil litigation cases do not apply to matters relating to SDA. Instead, costs associated with the SDA are governed under s.242 of the *Corporations Act* 2001 (C'th), which gives the court a *broad discretion* to decide how, when and against whom a costs order is to be made.[3]

In addition to the uncertainty in the recovery of costs, another reason why some shareholders may be reluctant to pursue a derivative suit could be because of the free rider problem. If there is a successful outcome in the SDA, non-participating shareholders will get a "free ride". These concerns are real and need to be addressed if the SDA is to be meaningful.

1 See, for example, s.24 of the *Supreme Court Act* 1986 (Vic.); s.65C of the *Civil Procedure Act* 2010 (Vic.); s.98 of the *Civil Procedure Act* 2005 (NSW); s.43(2) of the *Federal Court of Australia Act* 1976 (C'th).

2 The first is the party/party costs order, which is most common in practice where the successful party is only entitled to the costs that are reasonably incurred in the proceedings; and the second is the indemnity order, which is more generous as the successful party is entitled to be indemnified on all costs reasonably incurred. See also *Oshlack v. Richmond River Council* (1998) 193 CLR 72; [1998] HCA 11 for discussion of these two types.

3 *Re Hardy Bros Equipment Pty Ltd* [2021] NSWSC 1693, at [13–14] (Black J).

DOI: 10.4324/9781003430063-6

In Chapter 3, one of the purposes of the empirical study was to assess the judicial treatment of s.242. The study shows that in 55.4% of leave application cases (93 out of 168 applications) filed in the 20-year period 2000–2019, the applicants were successful in obtaining leave to bring an SDA. However, in 35.5% of those cases (33 out of 93), the grant of leave was on terms that the applicants would undertake to bear the costs of bringing the approved action and to indemnify the company against any adverse costs orders, including providing security for costs if necessary; while in 49.5% of the successful leave cases (46 out of 93), the courts reserved their power to consider the costs question at a later stage pending the outcome of the derivative action or they simply did not discuss the costs question. In both instances, the successful applicants were required to pay all costs in the interim with no certainty of recovering any of their costs.

In the remainder of the successful cases (15% or 14 out 93), the successful applicants for leave were also successful in obtaining a recovery for the *leave application*, either wholly or in part from the respondent opposing the application, or from a third party not named in the leave application who would potentially be a proposed defendant. In one instance, the company was required to pay the applicant the costs of both the leave application and the approved derivative action.[4] Overall, the empirical findings show that the number of orders made by the courts requiring the company to indemnify the applicant has been extremely low. The courts are generally reluctant to allow company funds to be used in derivative litigations.

In a derivative action, the court is often faced with two competing considerations. When an applicant has established the five criteria for leave to bring an SDA, the court must grant that leave.[5] There is no discretion for the court to deny or postpone that leave.[6] The other consideration is that in granting leave, the court must ensure that the company's financial resources are "protected",[7] which is the main reason for the court not to allow the company to fund the derivative action in most cases. On the whole, because of the uncertainty in the recovery of legal costs and expenses, there is very little incentive for aggrieved shareholders to apply to bring an SDA unless there is no other or better choice. Despite what the Explanatory Memorandum has stated, that the SDA could provide an "effective remedy" to shareholders and the applicant,[8] the reality is that the utility of the SDA has been compromised.

As noted in Chapter 1, academic literature on Australian SDA is very limited. Monichino is the only scholar and legal practitioner who has provided

4 *Wood v. Links Golf Tasmania Pty Ltd* [2010] FCA 570 (Finkelstein J).

5 *Connective Services Pty Ltd v. Slea Pty Ltd* [2018] VSCA 229, at [2].

6 *Zhu v. Orico Australia Pty Ltd* [2019] VSC 313, at [27] (Connock J); *Huang v. Wang* [2016] 114 ACSR 586, at [57] (Bathurst CJ, McColl JA and Barrett AJA agreeing).

7 *Steinier v. Sunlea Enterprises Pty Ltd* [2016] WASC 81, at [73] (Martino J); *Fiduciary Ltd v. Morningstar Research Pty Ltd* [2005] NSWSC 442, [56] (Austin J).

8 House of Representatives, *Explanatory Memorandum to the CLERP Bill* 1998, at 21.

his observations on the problems with s.242 and debated on whether the courts in Australia should move towards adopting the English *Wallersteiner* order.[9]

This chapter takes a different approach from that of Monichino and considers additional cases and explains why reform to the costs provision is desirable. The chapter suggests ways in which the US common fund/contingency fees arrangements and the substantial benefits/lodestar method may be implemented into the Australian SDA so as to allow successful applicants leave to recover some costs.

The central question to be addressed is: *Who* should pay for the leave application and the subsequent derivative action and *why*? This chapter is therefore structured as follows. Part 2 explains the scope of s.242 and the problems with the current costs structure in Australia. Part 3 provides some possible explanations for the approaches taken by Australian courts in requiring the successful applicants to bear the costs of derivative litigations. Part 4 explains why *successful* applicants should not have to pay for the approved action; but rather the company should bear the costs reasonably incurred; or in the alternative, those costs should be shifted to the acting solicitors or other entities. Part 5 then provides some suggestions for law reform, recommending the adoption of the US common fund doctrine, the substantial benefit test and the lodestar approach. The focus is on promoting a more effective use of the SDA without burdening the applicants with legal costs. Part 6 is the conclusion.

6.2 Problems with the current costs provision

6.2.1 The scope of s.242

Section 242 states that the court "may at any time make any order it considers appropriate about the costs of [the applicant, the company or any other party] ... in relation to proceedings brought or intervened in with leave under section 237". The provision also allows the court to make an order for "indemnification for costs". Section 242 is very broad indeed. As stated in the Explanatory Memorandum, the court has a "broad discretion" to decide on costs.[10] Section 242 has two key objectives:[11] (1) to enable the court to *protect a bona fide shareholder against liability for costs* by indemnifying them out of company funds; and (2) to provide an *additional safeguard* against unmeritorious or doubtful action.

9 Albert Monichino, "Costs in statutory derivative actions: The lingering ghost of Wallersteiner" (2015) 33 *Company and Securities Law Journal* 104.

10 House of Representatives, *Explanatory Memorandum to the CLERP Bill* 1998, at 25, [6.16].

11 House of Representatives, *Explanatory Memorandum to the CLERP Bill* 1998, at 26, [6.19] (emphasis added).

It is clear that the drafting of s.242 was not a mistake. The vagueness of the wording in s.242 was deliberate,[12] aiming to deny the successful applicant from recovering their reasonable costs of litigating on the company's behalf. The intention was to provide the court with greater flexibility in deciding on costs, and at the same time, provide the court with "an additional safeguard" to protect the company's resources by discouraging unmeritorious actions. The applicant is "at the mercy of the court" as to what is appropriate in respect to the recovery.[13]

Given its flexible wording, the judicial approach to s.242 is that "costs could be dealt with in a general way",[14] and the court is "free to approach matters... unconfined by statutory prescriptions".[15] In addition to the power to order one party to indemnify the other party,[16] the court can also make a costs order against a third party not named in the leave application, for example, the proposed defendant.[17] There is also no obligation on the court to consider making a costs order.[18]

It is submitted that s.242 fails to overcome the shareholder's disincentive to pursue an action stemming from the general costs rule that an unsuccessful party pays. When there is a successful outcome in the SDA, any compensation or benefit awarded by the court will accrue to the company to be enjoyed by all current shareholders. The applicant will not be entitled to the whole of the compensation. However, when a company loses, the applicant is potentially liable for all of the costs related to the derivative action. When a court has broad discretion to decide on costs under s.242, the implication is that it opens up a minefield of problems and uncertainties.

6.2.2 Conflicting judicial views on s.242

In understanding why s.242 is a major concern for prospective applicants, it is important to examine two conflicting views from the judiciary. The first is

12 Keith Fletcher, "CLERP and minority shareholder rights" (2001) 13 *Australian Journal of Corporate Law* 290, at 300.

13 Lang Thai, "How popular are statutory derivative actions in Australia? Comparisons with United States, Canada and New Zealand" (2002) *Australia Business Law Review* 30, at 136.

14 *Charlton v. Baber* [2003] NSWSC 745, at [73] (Barrett J). See also *McLaughlin v. Dungowan Manly Pty Limited* [2010] NSWSC 306, at [8–9] and *In the Matter of Wan Jia (Australia) International Development Pty Ltd* [2012] NSWSC 1007, at [13] where similar comments were made.

15 *Foyster v. Foyster Holdings* [2003] NSWSC 135, at [12] (Barrett J).

16 *In the matter of Jimmy's Recipe Pty Limited* [2018] NSWSC 1331, at [35]; *Carpenter v. Pioneer Park Pty Ltd* [2004] NSWSC 1007, at [45–46].

17 *MG Corrosion Consultants Pty Ltd v. Vinciguerra (No.2)* [2011] FCAFC 48.

18 The empirical study in Chapter 3 shows that in many of the leave application cases, the costs question was not discussed or referred to by the court and in many other cases, the court reserved its power to decide on costs at a later date. For example, in *White (Trustee) v. MWL Financial Group Pty Ltd (No.2)* [2019] FCA 364, at [2], [5], Davies J noted that the question of costs was subject to the outcome in the final judgment in the derivative proceedings.

from Barrett J in the NSW Supreme Court. In *Roach v. Winnote Pty Ltd,*[19] the shareholder applicant was successful in obtaining leave of the court to bring the proposed derivative action but was unsuccessful in his plea for legal costs to be borne by the company. Barrett J stated his reason as follows:[20]

> "It is thus clear that courts are concerned in some cases to ensure that the person granted leave under s.237 should bear, either wholly or in part, the burden of the company's costs in relation to the proceedings in which that person is to represent the company. Measures of that kind are intended to protect the company's financial resources and are merely part of the domestic arrangements within the company as to the basis on which the person concerned will be permitted to act for it."

In the same year, his Honour made a similar statement in another case. In *Sub Rosa Holding Pty Ltd v. Salsa Sudada Production Pty Ltd,*[21] Barrett J noted:[22]

> "It is common place for a person given permission to pursue a claim on behalf of a company to be required, in the first instance, to bear the burden of costs."

However, three years earlier in *Foyster v. Foyster Holdings Pty Ltd* [2003] NSWSC, Barrett J appeared to be supportive of the views of many scholars that shareholder applicants should be entitled to reimbursement of their costs. In that case, Barrett J stated:[23]

> "I must say that I find it difficult to see why [an applicant] who chooses to pursue litigation against a corporate defendant which happens to have a deadlocked board of directors should be expected to bear costs occasioned by that dislocation and by the need for statutory processes to be invoked. ... In the ordinary course, one would expect that a member or officer compelled to resort to s.237 to ensure that a defendant company was represented in proceedings should be protected, as to costs, by the company itself or by parties privy to the circumstances giving rise to the need for the s.237 application. Such a member or officer becomes, after all, the surrogate of the normal corporate decision makers whose decision has not been forthcoming."

This earlier case was not referred to by his Honour in his later decisions. In all three cases, however, including *Foyster,* the successful applicants

19 *Roach v. Winnote Pty Ltd* [2006] NSWSC 231.
20 *Roach v. Winnote Pty Ltd* [2006] NSWSC 231, at [29].
21 *Sub Rosa Holding Pty Ltd v. Salsa Sudada Production Pty Ltd* [2006] NSWSC 916.
22 *Sub Rosa Holding Pty Ltd v. Salsa Sudada Production Pty Ltd* [2006] NSWSC 916, at [49]
23 *Foyster v. Foyster Holdings Pty Ltd* [2003] NSWSC, at [13].

were ordered to pay for the leave application and the subsequent derivative proceedings, and there was no indication that they would recover any of their costs later. In effect, the company was not required to contribute to the applicants' costs. One conclusion that may be drawn from all this is that his Honour might have felt compelled to protect the company's assets because of the statement in the Explanatory Memorandum that s.242 was intended to provide "an additional safeguard" for the court to protect the company's resources and to discourage unmeritorious or doubtful actions.[24] In a first instance case, there is usually very little scope for the court to step outside the sphere.

Finkelstein J in the Federal Court of Australia has a different view. In *Wood v. Links Golf Tasmania Pty Ltd*, Finkelstein J made a costs order against the company, requiring the company to pay the "fair and reasonable costs" of running the derivative action.[25] In disagreeing with the approach of Barrett J, Finkelstein J said, "to be quite frank, it is by no means clear why this general approach ... has been adopted".[26] The reason provided is that:[27]

> "The purpose of permitting a person to bring an action in the name of the company is to prevent conduct which involves some element of harm. In most cases the wrongdoer will be in control of the company. That will be the reason the company itself is not bringing the action. ... In those circumstances, I can think of no reason why the company should not bear the costs. ... [but] this is not to suggest that a costs order will be made in all cases ... If a costs order is made and at any later time it turns out the claim is unmeritorious, the costs order can be recalled."

That case was decided in 2010 and Finkelstein J's approach has not been repeated since. However, this is not to say that his Honour's approach is bad. The approach seen in *Wood's case* is not inconsistent with the old common law practice, where the company was ordered to bear the initial costs of the derivative action,[28] with the proviso that the court could recall the original costs order if the action later turned out to have no merits.[29] The derivative plaintiff could be ordered to reimburse the company under common law. Some jurisdictions have statutory provisions to enable the successful applicant to recover some costs under limited circumstances;[30] and to some extent,

24 House of Representatives, *Explanatory Memorandum to the Corporate Law Economic Reform Program Bill* (1998) (C'th), at 26, [6.19].
25 *Wood v. Links Golf Tasmania Pty Ltd* [2010] FCA 570, at [12].
26 *Wood v. Links Golf Tasmania Pty Ltd* [2010] FCA 570, at [8].
27 *Wood v. Links Golf Tasmania Pty Ltd* [2010] FCA 570, at [9–12] (Finkelstein J).
28 See, for example, *Wallersteiner v. Moir* (No 2) [1975] QB 373 (Court of Appeal decision).
29 *Farrow v. Registrar of Building Societies* [1991] 2 VR 589.
30 For example, Canada and New Zealand.

the common law approach still has some use in the United Kingdom.[31] These will be canvassed further later in this chapter.

6.2.3 Other inconsistencies under s.242

It has become common practice that an applicant who seeks leave to bring a derivative action would be expected to bear the costs of maintaining the derivative action.[32] This is to ensure that the company will not have to pay for anything if it loses the court case, a way of making sure that the company's assets are protected. The courts have been reluctant to allow company funds to be used to pay for the derivative action, even where there are merits and the action is in the company's interests,[33] and even where the company is financially prosperous.[34] This part discusses some of the approaches used by the court in imposing costs on the applicant when granting leave. It considers how s.242 has been treated inconsistently.

6.2.3.1 Conditional grant of leave with costs

The most direct way for the court to impose costs on the applicant when making an order for leave is to make a conditional grant of leave, *on the condition* that the applicant bears the costs of the derivative action, including indemnifying the company against any adverse costs liability and providing security for costs if necessary.[35] The thinking is that if an applicant wishes to pursue a derivative action, they must pay for it. The grant of leave has "often been made conditional upon the applicant for leave indemnifying the company for its costs".[36] This type of leave is said to be necessary as a way of protecting the company's assets.[37] The company will not have to pay for anything if it loses the court case.

31 In the United Kingdom, there are statutory provisions governing the derivative action, but no statutory provision dealing with costs, which means that the common law approach on costs still has some relevance.

32 See *Cooper v. Myrtace Consulting Pty Ltd* [2014] FCA 480, at [31], where Davies J has noted that the grant of leave has "often been made conditional upon the applicant for leave indemnifying the company for its costs".

33 *Re Colorado Products Pty Ltd* (2014) NSWSC 64, where the applicant could not afford to pay.

34 See *Ehsman v. Nutectime International* [2006] NSWSC 887; *Pottie v. Dunkley* [2011] NSWSC 166. The dispute in both cases were held to be personal between shareholders.

35 *Stanisis v. Tracc Pty Ltd* [2022] WASC 281; *Power v. Ekstein* [2010] NSWSC 137, at [108]; *Vinciguerra v. MG Corrosion Consultants Pty Ltd* [2010] FCA 763, at [138]; *Fernandez v. True Value Solar Holdings Pty Ltd* [2012] VSC 430; *Re Fishinthenet Investments Pty Ltd and Coastal Waters Seafood Pty Ltd* [2014] NSWSC 260; *Stanton (WA) Pty Ltd (in liq.) v. Vasquez Investments Pty Ltd* [2017] NSWSC 128.

36 *Cooper v. Myrtace Consulting Pty Ltd* [2014] FCA 480, at [31] (Davies J).

37 *Steinier v. Sunlea Enterprises Pty Ltd* [2016] WASC 81, at para 73; *Re Colorado Products Pty Ltd (in provisional liquidation)* [2014] NSWSC 64, at [10]; *Cooper v. Myrtace Consulting Pty Ltd* [2014] FCA 480, at [31].

Under s.237(2)(c), it is a requirement that the applicant must prove to the court that the proposed derivative action "is in the best interests of the company". Given that it is not possible for an applicant to prove this element in absolute terms, because it is not possible to predict what the outcome of the case will be, it seems that the only logical alternative for the court to grant leave would be to grant it on the proviso that the applicant gives an undertaking that they will be liable for all costs and charges in bringing the proposed action. This is the only way that the court can be sure that the derivative action will be in the company's interests.

Given the difficulty in satisfying the court on the "best interests of the company" element, it is not unusual to see some cases where the applicants have voluntarily offered to indemnify the company on all costs associated with the bringing of the derivative action.[38] In *Re Poly Pacific Pty Ltd,* the applicant had gone to the extent of presenting to the court a draft consent order signed by both the applicant and the proposed defendant, detailing how the applicant would be responsible for paying the costs of the derivative action.[39] That draft consent order was submitted to the court at the beginning of the hearing. In that case, the court granted leave without considering too closely the leave criteria under s.237(2). Robson J was satisfied that the consent order in respect to costs was enough evidence for the court to declare that the proposed action was in the company's interest.[40]

6.2.3.2 Grant of leave with no costs order made

The second and equally common approach is where the court makes an order granting the applicant leave to bring the proposed action and, simultaneously reserving its power to decide on costs until such time that it considers appropriate, and this could possibly be at the conclusion of the substantive derivative proceedings. An interesting example is in the case of *Maher v. Honeysett & Maher Electrical Contractors Pty Ltd,*[41] where the court, in the hearing of the leave application, decided to reserve its power to decide on costs at a later time, and that later time was at the conclusion of the derivative action. Four years later in the follow up of that case, although the applicant had a successful outcome in the derivative action, with the judgment entered in favour of the company, the applicant failed on the application for a costs

38 *Zhu v. Orico Australia Pty Ltd* [2019] VSC 313; *App Shop Pty Ltd Jalal Bros Pty Ltd* [2019] NSWSC 490; *Li v. Dao* [2018] VSC 530; *Vlahos v. Vlahos* [2016] VSC 824.

39 *Re Poly Pacific Pty Ltd* [2013] VSC 670, at [60].

40 *Re Poly Pacific Pty Ltd* [2013] VSC 670, at [72]. Since then, no derivative action has been brought by the applicant. One possible reason could be that the applicant had successfully settled the dispute with the proposed defendant without further court intervention; the other explanation may be that the applicant had decided that litigation was too costly and that there was no certainty of any recovery at the end of the process.

41 *Maher v. Honeysett & Maher Electrical Contractors Pty Ltd* [2005] NSWSC 859.

order for the company to reimburse him because a successful outcome in that case did not amount to a substantial benefit to the company.[42] The compensation awarded in favour of the company was only a modest amount and the dispute between the parties was regarded as personal. It was held that the derivative action was used merely as a vehicle to settle that personal dispute.

It is also not unusual for the court to make an order granting leave but remaining quiet on the question of costs,[43] that is, the court may make an order for leave but may not wish to discuss the costs issue at all. In *Foyster v. Foyster Holdings* [2003] NSWSC 135, the applicant raised the issue of costs during the leave application stage, but Barrett J did "not consider it necessary to dwell on this question" at the time.[44] Similar to the conditional leave approach, an applicant who is successful in obtaining leave of the court to bring an action on behalf of the company is expected to find their own way to finance the action, and they could potentially be out of pocket.

The reason for these two approaches may be explained in *McLaughlin v. Dungowan Manly Pty Limited* where the court has said:[45]

> "it seems to me to be best for the question of who should bear the costs at first instance to be deferred until such time as proceedings have been commenced or at least until such time as an application [for costs] can be made with the benefit of a settled pleading, such that the judge hearing such an application will then be in a position better to assess what is in the best interests of the company in that regard."

It is clear that the court's priority is to protect the company's assets. This approach is more likely to be used where the court is confident that the proposed action has a strong "prospect of success".[46] Success in this context is based on the costs/benefits analysis.[47] It is dependent on whether the benefits of the proceeding are outweighed by the costs and risks that the company would suffer in bringing the action.[48] If the action is likely to produce a substantial financial return to the company, a benefit that is greater than the actual costs incurred in bringing and maintaining the action, then this could

42 *Maher v. Honeysett & Maher Electrical Contractors Pty Ltd* [2009] NSWSC 445.

43 See, for example, *Fitzpatrick v. Cheal* [2010] NSWSC 717; *Catalano v. Managing Australian Destinations Pty Ltd* [2014] FCAFC 55; *Connective Services Pty Ltd v. Slea Pty Ltd* [2018] VSCA 229.

44 *Foyster v. Foyster Holdings* [2003] NSWSC 135, at [12].

45 *McLaughlin v. Dungowan Manly Pty Limited* [2010] NSWSC 306, at [65].

46 *Huang v. Wang* [2016] NSWCA 164, at [60] (Bathurst CJ, with McColl and Barrett JJA agreeing). See also *Swansson v. RA Pratt Properties Pty Ltd* (2002) 42 ACSR 313; [2002] NSWSC 583.

47 *Blakeney v. Blakeney* [2016] WASCA 76, at [65].

48 *Daiwa Can Company v. Barokes Pty Ltd* [2016] VSC 296, at [61] (Sifris J) citing *True Value Solar Holdings Pty Ltd v. Fernandez* [2013] VSCA 27, at [13] (Osborn JA, with Neave JA and Priest JJA agreeing).

possibly be seen as a successful outcome for the company, in which case the applicant may be indemnified by the company. However, there is no certainty.

Similar to the conditional grant of leave, a derivative action would be in the company's interests if the company does not have to lose anything or pay anything.

6.2.3.3 Partial funding by the proposed defendant

There are very few cases where the courts have made an order for costs to be in favour of the applicants. *In the Matter of Jimmy's Recipe Pty Limited*,[49] in deciding that the applicant was entitled to her costs of the leave application to be paid by the three defendants who opposed the application, Brereton J of the NSW Supreme Court noted that his mind had "wandered to some extent between whether that should be contingent on the successful outcome of the ultimate proceedings or not".[50] His Honour concluded that because the leave application was regarded as final, and not interlocutory, a final order should be made now and not left to the judge determining the derivative proceedings.[51] His view in 2018 contradicted his earlier approach in 2009 in *Maher v. Honeysett & Maher Electrical Contractors Pty Ltd* where his Honour refused to make any costs order in favour of the successful applicant.[52]

The most unusual outcome was in the case of *Imperium Projects Pty Ltd*.[53] Although the applicant was successful in obtaining leave to commence the derivative action, the court held that the two proposed defendants only had to indemnify the applicant on half of the costs of the leave application, and this was only if the derivative action resulted in a successful outcome in favour of the company.[54] The case was treated as a personal dispute between the parties and that the company was used as a vehicle to settle their dispute. There was no mention as to who would be liable to pay for the derivative action or whether the applicant would be able to receive any indemnity.

6.3 Possible explanations why the courts require the applicant to pay

While there may be circumstances where it is appropriate for the applicants to bear the costs of the derivative action, there are equally compelling reasons why the company should be the one paying for it. This part discusses the approaches of the courts on s.242 and the possible explanations for their

49 *In the matter of Jimmy's Recipe Pty Limited* [2018] NSWSC 1331.
50 *In the matter of Jimmy's Recipe Pty Limited* [2018] NSWSC 1331, at [35].
51 *In the matter of Jimmy's Recipe Pty Limited* [2018] NSWSC 1331, at [35].
52 *Maher v. Honeysett and Maher Electrical Contractors Pty Ltd* [2009] NSWSC 445.
53 *In the Matter of Imperium Projects Pty Ltd* [2015] NSWSC 123.
54 *In the Matter of Imperium Projects Pty Ltd* [2015] NSWSC 123, at [16] (Black J).

approaches before moving on to the next part on why the company should be paying.

6.3.1 Circumstances where it is appropriate for the applicant to pay

There are some circumstances where it may be appropriate for the applicant to pay for the derivative action. Some examples are these.

(1) *Leave application pursued unsuccessfully* – If an applicant has been unsuccessful in the leave application, then it would be reasonable to require the applicant to bear the costs of that application.
(2) *Discontinuing or settling the derivation action* – If an applicant applies for leave to discontinue or compromise or settle the matter with the defendants as required under s.240, it would be reasonable for costs to be awarded against the applicant for initiating and bringing the action to the court in the first place.[55] The court may consider the case as one that could have been resolved amicably by the parties without the need for court intervention.
(3) *Company in liquidation* – If a company has gone into liquidation and a liquidator is unable to commence a court action due to a funding constraint, then it would be appropriate for a shareholder who wishes to bring a derivative action to pay for the action, subject to being allowed to recover his or her costs ahead of any payment to the creditors if the financial position of the company is improved as a result of the successful action. An insolvent company with limited funding cannot be expected to fund the action. By allowing leave to bring a derivative action in liquidation with the assurance that the shareholder's costs will be recovered if successful, a shareholder would be more inclined to prosecute the wrongdoer to recover more funds for the creditors.
(4) *Costs against the applicant as a penalty* – If the conduct of the applicant is considered unreasonable, such as causing delays and using up the court's time unnecessarily, it would be appropriate for the applicant to pay a penalty.[56]

55 In *Isak Constructions v. Faress* [2005] NSWSC 679, the applicant was successful in obtaining leave of the court to commence the SDA, but later decided not to proceed with the derivative proceeding and sought leave to discontinue it. The applicant was held liable to indemnify the company and the proposed defendant for all costs incurred. Similarly, in *Foyster v. Foyster* [2003] NSWSC 135, two directors were in a deadlock and one of them subsequently resigned from the company and applied for leave to bring an SDA, but the matter was subsequently settled and thus the court ordered the applicant to indemnify the company.
56 In *Jeans v. Deangrove Pty Ltd* [2001] NSWSC 84, at [13], the court held that "the present application which has occupied several days of court time, on an urgent basis, should never have been brought so belatedly". The applicant was ordered to pay the company's costs and

6.3.2 Other explanations why the courts would not allow the company to pay

Other possible explanations why the courts have not allowed the company to fund the derivative action are these.

6.3.2.1 Limited funds in the company

If a company is struggling financially, it is not possible for it to fund the derivative action, even where there are merits.[57] There is a line of authorities where the courts have exercised their inherent jurisdiction under the insolvency law to permit shareholder applicants to bring an action on behalf of the company in liquidation, on the condition that they pay for the court proceedings.[58] There must be evidence from the liquidator that the company is, in fact, unable to meet the costs of the proceedings which have precluded the liquidator from bringing the necessary actions.[59] In addition, the courts have insisted that a derivative action pursued by a shareholder applicant in liquidation would only be possible if there is strong evidence that some "distinct benefit" will accrue to the "general body of creditors".[60] The importance of it is to protect the assets of *not* the company *but* the company *in liquidation*.

6.3.2.2 The need to satisfy the "best interests of the company" criterion

Section 237(2)(c) requires the court to be satisfied that the proposed derivative action *is* in the best interests of the company, not that it *may* be, *appears* to be or *is likely* to be.[61] As discussed in Chapter 5, "in the best interests of the company" is the most difficult criterion for the applicants to satisfy the court due to the subjective nature of the test and the way in which the provision is phrased. One way for the court to be sure that the proposed derivative action is in the company's interests would be to make a conditional leave, on the proviso that the applicant bears the costs of the derivative proceedings.

In circumstances where the court is not satisfied that the proposed action is in the best interests of the company, which appears to have been the case

---

those of Commonwealth Bank, which was not a party to the proceedings but had been given a right to be heard.

57 *Re Colorado Products Pty Ltd (in prov liq)* [2014] NSWSC 64; *Re Sundara Pty Ltd* [2015] NSWSC 1694.

58 *Stanton (WA) Pty Ltd (in liq.) v. Vasquez Investments Pty Ltd* [2017] NSWSC 128; *Re Sundara Pty Ltd* [2015] NSWSC 1694; *Re Colorado Products Pty Ltd (in prov liq)* [2014] NSWSC 64; *Carpenter v. Pioneer Park Pty Ltd* [2004] NSWSC 1007.

59 In *Scuteri v. Lofthouse and Cauchi as liquidators of Fresh Start Australia Pty Ltd (in liq)* [2006] VSC 317, the company was wound up by reason of insolvency. One of the reasons the court granted shareholder derivative action was because the liquidator was able to find enough money to pay the creditors in full.

60 *Charlton v. Baber* [2003] NSWSC 745, at [74].

61 *Swansson v. RA Pratt Properties Pty Ltd* (2002) 42 ACSR 313; [2002] NSWSC 583, at [55] (Palmer J).

in many of the leave applications, then in granting leave, the court will most likely make a *conditional* order requiring the applicant to undertake to pay the company's costs of bringing the proceeding and indemnify the company against any adverse costs orders.

The courts have repeatedly said that where there are doubts as to the prospect of success, the courts will not allow company funds to be used to pay for the derivative action.[62] This is to ensure that the company's resources are "properly protected".[63] A derivative action is in the best interests of the company if the company does not lose anything if the action is pursued unsuccessfully.[64] In *Fiduciary Ltd v. Morningstar Research Pty Ltd*, Austin J explains the importance of considering the company's position if the action is pursued unsuccessfully:[65]

> "There is a balance to be struck between the prejudice that the company will suffer if the claims are pressed unsuccessfully on its behalf and there is an adverse costs order, and the advantage that it will gain, indirectly for the benefit of its shareholders, if the claims are successful."

In *Ananda Marga Pracaraka Samgba Ltd v. Tomar (No.3)*, Dodds-Streeton J considered the position of the company and concluded that the effect on the company and its operations would have been "extremely deleterious" if a costs order was to be made against the company.[66]

Robash Pty Ltd v. Gladstone Pacific Nickel Pty Ltd is one of the earlier cases where the court referred to costs as a significant matter for the consideration of whether granting leave would be in the best interests of the company. In that case, Ball J identified "other matters" to include:[67]

> "the prospects of success of the proposed action, the likely costs and likely consequences if it is not successful; and the nature of any indemnity the applicant has offered to the company. The likelihood of the company recovering under an indemnity is also relevant, as are the resources that the company will need to devote to the proceedings and the resources it has available."

62 *Huang v. Wang* [2016] NSWCA 164, at [60] (Bathurst CJ, with McColl J and Barrett AJ agreeing); *Swansson v. RA Pratt Properties Pty Ltd* (2002) 42 ACSR 313; [2002] NSWSC583.

63 *Fiduciary Ltd v. Morningstar Research Pty Ltd* [2005] NSWSC 442, [56] (Austin J).

64 *Fiduciary Ltd v. Morningstar Research Pty Ltd* [2005] NSWSC 442, [51] (Austin J); *Re Colorado Products Pty Ltd (in prov liq)* [2014] NSWSC 64.

65 *Fiduciary Ltd v. Morningstar Research Pty Ltd* [2005] NSWSC 442, at para 51. See also in *Steinier v. Sunlea Enterprises Pty Ltd* [2016] WASC 81, at [73].

66 *Ananda Marga Pracaraka Samgba Ltd v. Tomar (No.3)* [2012] FCA 184, at [61]. Leave was denied in this case because the amount offered by the two applicants to indemnify the company was inadequate for the court to consider the action to be in the company's best interests.

67 *Robash Pty Ltd v. Gladstone Pacific Nickel Pty Ltd* [2011] NSWSC 1235, at [57] (Ball J), cited in *Blakeney v. Blakeney* [2016] WASCA 76, at [55] (Buss AJ, Murphy J, Beech JA).

It is now common practice for the court to link the costs consideration with the best interests of the company criterion. In *Cooper v. Myrtace Consulting Pty Ltd*, Davies J stated:[68]

> "whether the proposed action is in the best interests of the company is whether the *company would be prejudiced by being exposed to the costs and expenses of litigation* and the risk of an adverse costs order. The grant of leave has often been made conditional upon the applicant for leave indemnifying the company for its costs of the proceeding and any adverse costs order against the company arising out of the proceeding. The case law emphasises *the importance of such an indemnity as a means of addressing the risk of prejudice to the company* from the commencement of the proceedings."

Consequently, in *Re Poly Pacific Pty Ltd*, the court granted leave without examining the best interests of the company element in detail and this was because the court had received a signed agreement with the proposed defendant, detailing the applicant's willingness to pay for the derivative action.[69] It was noted that a "pragmatic and practical approach is to be adopted".[70] In line with this approach, one could say that the approach now is that if an applicant is unable to satisfy the court that granting leave is in the best interests of the company, the other possible alternative in circumventing this problem would be to make an offer to indemnify the company on all costs and charges. However, if the amount offered is inadequate to safeguard the company against the risk of exposure to the adverse costs liability, the court can refuse leave, as seen in some cases.[71]

Even where there is no difficulty for an applicant to demonstrate that the proposed action is in the company's interests, based on the facts of the case, it has nonetheless become a habit for some courts to require the applicant to pay costs as a condition for the grant of leave.[72] This is to avoid the possibility

68 *Cooper v. Myrtace Consulting Pty Ltd* [2014] FCA 480, at [31]. See also *Fiduciary Ltd v. Morningstar Research Pty Ltd* [2005] NSWSC 441, at [51] where Austin J provided similar reasoning.

69 *Re Poly Pacific Pty Ltd* [2013] VSC 670, at [60]. Since then, no further reported case has been found on this matter. Possible explanations could be that the applicant had settled the dispute with the proposed defendant without further court intervention (in which case the leave application had a useful role, in that it was used as a threat of further litigation and possible liability), or the applicant had decided not to proceed with the approved derivative action due to, for example, funding constraint and the uncertainty in the recovery of costs at the end of the process.

70 *Re Poly Pacific Pty Ltd* [2013] VSC 670, at [64] (Robson J).

71 *Cooper v. Myrtace Consulting Pty Ltd* [2014] FCA 480; *Re Fishinthenet Investments Pty Ltd and Coastal Waters Seafood Pty Ltd* [2014] NSWSC 260; *Ananda Marga Pracaraka Samgba Ltd v. Tomar (No.3)* [2012] FCA 184.

72 *Zhu v. Orico Australia Pty Ltd* [2019] VSC 313; *Li v. Dao* [2018] VSC 530.

of the company facing a costs liability order if the derivative action later turns out to be unsuccessful. If there is no condition on costs in the grant of leave, the successful defendant would indirectly end up paying some or most of the costs through the company. In *Li v. Dao*,[73] the relevant facts show that the grant of leave was in the best interests of the company, in that:

- the applicant and the defendant opposing the application were both equal shareholders and were in a deadlock that only litigation could resolve the dispute;
- the company was no longer in business and a derivative action would not occupy any physical, human or other resources of the company other than the time and efforts put in by the applicant;
- the company had no creditors, and so any benefit acquired by the company from a successful outcome would only flow through to these two shareholders in equal proportion.

In making a conditional grant of leave, Connock J concluded that the "main purpose ... is to enable the trial judge to make such orders as to costs as he or she thinks appropriate *after* the final hearing".[74]

6.3.2.3 Personal disputes between shareholders

Personal disputes between shareholders are often regarded as having "no obvious interest" to the company.[75] If an applicant wishes to bring a derivative action to resolve a personal issue, that applicant is required to pay for the action and indemnify the company in respect to any adverse costs order. The courts will not allow company funds to be used in a derivative action to settle a personal dispute, regardless of the final outcome.[76] This is just part of the "domestic arrangements".[77] An example would be in a joint venture where both the applicant and the proposed defendant are equal shareholders experiencing a deadlock, and a derivative action is used as a means of resolving their personal differences.[78]

73 *Li v. Dao* [2018] VSC 530.
74 *Li v. Dao* [2018] VSC 530, at [184] *(emphasis added)*.
75 *In the matter of Imperium Projects Pty Limited* [2015] NSWSC 123, at [14] (Black J).
76 *Reale v. Duncan* [2006] NSWSC 227 and *Duncan Reale v. Cameda Investments* Pty Ltd [2006] NSWSC 1099 is one of three derivative action cases that went through to final judgment. The case involved a dispute between spouses with equal shareholding and directorship. Leave was granted to bring an SDA. Although the defendant was successful in the derivative action, he was unsuccessful in claiming for a recovering of his costs from the company. Instead, the court ordered both parties to pay costs equally and no company funds were used for this purpose.
77 *Roach v. Winnote Pty Ltd* [2006] NSWSC 231, at [29].
78 *Li v. Dao* [2018] VSC 530, at [89] (Connock J), citing *Ragless v. IPA Holdings Pty Ltd* (2008) 65 ACSR 700, para 35 (Debelle J, with Sulan and Vanstone JJ agreeing); *Ehsman v. Nutectime International* [2006] NSWSC 887.

In *In the Matter of Imperium Projects Pty Limited*, a conditional order was made requiring the proposed defendant to pay *only half* of the applicant's costs of the leave application and this was only if the derivative proceeding had a successful outcome in favour of the company.[79] The reason given by Black J was that:[80]

> "the proceedings involve a dispute between shareholders, in which the Company has no obvious interest, and any use of the Company funds to support the interests of one group of shareholders as against another raises matters of potential difficulty."

There is no further court hearing reported on this matter. What the statement means is that if there is no control on costs by the court, and if the defendant succeeds in the derivative action, there is a possibility that the successful defendant will indirectly end up paying some or most of the costs through the company, which is a scenario that the court attempted to avoid.

The case in *Vicad Pty Ltd – Pottie v. Dunkley*[81] reveals a long history of personal animosity amongst the siblings in a family-owned company. Although the company was financially stable, the court decided that the best way to resolve a family feud would be to grant leave to bring a derivative action, but the condition was that no company funds were to be used.

6.3.2.4 Overlap between a personal claim and a derivative claim

Another reason that the courts would not allow the company to pay for the derivative action is where there is some overlap between a personal claim and a derivative action. The applicant is able to make a personal claim, but decides to apply for and bring a derivative action instead, for example, where the shareholder applicant has alleged a breach of director's duties and oppression.

There are cases where the courts have allowed both a personal and a derivative claim to be combined and dealt with in the derivative action.[82] There are also cases where the courts have allowed the applicant to bring a derivative action if this is their preferred choice.[83] There are also cases where the courts have denied leave to bring a derivative action and required the applicant to bring a personal claim instead.[84] One thing that is common in

79 *In the matter of Imperium Projects Pty Limited* [2015] NSWSC 123, at [16].
80 *In the matter of Imperium Projects Pty Limited* [2015] NSWSC 123, at [14].
81 *Pottie v. Dunkley* [2011] NSWSC 166.
82 *Ehsman v. Nutectime International* [2006] NSWSC 887; *Cassegrain v. Gerard Cassegrain and Co Pty Ltd* [2012] NSWSC 403.
83 *Pottie v. Dunkley* [2011] NSWSC 166; *Vinciguerra v. MG Corrosion Consultants Pty Ltd* [2010] FCA 763.
84 *Blakeney v. Blakeney* [2016] WASCA 76; *LPD Holdings (Australia) Pty Ltd v. Phillips* [2013] QSC 225, at Para 51; *Vadori v. AAV Plumbing* [2010] NSWSC 274.

these three situations is that no company funds were permitted to be used in the derivative action. This appears to have been the outcome even where the company is prosperous.[85]

6.3.2.5 Additional safeguard

Another possible explanation that company funds cannot be used in a derivative action stems from the problem known as the "additional safeguard".[86] The company is the primary "beneficiary", so while the court has a broad discretion to decide on costs, the provision allows the court to turn away cases that have no merits or are doubtful.[87] These statements may have prompted the courts to protect the company's assets as seen in some cases.[88] If a company is in liquidation or in some form of insolvency, the company's assets will be preserved for the "general body of creditors".[89]

6.3.2.6 Historical reluctance

Historically, the courts have been reluctant to get involved in a company's internal management issues,[90] which is a source of shareholder litigation and SDA. This could be a reason that they have adopted a conservative approach in not permitting company funds to be used in the first instance.

6.3.3 Summary

After examining numerous cases in this area, it is fair to say that an applicant who is bringing an action on behalf of the company can almost be certain that their costs are unrecoverable from the company, even where the company ultimately succeeds in the action. The general sense is that the court will not permit company funds to be used in a derivative action.

The problem lies in s.242. The court has a *broad discretion* when making a costs order. The court is empowered to make any order it considers

85 *Ehsman v. Nutectime International* [2006] NSWSC 887; *Pottie v. Dunkley* [2011] NSWSC 166.

86 House of Representatives, *Explanatory Memorandum to the CLERP Bill* 1998, at 26, [6.19].

87 House of Representatives, *Explanatory Memorandum to the CLERP Bill* 1998, at 26, [6.19].

88 *Fiduciary Ltd v. Morningstar Research Pty Ltd* [2005] NSWSC 442, at [56]. See also *Roach v. Winnote Pty Ltd* [2006] NSWSC 231, at [29]; *Cooper v. Myrtace Consulting Pty Ltd* [2014] FCA 480, at [31].

89 *Charlton v. Baber* [2003] NSWSC 745, at [74]. See also *Re Colorado Products Pty Ltd (in provisional liquidation)* [2014] NSWSC 64; *Re Sundara Pty Ltd* [2015] NSWSC 1694.

90 See for example, *Burland v. Earle* [1992] AC 83; *Automatic Self-Cleansing Filter Syndicate Co Ltd v Cuninghame* [1906] 2 Ch 34. See also Ian Ramsay and Benjamin Saunders, "Litigation by shareholders and directors: An Empirical study of the Australian statutory derivative action" (2006) *Journal of Corporate Law Studies* 397, at 401, and Pearl Koh, "The statutory derivative action in Singapore: A critical and comparative examination" (2001) 13 *Bond Law Review* 64.

appropriate on costs, and this could be against the applicant, the company or any other party involved in the leave application or in the substantive derivative proceedings. It could also mean that the court is under no obligation to make any order at all.

Currently, there is no consistency in the treatment of s.242. When granting leave, the court is likely to make one of these two orders on costs: (i) granting a conditional leave *on the condition* that the applicant undertakes to pay for the derivative action and indemnify the company on any adverse costs order; or (ii) granting leave but *deferring* its power to make orders on costs until such time that the court is in a better position to assess what is in the best interests of the company. The first approach is often adopted in circumstances where the courts are *not* confident that the applicant has proven that granting leave is in the company's best interests. The courts have tended to link the costs consideration with the best interests of the company criterion. The overall default position in both approaches is that an applicant is expected to carry the burden of costs in running an action on behalf of the company.

It is questionable whether the SDA is an "effective" tool in obtaining shareholder relief. The applicants struggle not only with the need to satisfy the court with the leave requirement but also with recovering their costs. In almost twenty years since the SDA came into operation, only three derivative action cases have gone through to final judgment.[91] Although there are cases where the applicants have been successful in obtaining leave to bring an SDA, the reality is that a vast majority of these applicants have *not* in fact commenced the approved action, and there is no clear explanation for this phenomenon.

There are two possibilities. First, it is quite possible that some applicants may have settled their dispute with the proposed defendant without further court intervention, in which case the leave application may have a useful role, in that it was used as a threat of further litigation and possible liability. In this instance, the SDA, in particular the leave application in itself, could be construed as an "effective" remedy for shareholder applicants. A successful leave application could be used to force the proposed defendant to settle or to change their behaviour so as not to commit further breaches of their duties as directors. However, the second and other possibility is that some applicants may have decided not to proceed with the approved derivative action due to, for example, funding constraint and the uncertainty in the recovery of costs at the end of the process. Not all applicants can financially afford to bring the approved action. Litigation is costly and high costs of litigation may have forced some applicants to abort their further efforts.

This goes back to asking the circular questions: If the applicant has intended the SDA as a threat of liability and the applicant fails to execute that threat (because the defendant is unmoved by it and the applicant is unable to

91 This will be discussed in the latter part of this chapter.

financially afford further litigation), what is the next best option for the applicant? What now for the successful applicant? Where is the justification that the SDA is an "effective remedy" for shareholders when they cannot financially afford to go on to the next stage and pursue the approved action? The government report claims that the SDA could be used to provide an "effective remedy" for shareholders.[92] The courts have often denied company funds to be used in derivative actions. There seems to be no justification for making the applicant pay for the derivative action in the current model, particularly in circumstances where there are non-participating shareholders standing by to benefit from the successes in the derivative action.

The current costs structure in Australia is cold comfort for prospective applicants. They have no idea whether their costs in bringing an SDA are recoverable in the meantime. In one extreme case, *Maher v. Honeysett and Maher Electrical Contractors Pty Ltd*,[93] the court ordered the applicant, who was successful in both the leave application and the subsequent derivative proceedings, to pay half of the costs of the entire proceedings, and that no company funds were to be used. It is questionable whether the applicant should be burdened with costs in circumstances where the company is named as the plaintiff and where successes and benefits accrue only to the company.

6.4 Reasons in support of costs indemnities for the applicant

It is submitted that if an applicant has satisfied the court of the five criteria for leave under s.237(2), then the applicant should be entitled to a costs order as of right. In the first instance, the company would be a more appropriate funder of the approved action, unless it has become insolvent. The financial status of the applicant should not be relevant in deciding whether the proposed action is or is not in the company's interests. This part sets out reasons in support of the applicant's entitlement to costs indemnity orders, followed by suggestions for law reform in the next part to overcome Australia's rigid approach.

6.4.1 Derivative action "brought on behalf of" and "in the name of" the company

The main argument put forward is that the costs question should not be a determining factor in the leave application. The financial status of the applicant should not be relevant in the determination of the merits of the derivative action. The leave application and the costs question are two separate matters and should be treated separately. The argument is that where an applicant is successful in the leave application – that is, where the applicant has proven to

92 House of Representatives, CLERP Proposal No. 3, *Proposals for Reform: Directors' Duties and Corporate Governance: Facilitating Innovation and Protecting Investors* (1997), at 35.
93 *Maher v. Honeysett and Maher Electrical Contractors Pty Ltd* [2009] NSWSC 445.

be acting in good faith, the proposed action appears to be in the company's interests, and there is evidence that the company is unable or unwilling to pursue the action against the wrongdoer – the applicant should be entitled to a costs order or costs indemnity, either from the company or from other sources.

Under s.236(2), the provision says "proceedings brought on behalf of a company must be brought in the company's name". In essence, this is about derivative action brought by somebody and it must be in the company's name. It is indisputably clear that the company is the "proper plaintiff",[94] and if the action is successful, an order is given in favour of the company.[95] Logically, given that the action *has to be* in the company's name, and any success in the action accrues to the company, the company should be the bearer of the costs associated with that action in the first instance. An applicant who has been successful in the leave application is merely assisting and facilitating the company in resolving a dispute, particularly where there is a deadlock, through bringing the action on behalf of the company and for the benefit of all shareholders as a whole in the company.

Further support for this argument may be found through the reasoning of the English Court of Appeal in *Wallersteiner v. Moir*, where the applicant was entitled to a costs indemnity regardless of whether the company ultimately won or lost.[96] The conditions for costs indemnity are clear. Lord Buckley stated that the company should normally be liable for the claimant's costs provided that the claimant brings the derivative action in good faith and on reasonable grounds.[97] Lord Denning added that the initiation of the action must be a reasonable and prudent course to take in the interests of the company.[98] These conditions for a costs indemnity in *Wallersteiner v. Moir* are precisely the statutory conditions that an applicant must satisfy the court under s.237(2) in order to obtain leave. It is only fair that the applicant be entitled to costs indemnity from this point on.

This fairness element stems from considering the consequences of a derivative action and its eventual success or failure. Lord Denning has provided a logical reasoning:[99]

> "if the action succeeds, the wrongdoing director will be ordered to pay the costs: but if they are not recovered from him, they should be paid by the company. And all the additional costs (over and above party and party costs) should be taxed on a common fund basis and paid by the company.

94 *Foss v. Harbottle* (1843) 2 Hare 461.
95 *Spokes v. Grosvenor Hotel Co Ltd* [1897] 2 QB 124.
96 *Wallersteiner v. Moir* (No 2) [1975] QB 373.
97 *Wallersteiner v. Moir* (No 2) [1975] QB 373, at 403–404.
98 *Wallersteiner v. Moir* (No 2) [1975] QB 373, at 392.
99 *Wallersteiner v. Moir* (No 2) [1975] QB 373, at 391–392.

> ... But what if the action fails? ... the minority shareholder ... should not himself be liable to pay the costs of the other side, but the company itself should be liable, because he was acting for it and not himself. In addition, he should himself be indemnified by the company, in respect of his own costs even if the action fails."

This common law approach has been qualified in subsequent cases to bar wealthy shareholder claimants from obtaining indemnity; for example, both *Smith v. Croft* and *Farrow v. Registrar of Building Societies* took a more restrictive approach and held that interim costs orders should only be made if the minority shareholder claimant could show a genuine financial need.[100] It is submitted that the financial needs test is inappropriate and irrelevant, in that it defeats the purpose and intent of the SDA.[101] Furthermore, an applicant brings an action not for himself or herself but for the company named as the plaintiff and for the benefit of the company. It is very rare to have a situation where a wealthy applicant, with only a small token of shares in the company, would put their wealth at risk in litigating on behalf of other people. Despite the drawback, there are other cases showing continued support for costs indemnity under the *Wallersteiner* approach, including an Australian case in *Wood v. Links Golf Tasmania Pty Ltd* as discussed in the above.[102] The common law rule, as laid down in *Wallersteiner*, still has some use in the United Kingdom under strict circumstances, as will be explained later in this chapter.

6.4.2 Applicant's financial status is irrelevant in deciding merits of the action

The courts often take the view that the action will only be in the best interests of the company if the applicant can afford to pay.[103] The author has issues with this approach. It is not clear why consideration of the applicant's ability to pay is an important test of the company's interests element under s.237(2)(c), when clearly, there is no cross-reference made in the statute between s.237(2) leave criteria and the costs provision in s.242. Section 237(2) says that the court must grant leave if the five criteria referred to within that provision have been satisfied.[104] There is no mention of costs in the provision. Furthermore,

100 *Smith v. Croft* (No.1) [1986] 2 All ER 551 (English decision); *Farrow v. Registrar of Building Societies* [1991] 2 VR 589 (Australian decision).

101 One of the purposes of the SDA is enhancing directors' and managers' accountability as stated in the government report discussed in Chapter 2.

102 *Wood v. Links Golf Tasmania Pty Ltd* [2010] FCA 570, at [9–12] (Finkelstein J). These other cases and support from other jurisdictions will be discussed in the latter part of this chapter.

103 *Huang v. Wang* [2016] NSWCA 164, at [60] (Bathurst CJ, McColl JA and Barrett AJA agreeing); *Swansson v. RA Pratt Properties Pty Ltd* (2002) 42 ACSR 313; [2002] NSWSC583.

104 *Connective Services Pty Ltd v. Slea Pty Ltd* [2018] VSCA 229, at [2] (Ferguson CJ, Whelan and McLeish JJA); *Huang v. Wang* [2016] NSWCA 164, at [78] (Barrett AJA); *Carpenter v. Pioneer Park Pty Ltd* [2004] NSWSC 976. at [16].

s.238 allows substitution of another person if the original successful applicant is unable to proceed with the approved derivative action. If the original applicant is unsuccessful in the leave application because the court is too harsh in assessing the applicant's financial status, what chance is there for the second or subsequent applicant to apply for leave based on merits?

The courts' fixation on the conditional grant of leave seems to rule out some applicants who may be genuinely in need of court intervention and relief; for example, shareholders wishing to remedy the wrong done to the company due to directors' improper conduct. For the court to rule out these shareholders because they fail to prove their financial capability for leave is rather harsh. Respectfully noted, the current approach by many of the courts seems to focus not on the merits of the proposed action but on the wealth of the applicant as a test of their eligibility to bring the action. There is no logic in making the applicant pay for the action.

It is understandable that the court must try to balance the need to give shareholders an opportunity to bring an action to seek appropriate relief, and at the same time, to prevent actions that are unmeritorious or doubtful.[105] However, the leave criteria are already adequate in protecting the company's interests. The leave requirement alone is enough to filter out any unmeritorious and frivolous actions such that it is not necessary to make it any harder for the applicant to prove their financial capability for the purposes of demonstrating that the proposed action has merits and is worth pursuing.[106] Requiring the applicant to disclose their financial position could be argued as an invasion of personal privacy, considering that there is nowhere under the Act in Part 2F.1A that requires the applicant to undergo a financial means test as a condition for leave, for proof that the action is in the company's interests. Professor Keay argues that it seems unfair for the applicant to pay when they have "jumped over all of the hurdles".[107] Professors Kaplan and Elwood make a similar comment regarding interim funding in Canada that "it is curious that a test for interim funding would revisit the merits of the action, when the court will have already found that the action has sufficient merit to satisfy the interests of the company's requirement for leave".[108] Professor Ramsay argues that if an applicant has satisfied the court for leave, there should be a "mandatory requirement" for the company to pay.[109] Monichino has taken a

105 House of Representatives, *Explanatory Memorandum to the CLERP Bill* 1998, at 26, [6.19].

106 For detailed discussion of the high costs of derivative action and the complex reality faced by shareholders in deciding whether to bring an SDA, see Dan W. Puchniak, "The derivative action in Asia: The complex reality" (2012) 9 *Berkeley Business Law Journal* 1.

107 Andrew Keay, "Assessing and rethinking the statutory scheme for derivative actions under the Companies Act 2006" (2016) 16 *Journal of Corporate Law Studies* 39, at 57–58.

108 William Kaplan and Bruce Elwood, "The derivative action: A shareholder's 'bleak house'?" (2003) 36 *University of British Columbia Law Review* 443, at 465.

109 Ian Ramsay, "Corporate governance, shareholder litigation and the prospects for a statutory derivative action" (1992) 15 *NSW Law Journal* 149, at 164.

more flexible view and concludes that "the court should not be constrained by self-imposed rules", but rather should be free to adopt a fluid approach so as to make costs orders that are tailored to the particular facts before it.[110] The view of the author is that when the court is satisfied that the proposed action has merits, leave should be granted and the applicant be entitled to costs indemnity either from the company or from other sources.

6.4.3 Compensation and benefits accrue to the company

Another argument why the company should pay for the action stems from the concept of unjust enrichment. Under the current costs structure in Australia, when judgment is in favour of the company in the derivative action, any compensation or benefit received by the company will flow directly to all shareholders in the company, including the defendants if they are shareholders. For example, in *Zhu v. Orico Australia Pty Ltd*, the court found that the applicant had no collateral purpose in applying to bring the proposed action because the facts established that "the benefit that is sought to be gained for Orico Australia will benefit [the applicant] and [the defendant] in equal measure in their capacity as shareholders".[111] A similar reasoning is seen in *Li v. Dao*, where the court held that there was no collateral purpose on the part of the applicant in bringing the proposed action because the facts showed that the defendant with 50% shareholding would still "benefit from any successful outcomes that flow through to the two shareholders [the applicant and the proposed defendant]".[112] These were proof that the applicants were acting in good faith, had no collateral purpose and that the proposed action was in the company's interests. The unfortunate outcome for the applicants in these cases and many similar cases is that the applicants are still required to bear the costs initially, with no certain terms of any recovery.

Based on equitable principles, if a company is going to be the primary beneficiary and recipient of the compensation or benefits awarded in the successful action, the company should also be the bearer of costs in the running of that action. The applicant is merely an initiator and facilitator in the process. Indeed, while the applicant may have a greater interest in the outcome of the action, their ultimate receipt of compensation and benefit is limited to the proportionate amount of the shares they hold in the company. It is difficult to justify the company not having to pay for the action when the company is named as the plaintiff in the derivative action.

In recommending a mandatory requirement for the company to pay, Ramsay raises the concept of unjust enrichment as his further argument. If judgment is given in favour of the company in the action and if the company

110 Monichino, n 9, at 127.
111 *Zhu v. Orico Australia Pty Ltd* [2019] VSC 313, at [54] (Connock J).
112 *Li v. Dao* [2018] VSC 530, at [102], [74] (Connock J).

has not been required to pay the legal costs of the applicant, "this can be viewed as a form of unjust enrichment given that the company receives the benefit of the [applicant's] action".[113] Wilson takes a different approach to the unjust enrichment argument and suggests that legal costs be shifted to the solicitors acting for the company.[114] Solicitors, according to some scholars, are entrepreneurs;[115] and this means that they can align their interests with the interests of their clients.[116] The idea is to shift the risks of the costs to the solicitors who wish to take on the derivative action. The focus is to allow compensation awarded by the court to flow through to the solicitors first, as payment for their services, before passing on the remainder to the shareholders in the company. This would ultimately remove the burden of costs on the applicant.

6.4.4 Directors' accountability and corporate governance purpose

Another argument in support of the applicant's entitlement to costs indemnity stems from the public interest element. Chapter 2 discusses the role of the SDA. Its role is to enhance directors' accountability by allowing shareholders a means to deter managerial misconduct and breaches of directors' duties. These considerations are important not only for the company being the subject of litigation, but also for other related companies and for the community at large. A successful shareholder action, even if this means only a non-monetary relief being granted by the court, could possibly bring about positive changes in the behaviour of certain directors and in turn, improve the internal working of the company and other companies related to it, either directly or indirectly. A non-monetary relief could improve directors' accountability to the company by putting them on notice and encouraging them to practise good corporate governance. An applicant who is assisting the company in achieving these goals should not have to pay for the action.

6.4.5 Applicant granted leave to bring the approved action is an "agent"

An argument may be made that, in the context of litigation, the role of a successful applicant could be treated comparatively with that of the board of directors. That is, an applicant could be placed in "the same" position

113 Ramsay, n 109, at 164.

114 John D. Wilson, "Attorney fees and the decision to commence litigation: Analysis, comparison and an application to the shareholders' derivative action" (1985) 5 *Windsor Yearbook of Access to Justice* 142, at 177.

115 John C. Coffee, Entrepreneurial Litigation: Its Rise, Fall and Future (Harvard University Press, 2015); JR Macey and JP Miller, "The plaintiffs' attorney's role in class action and derivative litigation: Economic analysis and recommendations for reform" (1991) 58 *University of Chicago Law Review* 1.

116 Wilson, n 114, at 173–174.

as the company directors.[117] A successful applicant may be viewed as an "agent" acting on behalf of the company.[118] According to the agency theory, when the board of directors pursues an action on behalf of the company against a wrongdoer, the company pays for the action. By the same analogy, if an applicant has been successful in the leave application, and permission is given to bring the action, that applicant should be treated in the same way as the company board and be allowed a costs indemnity order.

6.4.6 Support for costs indemnity from other jurisdictions

There is support from other jurisdictions that the company should bear the costs of the derivative action. That is, some countries allow the applicants who have been successful in the leave application a right to costs indemnity if the company can afford it, and if circumstances seem fair and reasonable. Examples are from the United Kingdom, New Zealand, Canada and of course, the US.

6.4.6.1 The United Kingdom

Under the UK law, rule 19.9E of its *Civil Procedure (Amendment) Rules* 2007 states that:

> "The court may order the company, body corporate or trade union for the benefit of which a derivative claim is brought, to indemnify the claimant against liability for costs incurred in the permission application or in the derivative claim or both."

This is equivalent to the *Wallersteiner* principle as explained earlier.[119] Thus, the courts in the United Kingdom can make a conditional costs order based on the *Wallersteiner* principle.[120] However, the courts appear to have approached rule 19.9E with caution, only allowing the successful applicant to receive their costs indemnity from the company not as a lump sum payment but in stages and by incremental release.[121] This is to ensure that the applicant uses the SDA for a proper purpose and to prevent any potential abuse of the process. In *Boston Trust Co Ltd v. Szerelmey Ltd*, in granting

117 Arad Reisberg, "Funding derivative actions: A re-examination of costs and fees as incentives to commence litigation" (2004) 4 *Journal of Corporate Law Studies* 345, at 375.

118 *Wallersteiner v. Moir* (No 2) [1975] QB 373, at 391 (Denning LJ).

119 *Wallersteiner v. Moir* (No 2) [1975] QB 373.

120 *Wishart v. Castlecroft Securities Ltd* [2009] CSIH 65. See also Andrew Charman and Johan du Toit SC, *Shareholder Actions* (Bloomsbury Publisher, Second edition, 2018), Chapter 6 at [6.47].

121 *Boston Trust Co Ltd v. Szerelmey Ltd* [2020] EWHC 1136; *Kiani v. Cooper* [2010] EWHC 577 (Ch); *Stainer v. Lee* [2010] EWHC 1539; *Wishart v. Castlecroft Securities Ltd* [2009] CSIH 65.

leave to bring the derivative claims, the court also granted the successful claimant an indemnity order and set out terms for incremental release.[122] In a most recent decision, the court also made it clear that the indemnity order granted in favour of the successful claimant is "not a free pass" to engage in unnecessary or speculative work following the leave decision.[123] The defendant can challenge a claim for costs if the expenditure appears exorbitant, and as an example, an indemnity order would not automatically cover an inquiry into damages.[124] In *Stainer v. Lee*, the court held that the incremental release was necessary to monitor the spending, in recognition that "the amount of likely recovery is... uncertain, there is a concern that the claimant's costs could become disproportionate".[125]

However, a costs indemnity in favour of the applicant is not available in all cases. For example, where a dispute is personal between two shareholders and where an oppression action may be more appropriate in the circumstances, then a costs indemnity is not available to the applicant.[126] *In Zavahir v. Shankleman & Others*, after weighing up the risks and benefits of the proposed action, the court decided not the grant leave for an SDA, stating that such action would not be in the interests of the company.[127]

6.4.6.2 New Zealand

In New Zealand, its legislation states that if an applicant applies for a costs indemnity order, then the court must make that order for the company to pay unless it is "unjust or inequitable" for it to bear those costs.[128] The key test for a costs order is "unjust or inequitable". An award of costs is not automatic; an applicant is required to apply for costs indemnity.[129]

After an uncertain start to the operation of the SDA,[130] the courts in subsequent cases then allowed some applicants to recover their costs out of

122 *Boston Trust Co Ltd v. Szerelmey Ltd* [2020] EWHC 1136 (Ch); *Re Nexbell Ltd* [2021] EWHC 1258 (Ch).

123 *Boston Trust Co Ltd v. Szerelmey Ltd* [2022] EWHC 3055 (Ch), at [12] (Karet J).

124 *Boston Trust Co Ltd v. Szerelmey Ltd* [2022] EWHC 3055 (Ch), at [12] (Karet J).

125 *Stainer v. Lee* [2010] EWHC 1539, at [55–56] (Roth J). See also *Iesini v. Westrip Holdings Ltd* [2009] EWHC 2526 (Ch), [2010] All ER 108.

126 See for example, *Tonstate Group Ltd v. Wojakovski* [2019] EWHC 3363; *Bhullar v. Bhullar* [2016] 1 BCLC 106; *Hook v. Summer* [2015] EWHC 3820; *Hughes v. Weiss* [2012] EWHC 2363. See also *Re Nexbell Ltd* [2021] EWHC 1258 (Ch).

127 *Zavahir v. Shankleman & Others* [2016] EWHC 2772 (Ch).

128 Section 166 of the *Companies Act* 1993 (NZ).

129 In *Thorrington v. McCann* (1997) 8 NZCLC 261,564, the applicant did not apply for a costs order soon after the court had granted leave, and so was not entitled to a costs indemnity.

130 See for example, in *Vrij v. Boyle* [1995] 3 NZLR 763 (HC), where the court postponed all questions of costs and indemnities pending the outcome of the derivative action, which meant that the applicant must pay all costs in the interim. The New Zealand's SDA came into operation in 1993.

the company's funds where there was a need for indemnity.[131] Taylor, in her empirical study, reports that in 37.5% of the cases, the courts in New Zealand have awarded costs in favour of the applicant where they had applied for it soon after a decision was made in granting leave to bring an SDA; and in 40% of the cases, the applicants did not apply for a costs indemnity.[132] In *Presley v. CallPlus Ltd*, the court has said that there are "good policy reasons why the Act provides that ... the onus is on the respondent to satisfy the court that it would be unjust or inequitable for the company to bear those costs".[133] It is reasonable, therefore, to say that while the legislation allows the applicant a costs indemnity out of company funds, the court can decline the costs application where a derivative action is more about settling a personal dispute between shareholders and where an oppression action may be more suitable.

The approach in New Zealand does provide the applicant some certainty of outcome in their costs application under the "unjust and inequitable" ground, which could be helpful when making a decision as to whether to proceed with the approved derivative action, or even to decide at the very early stage whether to apply for leave to bring such action.

6.4.6.3 Canada

In Canada, its statute allows the court to make any order at any time in respect to requiring the company to pay reasonable costs incurred by the applicant in connection with the derivative action.[134] There is also a provision allowing the court to make *interim funding orders* if applied for by the applicant.[135] It seems that the applicant has a prima facie right to a costs indemnity where leave is granted, but the court retains the discretion to set terms as to when and how often the applicant can claim for interim funding.[136] In Canada, while the courts have tended to be cautious in awarding costs,[137] there are

131 See, for example, *MacFarlane v. Barlow* (1997) 8 NZCLC 261, at 470.

132 Lynne Taylor, "The derivative action in the Companies Act 1993: An empirical study" (2006) 22 *New Zealand Universities Law Review* 337, at 355 and 362. The study was for the period between July 1999 and April 2006.

133 *Presley v. CallPlus Ltd* [2008] NZCCLR 37.

134 Section 247(d) of the *Canada Business Corporation Act* 1990 states that "the court may at any time make any order it thinks fit including... (d) an order requiring the corporation or its subsidiary to pay reasonable legal fees and any other costs reasonably incurred by the complainant in connection with the [derivative] action".

135 Section 246(d) of the Canada *Business Corporation Act* 1990 states that "Where a complainant on an application can establish to the satisfaction of the court that an *interim order* for relief should be made, the court may make such order as it thinks fit".

136 For example, in *Turner v. Mailhot* [1985] 28 BLR 222, the court referred to the *Wallersteiner* principles and ruled that an applicant who has successfully obtained leave for an SDA establishes a prima facie right to an indemnity from the company.

137 Kaplan and Elwood, n 108, at 464.

instances where the court has ordered the company to pay for the SDA where the applicant has a financial need.[138]

6.4.6.4 Possible approach for Australia?

In order to remedy the rigid approach we have in Australia, some form of reconciliation with the *Wallersteiner* principle is necessary. One possible solution could be to amend s.242 with the effect that the broad discretionary power conferred on the court be restricted by making it clear that the successful applicant may be entitled to a costs indemnity from the company. A better approach would be to provide a system of incremental release of funds, based on either the stage in which the action is currently at or by periodic payment. It is necessary to have a balance to ensure that the courts are not too generous in making indemnity orders and at the same time not too harsh. The goal is not to "hinder valid claims" but to ensure that the wrongs done to the company are properly dealt with by the court.[139] A better wording for the new costs provision in Australia could be to allow the court the power to:

(i) *specifically* make orders requiring the company to bear the costs of the approved action (adopting the provisions in the United Kingdom, New Zealand and Canada); and
(ii) make orders in respect to interim funding, provided that the applicant applies for it (Canada) and that circumstances appear fair and equitable (New Zealand).

6.5 Suggestions for law reform

The suggestions made in the above discussion regarding the approaches from other jurisdictions relate to making the company pay for the derivative action; that is, allowing the successful applicant a right of indemnity from the company. This part now focuses on the US contingency fees arrangement, the idea of commercial litigation funding and the possibility of making public funding available. The idea is to shift the costs, or more appropriately the risks of costs, of litigation over to the solicitors or to the funders. The US approach is a preferred choice for reasons as explained below.

6.5.1 The US approach on derivative action fees

The US fees structure is superior, in that the shareholder plaintiffs are not liable to any costs, and in most cases, the company is also exempt from costs liability. The costs or the risks of costs are shifted to the solicitors acting for

138 See, for example, *Intercontinental Precious Metals Inc v. Cooke* [1994] WWR 66; *Primex Investments Ltd v. Northwest Sports Enterprises Ltd* [1996] 4 WWR 54.

139 Samantha Tang, "Shareholder remedies: Demise of the derivative claim?" (2012) 1 *UCL Journal of Law and Jurisprudence* 178, 203.

the clients. The structure is unique in many ways. The general rule in the US is that both parties bear their own legal costs regardless of the outcome in the action;[140] and because of this, the US attorneys depend on the contingency fees arrangement as payment for their services. They are entitled to retain anywhere between 20% and 30% of the amount they recover in a successful action or when the matter is settled.[141]

In derivative litigation, the US uses the contingency fees arrangement with two other approaches.[142] The first is called the "common fund" doctrine, which applies when the court awards a monetary compensation in a successful action or when the parties settle the matter with a monetary figure.[143] The attorneys may deduct an agreed sum from the total recovery amount based on the agreed percentage, with the remainder then paid to the company for distribution to the shareholders who are entitled to make their claims.[144] This common fund approach is equivalent to the contingency fees arrangement that applies to other forms of action.

The second approach, also commonly applied, stems from the "substantial benefits" test with the use of the "lodestar method".[145] This second approach applies where a successful derivative action leads to *non-monetary relief* that has substantial benefits to the company, in which case the "lodestar" method is used to calculate the attorneys' fees for services rendered. This method is simply a calculation of the attorneys' fees based on the number of hours reasonably spent on the work, multiplied by the applicable market hourly rate. This method may be adopted irrespective of whether a monetary fund is generated from the action.[146] Depending on a number of factors, such as novelty

140 See John C. Coffee, "The unfaithful champion: The plaintiff as monitor in shareholder litigation" (1985) 48 *Law and Contemporary Problems* 5, at 15–16; Dooley MP, *Foundation of Corporation Law*, Foundation Press 1995.

141 Herbert M. Kritzer, *Risks Reputations and Rewards: Contingency Fee Legal Practice in the United States*, (Stanford University Press, 2004).

142 For general discussion on the US and Australian derivative actions, see Thai, n 13; Lynden Griggs, "The statutory derivative action: Lessons that may be learnt from its past!" (2002) 6 *UWS Law Review* 63.

143 For a discussion of the origin of this common fund doctrine, see John P. Dawson, "Lawyers and involuntary clients: Attorney fees from funds" (1974) 87 *Harvard Law Review* 1597, at 1603–1612, which refers to two important US Supreme Court cases: *Trustee v. Greenough* 105 US 527 (1881), and *Central RR & Banking Co v. Pettus* 113 US 116 (1885).

144 M. J. Loewenstein, "Shareholder derivative litigation and corporate governance" (1999) 24 *Delaware Journal of Corporate Law* 1, at 14.

145 See, *Mill v. Electric Auto Lite Co* 396 US 375, at 392 (1970), where the US Full Supreme Court endorsed the "lodestar" method. It was held in that case that the shareholder plaintiff was entitled to attorneys' fees in the successful derivative action because by allowing "others to obtain full benefit from the plaintiff's efforts without contributing equally to the litigation expenses would be to enrich the others unjustly at the plaintiff's expenses".

146 *Southerland v. International Longshoremen's Union* 845 F 2d, 796, at 800–801 (9th Cir, 1987); *Levenson v. Overseas Shipholding Group Inc* 84 FRD 354, at 360 (SDNY 1979); *Sugarland Industry Inc. v. Thomas* 420 A 2d 142, at 149–150 (Del 1980).

and complexity of issues, quality of representation, risk and the like,[147] the court has the power to scrutinise and adjust the final figure calculated by the attorneys.[148]

Both the common fund doctrine and the lodestar method are the two most important mechanisms that dictate how the plaintiff's attorneys conduct the derivative action, who pays the attorneys' fees and how these fees are calculated.[149] The attorneys in the US operate more like "entrepreneurs";[150] they have as much interest in the outcome of the derivative action as the shareholder plaintiff. The benefit of the US fees structure, if adopted in Australia, is that if the proposed action appears to have no merits, it is unlikely that lawyers will take on the case, which is precisely in line with the statutory requirement in Australia's SDA that the proposed action has to be in the company's interests.

6.5.2 No floodgate problem in the US derivative action

At the time when the SDA came into operation, there was the intent of Parliament to minimise the possibility of a floodgate effect. This was made clear in the Explanatory Memorandum by pointing out that the court has a "broad discretion" to decide on the question of costs,[151] and that the costs provision in s.242 is intended as an "additional safeguard" against unmeritorious and doubtful actions.[152] It is a way of putting a tight control on who can bring a derivative action. This fear of the floodgate effect is unfounded.

When looking at the trend in the US derivative actions and the operation of the common fund doctrine and the lodestar method, there is no clear evidence of the floodgate problem in the US. Coffee, an eminent corporate law professor, points out the infrequent use of the derivative action in the US. His empirical study reveals that the number of derivative actions is declining while the number of shareholder class actions is steadily rising.[153] For example in 2012 alone, there were 52 derivative actions heard in the Delaware courts compared with 318 shareholder class actions in the same year in the same jurisdiction.[154] Dent made a similar observation 30 years earlier, noting

147 *Hensley v. Eckerhart* 461 US 424, at 434–436 (1983).

148 See generally, Alan Hirsch and Diane Sheehey, *Awarding Attorneys' Fees and Managing Fee Litigation* (Federal Judicial Center, 1994), Vol 19, citing *Hensley v. Eckerhart* 461 US 424, at 433 (1983).

149 Lang Thai, n 13, at 124.

150 Coffee, n 115.

151 House of Representatives, *Explanatory Memorandum to the CLERP Bill* 1998, at 25, [6.16].

152 House of Representatives, *Explanatory Memorandum to the CLERP Bill* 1998, at 26, [6.19].

153 Coffee, n 115, Ch 3 (derivative action) and Ch 4 (class action).

154 Coffee, n 115, at 47. Sometimes shareholders may have a choice between applying for leave to bring a derivative action or bringing a shareholder class action, and this choice is determined by the number of shareholders involved in the dispute and their efforts to join to form a representative group, which is discussed further in Chapter 7.

a decline in derivative actions in the US because of the need for approval by the independent litigation committee to bring a derivative action, which is not always easy to obtain.[155] The hurdle requirement for bringing a derivative action in the US is just as difficult.[156] The so-called independent directors appointed to the litigation committee to make a recommendation to the court to grant permission to bring the proposed action are not wholly independent and can never be independent.[157] Furthermore, the composition of those independent directors on the litigation committee can easily be challenged, as seen in the leading decision in *Zapata Corporation v. Maldonado*.[158] These are possible reasons that explain the attorneys' reluctance to pursue a derivative action in the US.

Other possible explanations for the decline in derivative action in the US are that: (i) companies are becoming larger and incorporated in a public form, resulting in more diverse share ownerships; and (ii) companies are increasing in size and membership. When considering these factors closely, it is almost impractical for one individual shareholder to apply for permission to bring a derivative action for the benefit of all shareholders in the company. These factors are just as relevant in Australia. It is submitted that adopting the US contingency fees arrangement and the lodestar method is unlikely to opening a floodgate to having more derivative actions in Australia. It would not get to the point where the SDA would be overly used, simply because there is the competing availability of other tools that shareholders can turn to, such as the class action and the oppression action. Unlike the SDA where there is the leave hurdle requirement, one important advantage of bringing a class action or an oppression action is that these have no such hurdle.[159]

155 George Dent, "The power of directors to terminate shareholder litigation: The death of the derivative suit" (1980) 75 *Newark University Law Review* 96, 111–113. See also Robert B. Thompson and Randall Thomas, "The public and private faces of derivative" (2004) 57 *Vanderbilt Law Review* 1747, at 1772–1777, where the authors examined all complaints filed in the Delaware courts in 1999–2000 and found that of 294 cases involving both private and public companies where a breach of fiduciary duty was alleged, only 56 cases were about derivative suits compared to 213 cases related to class actions, and 25 related to other direct suits.

156 For critical discussion of the leave process in the US, see Thai, n 13, at 119–123; Deborah A. DeMott, "Shareholder litigation in Australia and the United States: Common problems, uncommon solutions" (1987) 11(2) *Sydney Law Review* 259, 275–279; Kurt A. Goehre, "Is the demand requirement obsolete? How the United Kingdom modernised its shareholder derivative procedure and what the United States can learn from it" (2010) 28 *Wisconsin International Law Journal* 140, which compares the statutory derivative action in the United Kingdom and Australia with the US.

157 Dent, n 155, at 111–113.

158 *Zapata Corporation v. Maldonado* 430 a.2D 779 (Del) (1981). See also discussion in Deborah A. DeMott, *Shareholder Derivative Actions: Law and Practice*, (Thomson Reuters, 2014–2015), pp 761–764.

159 These other shareholder actions as an alternative are discussed in Chapter 7.

If the US fee structure is introduced into Australia, solicitors acting for the applicant in the SDA are more likely to think twice and weigh up the prospect of success before advising the applicant whether to apply for leave.

6.5.3 Third party commercial litigation funding

It may be possible for derivative actions to be funded by a third party commercial litigation funder, so that neither the applicant nor the company will be liable for costs. However, under the current situations, it may not be conducive for the funder to finance derivative actions. Three possible reasons are:

(a) The need for court permission to bring a derivative action, when currently there is much uncertainty in obtaining that leave;
(b) The uncertainty surrounding the recovery of legal costs under s.242; and
(c) The company involved in a derivative action tends to be small and closely held, which means that the funder is unlikely to earn large profits from a small handful of shareholder claimants.

The idea of commercial litigation funding was first approved by the High Court of Australia in 2006, in a class action case.[160] It was held that it would not be an abuse of the court's processes for a commercial funder to be involved in litigation. The idea is to bypass the US contingency fees arrangement, which is prohibited in Australia.[161] This funding concept is still largely unregulated. There is no specific legislation regulating the funder's commission rate. More recently, some courts have felt the need to step in and intervene,[162] while other courts felt they have no jurisdiction to amend the commission rate.[163] There are also no appropriate rules dealing with this tripartite arrangement involving solicitors, the commercial funder and the client, nor are there clear rules dealing with potential or perceived conflicts.

160 *Campbells Cash and Carry v. Fostiff* (2006) 229 CLR 386. This position was reaffirmed by the same Court three years later in another case, *Jeffrey and Katauskas Pty Ltd v. Richard Constructions Pty Ltd* (2009) 83 ALJR 1180.

161 Lang Thai, "Commercial litigation funding: The need to impose regulations to improve the outcome of the shareholder class actions" (2011) 4 *Journal of the Australasian Law Teachers Association* 1–16.

162 In *Blairgowrie Trading Ltd v. Allco Finance Group Ltd (Receivers and Managers Appointed) (in liq.) (No.3)* [2017] FCA 330, at [110], Beach J decided to exercise his discretion and adjust the funder's agreed commission rate from 32.5% to 22.1%.

163 In *Clarke v. Sandhurst Trustees Limited (No.2)* [2018] FCA 511, at [12], Lee J decided that the court has no power to "upset the bargain struck between the funder and group members", and so allowed the funder to keep the agreed commission rate at 30%, while the law firm pocketed 31% and the remainder was passed on to the group members as their compensation recovery.

Commercial funders are attracted to class actions, such as shareholder class actions, because they make their profits through collecting revenues from a large pool of shareholders who have common or similar claims against the company.[164]

For this funding concept to work in SDAs, industry regulation is necessary. Currently, governments are considering proposals for regulating third party commercial funding for class actions.[165] Funding regulation for SDA may be possible if provisions are structured with the intent of enabling applicants *a chance* to bring the approved action, for example:

- funder must not deny funding if there is strong evidence that the applicant is likely to obtain permission from the court to proceed with the action (providing the applicant *a chance* to bring the proposed action and seek appropriate relief);
- funder is only permitted to charge a commission rate based on the normal market bank interest rate (allowing the funder to make a profit but at the same time putting a cap on the amount it can earn);
- with approval of the court, funder may be permitted to retain the whole of the company's awarded compensation (again providing the applicant *a chance* to bring the proposed action; approval would depend on a number of factors, including the interest rate capped in the funding contract, the applicant's purpose in bringing the action, etc.)

This suggested proposal, regulation of commercial funders in the context of applying to derivative action, may be feasible if the intent of the applicant is to prosecute the wrongdoing directors with a view to deterring them from committing further misconduct. The drawback is that any compensation awarded by the court or received by way of settlement with the other side will need to be deducted twice – payment to the funder and payment to the solicitors – before the remaining sum goes to the company. As discussed above, the US contingency fees structure is more appropriate for derivative actions because only one sum is paid to the solicitors, and it minimises the problem of free riding by non-participating shareholders.

164 Lang Thai, "Class Action Procedure in Australia – Issues and Challenges" in (Chapter 11) in Colin Picker and Guy Seidman (eds.), *The Dynamism of Civil Procedure: Global Trends and Developments (Ius Gentium: Comparative Perspectives on Law and Justice series)*, 215–236 (Springer, 2016); Michael Legg, "Class action settlements in Australia – The need for greater scrutiny" (2014) 38(2) *Melbourne University Law Review* 590. Claims in shareholder class actions tend to be about directors providing misleading or deceptive information on shares or failing to adequately disclose information or about breach of directors' duties.

165 See Australian Law Reform Commission ("ALRC"), "Inquiry into Class Action Proceedings and Third Party Litigation Funders" (Final Report, submitted to the Attorney-General on 21 December 2018); Victorian Law Reform Commission ("VLRC"), "Access to Justice – Litigation Funding and Group Proceedings" (Final Report, March 2018).

6.5.4 Should public funding be used?

Reisberg suggests that public funding of derivative action might be an option in some countries and puts forward arguments for and against that idea.[166] He provides an example from Israel where, in that jurisdiction, there is provision in its legislation that enables its corporate regulator to fund an SDA and that the regulator has the discretion to decide on a case-by-case basis. The test for possible public funding is that the action must have a "public interest" element and the court is satisfied that the proposed action has a "reasonable prospect of success" that leads the court to grant leave to the shareholder applicant to bring that action.[167]

The public interest element may be argued from the point of fulfilling the other function that a derivative action has, which is improvement of corporate governance and corporate social responsibilities, as discussed in Chapter 2. A successful derivative action may lead to greater directors' accountability to the company and to its employees, customers and other stakeholders who might have been in some way affected by the directors' improper conduct. By making the directors accountable for their improper conduct, a successful action may have an important deterrent effect not only on those who have been prosecuted for the wrong done to the company, but also on those who are in a similar position. By making public funding possible, it is one way for Parliament to show formal recognition of the importance of good corporate governance and corporate social responsibility.

Whether Australia should make such public funding available for derivative actions is questionable. ASIC, the main corporate regulator in Australia, is already operating within a tight annual budget, so it would be difficult for ASIC to stretch its resources further.[168]

6.5.5 Minimising the free rider problem

The free rider problem is unavoidable in all derivative actions, unless it is minimised by passing a legislative provision that would specifically prevent compensation passing on to the non-participating shareholders. Empowering the court to make orders for compensation to be paid *directly* to the affected shareholder applicants *rather than to the company* would help to minimise this problem. The benefit of such a provision is to give shareholder applicants an incentive to prosecute directors who have wronged the company, thereby making them accountable for their actions. By giving the affected shareholder

166 Arad Reisberg, "Access to justice or justice not accessed: Is there a case for public funding of derivative claims?" (2012) 37 *Brooklyn Journal of International Law* 1021, at 1038.

167 Sections 205 and s.205A of the *Companies Law* 1999 (Israel) as introduced in May 2011, cited in Reisberg, n 163, at 1038.

168 See Australian Securities and Investment Commission Annual Report 2017–2018: https://asic.gov.au/Annual-report-2017-18/ASIC-AR-introduction.html (viewed 12 July 2019).

applicants more power through allowing them to receive benefits and compensation directly from the court, it would mean that they are more likely to want to assist the company in deterring directors from committing similar misconduct. Conversely, with the knowledge that shareholders have greater power, directors are less likely to commit offences in the first place. Canada and Israel have provisions to these effects.[169] Compensation and benefits awarded directly to the successful applicants would give a more meaningful use to the SDA and its role and function.

6.6 Conclusion

This chapter has explored the fundamental flaws in the operation of the costs provision under s.242. The current practice is that the court either makes a conditional grant of leave requiring the applicant to bear the costs of the action or grants leave to bring the action but reserves its power to decide on the question of costs at a later time, without stating when that may be. This is the only way that the courts can be satisfied that the proposed action is in the company's interests as per the s.237(2)(c) requirement. The idea is that the action will be in the company's interests only if the company does not have to pay for anything and will not lose anything if the action is pursued unsuccessfully. This approach is harsh. It rules out bona fide applicants who cannot afford to pay for the action to seek the appropriate relief needed. Even for shareholders who are financially capable, there is no incentive for them to commence the action knowing that their expenses are unrecoverable.

These approaches seem to have overlooked the fundamental role of the SDA. A derivative action is an action brought on behalf of the company for the purposes of remedying the wrong done *to the company* with the view of deterring directors from committing further misconduct and ensuring the maintenance of good corporate governance. These purposes are for the public good. In order to achieve these purposes, in circumstances where public enforcement by ASIC is not possible due to its limited resources and its need to prioritise matters, shareholders should be given the necessary support to bring the required action to protect the company's interest.

This chapter has explored a number of options, one of which is to recommend a mandatory requirement for the company to pay where the court has granted leave. Leave should be given *not* that the action *is* in the company's interests, because one can never be certain of the outcome in a court case, but based on a proper test that the action *appears to be* in the company's interests. Furthermore, making the company pay for the derivative action would seem to accord with the original legislative intent that costs should follow the event.

169 In Canada, s.246(d) 246(d) of the *Canada Business Corporations Act* 1990; In Israel, s.201 of the *Companies Law* 1999.

The preferred option should be to adopt the US common fund doctrine and the lodestar method based on the substantial benefits test in order to allow the successful applicant to recover their costs. Both parties should be liable for their own solicitors' costs, and payment of solicitors' fees will be contingent on the successful outcome of the derivative action. If the action generates monetary relief, legal fees will be paid at a fixed percentage on the amount recovered. If the action results in a substantial non-monetary benefit to the company, legal fees will be paid out of company funds for the work done. The US approach is superior to the idea of commercial litigation funding. Under the US fees structure, shareholders have certainty of litigation funding, solicitors will operate on a "no win no fee" basis, and they can be certain that only a portion of their compensation will go to the acting solicitors. The fear of the floodgate effect in SDA under the US fees structure is unfounded as this has not been a problem in the US. Similar to Australia, attorneys acting for shareholders in the US also have to pass the leave hurdle before they can proceed with the derivative action, forcing them to weigh the prospects of success before advising their clients and making decisions to apply for leave.

7 Inspection of company books and other factors affecting the use of SDA

7.1 Introduction

The preceding chapters focused on three key issues in respect to the statutory derivative action ("SDA") and provided some suggestions for law reform in order to improve its utility as a shareholder remedy. This chapter aims to discuss other factors affecting the use of the SDA; namely, uncertainty in obtaining an order for inspection of company books and documents, and the availability of alternative actions, such as oppression/unfair prejudice action and shareholder class action.

In some circumstances, an applicant seeking leave to bring an SDA may also need to apply to the court for permission to inspect company books under s.247A of the *Corporations Act* 2001 (C'th) to determine whether they have enough evidence to succeed in a derivative action. A passive shareholder may have a reasonable suspicion that a director has committed a breach of directors' duties but may not be able to prove it due to a lack of knowledge of the internal workings in the company and the extent of internal irregularities. A court order under s.247A is not often forthcoming. Thus, where there are choices, "shareholders are likely to choose the path of least resistance and use other methods to address grievances".[1] An oppression action is one of two important alternatives. Its attractive features are that court approval is not required to commence the action and, if oppression is established, there will be a range of suitable remedies that the court can make in favour of the oppressed party. A class action is another important alternative. A class action is different to an SDA, in that a class action involves aggrieved shareholders suing the company and the directors who are responsible for the wrong done to the company. In other words, a class action is not an action brought on behalf of the company, rather in Australia it is brought by a group of at least seven shareholders with similar or related claims against the company.[2] A self-funded class action could be a good source of remedy for aggrieved shareholders in small private companies.

1 Martin Gelter, "Why do shareholder derivative suits remain rare in continental Europe?" (2012) 37 *Brooklyn Journal of International Law* 843, at 891.
2 *Federal Court of Australia Act* 1976 (C'th), Part IVA

DOI: 10.4324/9781003430063-7

This chapter is structured as follows. Part 2 discusses the difficulty that an applicant may have in obtaining a court order for inspection of company books and documents under s.247A of the *Corporations Act* 2001 (C'th) ("CA").[3] Part 3 explains the availability of oppression/unfair prejudice action and its attractive features as an alternative shareholder remedy. Part 4 discusses the availability of shareholder class action as the other important shareholder remedy. This part will consider why shareholder class action is more popular than the SDA. Its main attraction is that a commercial funder is more willing to finance a class action than an SDA, due to the fact that there is no leave requirement. Class action is commonly used where the number of claimants is large. Shareholders in small private companies can still utilise the class action procedure, provided that they can form a group of seven class members and bring a self-funded action if they cannot secure funding support from a commercial funder. This part will also consider the role of commercial litigation funding and the current reform proposals that address issues relating to litigation funding. Part 5 provides some concluding remarks.

7.2 Limited access to company information

7.2.1 Preliminary

One of the difficulties for a shareholder applicant seeking leave to bring an SDA is the lack of access to company information to establish a cause of action. When there is insufficient evidence, there is not much for the applicant to go on. A shareholder who has very little to do with the internal governance of the company (for example, a non-director shareholder) and who has difficulty gathering evidence to prepare the case properly is likely to face the challenge of deciding whether to make an application for leave.

Pre-action discovery of documents is generally unavailable under common law unless the *Corporations Act* 2001 (C'th) ("CA") provides some exceptions for discovery or the company's constitution provides members with a right of discovery, but even so, these types of discovery are heavily controlled by the majority shareholders and directors. For example, under the CA, s.247D provides that the directors of a company, or the company by a resolution passed at a general meeting, may authorise a member or shareholder to inspect company books.[4] This provision only requires "a resolution"; that is, it does not require a "special resolution",[5] which means only a

3 Hereinafter, references to a section are to the *Corporations Act* 2001 (C'th), unless stated otherwise.

4 *Corporations Act* 2001 (C'th), s.9 defines "books" to mean just about all materials available in the company. This is further explained below in Part 7.2.2 below.

5 *Corporations Act* 2001 (C'th), s.9 defines "special resolution" as a resolution that has been passed by at least 75% of the votes cast by members entitled to vote.

majority vote is required. This provision is also a "replaceable rule",[6] which means that the majority shareholders can remove this provision and replace it with some other clause in the company's constitution by passing a special resolution. In effect, the provision is broad enough for the majority shareholders and directors to impose limitation on inspection by a shareholder/member. Majority shareholders may also be able to displace s.247D and insert some other clause into the company's constitution in order to limit inspection by minority shareholders.[7]

In theory, it seems reasonable for a shareholder to have some rights of inspection of company books and documents, for example, a right to inspect minutes relating to shareholders' meetings under s.251B, a right to inspect the company's registers under s.173 and a right to obtain a copy of the company's constitution under s.139. However, the reality is that the minority shareholder's rights to such general information are very limited. These records are not likely to contain any substantial evidence of corporate wrongdoings. The majority shareholders and directors who are in control of the company may find ways and means to prevent or delay the release of information that may be sensitive or damaging to their position. For example, the controller of the company may require the member requesting information to identify the exact document for inspection as a scheme to buy time and find ways to block the release of such a document containing sensitive and incriminating information. One scholar argues that the absence of a wide-ranging discovery procedure makes derivative action more difficult,[8] while another scholar asserts that a minority shareholder suffers serious "informational disadvantages" compared to the board, in the sense that their lack of access to company information would prevent them from assessing accurately whether to institute a derivative action.[9] Another scholar points out that, as passive shareholders, they are "unfairly penalised" when they are denied detailed information on the company's operation.[10] Others have argued that, without court intervention, it is almost impossible for non-director shareholders to informally obtain evidence of any internal misconduct or wrongdoing.[11]

6 See *Corporations Act* 2001 (C'th), s.135(2).

7 This is possible if the majority shareholders can pass a "special resolution" as required under s.136, with 75% of the votes from members in attendance, to insert a new clause or to change the existing clause in the company's constitution.

8 Gelter, n 1, at 872.

9 Arad Reisberg, *Derivative Actions and Corporate Governance: Theory and Operation* (Oxford University Press, 2007) at 86.

10 Samantha S. Tang, "Corporate avengers need not be angels: Rethinking good faith in the derivative action" (2016) 16 *Journal of Corporate Law Studies* 471, at 477.

11 Christopher Hare, "Shareholder remedies: Personal rights, corporate rights and the derivative action", in Peter Watts, Neil Campbell and Christopher Hare (eds.), *Company Law in New Zealand* (LexisNexis, 2011), 741; Dennis H. Peterson and Matthew J. Cumming, *Shareholder Remedies in Canada* (Looseleaf services, 2nd ed, LexisNexis, 2009), at [16.43].

A shareholder has a right under s.1274 to obtain information about the company in respect to the documents lodged with the Australian Securities and Investments Commission ("ASIC"), but it is worth noting too that not all company documents are available at ASIC. For example, a small proprietary company does not need to lodge a copy of the company's constitution or a resolution with ASIC.[12]

If a shareholder is unable to obtain inspection of books and documents from the company directly, the other option in seeking inspection is by making an application to the court under s.247A. However, an inspection via a court order is equally challenging;[13] there are at least three hurdles under s.247A, as explained further below.

7.2.2 Uncertainty in obtaining inspection under s.247A

7.2.2.1 Scope of the inspection provision

Applying for an inspection order under s.247A is not a smooth process.[14] Section 247A provides that on application by a member of a company, the court may make an order authorising the applicant or another person on behalf of the applicant to inspect "books" and documents of the company.[15] The provision further states that "[t]he Court may only make the order if it is satisfied that the applicant is *acting in good faith* and that the inspection is to be made *for a proper purpose*".[16]

"Books" is defined as including all registers and all records of information, financial reports and records and any document, however compiled, recorded and stored.[17] This definition is wide enough to include all materials that are retrievable by a computer, whether stored in the computer or in a remote location.[18]

Section 247A(3) and (4) state that a person who applies for leave to bring an SDA under s.237 or is granted leave to bring such action or is eligible to apply for leave under that section, may apply to the court for an order authorising the applicant or another person on behalf of the applicant to inspect books of the company; and s.247A(5) provides that the court "may make the

12 See s.136(5) of the *Corporations Act* 2001 (C'th), comparing with a public company's mandatory requirement.

13 Lang Thai and Matt Berkahn, "Statutory derivative actions in Australia and New Zealand: What can we learn from each other?" (2012) 25 *New Zealand University Law Review* 370, at 394.

14 The inspection provision was introduced in 1985 under the old s.256B of the Companies Code 1985 and has since been amended and re-numbered and is now contained in s.247A of the *Corporations Act* 2001 (C'th).

15 The word "books" is defined in s.9 of the CA.

16 Emphasis added.

17 *Corporations Act* 2001 (C'th), s.9.

18 Robert P. Austin and Ian M. Ramsay, *Ford, Austin and Ramsay's Principles of Corporations Law* (LexisNexis Butterworths, 17th ed., 2018), at 936; looseleaf services, 2019, at [10.420].

order only if it is satisfied" that the applicant is acting in good faith and the inspection is made for a purpose connected with the application for leave under s.237, or with bringing or intervening in proceedings pursuant to leave granted under that section.[19] In essence, the intention of bringing an SDA or applying to bring an SDA may be a relevant factor, but the applicant must still pass the "good faith" and the "proper purpose" tests, and the grant of an inspection order is still within the court's power to decide.

A further limitation is that only a current member of the company has standing to apply for inspection. This is in reference to the word "member" in s.247A (as opposed to a "former member" in s.236(1) in relation to an SDA). This is confirmed in *Leadenhall Australia Pty Ltd v. Cape Lambert Resources Ltd* where Charleston J stated that s.247A is available only to a "current" shareholder of the company.[20] Thus, there is a presumption that a former member would not be acting in good faith in the inspection and that his or her inspection would not be for a proper purpose.

There are at least three hurdles under s.247A: (i) the need to show "good faith" and "proper purpose"; (ii) the grant of inspection is at the court's discretion; and (iii) the likely need to show "special interest" for inspection. It is possible to apply for an inspection order and an order to bring an SDA simultaneously.[21]

7.2.2.2 The need to show "good faith" and "proper purpose"

It has been said that the onus is on the applicant to demonstrate "good faith" and "proper purpose" before the court would consider whether to grant an inspection order.[22] The applicant is required to prove them objectively.[23] These terms are not defined in the legislation. There is also no clarity in the judicial interpretation of these terms.

There is some uncertainty as to whether these two elements are a composite test or two separate requirements.[24] In some cases, the court has con-

19 Section 247A is reproduced in Appendix A. It is not within the SDA provisions in Part 2F.1A. Subsections 247A(3), (4) and (5) were introduced into the CA at the same time as the SDA provisions.

20 *Leadenhall Australia Pty Ltd v. Cape Lambert Resources Ltd* (2018) 125 ACSR 484; [2018] FCA 558, at [35] (Charlesworth J).

21 Re Akierman Holdings Pty Ltd [2015] NSWSC 1395.

22 *Acehill Investment Pty Ltd v. Incitec Ltd* [2002] SASC 344, at [29] (Debelle J), cited in *Leadenhall Australia Pty Ltd v. Cape Lambert Resources Ltd* (2018) 125 ACSR 484; [2018] FCA 558, at [32] (Charlesworth J), in *In the Matter of Sirrah Pty Limited* [2017] NSWSC 1683, at [22] (Black J), and in *In the matter of Tolco Pty Limited* [2016] NSWSC 1069, at [15–16] (Brereton J).

23 *Leadenhall Australia Pty Ltd v. Cape Lambert Resources Ltd* (2018) 125 ACSR 484; [2018] FCA 558, at [32] (Charlesworth J), citing *Acehill Investment Pty Ltd v. Incitec Ltd* [2002] SASC 344 and *Barrack Mines Ltd v. Grants Patch Mining Ltd* [1988] 1 Qld R 606 (Full Court).

24 See discussion in Christos Mantziaris, "The member's right to inspect the company books: Corporations Act, s.247A" (2009) 83 *Australian Law Journal* 621, at 627–628.

sidered them as one composite requirement;[25] while in other cases, the court has construed them as two separate tests.[26] In the most recent decision, the Full Federal Court of Australia in *Enares Pty Limited v. Nimble Money Limited* was critical of the structure of s.247A, noting the wording in that provision as "awkward",[27] and went on to state that the two elements in that provision "will regularly involve overlapping considerations".[28] In *Mesa Minerals Ltd v. Mighty River International Ltd*, the Full Federal Court held that these two elements take the form of "a composite notion rather than two distinct requirements".[29] However, the idea of applying these two tests as "composite" seems unclear. The composite notion suggests that an applicant for inspection of company documents is required to demonstrate "a case for investigation".[30] While some courts have taken a more balanced approach,[31] other courts have considered "proper purpose" as a more important element than "good faith",[32] and other courts have considered only the test of "good faith".[33] Thus, the approach overall has been inconsistent.

For example, in *Leadenhall Australia Pty Ltd v. Cape Lambert Resources Ltd*, Charleston J in the Federal Court of Australia considered only the "proper purpose" test and did not refer to "good faith" in his deliberation.[34] The court denied inspection based heavily on the fact that the other shareholder applicant, who held a greater proportion of shares in the company at the time the inspection application was made, had subsequently sold all their shares. Consequently, the court held that an inspection applied for by the

25 *Enares Pty Limited v. Nimble Money Limited* [2022] FCAFC 126, at [38] (Farrell, Markovic and Derrington JJ); *Hanks v. Admiralty Resources NL* [2011] FCA 891, at [32] (Gordon J); *Acehill Investment Pty Ltd v. Incitec Ltd* [2002] SASC 344, at [29] (Debelle J); *Knightswood Nominees Pty Ltd v. Sherwin Pastoral Co* (1989) 15 ACLR 151, at 156 (Brooking J).

26 *Vinciguerra v. MG Corrosion Consultants Pty Ltd* [2007] FCA 503; *McNeill v. Hearing & Balance Centre Pty Ltd* [2007] NSWSC 942.

27 *Enares Pty Limited v. Nimble Money Limited* [2022] FCAFC 126, at [36] (Farrell, Markovic and Derrington JJ).

28 *Enares Pty Limited v. Nimble Money Limited* [2022] FCAFC 126, at [38] (Farrell, Markovic and Derrington JJ).

29 *Mesa Minerals Ltd v. Mighty River International Ltd* [2016] FCAFC 16 at [22] (Katzmann J, with Siopis and Gilmour JJ agreeing). See also *Leadenhall Australia Pty Ltd v. Cape Lambert Resources Ltd* (2018) 125 ACSR 484; [2018] FCA 558, at [32] (Charlesworth J); *In the Matter of Tolco Pty Limited* [2016] NSWSC 1069, at [15] (Brereton J); *Acehill Investment Pty Ltd v. Incitec Ltd* [2002] SASC 344, at [29] (Debelle J).

30 *Praetorin Pty Ltd v. TZ Ltd* [2009] NSWSC 1237; 76 ACSR 236, at [39] (Barrett J). See also *In the Matter of Sirrah Pty Limited* [2017] NSWSC 1683, at [23], [36]; *London City Equities Ltd v. Penrice Soda Holdings Ltd* [2011] FCA 674; (2011) 84 ACSR 573, at [29], [36–38].

31 *In the Matter of Tolco Pty Limited* [2016] NSWSC 1069 (Brereton J).

32 *Leadenhall Australia Pty Ltd v. Cape Lambert Resources Ltd* (2018) 125 ACSR 484; [2018] FCA 558 (Charleston J).

33 *Quinlan v. Vital Technology Australia Ltd* (1987) 5 ACLC 389.

34 *Leadenhall Australia Pty Ltd v. Cape Lambert Resources Ltd* (2018) 125 ACSR 484; [2018] FCA 558.

remaining applicant, who held a small parcel of shares in the company, was not for a proper purpose.[35] In contrast, in the case of *In the Matter of Tolco Pty Limited*,[36] Brereton J of the NSW Supreme Court took a more balanced approach by referring to both elements. His Honour noted that the applicant had 50% shares in the company, a fact that indicated good faith. The court then went on to consider the purpose and scope of inspection, and granted inspection on the ground that there was clear indication that the applicant had plans to apply for leave to bring an SDA.[37] In both cases, the applicant's purpose for inspection seems to be the determining factor in the court's exercise of its discretion to grant or not to grant inspection.

In other instances where good faith is absent, it has been said that it is not necessary for the court to consider whether the purpose for inspection is proper.[38] In one case, the court found that the applicant had acquired a small parcel of shares in the company in order to inspect company books and held that it was not necessary to consider the case further.[39] In another case, an applicant with just over 5% of shares in the company was said to have acted in good faith in making the application for inspection.[40] Generally, the presence of hostility towards the other party is considered normal in litigation and is not a sign of acting in bad faith.[41]

The "proper purpose" test refers to a "purpose connected with the proper exercise of the rights of a shareholder" and "not ... as a litigant in proceedings against the company";[42] meaning that a shareholder cannot apply for inspection with the purpose of litigating against the company. Pursuing a reasonable suspicion of breach of directors' duty is a proper purpose under s.247A.[43] As for "good faith", an applicant who has significant shareholding

35 *Leadenhall Australia Pty Ltd v. Cape Lambert Resources Ltd* (2018) 125 ACSR 484; [2018] FCA 558, at [67–70].

36 *In the Matter of Tolco Pty Limited* [2016] NSWSC 1069.

37 *In the Matter of Tolco Pty Limited* [2016] NSWSC 1069, at [20–25] (Brereton J).

38 *Keenfern Pty Ltd v. Thorlock International Ltd* (2002) 20 ACLC 1,322, at [9-11].

39 *Quinlan v. Vital Technology Australia Ltd* (1987) 5 ACLC 389.

40 *Coates v. Classic Minerals Ltd* [2016] WASC 371.

41 In *Vinciguerra v. MG Corrosion Consultants Pty Ltd* [2007] FCA 503, at [70], Gilmour J in the Federal Court of Australia noted that threatening to "destroy the company" was not sufficient to say that the applicant seeking inspection was acting in bad faith. See also *Re 383 Latrobe Street Development Pty* Ltd [2021] VSC 655, at [40] (Connock J); *Humes Ltd v. Unity APA Ltd* (No 2) [1987] VR 474, at 479.

42 *Mesa Minerals Ltd v. Mighty River International Ltd* [2016] FCAFC 16 at [22] (Katzmann J, with Siopis and Gilmour JJ agreeing). See also, *Cescastle Pty Ltd v. Renak Holdings Ltd* (1991) 9 ACLC 1333, at 1335. A good example is in *Keenfern Pty Ltd v. Thorlock International Ltd* (2002) 20 ACLC 1,322, where the court dismissed the application for an inspection order because the purpose of inspection was improper, in that the applicant sought to inspect company books in order to determine whether the defendant company was insolvent.

43 *Smartec Capital Pty Ltd v. Centro Properties Ltd* [2011] NSWSC 495; *Leadenhall Australia Pty Ltd v. Cape Lambert Resources Ltd* (2018) 125 ACSR 484; [2018] FCA 558, at [32] (Charlesworth J); *McNeill v. Hearing & Balance Centre Pty Ltd* [2007] NSWSC 942, at [17], citing *Bar-*

and has been a shareholder for "some considerable time" would be able to establish good faith more easily than someone who has recently acquired a token shareholding.[44]

The implication of all these is that there is no clarity as to how an applicant can satisfy the court of these two elements, both of which are equally important, and yet whether one element receives more emphasis than the other really depends on the facts of each case. As noted in *In the Matter of Sirrah Pty Limited*, the court will determine whether each has been demonstrated by applying an objective test.[45]

7.2.2.3 Granting inspection is at the court's discretion

The other concerning factor is that there is no certainty that the court will allow inspection even where an applicant has successfully established "good faith" and "proper purpose" under s.247A. The courts have made abundantly clear that they have full discretion whether to order inspection. Under s.247B, the court also has the power to make "any other orders it considers appropriate" in relation to limiting the scope of inspection. By this, the court has the power to decide on the terms of the inspection order,[46] including the power to order the applicant to provide a copy of the inspected documents to an appropriate regulator for monitoring the progress of the proposed derivative action.[47]

In *Majestic Resources NL v. Caveat Pty Ltd*, Templeman J of the Western Australian Court of Appeal stated that:[48]

> "in considering whether to make an order under s.247A, the Court is required to exercise a discretion. ... In my view, the exercise of the discretion requires the Court to consider not only whether it is appropriate

---

rack Mines Ltd v. Grants Patch Mining Ltd [1988] 1 Qld R 606 (Full Court); *Engel v National Biodiesel Ltd* [2015] FCA 1114.

44 *Mesa Minerals Ltd v. Mighty River International Ltd* [2016] FCAFC 16 at [22] (Katzmann J, with Siopis and Gilmour JJ agreeing); *McNeill v. Hearing & Balance Centre Pty Ltd* [2007] NSWSC 942, at [14] (Hammerschlag J). Cf *Quinlan v. Vital Technology Australia Ltd* (1987) 5 ACLC 389, at 393.

45 *In the Matter of Sirrah Pty Limited* [2017] NSWSC 1683, at [22] (Black J), citing *Acehill Investment Pty Ltd v. Incitec Ltd* [2002] SASC 344, at [29] (Debelle J).

46 *In the Matter of Tolco Pty Limited* [2016] NSWSC 1069, at [16] (Brereton J); *Vinciguerra v. MG Corrosion Consultants Pty Ltd* [2007] FCA 503, at [37] (Gilmour J); *Majestic Resources NL v. Caveat Pty Ltd* [2004] WASCA 201, at [20–25] (Templeman J); *Acehill Investments Pty Ltd v Incitec Ltd* [2002] SASC 344 at [29] (Debelle J)

47 *Knightswood Nominees Pty Ltd v. Sherwin Pastoral Co* (1989) 15 ACLR 151 (Brooking J). This order made in this case is consistent with s.247C of the *Corporations Act* 2001 (C'th), where the court may require the applicant to disclose to ASIC information acquired from the inspection.

48 *Majestic Resources NL v. Caveat Pty Ltd* [2004] WASCA 201, at [21] (Templeman J, with Malcolm CJ and Wheeler J agreeing).

> to make an order for inspection but also to consider which of the books of the company should be made available for that purpose."

Similarly, in *Merim Pty Ltd v. Style Ltd*, Goldberg J of the Federal Court of Australia stated:[49]

> "In granting an order for inspection under s 247A, it is not appropriate to allow a wholesale and general inspection of Style's books. This would cause unnecessary disruption to the company. In any event the books to be inspected should be books that bear on, and be particularly relevant to, the purpose for which the inspection is sought."

The approach of Goldberg J has been cited with approval in subsequent cases.[50] The expectation is that the applicant must specify the documents to be inspected and the nature of that inspection.[51] The court will not allow an applicant for inspection to go on a fishing expedition. In *Acehill Investment Pty Ltd v. Incitec Ltd*, Debelle J of the South Australian Supreme Court noted that "as a general rule, inspection will be confined to, say, the results of decisions of directors rather than all the documents such as board papers leading to decisions".[52] However, in this case, the court allowed the applicant to inspect board papers but coupled with an order limiting the use of the information. The applicant had successfully argued that the inspection of board papers was necessary for the stated purpose, which was the valuation of shares.[53]

7.2.2.4 The applicant's "special interest" for inspection

Under common law, there used to be a test known as "special interest" for inspection, that the court would allow inspection only if the applicant was able to prove "special interest" in the matter greater than the interest of many other shareholders in the company, and only if the applicant was able to specify with sufficient details the exact documents to be inspected.[54] It is not clear to what extent this common law "special interest" test is still relevant, since the statutory inspection was introduced in 1985. Professor Jennifer Hill

49 *Merim Pty Ltd v. Style Ltd* [2009] FCA 314; 255 ALR 63, at [71] (Goldberg J).

50 See for example, *Mesa Minerals Limited v. Mighty River International Limited* [2016] FCAFC 16, at [83–84] (Katzman J, with Siopis and Gilmour JJ agreeing); *Engel v. National Biodiesel Ltd* [2015] FCA 1114 at [10] (Markovic J); *London City Equities Ltd v. Penrice Soda Holdings Ltd* [2011] FCA 674 at [47] (Robertson J).

51 *In the Matter of Tolco Pty Limited* [2016] NSWSC 1069, at [26] (Brereton J).

52 *Acehill Investment Pty Ltd v. Incitec Ltd* [2002] SASC 344, at [29].

53 *Acehill Investment Pty Ltd v. Incitec Ltd* [2002] SASC 344, at [39–40].

54 See, for example, *R v. Merchant Tailors* (1831) 109 ER 1086; and *Edman v. Ross* (1922) 22 SR (NSW) 351.

notes that the common law attitude to inspection is "not a generous one".[55] Mantziaris observes that the "special interest" requirement has been shifted to being a "relevant consideration".[56] Although the common law test is no longer a requirement, the court may still consider the test as relevant in considering whether to grant an inspection order.[57]

On the whole, the current state of the law is that the courts will not allow applicants to go on a fishing expedition or to engage in a "wholesale" inspection.[58] In limiting the scope of inspection, the Full Federal Court of Australia in the most recent case, *Enares Pty Limited v. Nimble Money Limited,* has noted that the inspection provision:[59]

> "does not permit inspection by shareholders who are unsure about whether the directors have complied with their duty and merely wish to examine the company's books to satisfy themselves that no breach has occurred ... there needs to be something akin to some tangible support for the concern being something beyond mere belief or assertion."

The Court in that case went on to explain that the shareholder's concern for the company has to be "more than curiosity or general suspicion of a company's management... it is not enough for an applicant to say that it 'just wanted to check it out that no-one had done anything wrong, because I have a circularity problem'".[60] Therefore, by not having the "special interest" test as a prerequisite but as a relevant consideration, the test provides the court with the additional flexibility in denying inspection or limiting the scope of inspection.

One argument in support of this test relates to the protection of innocent third parties named in the documents,[61] a need to guard against any misuse of company documents and to maintain privacy as far as possible. The other argument for limiting inspection relates to giving recognition to the importance of the internal management rule and the rule against shareholder interference, that the management has the power to conduct the business of the

55 Jennifer Hill, "Companies – Inspection by shareholders of corporate books and documents" (1987) 61 *Australian Law Journal* 657, at 657.

56 Mantziaris, n 24, at 631–633 (discussing the effects of the decision in *Rowland v. Meudon* (2008) 220 FLR 362 where Bryson AJ referred to the "special interest" test as still a "relevant consideration" in matters relating to the grant of an inspection order).

57 This position has been confirmed by the Full Federal Court in *Mesa Minerals Ltd v. Mighty River* International Ltd [2016] FCAFC 16, at [23–25] (Katzmann J, with Siopis and Gilmour JJ agreeing).

58 *Merim Pty Ltd v. Style Ltd* [2009] FCA 314; 255 ALR 63, at [71] (Goldberg J).

59 *Enares Pty Limited v. Nimble Money Limited* [2022] FCAFC 126, at [46–47] (Farrell, Markovic and Derrington JJ).

60 *Enares Pty Limited v. Nimble Money Limited* [2022] FCAFC 126, at [47] (Farrell, Markovic and Derrington JJ), citing *Rasley v. Financial & Energy Exchange* [2020] FCA 1462, at [28].

61 *Acehill Investments Pty Ltd v. Incitec Ltd* [2002] SASC 344 at [29] (Debelle J).

company, and individual shareholders are prohibited from interfering.[62] Tight control on inspection is said to be necessary to ensure that the business of the company will not be disrupted unnecessarily.[63]

7.2.3 Summary and examples of cases

It is important to note that even where an applicant has established good faith (for example, having significant shareholding in the company over a considerable period) and has established that the inspection is for a proper purpose (such as in connection with the bringing of an SDA under s.237), there is no guarantee that the applicant will be given an inspection order. The court has broad discretion under ss.247A and 247B to decide whether to grant an inspection order, and if such is granted, the court has the power to limit the scope of that inspection.

Furthermore, based on the common law principle of internal management and privacy principles, the court may need the applicant to show that their interest in inspection is more special than the interest of other members in the company. Courts generally do not allow the applicant to go on a fishing expedition.

Sections 247A and 247B have been described as "remedial" provisions that should only be used as a last resort.[64] Just as the courts have limited the scope of inspection,[65] the courts have also denied shareholder applications for inspection on the ground that the applicant lacked "special interest" in the subject matter;[66] and on the ground that the type of inspection applied for was too broad or too general to be for a proper purpose.[67] The courts have also rejected the shareholder's applications for inspection on the basis that the applicant had not provided sufficient evidence to demonstrate the need for inspection and had not fully identified the reasons why inspection was necessary.[68]

In *In the Matter of Sirrah Pty Limited*,[69] the two applicants, appointed as executors of their late mother's estate and having 47.2% of the shares, informally requested inspection from the company of a list of 38 categories of

62 *Automatic Self-Cleansing Filter Syndicate Co Ltd v. Cunninghame* [1906] 2 Ch 34; *John Shaw and Sons v. Peter Shaw and John Shaw* [1935] 2 KB 113.

63 *Merim Pty Ltd v. Style Ltd* [2009] FCA 314; 255 ALR 63, at [71] (Goldberg J).

64 *Czerwinski v. Syrena Royal Pty Ltd* [2000] VSC 125.

65 See, for example, *Majestic Resources NL v. Caveat Pty Ltd* [2004] WASCA 201, and *London City Equities Ltd v. Penrice Soda Holdings Ltd* [2011] FCA 674.

66 See, for example, *Hanks v. Admiralty Resources NL* (No.2) [2011] FCA 1464, at [24].

67 See *Smartec Capital Pty Ltd v. Centro Properties Ltd* [2011] NSWSC 495, at [66]–[67].

68 In *Keenfern Pty Ltd v. Thorlock International Ltd* (2002) 20 ACLC 1,322, at 1,323, the court refused to allow inspection of documents because it found that the information to be acquired was for the applicant to decide whether to file for a winding up of the company and this was noted by the court as an improper purpose.

69 *In the Matter of Sirrah Pty Limited* [2017] NSWSC 1683.

documents. The board of directors denied their request for inspection on most of the listed documents. The applicants applied for court intervention under s.247A on the grounds that they had not received dividends for quite some time, that they suspected breaches of directors' duties and that their intended purpose for inspection was to consider bringing a derivative action under s.237. Black J in the NSW Supreme Court considered the 38 categories individually and allowed inspection on not all, but a wider list of documents than those previously permitted by the board of directors.[70] Unfortunately, however, the applicants were required to pay the costs of the inspection application.[71]

It is worth noting briefly that not all shareholders who had applied for leave to bring an SDA under s.237 had also applied for inspection. One possible explanation could be due to costs and expenses in pursuing a court action. There may well be shareholders who simply do not wish to spend money litigating on matters where they receive only a small financial benefit in return. The other possible explanation could be that many of the applicants who applied for leave were also directors of the company, and so they already had some information to commence their leave application. If an applicant has just enough evidence to establish a ground for a derivative action under s.237 and succeeds in obtaining leave, then a section 247A application may be redundant as they could later rely on utilising the discovery and interrogatory process through the general civil procedure channel. Section 247A may be useful for those non-director shareholders who are trying to prove breaches of directors' duties. One legal practitioner observes that s.247A applications do not always reach judicial determination; a threat of an inspection order may be a factor contributing to speedy settlement.[72]

7.3 Availability of oppression action

Another factor affecting the use of the SDA could be due to the availability of oppression action, also known as an unfair prejudice action in some jurisdictions.[73] There are a number of reasons why an oppression action may be more attractive for a shareholder complainant, one of which is that leave of the court is not required to bring an oppression claim. This part provides a brief account of what an oppression action is, explains the range of remedies available for relieving oppression, and then provides a summary of the advantages of bringing an oppression action. This part will also make some comparison with the SDA procedure.

70 *In the Matter of Sirrah Pty Limited* [2017] NSWSC 1683, at [61] (Black J).
71 Detailed discussion on the lack of use of s.247A is beyond the scope of this book.
72 Mantziaris, n 24, at 624.
73 Example, in New Zealand, Singapore and the United Kingdom.

7.3.1 What is an oppression action?

The procedure for bringing an oppression action is contained in Part 2F.1 (sections 232-235) of the *Corporations Act* 2001 (C'th). Under s.232, the court may make an order to relieve oppression if:

(a) the conduct of the company's affairs;[74] or
(b) an actual or proposed act or omission by or on behalf of a company; or
(c) a resolution, or a proposed resolution, of members or a class of members of a company; is either:
(d) contrary to the interests of the members as a whole; or
(e) oppressive to, unfairly prejudicial to, or unfairly discriminatory against, a member or members whether in that capacity or in any other capacity.

One of the attractions for bringing an oppression action rather than an SDA is that a shareholder complainant has greater flexibility in framing their grievances. Section 232 provides a wide range of circumstances as to when the conduct of the company's "affairs" is contrary to the interests of the members as a whole or is oppressive or unfair to a member. This means that an oppression remedy may be sought for an action, a proposed action or an omission by the company board or by members in passing a resolution at a general meeting. The provision focuses on "oppression in terms of its impact on the oppressed, not in terms of the impact of the oppressor".[75] Oppression may also occur even where there is no contravention of the fiduciary requirements of good faith and proper purpose on the part of the directors.[76]

A current and former member of the company, including a person who has shares transmitted by will or by operation of law or any other person that ASIC "thinks appropriate", may make a claim to the court for an oppression order.[77] The oppression provision is applicable to all types of companies, but it is most commonly used in small private or closely held companies where a minority shareholder cannot satisfactorily deal with the other shareholders.[78]

74 The "affairs" of the company is defined in s.53 of the CA to include a wide range of circumstances, including the formation of the company, its membership, trading activities, profits and losses, the internal management, and the exercise of voting rights.

75 *Re Quest Exploration Pty Ltd* (1992) 6 ACSR 659, at 669. See also *Fexuto Pty Ltd v. Bosnjak Holdings Pty Ltd* (1998) 28 ACSR 688, at 703 and *Popovic v. Tanasijevic* (No.5) (2000) 34 ACSR 1, at 71.

76 *Gerard Cassegrain & Co Pty Ltd v. Cassegrain* [2011] NSWSC 1156, at [49].

77 *Corporations Act* 2001 (C'th), s.234.

78 Ian M. Ramsay, "An empirical study of the use of the oppression remedy" (1999) 27 *Australian Business Law Review* 23, at 27; Ryan J. Turner, "Directors' fiduciary duties and oppression in closely held corporations" (2013) 31 *Company and Securities Law Journal* 278, at 286.

A further reason for its popularity is that the courts do not require that the conduct of the company's affairs be commercially unfair.[79] A shareholder in a small privately owned company could easily make a claim for oppression. There is court recognition that dealings between family members are often informal and may not necessarily be made on commercial terms and that one member may assume dominance over the other members. Conduct that may be fair between two competing business partners may not always be fair between members in a family-owned company.[80]

It is possible for a shareholder to make an oppression claim and to apply to bring an SDA concurrently.[81] This is confirmed in a note in s.236 that an applicant for a derivative action is not prevented from bringing a personal action.[82]

7.3.2 Flexibility in the interpretation of oppression

The courts' interpretation of the oppression provision appears to have been consistent and flexible. The focus is on proof of "unfairness".[83] The decision handed down by the High Court of Australia in *Wayde v. New South Wales Rugby League Limited* is still the leading authority in this area.[84] Brennan J, who delivered the leading judgment, considered the oppression provision from the perspective of whether the decision made by the directors was "unfair" on the member. What constitutes "oppressive conduct" or conduct that is "unfairly prejudicial" or "unfairly discriminatory" has been described as not alternatives, but as a "composite" requirement, the essence of which relates to "unfairness", which has a detrimental effect on the interests of a

79 *Exton v. Exton Pty Ltd* [2017] VSC 14, at [39] (Sifris J); *Australian Institute of Fitness Pty Ltd v. Australian Institute of Fitness (Vic/Tas) Pty Ltd* (No.3) [2015] NSWSC 1639, at [83]; *Turnbull v. NRMA Ltd* [2004] NSWSC 577. Cf. *Morgan v. 45 Flers Avenue Pty Ltd* (1986) 5 ACLC 222, at 233 (Young J) where previously, the test was that the conduct must involve "commercial unfairness".

80 *Exton v. Exton Pty Ltd* [2017] VSC 14, at [48] (Sifris J noted that "conduct that may appear unfair may be fully justified").

81 See for example, *White (Trustee) v. MWL Financial Group Pty Ltd* (No.2) [2019] FCA 364; *Connective Services Pty Ltd v. Slea Pty Ltd* [2018] VSCA 229; *In the Matter of Jimmy's Recipe Pty Limited* [2018] NSWSC 1331; *Pottie v. Dunkley* [2011] NSWSC 166. For other examples of overlap between the SDA and the oppression action, see Turner, n 78, at 289–291.

82 The Note in s.236 states that "[t]his section does not prevent a person bringing, or intervening in, proceedings on their own behalf in respect of a personal right", which means that an applicant can also bring a personal action such as making a claim for an oppression remedy.

83 *Wayde v. New South Wales Rugby League Limited* (1985) 3 ACLC 799, at 806 (Brennan J). His Honour went on to say that: "The Court must determine whether reasonable directors, possessing any special skills, knowledge or acumen possessed by the directors and having in mind the importance of furthering the corporate object on the one hand and the disadvantage, disability or burden which their decision will impose on a member on the other, would have decided that it was unfair to make that decision".

84 *Wayde v. New South Wales Rugby League Limited* (1985) 3 ACLC 799.

member or members in the light of the history and structure of the particular company and the reasonable expectation of the members.[85]

This approach has been applied in numerous subsequent cases.[86] More recently in *Lukaszewicz v. Polish Club Ltd*,[87] Black J in the New South Wales Supreme Court quoted a Full Federal Court decision in *Catalano v. Managing Australia Destinations Pty Ltd*:[88]

> "The test of unfairness requires an objective assessment of the conduct in question … The question is whether objectively in the eyes of the commercial bystander there has been unfairness, namely conduct that is so unfair that reasonable directors who consider the matter would not have thought the conduct or decision fair. As the test is objective, whether or not the conduct is oppressive will not depend upon the motives for what was done. It is the effect of the act that is material."

The test is, therefore, objective.[89] A finding of oppression is determined by reference to accepted standards of corporate behaviour or by how reasonable directors would act in attending to the affairs of the company.[90] In *Polish Club*, the board of directors were found to have rejected a large number of applicants for admission to membership. They had also excluded other members from attending the general meeting who did not share the same views as the board. The court found that, although the board of directors had not breached the company's constitution and had not acted with improper motive, they had nonetheless engaged in oppressive conduct. They actively sought and admitted new members who were known to share the same views

85 On this point, the High Court of Australia in *Wayde v. New South Wales Rugby League Limited* (1985) 3 ACLC 799 adopted the New Zealand Court of Appeal decision in *Thomas v. HW Thomas Limited* [1984] 1 NZLR 686; (1984) 2 ACLC 610, at 618 (Richardson J). See also in *Morgan v. 45 Flers Avenue Pty Ltd* (1986) 5 ACLC 222, at 233 where Young J referred to these expressions in the s.232 equivalent as "a composite whole … the section should be considered merely as different aspects of the essential criterion", which was subsequently quoted in *Joint v. Stephens* [2008] VSCA 210, at 134, in *Exton v. Exton Pty Ltd* [2017] VSC 14, at [48] and in many other cases.

86 For example, *Australian Institute of Fitness (Vic/Tas) Pty Ltd* (No.3) [2015] NSWSC 1639 at [81–101]; *Hillam v. Ample Source International Ltd* (No.2) [2012] FCAFC 73, at [4] (Emmett, Jacobson and Buchanan JJ); *Tomanovic v. Argyle HQ Pty Ltd* [2010] NSWSC 152, at [39]; *Fexuto Pty Ltd v. Bosnjak Holdings Pty Ltd* [2001] NSWCA 97, at [89].

87 *Lukaszewicz v. Polish Club Ltd* [2019] NSWSC 446.

88 *Lukaszewicz v. Polish Club Ltd* [2019] NSWSC 446, at [12] (Black J), quoting from *Catalano v. Managing Australia Destinations Pty Ltd* [2014] FCAFC 55 at [9].

89 *Wilmar Sugar Australia Limited v. Mackay Sugar Limited* [2017] FCAFC 40; *Exton v. Exton Pty Ltd* [2017] VSC 14, at [48] (Sifris J); *Morgan v. 45 Flers Avenue Pty Ltd* (1986) 5 ACLC 222, at 233 (Young J). See also Robert Baxt, "The Federal Court confirms that the test of oppression is objective" (2016) 1 *Baxt Report* 12.

90 *Australian Institute of Fitness Pty Ltd v. Australian Institute of Fitness* (Vic/Tas) Pty Ltd (No.3) [2015] NSWSC 1639, at [84].

as them and excluded those unknown to them personally, and they exercised their disciplinary powers against the existing members who did not share the same views. It was held that the directors' conduct in stacking up membership that shared similar views and diluting the influence of dissenting members amounted to oppressive conduct.

The decision in *Polish Club* illustrates that the intention of the defendant in breaching s.232 is irrelevant;[91] only the effect of the conduct is important.[92] This case involved a non-profit company. Its outcome indicates that the test of unfairness does not necessarily involve commercial unfairness. The decision is equally relevant to cases involving a small privately owned or family-owned company where there is often a lack of formality and lack of discussion on commercial terms, which could lead to a case of oppression against the minority.

In circumstances where there are two business partners with equal shareholdings in the company, it is possible for one partner to make a claim of oppression. The usual approach is the "reasonable expectations" of shareholders by considering the interests and behaviour of both parties based on the company's background and history.[93] The oppression provision is a "remedial provision designed to allow the court to intervene where there is a visible departure from the standards of fair dealing".[94] In other words, the plaintiff's conduct is as relevant as the conduct of the alleged oppressor.[95] In *Paterson v. Humfrey*, Le Miere J stated that:[96]

> "There is no reason in principle why a holder of 50% of the shares of a company should be denied relief under s 232. In general, the statutory power to intervene in the internal affairs of a company is necessary only where an applicant does not itself have the power to prevent oppression."

Justice Chesterman, writing as a commentator, reviews some court decisions and notes that oppression could occur in a 50/50 company not because of a

91 See also *Joint v. Stephens* [2008] VSCA 210, at [138].

92 *Lukaszewicz v. Polish Club Ltd* [2019] NSWSC 446, at [12] (Black J), quoting from *Catalano v. Managing Australia Destinations Pty Ltd* [2014] FCAFC 55 at [9]. See also *Tomanovic v. Global Mortgage Equity Corporation Pty Ltd* [2011] NSWCA 104, at [217–224] (Campbell JA).

93 Boyd v. Feeney [2017] NSWSC 1595; *Wayde v. New South Wales Rugby League Limited* (1985) 3 ACLC 799.

94 Jennifer Hill, "Protecting minority shareholders and reasonable expectations" (1992) 10 *Company and Securities Law Journal* 86, at 100, citing *Thomas v. HW Thomas Limited* [1984] 1 NZLR 686; (1984) 2 ACLC 610, at 618.

95 See, *Exton v. Exton Pty Ltd* [2017] VSC 14, at [44] (Sifris J), citing *Joint v. Stephens* [2008] VSCA 210, at [136] (Nettle, Ashley, Neave JJA).

96 *Paterson v. Humfrey* [2014] WASC 446, at [53]. See also *Tomanovic v. Global Mortgage Equity Corporation Pty Ltd* [2011] NSWCA 104, at [321] (Young JA).

majority of shares but because of a *majority of votes*.[97] *Exton v. Exton Pty Ltd* is a good illustration of the approach of reasonable expectation.[98] In that case, the facts reveal that the relationship between two brothers had broken down when one sibling, Peter, alleged that the other sibling, Ian, had stopped treating him as an equal in the business. Peter claimed that he had been oppressed on the basis that Ian had diverted company funds to himself or for his benefit and sought an order in the form of buying out Ian's shares. In defence, Ian sought an order to wind up the company on the just and equitable ground. The court found that there was oppression and that oppression had stopped when Ian applied for a winding up order. The court held that the most appropriate remedy would be to buy out Ian's shares. A winding up order would not be appropriate given that the company was solvent and still doing well, and that Ian did not have clean hands when he filed an application for a winding up order. Further, evidence from cross-examination indicated that Ian was willing to have his shares bought out.

The decision in *Exton v. Exton Pty Ltd* shows that one business partner with 50% shares in the company can make an oppression claim under ss.232 against the other 50% partner. Whether an equal shareholder chooses to bring an oppression claim or apply for leave to bring an SDA, the outcome is likely to be the same, that is, for one partner to buy out the other partner. The practical differences between an oppression claim and a derivative action are in the process and in the costs. Bringing an oppression action is considerably simpler, easier to use and less convoluted. There is no need for that extra step in applying for leave as there is in an SDA, and overall, the costs of bringing an oppression claim are far less than in a derivative action.

7.3.3 Oppression action brought for derivative wrongs

It is generally easier to prove an infringement of personal rights in a personal action than to prove a corporate wrong done to the company in an SDA. An oppression claim is an example of a personal action. It is relatively common, therefore, for a shareholder to choose to bring an oppression action for a derivative wrong. As discussed above, the test for an oppression remedy is proof of "unfairness" to a member or members, as opposed to proof of a corporate wrong done to the entire company. An alleged corporate wrongdoing could easily be framed as a wrong that has resulted in an unfair outcome for the shareholder complainant.[99]

97 Justice R.N. Chesterman, "Oppression by the majority – Or of it?" (2004) 25(2) *Australian Bar Review* 103.

98 *Exton v. Exton Pty Ltd* [2017] VSC 14.

99 *Drew v. Lynch* [2019] FCA 632; *Blong Ume Nominees Pty Ltd v. Semweb Nominees Pty Ltd* [2017] SASC 137; *Victory Projects Pty Ltd v. AAA Self Storage Pty Ltd* [2016] NSWSC 1758; *Re JGS Investment Holdings Pty Ltd* [2014] NSWSC 1532; *LPD Holdings (Aust) Pty Ltd v. Phillips* [2013] QSC 225; *Vadori v. AAV Plumbing Pty Ltd* [2010] NSWSC 274; *Gerard*

For example, where a company has failed to declare dividends for several years, this could be because the directors have paid excessive remuneration to themselves instead, in which case they have committed a breach of directors' duties warranting a derivative action to be brought. However, given the failure to declare dividends is a wrong done not only to the company but also to the shareholders personally, a shareholder in this example could choose to bring an oppression claim against the majority shareholders and directors.[100] A wrong done to the company may well have an adverse impact on the individual shareholder's investment.

One scholar provides instances where it may be difficult to distinguish between a corporate wrongdoing that warrants a derivative action and a wrong done to individual shareholders that gives rise to a personal action only.[101] Another scholar notes that a shareholder complainant could frame a corporate wrongdoing as a wrong affecting the shareholder personally that fits into the broad language of oppression provided in s.232.[102] The latter view is preferred. There is judicial support for a broad interpretation and application of the oppression provisions. In *Campbell v. Backoffice Investments Pty Ltd*, French CJ of the High Court of Australia stated that the language and history of the remedy indicates that "ss 232 and 233 are to be read broadly" and that any imposition of limitations by the courts on the remedy "is to be approached with caution".[103] As an example, in *In the matter of Anna Bay Resort Pty Ltd*,[104] the plaintiff made a claim of oppression under s.232. The outcome was that the court granted leave to bring a derivative action not under s.237 but under s.233, as one of the possible remedies derived from an oppression claim. It is therefore possible to bring an oppression action to then request the court for a derivative action as a form of remedy, in effect short circuiting the need to establish the leave requirement under s.237.

However, it should be noted that the courts have tended not to order a statutory derivative action as a remedy under an oppression claim if other types of remedy are more appropriate. In *Zong v. Lin*, the New South Wales Court of Appeal upheld the trial court's decision by not permitting a derivative action

Cassegrain & Co Pty Ltd v. Cassegrain [2010] NSWSC 91; *Prudential Assurance Co. Ltd v. Newman Industries Ltd* (No.2) [1982] Ch 204.

100 See, for example, *Re Optimisation Australia Pty Ltd* [2018] NSWSC 31; *Wambo Coal Pty Ltd v. Sumiseki Materials Co Ltd* [2014] NSWCA 326; *Sandford v. Sandford Courier Service Pty Ltd* (1986) 10 ACLR 549.

101 Pamela Hanrahan, "Distinguishing corporate and personal claims in Australian company litigation" (1997) 15 *Company and Securities Law Journal* 21.

102 Elizabeth Boros, "Remedies for oppression cases for derivative wrongs" (2014) 32 *Company and Securities Law Journal* 151.

103 *Campbell v. Backoffice Investments Pty Ltd* [2009] HCA 25; (2009) 238 CLR 304, 334 at [72] (French CJ). See also *Campbell v. Backoffice Investments Pty Ltd* [2008] NSWCA 95.

104 *Re Anna Bay Resort Pty Ltd* [2022] NSWSC 331 (Rees J).

applied for under s.237, stating that the court would "choose the remedy which is least intrusive " to the company.[105] The plaintiff in this case brought an oppression claim under s.232 and simultaneously applied for leave to bring an SDA under s.237.

Other instances where the same conduct has caused a wrong to both the company and individual shareholders and where the shareholder complainant has successfully pursued an oppression claim include:

- Directors misappropriating company funds;[106]
- Directors' excessive payments to themselves as salaries, and not paying dividends to shareholders;[107]
- Amendment of a constitution in order to remove the right of a member to participate in the appointment of directors;[108]
- Diversion of corporate/business opportunities;[109]
- Abuse of majority power,[110] including where a member is excluded from management of the company;[111]
- Deadlock between two business partners, with one partner excluded from management.[112]

7.3.4 Non-exhaustive list of available remedies

Another benefit for a shareholder choosing to pursue an oppression action rather than applying for an SDA is the availability of a range of remedies. If a court finds that oppression has occurred, it has the power to make any order it "considers appropriate" under s.233 and these include an order to:

- wind up the company;[113]
- modify or repeal the company's constitution;
- regulate the conduct of the company in future;
- compel other members to purchase the shares of a member (potentially at a price determined by the court);
- compel the company to commence or defend a legal action;

105 *Zong v. Lin* [2022] NSWCA 136, at [79] (Gleeson JA, with Leeming JA and Kirk JA agreeing).
106 *Cowling v. Mekken* [2015] VSC 196.
107 *Re Optimisation Australia Pty Ltd* [2018] NSWSC 31; *Wambo Coal Pty Ltd v. Sumiseki Materials Co Ltd* [2014] NSWCA 326
108 *Wilmar Sugar Australia Limited v. Mackay Sugar Limited* [2017] FCAFC 40.
109 *Fexuto Pty Ltd v. Bosnjak Holdings Pty Ltd* [2001] NSWCA 97; *Catalano v. Managing Australia Destinations Pty Ltd* [2014] FCAFC 55.
110 *Hillam v. Ample Source International Ltd* (No.2) [2012] FCAFC 73.
111 *Nassar v. Innovative Precasters Group Pty Ltd* [2009] NSWSC 342; *Joint v. Stephens* [2008] VSCA 210.
112 *Exton v. Exton Pty Ltd* [2017] VSC 14.
113 A winding up order is usually the last resort and is often based on the "just and equitable" ground: see, for example, *Re Yenidje Tobacco Co Ltd* [1916] 2 Ch 426.

- authorise a member to commence an action on behalf of and in the name of the company (a derivative action);
- appoint a receiver manager;
- restrain a person from engaging in certain conduct (an injunction order);
- require a person to do certain act.

The list referred to in s.233 is non-exhaustive. The court can make any other order not listed in s.233.[114] The main objective is to make an order that is most appropriate in the circumstances in order to relieve oppression or unfair conduct.[115] Although monetary compensation is not listed in s.233, the court can make a compensation order in favour of the oppressed claimant,[116] and if necessary, in favour of the company.[117] In *LPD Holdings (Australia) Pty Ltd v. Phillips*, McMurdo J stated that:[118]

> "the claim for compensation against those directors ... might extend to conduct which is not actionable by the company. In such a case, the court could make some compensatory order under s.233 against those who caused the company's affairs to be conducted in a manner which engaged s.233. That is because one of the recognised purposes of so-called oppression proceedings is to compensate the member or members for the oppressive conduct."

However, even where a shareholder has successfully established oppression, the court is not under any obligation to grant any remedy. The court has the power to decide whether to grant an oppression remedy under s.233.[119] In *Falkingham v. Peninsula Kingswood Country Golf Club*, the Victorian Court of Appeal upheld the decision of the lower court, saying that Robson J was within his power not to grant relief for oppression.[120] In that case, oppression had been proven, but the court refused to grant relief due to the considerable delay on the part of the shareholder in bringing the claim to the court.[121]

114 *Turnbull v. NRMA* [2004] NSWSC 577, at [42]; *Solanki v. Cufari* [2014] VSC 345, at [65].
115 *Ehsman v. Nutectime International Pty Ltd* (No.2) [2009] NSWSC 1096.
116 *Fexuto Pty Ltd v Bosnjak Holdings Pty Ltd* [2001] NSWCA 97; *McCausland v. Surfing Hardware International Holdings Pty Ltd* [2013] NSWSC 902; *Re JGS Investment Holdings Pty Ltd* [2014] NSWSC 1532.
117 *LPD Holdings (Australia) Pty Ltd v. Phillips* [2013] QSC 225, at [51] (McMurdo J). See also *Blong Ume Nominees Pty Ltd v. Semweb Nominees Pty Ltd* [2017] SASC 137, at [56–57].
118 *LPD Holdings (Australia) Pty Ltd v. Phillips* [2013] QSC 225, at [56].
119 *Falkingham v. Peninsula Kingswood Country Golf Club* [2015] VSCA 16 (Whelan JA, with Warren CJ and Beach J agreeing); *Crawley v. Short* [2009] NSWCA 410; *Shelton v. NRMA Ltd* [2004] FCA 1393 at [15] (Tamberlin J).
120 *Falkingham v. Peninsula Kingswood Country Golf Club* [2015] VSCA 16, Whelan JA (with Warren CJ and Beach J agreeing).
121 *Re Peninsula Kingswood Country Golf Club* [2014] VSC 437 (Robson J).

In contrast, in *Exton v. Extons Pty Ltd*,[122] although the oppressive conduct had stopped when the other 50% shareholder filed an application for winding up the company that was still solvent, Sifris J granted relief in favour of the oppressed shareholder by permitting the oppressed party to buy out the shares of the other 50% shareholder.[123] His Honour did not allow the company to be wound up.

7.3.5 An oppression action is a cheaper option

Another advantage of bringing an oppression action is that it may be a cheaper option than an SDA. Leave of the court is not required to bring an oppression action, which means that there will be less time and money spent on the case, and the process in obtaining relief could possibly be less stressful for the shareholder overall.

There are two stages for bringing an SDA – the leave application stage, and if leave is granted, the substantive derivative action stage. An oppression action does not suffer the same problem. It does not have the same procedural hurdle, and so an oppression action may be more affordable.

7.3.6 Overlapping with derivative action

The other remedies that a court can make, as a way of removing oppression, are an order directing the company to bring a court action under s.233(1)(f) and an order authorising a shareholder to bring a derivative action on behalf of and in the name of the company under s.233(1)(g). These provisions have been in existence long before the SDA came into effect. The inclusion of these as an oppression remedy was a response to law reform recommendations acknowledging that oppression or unfair prejudice could exist where a wrong has been done to a company but control over legal actions by the company is in the hands of the majority that has improperly prevented the action being taken against the wrongdoer.[124]

These remedial provisions appear to have been rarely used. *Re Overton Holdings Pty Ltd* is one of the very few reported decisions where the court granted a derivative action as a form of remedy to relieve oppression.[125] In that

122 *Exton v. Extons Pty Ltd* [2017] VSC 14.

123 *Exton v. Extons Pty Ltd* [2017] VSC 14, at [87–91].

124 Austin and Ramsay, n 18, at 843 citing from the UK's Jenkins Committee Report (Report of the Company Law Committee 1962 Cmnd, UK), at [207–208]. For further discussion of the historical development of the statutory oppression remedy, see Jennifer Hill, "Protecting minority shareholders and reasonable expectations" (1992) 10 *Company and Securities Law Journal* 86, at 92–95; Elizabeth Boros, *Minority Shareholders Remedies* (Oxford University Press, 1995), at 113–120; A.J. Boyle, *Minority Shareholder Remedies* (Cambridge University Press, 2002), at 90–118.

125 *Re Overton Holdings Pty Ltd* (1984) 9 ACLR 225.

case, the reasoning of the court was that the oppression provision provided the court with an "extremely wide" power and that power "gives statutory force to the exception to the rule in *Foss v. Harbottle*".[126]

It is not clear why the courts have rarely made an order for a derivative action in an oppression claim. There are two possible explanations. First, due to the derivative action being an action brought on behalf of the company, the courts may have attempted to preserve the unique feature inherent in the derivative proceeding by requiring the applicant to apply for leave to bring the derivative action. If such order is granted under s.233, the effect would be that the shareholder would not have to apply and prove the tests for leave under s.237(2), and this would ultimately defeat the purpose of having the SDA provisions in the legislation and would potentially make it far too easy for a shareholder to bring a derivative action. The courts may have attempted to prevent the erosion of the SDA procedure in Part 2F.1A.

Second, there is no provision in Part 2F.1 that allows an oppressed party to recover their legal costs for bringing a derivative action. An oppression action is a type of personal action, and so the normal rules relating to "costs following the event" would apply. A shareholder complainant can expect to get their costs recovered only if they succeed in the oppression action. If a derivative action is ordered as a form of remedy for oppression, then it may be fair that the court also makes an order allowing an indemnity for the costs of the derivative proceedings for the reason that the action is no longer personal in nature but is now brought on behalf of the company. Given that the courts have rarely awarded costs in favour of the applicant for leave to bring the approved SDA under s.237,[127] it is unlikely that the court would make an order for a derivative action under the oppression provision and a costs indemnity order at the same time.

7.3.7 Limitation in bringing an oppression action

Despite its flexibility, the oppression claim does have one major limitation. An oppression claim can only be made against a company or its current directors or controllers. This is due to the wording in s.232. An oppression action is not available against a third party or a former director or former officer of the company. The rationale for this is that if an oppressor has left the company, then oppression is no longer continuing and s.232 is no longer an option. If an aggrieved shareholder wishes to pursue the matter, they may need to apply for leave to bring an SDA under s.237 instead.

Generally, an oppressed shareholder will try to enforce a contractual right that he or she has with the company or to enforce a corporate right in circumstances where the directors have breached their duty to the company

126 *Re Overton Holdings Pty Ltd* (1984) 9 ACLR 225 at 231.
127 This point has been discussed in Chapter 6 under costs.

which has resulted in an unfair outcome imposed on the shareholder personally.[128] Given the recognition of a fiduciary relationship between shareholders and directors,[129] it is now also possible for an oppression action to be brought against directors for breach of a fiduciary duty to shareholders in the company.[130]

7.3.8 Summary of the advantages

There are many good reasons why an oppression action is preferred over an SDA if a shareholder litigant has a choice between the two, and often they do have that choice. As noted in the above discussion, where a wrong done to a company that warrants an SDA to be brought, a shareholder may also be able to bring an oppression claim, provided that the outcome of that wrong is framed as oppressive or unfair to the shareholder. When comparing with an SDA, the advantages of bringing an oppression action may be summarised as follows:

- There is no procedural obstacle in commencing an oppression action, as there is in an SDA. The grounds for which the court can declare that oppression has occurred are very broad under s.232;
- Oppression action is more likely to be a cheaper and more efficient option because, unlike the SDA, there is no need to pass any screening test to satisfy the court of the criteria for leave;
- The list of remedies that the court can make in an oppression action is very broad under s.233, including making an order for monetary compensation if this is most appropriate. By comparison, in an application for leave to bring an SDA, the actual remedy is leave to bring an SDA, which then requires the applicant to go on and bring the approved action, which, in real terms, may be slow, inefficient and a costly process;
- Proving a breach of the oppression provision under s.232 is easier than showing that the proposed SDA is in the best interests of the company under s.237(2). For example, s.232 relates to proof of "unfairness", not necessarily commercial unfairness, but just general unfairness directed at a member or members of the company. An oppressed shareholder is only required to prove unfairness or prove oppressive conduct inflicted on himself or herself for the court to grant an appropriate relief. In an SDA, however, an applicant is required to establish harm inflicted on the

128 *Gambotto v. WCP Ltd* (1995) 182 CLR 432 (this is a case about shares being acquired by the company without complying with the rules relating to procedural and substantive fairness).

129 *Mesenberg v. Cord Industrial Recruiters Pty Ltd* (1996) 39 NSWLR 128; *Brunninghausen v. Glavanics* (1999) 46 NSWLR 538.

130 See, for example, *Brunninghausen v. Glavanics* (1999) 46 NSWLR 538, at 549 (where Handley JA noted that oppression arose "from the bare facts of the relationship" between the two parties). See also, *Jones v. Jones* [2009] VSC 292, at [36–41] (Judd J).

entire company as a whole, inclusive of the prospective members of the company, which is a heavier burden on the applicant to satisfy the court;
- A shareholder who is successful in an oppression claim is likely to have their costs recovered from the losing party through the general civil litigation process;
- An oppression action may be brought either against the company or against its directors or its majority shareholders/oppressors.

7.4 Availability of funded shareholder class action

Another factor that affects the use of the SDA is the availability of the class action procedure, coupled with the availability of commercial litigation funding. This part aims to explain what class action is, why shareholder class action is more popular in Australia than the SDA, the operation of external litigation funding, and why it may still be of benefit to shareholders in small private companies to bring a class action rather than an SDA.

7.4.1 What is class action?

The class action procedure in Australia has been in effect since 4 March 1992. It is located in Part IVA of the *Federal Court of Australia Act* 1976 (C'th) ("FCAA"). To commence a class action, s.33C of the FCAA provides two essential criteria: (i) at least seven persons must agree to form a class; and (ii) those seven members must have a claim or claims against the same defendant arising from the same, similar or related circumstances.[131] When one member decides to take the lead and represents six other members in the class, there is a very high chance that the lead plaintiff will also be representing other eligible class members who have not come forward, both known and unknown to him. The class members will appear when litigants from both sides are about to settle the case, either in court or by way of an out of court settlement (the latter being subject to the court's approval). Ultimately, the list of class members who are entitled to compensation will be restricted to those who can prove their claim or claims arising from the same, similar or related circumstances. The list of eligible claimants will therefore be restricted to shareholders directly affected by, for example, a breach of directors' duties and will not include future shareholders. Bringing a class action is not about the claim being in the best interests of the company as in the SDA; rather, it is about remedying the wrong done to the affected group of shareholders.

The class action in Australia operates by way of an "opt out" mechanism. Under s.33J of the FCAA, any person who has a claim or claims against the same defendant arising from the same, similar or related circumstances will automatically be included in the list of eligible claimants (provided they can

131 Federal Court of Australia Act 1976 (C'th), s 33C.

prove their eligibility), unless they expressly choose to opt out by notifying the court of their intention.[132] The effect of the "opt out" provision is that the decision of the court will not be binding on those who have opted out and that they can bring a separate court action later if they wish.[133]

The class action procedure has a general application and can be used by any person in any context. For example, in shareholder cases, class actions are commonly used in matters involving the company failing to provide full disclosure on share values and share prices, in particular, contravention of the prohibition against misleading or deceptive conduct,[134] and contravention of the continuous disclosure obligations.[135] Both are in effect an extension of the breach of directors' duties. Claims for compensation are initiated by a shareholder representative acting on behalf of himself and other shareholders in the company. A class action is different from an SDA in the sense that the class representative and the members sue the company as the defendant for contravention of the law. Some directors and officers who have breached their duties to the company may also be included as the defendant.

A class action is a representative action or group action involving multiple class members coming together to make a claim or claims, both known and unknown to the representative. Thus, when a lead plaintiff commences a class action, that action cannot be withdrawn, discontinued, compromised or settled without the approval of the court.[136] This is similar to the case in SDA. The approval of the court is necessary to ensure that the lead plaintiff will not be entering into any undisclosed compromise with the defendant, but to act in the interests of all affected class members.

Currently, three states in Australia have introduced their own class proceedings:[137] Victoria in 2000, which has provisions mirror-imaged to the FCAA;[138] New South Wales in 2011;[139] and Queensland in 2017.[140] Other state jurisdictions have no detailed class action procedure.[141]

132 *Federal Court of Australia Act* 1976 (C'th), s 33J. See also, Lang Thai, "Is there a need to reform the corporate class action procedure in Australia?" (2011) 8 *Macquarie Journal of Business Law* 134 for discussion of shareholder class actions.

133 Lang Thai, "Class action procedure in Australia – Issues and challenges" in Colin Picker and Guy Seidman (eds.), *The Dynamism of Civil Procedure: Global Trends and Developments*, Ius Gentium: Comparative Perspectives on Law and Justice series (Springer, 2016), at 215-236.

134 Corporations Act 2001 (C'th), ss.670A, 953A, 1022A, 1041E, 1041F, 1041H, 1308 and 1309; and Australian Securities and Investments Commission Act 2001 (C'th), s.12DA.

135 Chapter 6-6D of the *Corporations Act 2001* (C'th) covers continuous disclosure obligations.

136 *Federal Court of Australia Act* 1976 (C'th), ss. 33W, 33V and 33T.

137 For ease of discussion, only the FCAA will be referred to in this chapter.

138 *Supreme Court Act* 1986 (Vic.), Part 4A, with number sections almost identical to the FCAA.

139 *Civil Procedure Act* 2005 (NSW), Part 10

140 *Civil Proceeding Act* 2011 (Qld), Part 13A

141 In these other jurisdictions, representative actions based on practices of the Supreme Court civil procedure rules are available to run pseudo-class actions: Michael Legg, "Public and

The objective of the class action procedure is to provide access to justice by allowing members to consolidate their resources and resolve their disputes collectively and more efficiently, to avoid the defendants facing multiple lawsuits from plaintiffs with similar or related claims, thereby reducing the risk of inconsistent findings; and to reduce costs for the parties and the courts.[142] As more recently referred to, it could also have the effect of deterring corporate wrongdoings,[143] in addition to providing compensation to the injured members.

7.4.2 Popularity of shareholder class actions

Professor Morabito in his 2017 study has found that class actions have been on the rise since 1992, with an even greater increase from 2006 onward,[144] which is the year when the High Court of Australia embraced the idea of commercial litigation funding to apply in class action cases.[145] The three main reasons for their increasing popularity may be these.[146]

7.4.2.1 Leave of the court is not required

First, there is no need for a shareholder plaintiff to apply for leave of the court to commence a class action. There is no convoluted procedural obstacle or pre-trial complexity in the class action as there is in an SDA. A shareholder can simply commence a class action if he or she is able to identify at least six other shareholders who have a claim or claims against the same defendant arising from the same, similar or related circumstances.

---

private enforcement: ASIC and the shareholder class action", in Michael Legg (eds), *Regulation, Litigation and Enforcement* (Thomson Reuters, 2011), at 152.

142 Second Reading Speech by the Australian Attorney-General, Federal Court of Australia Amendment Bill 1991 (C'th), House of Representatives, Parliamentary Debates (Hansard), 14 November 1991, at 3176. See also *Bright v. Femcare Ltd* (2002) 195 ALR 574, at [152].

143 Access to Justice Taskforce, Federal Attorney-General's Department, A Strategic Framework for Access to Justice in the Federal Civil Justice System (September 2009), at 114.

144 Vince Morabito, "The First Twenty-Five Years of Class Actions in Australia: An Empirical Study of Australia's Class Action Regimes, Fifth Report" (July 2017), at 28–29 where the study found (at Table 7 and Table 2.4) that when comparing the periods of 1992–2004 (non-funding period) and 2005–2017 (commercial litigation funding period), shareholder class actions went from 5% (15) to 23.4% (70) of all filed class action proceedings and in the past five years, shareholder class actions have grown even more to represent 34.2% (37) of all filed class actions. See also Jenny Campbell and Jerome Entwisle, "The Australian shareholder class action experience: Are we approaching a tipping point?" (2017) 36(2) *Civil Justice Quarterly* 177.

145 Part 7.4.4 below further discusses the role of commercial litigation funding.

146 The first significant shareholder class action was in *Dorajay Pty Ltd v. Aristocrat Leisure Ltd* (2005) 147 FCR 394 and [2009] FCA 19, where, after protracted litigation, the defendant agreed to pay a sum of $144.5 million in settlement of all claims approved by the court. Since then, there have been numerous other shareholder class actions, with the defendant generally agreeing to an approved out of court settlement sum. For further discussion and other subsequent cases, see, Thai, n 133, at 215–236; Michael Legg and Samuel J. Hickey, "Finality and fairness in Australian class action settlements" (2019) 41 *Sydney Law Review* 185.

Once the plaintiff has commenced the class action, the usual rights of discovery and interrogatory apply in the same way as any other general civil litigation. The only requirement for the class action to continue is to ensure that there are at least seven relevant class members and that they have not opted out of the action during the proceedings.[147]

7.4.2.2 Certainty in recovering legal costs

Second, there is some certainty in obtaining a recovery of legal costs and expenses in a successful class action. The court has the power to make an order in relation to costs in favour of the successful party, including an order indemnifying the lead plaintiff.[148] In the majority of shareholder class actions, the costs of the plaintiff are paid out of the settlement sum approved by the court. The settlement sum is divided into three components – the acting law firm receives a portion as services rendered, the commercial litigation funder receives a percentage as commission for providing funding support and the remainder goes to the eligible class members as compensation for their losses and injuries.[149]

The flexible and generous costs provisions in the class action have made it possible for shareholder plaintiffs to step up and lead the class action, which is quite different from the situation under the SDA, where the successful applicants for leave are expected to bear the costs of the substantive derivative proceedings in the majority of cases.

7.4.2.3 Ease in obtaining funding support from an external litigation funder

Third, a shareholder plaintiff is more likely to be successful in obtaining funding support from an external funder for a class action than a derivative action. This is because the external funder can be sure that once funding is provided to the lead plaintiff, a class action can be commenced almost immediately. Of course, the funder would only be willing to fund a class action after it has done some preliminary investigation into the matter and is confident of a successful outcome,[150] in the sense that the funder is likely to make a profit from financing the action.

147 *Federal Court of Australia Act* 1976 (C'th), ss. 33C and 33J.

148 *Federal Court of Australia Act* 1976 (C'th), s.33ZJ and s.33V.

149 For example, in *Clarke v. Sandhurst Trustees Limited* (No.2) [2018] FCA 511, Lee J in the Federal Court of Australia approved the settlement sum of $16.85 million, of which the acting lawyers received 31% as legal fees, the commercial funder received 30% as commission for financing the action, and group members received 39% as their total compensation. In *Blairgowrie Trading Ltd v. Allco Finance Group Ltd* (Receivers and Managers Appointed) (in liq.) (No.3) [2017] FCA 330, Beach J approved the settlement sum of $40 million, of which 26.5% went to the acting lawyers, 22.1% to the litigation funder and 51.5% to be divided amongst 5,130 shareholders.

150 In nearly all of the shareholder class actions in Australia, the matters ended with an out of court settlement approved by the court, with the defendant companies agreeing to pay compensation and legal costs, including covering the costs of the litigation funder.

7.4.3 Shareholders in small private companies

It is not impossible for shareholders in small private companies to bring a class action under Part IVA of the FCAA, provided the shareholder plaintiff can gather support from six other shareholders in the company who have the same, similar or related grievances to form a class. Obtaining funding support from an external funder may not be easy given the small class size and hence, the small profit margin for the funder, but this should not prevent shareholders from bringing a self-funded class action against the company and other directors who have breached the directors' duties. The benefit of bringing a self-funded class action as opposed to bringing an SDA is that there is no statutory leave requirement or other such procedural obstacles.[151] All that is required in a class action is that there are at least seven class members with the same, similar or related circumstances.

When shareholders bring a class action, the company will become the defendant, along with the directors and other officers who have been responsible for the action or inaction of the company. For example, some directors may have failed to comply with the continuous disclosure obligations or engaged in misleading or deceptive conduct or failed to declare payment of dividends or have improperly diverted company assets or committed other wrongdoings that caused losses to the company.

A commercial funder is generally unwilling to provide funding support to bring an SDA owing to the uncertainty in obtaining leave of the court under s.237(2) of the CA and the uncertainty in the recovery of costs under s.242. Perhaps one way of incentivising an external funder to take on and finance a class action involving a small private company is to make a promise that the funder can get to keep all of the earnings from the successful action. This will hopefully do the trick if the purpose of the shareholder class members is not really looking to obtain compensation from the successful class action but to hold directors accountable for their wrongdoings and to improve the overall corporate governance.

7.4.4 The role of commercial litigation funding

For the first time in history, the High Court of Australia in 2006 permitted a class action to be funded by an external commercial litigation funder.[152] The decision to permit external funding was affirmed and applied again by the High Court in 2009.[153] In both cases, there was recognition that the costs of litigation are beyond the means of many ordinary people and that commer-

151 Michael Duffy, "Procedural dilemmas for contemporary shareholder remedies – Derivative action or class action" (2004) 22 *Company and Securities Law Journal* 46, at 68. See also *Dorajay Pty Ltd v. Aristocrat Leisure Ltd* (2005) 147 FCR 394; *Dawson Nominees Pty Ltd v. Brookfield Multiplex Ltd* (No 4) [2010] FCA 1029.

152 *Campbells Cash and Carry v. Fostif Pty Ltd* (2006) 229 CLR 386.

153 *Jeffrey and Katauskas Pty Ltd v. Rickard Constructions Pty Ltd* (2009) 83 ALJR 1180.

cial litigation funders have an important role to play in ensuring that these people can get access to justice.[154] A class action funded by a non-party funder would not contravene any public policy and the action would not constitute an abuse of the court's process.[155]

However, the litigation funding industry is still largely unregulated in Australia.[156] Commercial funders are free to set their own terms and conditions in the funding agreement. The funder is usually a corporate entity that agrees to assist a plaintiff to commence a court action by providing funding support. In return, the funder expects to retain an agreed percentage of any compensation awarded by way of approved settlement or court order. If the lead plaintiff decides to withdraw the class action or a class member decides to opt out of the class action, the funding provider can insist on the return of the fund with interest.

Generally, a funder would want to get involved in a court action only if the class members have a legitimate claim against the defendant and there is a high probability of success – or a high probability that the defendant is likely to negotiate for a settlement at the earliest opportune time. Thus, the funder will independently conduct its own investigation into the issue before making an offer to assist with funding the court action. The funding agreement is usually a tripartite arrangement amongst the class members, the litigation funder and the class members' lawyers. Depending on the terms of the agreement, as this can vary from case to case, litigation funding includes lawyers' fees, court fees and expenses, project management fees, investigation fees and may include security for costs. The funder's sole purpose is to make a commercial gain from the litigation of others. Depending on how the funding agreement is phrased, the funder may or may not have any direct control over the court action.

There is no legislative provision dealing with the commission or the percentage of earnings that a litigation funder is entitled to retain. Since 2006, only some regulations have been put in place, and these deal only with issues relating to potential conflicts of interests amongst the class members, the litigation funder and the class members' lawyers.[157]

154 *Campbells Cash and Carry v. Fostif Pty Ltd* (2006) 229 CLR 386, at 434, 468, 407 (Gleeson CJ, Gummow, Kirby, Hayne and Crennan JJ).

155 *Campbells Cash and Carry v. Fostif Pty Ltd* (2006) 229 CLR 386, at 434, 468 (Gummow, Kirby, Hayne and Crennan JJ, with Gleeson CJ agreeing at 407), and with Callinan and Heydon JJ dissenting at 484-486 on the grounds that the arrangement constituted maintenance and champerty, a form of abuse of the court's process. For detailed analysis of these two cases, see Lang Thai, "Commercial litigation funding: The need to impose regulations to improve the outcome of shareholder class actions" (2011) 4 *Journal of the Australasian Law Teachers Association* 1–16.

156 There is no specific legislation governing the regulation of litigation funding or funders. The industry is self-regulated, managed by the Australian Association of Litigation Funders.

157 These conflict rules applicable to litigation funding arrangements came into effect on 12 July 2013, now located in Part 7.6 of the *Corporations Regulations* 2001 (C'th). The introduction of these rules was a result of the High Court of Australia decision in *International Litigation*

The commission rate set by a commercial funder is usually between 20% and 30%.[158] Whether the court has the power to amend the commission rate is controversial. One view is that because the court has the protective and supervisory role in the class action, in the sense that it has the power to approve settlement under s.33V and the power to make any order under s.33ZF, it should also have the power to amend the commission rate.[159] In *Blairgowrie Trading Ltd v. Allco Finance Group Ltd (in liq.) (No.3)*, Beach J adjusted the contractually agreed commission rate from 32.5% to about 22.1% in the final calculations.[160] The other view is that because a litigation funding agreement is a commercial contract, the court has no power to amend the terms of the litigation funding agreement.[161] In *Clarke v. Sandhurst Trustees Limited (No.2)*, Lee J in the Federal Court of Australia held that the protective and supervisory role of the court is to facilitate settlement but not to amend the commission rate; to do so would "upset the bargain struck between the funder and group members".[162] His Honour approved the settlement sum of $16.85 million, of which the funder received 30%, lawyers 31% and group members 39%.[163] Currently, there is no fixed rule for deciding what percentage a commercial funder is entitled to retain.

A commercial funder is more willing to fund a class action than an SDA possibly because of these four main reasons:[164]

(i) Unlike an SDA where there are procedural obstacles, there is no leave hurdle for commencing a class action;

Partners Pte Ltd v. Chameleon Mining NL (receivers and managers appointed) [2012] HCA 45 where it was held that the term "managed investment scheme" did not apply to litigation funders and therefore the litigation funder was exempt from needing an Australian Financial Services Licence under the *Corporations Act* 2001 (C'th).

158 It has been known to be higher in the earlier years: See Stuart Clark and Michael Legg, "The continued rise of litigation funding" (2006) 22(9) *Company Director* 34, at 36.

159 *Money Max International Pty Ltd v. QBE Insurance Group Ltd* [2016] FCAFC 148, at [7-14]; *Mitic v. Oz Minerals Limited (No.2)* [2017] FCA 409, at [28–29]; *Blairgowrie Trading Ltd v. Allco Finance Group Ltd* (Receivers and Managers Appointed) (in liq.) (No.3) [2017] FCA 330, at [110].

160 *Blairgowrie Trading Ltd v. Allco Finance Group Ltd* (Receivers and Managers Appointed) (in liq.) (No.3) [2017] FCA 330.

161 Justice Michael B. J. Lee, "Varying Funding Agreements and Freedom to Contract: Some Observations" (1 June 2017) published on the Federal Court of Australia website www.fedcourt.gov.au/digital-law-library/judges-speeches/justice-lee/lee-j-20170601 (viewed 20 September 2020). See also *Caason Investments Pty Limited v. Cao* (No.2) [2018] FCA 527 (Murphy J); *Clarke v. Sandhurst Trustees Limited (No.2)* [2018] FCA 511 (Lee J); *Perera v. Getswift Limited* [2018] FCA 732 (Lee J).

162 *Clarke v. Sandhurst Trustees Limited (No.2)* [2018] FCA 511, at [12] (Lee J).

163 Compare with another case in *Caason Investments Pty Limited v. Cao (No.2)* [2018] FCA 527, where Murphy J approved the settlement sum of $19.25 million, of which the funder received 30%, lawyers 43% inclusive of costs, and class members 27%.

164 Thai, n 133, at 250–251.

(ii) In a successful class action, the class representative is expected to seek recovery of costs from the unsuccessful defendant, and the recovery of these costs will ultimately go back to the commercial funder who initially funded the class action;
(iii) In a shareholder class action, the defendant is the "company", which means that the commercial funder is well aware that the company can "afford" to pay for the compensation. Thus, after a period of protracted litigation and with some pressure placed on the defendant, the directors (including those wrongdoers in the company) will tend to agree to an out of court settlement approved by the court, as seen in many of the shareholder class action cases;[165]
(iv) Where there is a large pool of shareholders in the company, a commercial funder could expect to receive from individual shareholders a large proportion of profits at the end of a successful class action.

A commercial litigation funding agreement is different from the contingency fees arrangement commonly used in the US. In a litigation funding agreement as described in this chapter, a third party, usually a corporate entity, provides funding. In a contingency fees arrangement, the acting law firm provides funding support,[166] and this arrangement is prohibited in Australia.[167] A law firm representing class members cannot be a funding provider.

7.4.5 Proposed reforms to overcome issues in "funded" shareholder class action

It is worth noting briefly that the Australian "opt out" class action is not without flaws. Similar to the SDA, the effect of free riding by non-participating members in a class action is unavoidable. There are other issues relating to the "funded" class action. The lead plaintiff and class members are not free to

165 For example, in *Kirby v. Centro Properties Limited* (No 6) [2012] FCA 650, Middleton J of the Federal Court of Australia approved a settlement sum of $200 million, of which a large portion went to the commercial funder and the acting law firm, and the remainder was distributed to about 6000 shareholders. It is still the largest shareholder class action in history in terms of the size of the settlement sum.

166 A contingency fees arrangement comes about when a law firm representing a client agrees to deduct a portion of the recovery only if there is a successful outcome in the court action. For further reading on contingency fees in the US, see Lester Brickman and Lawyer Barons: What their contingency fees really cost America? (Cambridge University Press, 2011); Herbert M. Kritzer, *Risks, Reputations and Rewards: Contingency Fee Legal Practice in the United States* (Stanford University Press, 2004); K.A. Lambert, "Class action settlements in Louisiana", (2000) 61 *Louisiana Law Review* 89.

167 See, *Legal Profession Act* 2004 (Vic) s 3.4.29(1)(b); *Legal Profession Act* 2006 (ACT) s 285; *Legal Profession Act* 2004 (NSW) s 325(1)(b); *Legal Profession Act* 2006 (NT) s 320(1); *Legal Profession Act* 2007 (Qld) s 325; *Rules of Professional Conduct and Practice* 2003 (SA) r 42; *Legal Profession Act* 2007 (Tas) s 309(1); *Legal Profession Act* 2008 (WA) s 285(1).

negotiate settlement with the defendant as the funding provider often controls this matter indirectly. For example, the lead plaintiff may wish to negotiate further to obtain a better recovery or to proceed to trial while the funding provider on the other hand decides that it would be in everybody's interests to accept an early settlement offer. Furthermore, class members are not free to negotiate the commission rate with the funding provider when they are desperate to have the class action up and running. There is also confusion over the terms "opt in" and "opt out", in that the legislation favours the "opt out" mechanism while the funding provider requires enough class members to "opt in" to the funding agreement for a class action to be funded.[168] There are now variations of the "opt out" procedure".[169]

Reform proposals are underway to overcome these and many other problems relating to "funded" shareholder class actions, with the objective of providing better outcomes and compensation for class members. As a result of extensive discussions since 2014,[170] the Australian Government has recently released its first draft Bill for public consultation in this matter,[171] incorporating many of the recommendations made in the Australian Law Reform Commission's Final Reports, including:[172]

- amending the class action procedure in order to provide the court with more power to make a costs order against the funding provider;
- improving detection and monitoring of conflicts of interests between the funding provider and class members' solicitors;
- improving licensing and regulation of funding providers and all other commercial funders;
- requiring leave of the court if a class action involves third party funding; and
- allowing contingency fees arrangement in class actions (as an alternative to third party litigation funding).

It has been proposed that only funded class actions will require leave of the court to commence.[173] This is to ensure that the terms of the funding

168 Thai, n 155, at 13–14.

169 Legg and Hickey, n 146, at 203–206.

170 See, Productivity Commission, Access to Justice Arrangements (Inquiry Report, No. 72, Volumes 1 and 2, 2014); VLRC, Access to Justice – Litigation Funding and Group Proceedings (Final Report, March 2018); ALRC, Inquiry into Class Action Proceedings and Third Party Litigation Funders (Discussion Paper, June 2018, and Post-Submission Seminar Presentation, September 2018; ALRC, Integrity, Fairness and Efficiency – An Inquiry into Class Action Proceedings and Third Party Litigation Funders (Report 134, January 2019).

171 Australian Government Treasury, Treasury Laws Amendment (Measures for Consultation) Bill 2021: Litigation funders – Draft exposure (October 2021): https://treasury.gov.au/consultation/c2021-211417 (viewed 18 September 2022).

172 ALRC, Integrity, Fairness and Efficiency – An Inquiry into Class Action Proceedings and Third Party Litigation Funders (Report 134, January 2019).

173 ALRC, Inquiry into Class Action Proceedings and Third Party Litigation Funders (Supplementary note: Leave to Proceed, September 2018).

agreement will be fair and reasonable, particularly for the class members. This reform proposal is unlikely to have much impact on shareholders in small private companies planning on bringing self-funded class actions.

7.5 Conclusion

This chapter has considered other factors that may have contributed to the infrequent use of the SDA. The denial of access to company information is one of the main stumbling blocks for shareholder litigants. Without adequate evidence to decide on the strength of the claim, there is very little for minority shareholders to justify a case for a derivative action. Shareholders who have never acted as director of the company, who have had no involvement in the management and who suspect breaches of directors' duties would have very little hope of getting hold of evidence to show that the proposed derivative action is in the best interests of the company. It would be difficult to show that there is a serious question to be tried where shareholders are denied information to establish a breach of directors' duties. Making an application to the court for inspection of company books and documents is probably as challenging as making an application for leave to bring an SDA, for the reason that, even if the applicant has established good faith and proper purpose for inspection, the court still has full discretion to decide whether to grant an inspection order. The grant of an inspection order is discretionary, based on other equitable grounds, such as preservation of third party privacy and confidentiality and restricting unnecessary disruption to the company's business. Even where the court grants an inspection, the order often contains conditions and limitations.

It is understandable that where there are choices, shareholders would look for the path of least resistance and turn to an oppression action or even a class action if they can gather support from at least six other class members.[174] These days, shareholders have become more confident in pursuing cases against directors for improper behaviour in the company or on the grounds that directors owe a fiduciary duty to the shareholders in discharge of their duty to the company. Apart from making an application to the court for leave to bring an SDA, which appears too difficult, too time consuming and too costly, they have other choices in asserting their personal rights in the company and rectifying the injury done to them personally. In the end, regardless of which path they choose, one thing common amongst these actions is that they all aim to provide shareholders with some degree of protection

174 There are other additional alternatives, such as an application to the court for a statutory injunction; however, the court has complete discretion to decide whether to issue an injunction: See Lang Thai, "Statutory injunction – Call for amendment to s 1324 of the Corporations Act" (2006) 24 Company and Securities Law Journal 41. See also McCracken v. Phoenix Constructions (Qld) Pty Ltd (2012) 289 ALR 710; [2012] QCA 129; Re Colorado Products Pty Ltd (in prov liq) [2014] NSWSC 789.

and enhancement of corporate governance. One way or another, directors in the wrong will become accountable for their inappropriate behaviour. However, given the considerable flexibility and ease in the use of the oppression action and the class action, and if the SDA procedure is left unmonitored and unchanged, there is a possibility that the SDA will slip into further disuse and become redundant, or just another inconvenient shareholder remedy only to be used as a last resort.

8 Summary and conclusion

8.1 Introduction

As noted in the beginning, the purpose of this book is to inform the world about the uniqueness of the Australian statutory derivative action, and how other countries can learn from it. The book has explored how the statutory derivative action ("SDA") for Australia could be reformed to provide shareholders with better protection against corporate misconduct, and in turn, promote directors' accountability and good corporate governance. In this concluding chapter, Part 2 summarises the findings and the reform recommendations. Part 3 includes suggestions for future research based on other questions identified during the writing of this book. Part 4 provides some final remarks.

8.2 Answers to the research questions

As noted in Chapter 1, the objective of the book was to investigate whether there is a need for reform to the SDA in Australia, and if so why, and how. In doing so, the book addressed the two related research questions:

(1) Has the SDA been effective as a shareholder remedy and as a tool for deterring corporate wrongdoings, with a view to bringing about enhancement of directors' accountability and corporate governance as intended by the legislation?
(2) Which of the SDA provisions might benefit from reform to achieve the intended purposes?

The first research question deals with the effectiveness of the SDA in its current form, while the second research question is about a possible reform to the SDA and how this could be achieved. The book has established a case for law reform to the SDA. Based on the empirical evidence, case law analysis and comparative analysis with other jurisdictions, the book contends that the SDA has not really been effective as a tool for shareholder remedy and access to justice. The SDA provisions in Part 2F.1A of the *Corporations Act* 2001 and the courts' strict interpretations of these provisions have not greatly improved

DOI: 10.4324/9781003430063-8

the shareholders' position in the company, and reform is necessary to provide them with greater protection against corporate misconduct. If shareholders are awarded the appropriate remedy, this could indirectly enhance directors' accountability and corporate governance.

8.2.1 Empirical findings identifying and confirming problem areas in SDA: Summary

The empirical findings reported in Chapter 3 contribute new knowledge in the area of statutory derivative action, as explained below. This book is the first of its kind in Australia that has comprehensively assessed all 168 cases relating to the leave application decided over the 20-year period from 13 March 2000 (the date the SDA came into operation) to 28 December 2019. The empirical data have identified areas that need further consideration and confirmed the propositions in Chapters 1 and 2 and the similar comments made by other corporate law scholars that there are "still issues relating to the application of Part 2F.1A that require resolution".[1] The need to untangle the "entanglement" between the leave requirement and the costs provision is one important example.[2] Furthermore, the empirical findings have identified "good faith" and "in the best interests of the company" as the two most challenging criteria for shareholder applicants to satisfy the court for leave to bring an SDA, coupled with the difficulty in obtaining a recovery of costs.

Chapter 2 reviewed the literature on the historical developments of the derivative action, including the reasons for introducing the statutory framework given in the government reports and in the Explanatory Memorandum that introduced the SDA. This exercise was necessary as a way of comparing the SDA with the old system and identifying areas that need further consideration and reform. It was intended that the SDA would provide shareholders with an "effective remedy" and that it could bring about directors' accountability and enhancement of corporate governance.[3] However, the key propositions put forward in Chapter 2 were that the preconditions for leave in s.237(2) for bringing an SDA are too onerous and that the costs provision in s.242 is too uncertain for it to have any meaningful impact on shareholder litigation.

1 Geoffrey Egert, Colin Anderson and Scott Kiel-Chisholm, "The application of the statutory derivative action in Pt 2F.1A of the Corporations Act to companies in liquidation under Ch 5: Well oiled machine or is Pt 2F.1A in need of a tune up?" (2011) 25 *Australian Journal of Corporate Law* 318, at 318; Lang Thai, "Calling for reform to the statutory derivative action in Australia: Critical analysis and suggestions for reform" (2013) 21 *Insolvency Law Journal* 242.

2 Albert Monichino, "Costs in statutory derivative actions: The lingering ghost of Wallersteiner" (2015) 33 *Company and Securities Law Journal* 104, at 115.

3 See, for example, House of Representatives, *Explanatory Memorandum to the CLERP Bill* 1998, at 21; CASAC, *Statutory Derivative Action* (Report, 1993), at 4; CLERP Proposal Paper No. 3, *Proposals for Reform: Directors' Duties and Corporate Governance* (1997), at 32–33.

This book contains the first extensive empirical study to assess the patterns of use of the SDA. The study measured how difficult it was for applicants to obtain leave of the court to bring an SDA and which of the five criteria in s.237(2) have posed obstacles for applicants to satisfy the court for leave. This was done by adding up the number of successful and unsuccessful leave applications during the 20-year period from 2000 to 2019 and then assessing why those unsuccessful applicants have not been able to obtain leave, based on the percentage of failures against each of the five criteria in s.237(2). The empirical findings reported in Chapter 3 provided some new insights to the understanding of the SDA, and provided confirmation that the SDA framework has not significantly improved the shareholders' position when compared with the previous rules under common law.[4] The empirical research has shown that 44.6% of the applicants failed to obtain leave to bring an SDA, which is very high when considering in terms of 75 unsuccessful leave applications out of a total of 168 leave cases during the 20-year period; and of that, the majority of applicants had found "good faith" and "in the best interests of the company" to be most difficult to establish for leave.[5]

Another important insight was that in 55.4% of the successful leave applications, a great majority of applicants were not entitled to an indemnity order in respect to the leave application (85.0%) and were expected to bear the costs of bringing the approved derivative action (98.9%). That is, the great majority of successful applicants for leave were required to pay costs in respect to the leave application and in respect to the bringing of the SDA, with the effect that no company funds were to be used to finance the action. An interesting discovery was that only three SDA cases (1.8%) over a period of 20 years have gone all the way to final judgment, and none of the successful parties has been successful in recovering their legal costs. In effect, the courts declined to allow the company to fund the action. These outcomes are the product of the courts having a broad discretion to decide on costs under s.242.[6]

A further new insight was that a great majority of applicants were *current* shareholders (92.9%), either as current shareholder and director or as current shareholder and former director or as current shareholder with support of other current shareholders. This high percentage suggests that a *former* shareholder might not have been confident enough to seek leave to bring an SDA due to the anticipated difficulty in establishing their good faith to the court. The good faith requirement is an extension of proof of the applicant's eligibility to bring an action on behalf of the company.

Furthermore, the research has revealed that the majority of defendants opposing the leave application were directors of the company (65.5%), and the majority of claims against them concerned breaches of directors' duties

4 See Chapter 3.
5 See Chapters 3, 4 and 5.
6 See Chapters 3 and 6.

(57.7%). This suggests that there is potential for the SDA to become an effective tool for deterring misconduct and bringing about some improvement to corporate governance. However, this may only be possible if there is enough incentive for shareholder applicants to pursue their SDAs all the way to final judgment. Based on the empirical evidence and given that only three SDA cases have gone all the way to final judgment in the period March 2000 to December 2019, it is reasonable to assume that all other successful applicants had decided not to go on and bring the approved derivative action. It could be that some might have used the successful leave application as a bargaining tool for negotiating a settlement and some might have walked away and done nothing more. This is not surprising in light of the fact that litigation is costly and that they have not been successful in obtaining an indemnity order to ensure a recovery of their costs.

8.2.2 The leave requirement issue coupled with the costs issue: Summary of analyses

8.2.2.1 Contributions to knowledge

The empirical evidence was used to further support the arguments on why law reform to the Australian SDA is necessary. The book offered some explanations, through case law analysis in Chapters 4, 5 and 6, as to why 44.6% of those applicants had failed on those two criteria and why many others were successful in obtaining leave to bring an SDA but did not go on to bring the approved action. The book engaged in a qualitative analysis to explain the correlations between the successful and unsuccessful leave applications, and the underlying reasons why some applications were successful and some not. One of the focal points in those three chapters was to explain the "why" component, in answer to the first research question. The other focal point was to provide some suggestions for law reform, as summarised in 8.2.4 below.

As noted in Chapter 1, research in this area has been in short supply in the past 20 years or more. The "good faith" and "in the best interests of the company" criteria in the context of the Australian SDA have thus far not been the subject of extended scholarly analysis. The research and analysis undertaken in Chapters 4 and 5 therefore provide new knowledge and insights in the understanding of the extent of difficulty in these areas and how these provisions could be reformed in moving forward to provide shareholders with better access to justice and a more effective remedy.

As for the costs provision in s.242, there has been one publication by a legal practitioner providing his observations on the problems with the costs provision and debating on whether the courts in Australia should move towards adopting a more flexible approach as seen in the UK courts based on the *Wallersteiner* order.[7] The analysis undertaken in Chapter 6 in this book

7 Monichino, n 2.

has taken a different path and suggested incorporation of the US common fund/contingency fees arrangements and the substantial benefits/lodestar method into the legislation to allow successful applicants leave to recover some costs.

8.2.2.2 The "good faith" requirement

Australia is one of the very few countries that have the most onerous leave requirement. In Chapter 4, case law analysis informed us that there is no standard test for determining whether an applicant is acting in "good faith" under s.237(2)(b) when making an application for leave to bring an SDA. Judicial approaches to the term "good faith" have been varied, lacking clarity, with the courts adopting a range of explanations to assist with interpretation. For example, terms that have been used to explain are "collateral purpose", "ulterior motive", show of "animosity and malice", whether significant efforts had been shown by the applicant when applying for leave, the size of the applicant's shareholding, comparison with the directors' duty of good faith, and whether the leave application included an oppression claim. In the end, one set of rules applicable in one particular case was not necessarily relevant in another case.

The book also put forward arguments as to why the inclusion of good faith is redundant in the SDA, focusing on the fact that five criteria to establish for leave are already too many, more than in many other jurisdictions; and some of these criteria overlap with the others, making the requirement of good faith unnecessary.[8] For example, the empirical research has shown that when an applicant fails on the "in the best interests of the company" criterion, the same applicant is likely to fail on the "good faith" criterion. Indeed, consideration of "good faith" is relevant, but its inclusion in the legislation is unnecessary. The applicant's good faith may be shown indirectly through other means and other existing criteria. Due to the difficulty in defining what good faith is, its express inclusion only adds another burden on shareholders, deterring them from coming forward to make a case for a derivative action. Some countries, such as New Zealand and Hong Kong, do not have "good faith" as a requirement in their SDAs and the absence of that element has not resulted in an overflow of leave applications in their judicial system. Those countries that do not have "good faith" in their legislation do not appear to experience any unwarranted abuse of the SDA process. It is recommended that Australia remove the test of "good faith" in Part 2F.1A of the *Corporations Act* 2001.

8.2.2.3 Flaws in the "in the best interests of the company" requirement

The other problematic criterion identified is the need of an applicant to demonstrate the proposed derivative action "is in the best interests of the company"

8 See Chapter 4.

under s.237(2)(c). This criterion has been found to be most challenging (62.6%). As explained in Chapter 5, there are three issues with this criterion: (i) uncertainty and confusion in the interpretation of "best interests"; (ii) a lack of clarity on how much evidence or what evidence is required to demonstrate that the proposed derivative action "is in the best interests of the company"; and (iii) a lack of clarity on who the people or entities are that make up the "company", whether the applicant only needs to consider the shareholders as a whole or whether they are required to also consider other stakeholders. The sticking point relating to this criterion is in the words "is" and "best". Essentially, it is impossible for anyone to predict what the outcome of an SDA is.

The courts' interpretations of s.237(2)(c) have been circular and varied, and at times, inconsistent, similar to the "good faith" dilemma. In determining whether the proposed action "*is* in the *best* interests of the company", the courts have taken into account factors such as the character and scale of the company, the nature of its operation and business, whether other or alternative remedies are available to the applicant, the relationship between the parties and their respective relationship with the company, the financial position of the company, the extent of disruption to the company if the court were to grant leave, and most importantly, the costs of the proposed action relative to the potential benefits to the company. The last point, costs/benefits analysis, has been the pivotal point in the court's decision to grant or not to grant leave in numerous cases.

The most difficult part of the test in s.237(2)(c) lies in the standard of proof. The inclusion of the word "is" indicates that the applicant has to establish on a balance of probabilities that the proposed derivative action must be "in the best interests of the company". Even where an applicant is armed with voluminous evidence to prove a strong chance of winning, there is still no certainty in the outcome of the leave application. A successful outcome in an SDA is not representative of the outcome being in the company's best interests. A derivative action may have a successful outcome, but if the compensation is of a modest amount, outweighed by the cost of litigation,[9] then this form of relief may not be in the best interests of the company overall.

8.2.2.4 Overlapping effects and costs implications

An important finding in the research was that, in nearly all successful leave cases, the court granted leave on the proviso that the applicant be responsible for all costs, charges and expenses in running the action and that there was

9 A good example is seen in *Maher v. Honeysett and Maher Electrical Contractors Pty Ltd* [2009] NSWSC 445 where a modest amount was awarded as compensation in the final judgment in the SDA, but the costs of both parties were added together and both were then required to contribute the same amount each, with no company funds being used to fund the action.

evidence that the applicant could financially afford to bring the proposed action. In other words, the applicant would be able to satisfy the court of the requirements of "good faith" and "in the best interests of the company" if they were willing and prepared to cover the costs of the leave application and the proposed derivative action, assuring the court that the company would not have to fund the action. The real difficulty is not knowing how much evidence or what evidence is necessary to satisfactorily establish these leave criteria, apart from undertaking to pay for the action to be brought.

The rationale for refusing to have the company finance the SDA is predominantly to protect the company's interests and its financial resources and to prevent potential abuse of the SDA process. This approach, as adopted by the courts, has been a way of giving effect to the statement in the Explanatory Memorandum that introduced the SDA, that the costs provision in s.242 is designed to provide the court with an "additional safeguard".[10] However, the present research has shown that such fears reported in the Explanatory Memorandum,[11] coupled with the cautionary note provided and, in response, the harsh approach adopted by the Australian courts on the interpretation of the leave requirement under s.237(2) and the costs provision under s.242, are unnecessary, as explained in Chapter 6. Overseas experiences have shown that their SDAs have not resulted in a flood of cases in their courtrooms.

Indeed, it is important to protect the company's interests and its financial resources, but at the same time, it is equally important to make way for genuine shareholder applicants to bring a derivative action without burdening them with heavy costs and onerous leave criteria. After all, a derivative action is an action brought on behalf of the company for the benefit of all shareholders in the company. An applicant's financial status should not be a factor in determining the merits of the proposed action. A genuine applicant should not be burdened with costs where they have offered their time and energy trying to assist the company to rectify the wrong done to it.[12]

It is worth noting that due to the uncertainty in the leave requirement and the recovery of costs, coupled with the uncertainty in obtaining an order for inspection of company books,[13] some shareholders may turn to another alternative for relief instead. The most popular one has been an oppression/unfair prejudice action or even a class action (if they can gather support from at least six other class members), as explained in Chapter 7. These alternatives may be simpler and cheaper as there is no leave requirement for commencing these actions. In an oppression action, there is no procedural obstacle and the remedy granted by the court is generally personal to the plaintiff. A class

10 House of Representatives, *Explanatory Memorandum to the CLERP Bill* 1998, at 26, [6.19].

11 For example, using statements referring to the need to prevent "unmeritorious" or "vexatious" or "frivolous" actions.

12 As explained with supporting reasons in Chapters 5 and 6.

13 Section 247A of the *Corporations Act* 2001 is explained in Chapter 7.2 in this book.

action is more commonly used in larger companies; however, class action could still be used in a small private company provided that there are at least seven shareholders sharing similar or related grievances to form a class.

8.2.2.5 Comparative analysis and implications for Australia

Research has shown that Australia is one of the very few countries that has the strictest leave requirement. Comparative analysis with other jurisdictions has provided important insights into how best to improve the Australian SDA, and also for other countries that consider implementing the SDA into their own country to learn from the experiences. Ideas and suggestions included in Chapters 4, 5 and 6 can be summed up as these:

- While an Australian applicant must demonstrate with certainty that the proposed action on behalf of the company will have a guaranteed success for the company by the use of the words "is" and "best" in s.237(2)(c), a test that is impossible to establish satisfactorily in practical terms, other countries do not have a similar issue.[14] Other countries have a lower threshold by using the expression "appears to be in the interests of the corporation" as seen in Canada,[15] or "appears to be prima facie in the interests of the company", as in Singapore[16] or a variation of other expressions with a similar effect.[17]
- Interestingly, British Columbia (a province in Canada) has a provision that requires the shareholder applicant to show to the court's satisfaction that the proposed derivative action "appears to the Court that it is in the best interests of the company" (that is, it has the word "appears" instead of the Australian version that has the word "is"). The courts in British Columbia, however, seem to follow Canada's federal approach, which has a much lower threshold, and that provision is equivalent to asking whether the applicant can show that there is an "arguable" case or there is a "reasonable prospect of success" in the proposed action.[18] This is the same as asking whether "there is a serious question to be tried" under the Australian s.237(2)(d).[19]
- New Zealand did not see the need to have "good faith" as a test in its legislation. It is a relevant factor for consideration, but not a necessary

14 See Chapter 5.
15 *Canada Business Corporations Act,* R.S.C. 1985, s.239(2)(c).
16 *Companies Act* 1993 (Singapore, Chapter 50, 2006, revised ed), s.216A(3)(c).
17 See, for example, *Companies Act* 1993 (New Zealand), s.165(3); *Companies Act* 2006 (UK), s.263(3).
18 See Chapter 5, as decided in *Jordan Enterprises Ltd v. Barker* 2015, BCSC 559 at [33–36]; *Gill v. Kalgidhar Darbar Sahib Society*, 2018 BCSC 813, at [46]; *Luft v. Ball* 2013, BCSC 574 at [54]; *Holdyk v. Adolph* 2012, BCCA 37, at [19]; *Gartenberg v. Consolidated Stone Industries Inc.* 2005 BCCA 462, at [26].
19 See Chapter 5.

prerequisite for leave in New Zealand. By comparison, Singapore has the "good faith" requirement in its legislation, but the application of that requirement was thrown into confusion when the Singapore Court of Appeal in recent years overturned its original approach and adopted a stricter approach. The implication for Australia is that the "good faith" requirement may need to be reconsidered; the book has argued, in Chapter 4 that, although "good faith" is a relevant consideration, it should not be made as a precondition for leave to be granted.[20]

- Some jurisdictions, such as Canada, New Zealand and the United Kingdom, allow successful applicants to recover some costs if circumstances appear just and equitable and if the company can afford it. Furthermore, Canada and New Zealand allow the court to make an order compensating not the whole company but the shareholders who have been adversely affected by the wrong done to the company. In effect, their provisions allow the court to filter out free riders and other members not deserving or not entitled to compensation, depending on the role they play in the company. For example, majority shareholders who have injured the company or prospective shareholders who recently joined the company would not be entitled to a share of the compensation.[21]
- Some jurisdictions such as Canada, Singapore and Hong Kong have *fewer* leave criteria.[22]

The insights acquired from these jurisdictional comparisons, as explained in the book, are that Canada, Singapore, New Zealand, the United Kingdom, Hong Kong and the US have an SDA that is more user-friendly to shareholders, to a varying degree, making it less onerous on the shareholder to apply for leave. Their systems seem to favour a stronger desire to cultivate and promote directors' accountability and corporate governance, which is something that Australia may be able to learn from, for the purposes of amending the Australian law relating to the SDA.

8.2.3 Justification for retention of SDA

As noted in Chapter 1, the book submits that the SDA should be retained, but in a modified form. There are two reasons. First, as a private enforcement tool, an SDA is a means by which a shareholder can enforce corporate rights to protect the company against a director for breach of directors' duties. SDA is an important source of shareholder remedy for the company, even if shareholders are entitled only to a *pro rata* benefit of the total recovery in a successful action. Apart from relying on a public regulator, such as ASIC,

20 See Chapter 4.
21 See Chapter 6.
22 See Chapter 5.

to prosecute an offending director (which it may lack the resources to do), a well-designed SDA could give shareholders a means to obtain relief that would benefit the whole of the company rather than for them individually looking out to protect their own interests. Forcing powerless shareholders to take a different path because the SDA procedure is too cumbersome and/or too costly may, in the long haul, bring about some unintended consequences to the company, while in the meantime, directors who have wronged the company may continue with their bad behaviour and not be brought to justice.

Second and following on from the first point, on occasions, where claims from individual shareholders overlap because of similar facts or circumstances, it may be more cost-effective and less cumbersome if an SDA is brought instead of multiple oppression actions or other multiple personal claims. A class action may also be available if there are seven or more shareholders involved in a similar or related claim, but this type of lawsuit would not be helping the company since a class action is usually an action brought *against* the company. An SDA may be a useful tool if these individual shareholders are willing and prepared to contribute to the overall costs in bringing a derivative action if the court does not allow company funds to be used. However, one can only hope that the legislature would amend the costs provision to ease the pressure on the shareholder applicant.

8.2.4 The way forward

In answer to the second research question, the recommended law reform proposals are summarised as follows:

- Removal of "good faith" in s.237(2)(b) – Whether it is necessary to have good faith included as a prerequisite in Part 2F.1A of the Australian *Corporations Act* 2001 (C'th) is debatable. However, as explained in Chapter 4 and the key points summarised in this chapter above, it is the view of the author that the "good faith" requirement is unnecessary and should be removed from the SDA.
- Amending s.237(2)(c) relating to the term "in the best interests of the company" – As explained in Chapter 5 and the key reasons noted in this chapter, it is the author's recommendation that the troubling words "is" and "best" be removed from s.237(2)(c) and that the provision be replaced with a new expression that reads "appears to be in the interests of the company". This would also be in line with many of the overseas current practices.
- Recovery of legal costs and s.242 – As explained in Chapter 6 in detail and the key points summarised in this chapter above, it is recommended that the broad power conferred on the court to award costs in s.242 be removed and replaced by a new provision that enables successful applicants to recover some costs. One option is to adopt the US common

fund/contingency fees arrangements and the substantial benefit/lodestar method. If the action generates monetary relief, legal fees will be paid at a fixed percentage of the amount recovered whether by judgment or settlement. If the action results in a substantial non-monetary benefit to the company, legal fees will be paid out of the company's funds on the services rendered at an hourly rate. The other option is to adopt the Canadian or New Zealand provision to allow the successful applicant to apply for an indemnity order based on "just and equitable" grounds for the company to bear those costs.[23] The UK approach is another option where the courts have been seen to make orders relating to periodic releases of company funds if circumstances appear just and equitable.

- Minimising the free rider problem – One way of minimising the free rider problem could be to adopt the Canadian or New Zealand approach by including a provision in Part 2F.1A of the Australian *Corporations Act* 2001 (C'th) to allow only the *injured* shareholders to benefit from the company's successes in the derivative action, as explained in Chapter 6.
- Clarifying the scope of "company" and company in liquidation – In the current form, there is a lack of clarity in the word "company" and its usage. As explained in Chapter 5, it is not clear whether a shareholder applicant for leave is required to consider a wider group of interests to include other stakeholders. Further, the general judicial approach is that Part 2F.1A does not apply to a company in liquidation; rather, the courts have been seen to exercise their inherent discretion under the insolvency law to grant the applicant leave to bring a shareholder derivative action. If the intention is for Part 2F.1A to apply to insolvency cases, then clarity is necessary by including terms such as "in liquidation".
- Too many criteria – The Australian SDA has five criteria for leave, far more than some other countries. As noted, Australia is one of the very few countries that have the strictest leave requirement. Perhaps the requirement relating to "there is a serious question to be tried" in s.237(2)(d) could be removed so as to minimise the overlap with the revised requirement relating to "in the interests of the company", as explained in Chapter 5.
- Related third party and presumption of good business judgment in s.237(3) – It is debatable whether this provision is necessary. The existence of this provision hinders the effective use of the derivative action provisions. There are enough provisions in the *Corporations Act* that allow directors' defences, including the business judgment rule contained in s.180(2), as described in Chapter 5. If, for example, a director who has resigned from the company because of an allegation of breaches of directors' duties, a shareholder applicant seeking to assert their corporate rights and pursue an action against the former director should be permitted to apply to the court for leave in the same way

23 See *Companies Act* 1993 (New Zealand), s.166.

that an applicant would apply for leave to sue against a current director. A shareholder applicant should not be burdened with that extra need to establish whether the former director is a "related party" (hence, exempting the application of s.237(3) or whether the former director is a "third party", in which case, the shareholder applicant is under extra pressure to rebut the presumption in s.237(3)).[24] Under the current law, whether a former director is a "related party" or a "third party" is dependent on whether the leave application is made within the six months since the person's departure or outside that period. It seems unreasonable to impose that extra burden on the applicant to rebut the presumption set out in s.237(3) that the board of directors had made a good business decision not to litigate, as explained in Chapter 5.

It is understandable that there is a need in the law to balance between, on the one hand, allowing a derivative action to proceed, and on the other hand, protecting the company against unmeritorious or frivolous action. However, the book has shown that the less rigid approach adopted in some jurisdictions with strong economies (such as Canada, Singapore, New Zealand, the United Kingdom and Hong Kong) has not resulted in any unwarranted abuse of the SDA process or created a flood of cases. The fears foreseen in the government reports and in the Explanatory Memorandum that introduced the SDA were unfounded.

8.3 Areas for future research

There are a number of areas for future research. One area could be to investigate whether the law should allow employees to apply to the court for leave to bring an SDA. This would involve answering research questions such as:

- Will there be any interests for employees to get involved in the SDA, and if so, what type of interests recognised in law would provide them with some incentive to bring an SDA?[25]
- What type of employees should be permitted to bring an SDA, and how long should they have been with the company in order to establish good faith, loyalty to the company and impartiality?
- How should employees' interests be given recognition and protection under corporate law and how would these intersect under labour law?

24 See Chapter 5.

25 It has been argued that employees could be regarded as human capital to the company, and because they add value to the company, they should be given some financial interest and property rights in the company in the same way as the shareholders: Wanjiru Njoya, *Property in Work: The Employment Relationship in the Anglo-American Firm* (Ashgate Publishing Limited, 2007); Howard Gospel and Andrew Pendleton, *Corporate Governance and Labour Management: An International Comparison* (Oxford University Press, 2006).

The advantages of allowing ordinary employees to bring an SDA are that they are more likely to have better inside knowledge of the company and of the breaches of directors' duties, and that they are likely to be in a better position to show the court that the proposed action would be in the interests of the company. This research area would involve corporate law and labour law intersection, and the concepts of corporate social responsibility, the stakeholder approach and the use of German co-determination and supervisory board principles.

Another related area for future research could be to bridge the gap between the SDA provisions and the insolvency provisions, which is beyond the scope of this book. The implications of the SDA in Part 2F.1A and the insolvency provisions relating to company liquidation need to be reconciled in order to establish a system that would enable bona fide shareholders affected by the insolvency to have some rights to claim for compensation in insolvency. Currently, an applicant may be given leave to bring shareholder derivative action under the insolvency provisions through the court's inherent discretion under the insolvency provisions,[26] but there is no certainty of any recovery in compensation or in costs. Creditors are still the dominant claimants in insolvency proceedings. The relevant research questions to include could be:

- What characteristics should bona fide shareholders possess to be entitled to a claim of recovery in shareholder derivative action?
- What are the costs to the community and what impact does it have on the community and on corporate governance if directors' wrongdoings go unnoticed or unmonitored because neither the liquidator nor the shareholder can financially afford to bring a derivative action?
- What should be a fair and reasonable proportion of recovery given to shareholders in a *shareholder* derivative action in liquidation?

Another area for future research could be to locate applicants for leave and conduct a questionnaire-type survey in order to understand why many successful applicants have abandoned their pursuit of SDA and to find out what unsuccessful applicants have done to obtain justice elsewhere for the company. There is a gap in understanding why a vast majority of successful applicants for leave did not commence the approved derivative action. One can only assume that it could be due to the high costs of litigation and the uncertainty of recovering those costs. Some applicants might have been fortunate enough to use the successful leave application as a bargaining tool

26 It has been established in the past ten years or so that the SDA procedure in Part 2F.1A of the Australian *Corporations Act* 2001 (C'th) is not applicable to shareholders where a company has been placed into liquidation: see, for example, *Chahwan v. Euphoric Pty Ltd* (2008) 65 ACSR 661; [2008] NSWCA 52; *Ragless v. IPA Holdings Pty Ltd (in liq)* (2008) 65 ACSR 700; [2008] SASC 90 (South Australian Court of Appeal decision).

to negotiate a favourable settlement, in which case one might argue that the current SDA has achieved its purpose in the enhancement of corporate accountability; while others might have abandoned their efforts to pursue further. Such a questionnaire-type survey could provide some further useful evidence and insights into other ways to promote and maintain good corporate governance.

8.4 Concluding remarks

This book is the first comprehensive and detailed study of the operation of the SDA in Australia. No other scholar has attempted a similar approach on the Australian SDA in such depth and detail, which includes a comprehensive empirical study covering a period of 20 years, combined with detailed case law analysis and comparisons with other jurisdictions.

It is submitted that the SDA has not been working as well as was intended by the legislature. This book provides some suggestions and recommendations for law reform. The adoption of these reforms would provide minority shareholders with better protection against managerial misconduct and breaches of directors' duties. An improved SDA mechanism would indeed deter directors from committing any wrongdoing, and in turn, promote good corporate governance overall. A shareholder applicant who is willing and prepared to step up to facilitate the company in prosecuting the offenders should not be over-burdened with the need to demonstrate good faith and be subjected to pay the costs of the derivative proceedings.

It is hoped that the suggestions and recommendations provided in this book will be useful for countries that have adopted the SDA and are considering revising their framework, and for countries that are planning on introducing the SDA for the first time. SDA, if properly designed, could possibly be seen as a powerful tool for promoting good corporate governance. It should not be viewed as a cumbersome shareholder remedy only to be used when there is no better choice.

Bibliography

Anderson, Helen, "Directors' Liability for Fraudulent Phoenix Activity: A Comparison of the Australian and UK Approaches" (2014) 14 *Journal of Corporate Law Studies* 139

Anderson, Helen, Michelle Welsh, Ian Ramsay and Peter Gahan, "Shareholder and Creditor Protection in Australia: A Leximetric Analysis" (2012) 30 *Company and Securities Law Journal* 366

Armour, John, Bernard Black, Brian Cheffins and Richard Nolan, "Private Enforcement of Corporate Law: An Empirical Comparison of the United Kingdom and the United States" (2009) 6 *Journal of Empirical Legal Studies* 687

Bainbridge, Wesley and Tim Connor, "Another Way Forward? The Scope for an Appellate Court to Reinterpret the Statutory Business Judgment Rule" (2016) 34 *Company and Securities Law Journal* 415

Balp, Gaia and Giovanni Strampelli, "Institutional Investor Collective Engagements: Non-Activist Corporation vs Activist Wolf Packs" (2020) 14(2) *Ohio State Business Law Journal* 135

Banta, P. F., "New Indiana Business Corporation Law: Reckless Statute or New Standard" (1987) *Columbia Business Law Review* 233

Baxt, Robert, "A Body Blow to Section 1324 of the Corporations Law: Will the Derivative Action Get a New Lease of Life?" (1996) 14 *Company and Securities Law Journal* 312

Baxt, Robert, "The Federal Court Confirms that the Test of Oppression Is Objective" (2016) 1 *Baxt Report* 12

Baxt, Robert, "The Rule in Foss v Harbottle Rears its Ugly Head: The Case for a Statutory Derivative Action Gathers Strength" (1996) 14 *Companies and Securities Law Journal* 174

Baxt, Robert, "The unwillingness of courts to correct directors' mistakes – Especially where minorities are involved" (1997) 15 *Company and Securities Law Journal* 65

Beck, S. M., "The Shareholder's Derivative Action" (1974) 52 *Canadian Bar Review* 159

Berkahn, Matthew, "The Derivative Action in Australia and New Zealand: Will the Statutory Provisions Improve Shareholders' Enforcement Right?" (1998) 10 *Bond Law Review* 1

Berkahn, Matthew and Lindsay Trotman, "Public and Private Enforcement of Company Law in New Zealand 1986–1990" (2000) 7 *Canterbury Law Review* 516

Black, Bernard S., "Shareholder Passivity Re-examined" (1990) 89 *Michigan Law Review* 520, 527–528.

Boros, Elizabeth, "Remedies for Oppression Cases for Derivative Wrongs" (2014) 32 *Company and Securities Law Journal* 151
Boros, Elizabeth, "Clarification regarding past oppression: *Exton v. Exton Pty Ltd*" (2017) 35 *Company and Securities Law Journal* 391
Bottomley, Stephen, "Shareholder Derivative Actions and Public Interest Suits: Two Versions of the Same Story?" (1992) 15 *University of New South Wales Law Journal* 127
Brockett, Richard, "The Valuation of Shareholdings in an Oppression Context: A Contemporary Review" (2012) 24 *Bond Law Review* 101
Broderick, Matthew, "Statutory Derivative Actions in Company Liquidations" (2008) 16 *Insolvency Law Journal* 7
Campbell, Jenny and Jerome Entwisle, "The Australian Shareholder Class Action Experience: Are We Approaching a Tipping Point?" (2017) 36(2) *Civil Justice Quarterly* 177
Cassim, Maleka, "The Statutory Derivative Action under the Companies Act of 2008: The Role of Good Faith" (2013) 130 *South African Law Journal* 496
Cheffins, Brian R., "Reforming the Derivative Action: The Canadian Experience and British Prospects" (1997) 2 *Company Financial & Insolvency Law Review* 227
Cheffins, Brian R. and Bernard S. Black, "Outside Director Liability Across Countries" (2006) 84 *Texas Law Review* 1385
Cheffins, Brian R. and J. M. Dine, "Shareholder Remedies: Lessons from Canada" (1992) 13 *Company Lawyer* 89
Chesterman, Justice R. N., "Oppression by the Majority: Or of it?" (2004) 25(2) *Australian Bar Review* 103
Choo, Pearlie K. M., "The Statutory Derivative Action in Singapore: A Critical and Comparative Examination" (2001) 13 *Bond Law Review* 64
Choo, Pearlie K. M., "Of Links and Legal Merits: Good Faith in the Statutory Derivative Action in Singapore" (2014) 14 *Oxford University Commonwealth Law Journal* 225
Chumir, S., "Challenging Directors and the Rule in Foss v. Harbottle" (1965) 4 *Alta Law Review* 96
Clark, Stuart and Michael Legg, "The Continued Rise of Litigation Funding" (2006) 22(9) *Company Director* 34
Coffee, John C., "The Unfaithful Champion: The Plaintiff as Monitor in Shareholder Litigation" (1985) 48 *Law and Contemporary Problems* 5
Coffee, John C. and Donald E. Schwartz, "The Survival of the Derivative Suit: An Evaluation and a Proposal for Legislative Reform" (1981) 81 *Columbia Law Review* 261
Davis, Kenneth, "The Forgotten Derivative Suit" (2008) 61 *Vanderbilt Law Review* 387
Dawson, J. P., "Lawyers and Involuntary Clients: Attorney Fees from Funds" (1974) 87 *Harvard Law Review* 1597
DeMott, Deborah A., "Shareholder Litigation in Australia and the United States: Common Problems, Uncommon Solutions" (1987) 11(2) *Sydney Law Review* 259
Dent, George, "The Power of Directors to Terminate Shareholder Litigation: The Death of the Derivative Suit" (1980) 75 *Newak University Law Review* 96
Dodd, Merrick, "For Whom are Corporate Managers Trustees?" (1932) *Harvard Law Review* 45
Duffy, Michael, "Procedural Dilemmas for Contemporary Shareholder Remedies: Derivative Action or Class Action" (2004) 22 *Company and Securities Law Journal* 46

Egert, Geoffrey, Colin Anderson and Scott Kiel-Chisholm, "The Application of the Statutory Derivative Action in Pt 2F.1A of the Corporations Act to Companies in Liquidation under Ch 5: Well Oiled Machine or is Pt 2F.1A in Need of a Tune up?" (2011) 25 *Australian Journal of Corporate Law* 318

Fischel, Daniel R. and Michael Bradley, "The Role of Liability Rules and the Derivative Suit in Corporate Law: A Theoretical and Empirical Analysis" (1983) 71 *Cornell Law Journal* 261

Fletcher, Keith L., "CLERP and Minority Shareholder Rights" (2001) 13 *Australian Journal of Corporate Law* 290

Fridman, Saul, "Ratification of Directors' Breaches" (1992) 10 *Company and Securities Law Journal* 252

Geis, George S., "Shareholder Derivative Litigation and the Preclusion Problem" (2014) 100 *Virginia Law Review* 261

Gelter, Martin, "Why Do Shareholder Derivative Suits Remain Rare in Continental Europe?" (2012) 37 *Brooklyn Journal of International Law* 843

Gevurtz, F. A., "Who Represents the Corporation? In Search of a Better Method for Determining the Corporate Interest in Derivative Suits" (1995) 46 *University of Pittsburgh Law Review* 265

Gibbs-Kneller, David and Chidiebere Ogbonnaya, "Empirical Analysis of the Statutory Derivative Claim: De facto Application and the sine quibus non" (2019) 19(2) *Journal of Corporate Law Studies* 303

Gibson, Belinda and Diane Brown, "ASIC's Expectations of Directors" (2012) 35 *University of New South Wales Law Journal* 254

Goehre, Kurt A., "Is the Demand Requirement Obsolete? How the United Kingdom Modernised its Shareholder Derivative Procedure and What the United States Can Learn from it" (2010) 28 *Wisconsin International Law Journal* 140

Goo, Say H., "Multiple Derivative Action and Common Law Derivative Action Revisited: A Tale of Two Jurisdictions" (2010) 10 *Journal of Corporate Law Studies* 255

Gray, Anthony, "Good Faith in Australian Contract Law after Barker" (2015) 43 *Australian Business Law Review* 358

Griggs, Lynden, "The Statutory Derivative Action: Lessons That May Be Learnt from its Past" (2002) 6 *University of Western Sydney Law Review* 64

Griggs, Lynden and J. P. Lowry, "Minority Shareholder Remedies: A Comparative View" (1994) *Journal of Business Law* 463

Hale, Christopher, "What's Right with the Rule in Foss v. Harbottle?" (1997) 2 *Company Financial Insolvency Law Review* 219

Hanrahan, Pamela, "Distinguishing Corporate and Personal Claims in Australian Company Litigation" (1997) 15 *Company and Securities Law Journal* 21

Hargovan, Anil, "Under Judicial and Legislative Attack: The Rule in Foss v. Harbottle" (1996) 113 *South African Law Journal* 631

Hargovan, Anil and Jason Harris, "Sons of Gwalia Ltd *v*. Margaretic: The Shifting Balance of Shareholders' Interests in Insolvency: Evolution or Revolution?" (2007) 31 *Melbourne University Law Review* 591

Harper Thomas, Carmen, "Limited Liability Companies Are Off and Running: Historic Charleston Holdings, LLC v. Mallon, Accountings, and Derivative Actions in LLC Litigation" (2006) 57 *South Carolina Law Review* 441

Harris, Jason and Anil Hargovan, "Still a Sleepy Hollow? Directors' Liability and the Business Judgment Rule" (2016) 31 *Australian Journal of Corporate Law* 319

Hayne, Justice K. M., "Directors' Duties and a Company's Creditors" (2014) 38 *Melbourne University Law Review* 795

Hill, Jennifer G., "Subverting Shareholder Rights: Lessons from News Corp's Migration to Delaware" (2010) 63 *Vanderbilt Law Review* 1; Working Paper No. 143/2010, European Corporate Governance Institute Working Paper Series in Law, March 2010)

Hill, Jennifer G., "Companies: Inspection by Shareholders of Corporate Books and Documents" (1987) 61 *Australian Law Journal* 657

Hill, Jennifer G., "Protecting Minority Shareholders and Reasonable Expectations" (1992) 10 *Company and Securities Law Journal* 86

Hofmann, Melissa, "The Statutory Derivative Action in Australia: An Empirical Review of its Use and Effectiveness in Australia in Comparison to the United States, Canada and Singapore" (2005) *Corporate Governance eJournal* 1

Israels Carlos, L., "The Sacred Crow of Corporate existence: Problems of Deadlock and Dissolution" (1952) 19 *University of Chicago Law Review* 778

Jackson Howell, E. and Mark J. Roe, "Public and Private Enforcement of Securities Laws: Resource-Based Evidence" (2009) 93 *Journal of Financial Economics* 207–

Jones, Renee M. and Michelle Welsh, "Toward a Public Enforcement Model for Directors' Duty of Oversight" (2012) 45 *Vanderbilt Journal of Transnational Law* 343–404

Kaplan, William and Bruce Elwood, "The Derivative Action: A Shareholder's "Bleak House"?" (2003) 36 *University of British Columbia Law Review* 443

Keay, Andrew, "Can Derivative Proceedings be Commenced Where the Company Is in Liquidation?" (2008) 21(4) *Insolvency Intelligence* 49

Keay, Andrew, "Ascertaining the Corporate Objective: An Entity Maximisation and Sustainability Model" (2008) 71 *Modern Law Review* 663

Keay, Andrew, "Assessing and Rethinking the Statutory Scheme for Derivative Actions under the Companies Act 2006" (2016) 16 *Journal of Corporate Law Studies* 39

Keay, Andrew and Joan Loughrey, "Derivative Proceedings in a Brave New World for Company Management and Shareholders" (2010) *Journal of Business Law* 151

Keay, Andrew and Joan Louhrey, "Something Old, Something New, Something Borrowed: An Analysis of the New Derivative Active Action under the Companies Act 2006" (2008) 124 *Law Quarterly Review* 469

Kluver, John, "Derivative Actions and the Rule in *Foss v Harbottle*: Do We Need a Statutory Remedy?" (1993) 11 *Companies and Securities Law Journal* 7

Koh, Alan K., 'Searching for Good Faith in Singapore's Derivative Action: Much Ado About Something? Wong Kai Wah v Wong Kai Yuan, Ang Thiam Swee v Low Hian Chor (2015) 36 *Company Lawyer* 207

Koh, Pearlie, "Of links and Legal Merits: Good Faith in the Statutory Derivative Action in Singapore" (2014) 14 *Oxford University Commonwealth Law Journal* 225

Lam, Daniel T. L., "Statutory Derivative Action in Hong Kong: So Far so Good?" (2009) 23 *Australian Journal of Corporate Law* 26

Lambert, K. A., "Class Action Settlements in Louisiana", (2000) 61 *Louisiana Law Review* 89

Legg, Michael, "Class Action Settlements in Australia: The Need for Greater Scrutiny" (2014) 38(2) *Melbourne University Law Review* 590

Legg, Michael and Samuel J. Hickey, "Finality and Fairness in Australian Shareholder Class Action Settlements" (2019) 41 *Sydney Law Review* 185

Loewenstein, M. J., "Shareholder Derivative Litigation and Corporate Governance" (1999) 24 *Delaware Journal of Corporate Law* 1

Lombard, Sulette and Tronel Joubert, "The Legislative Response to the Shareholders v Stakeholders Debate: A Comparative Overview" (2014) 14 *Journal of Corporate Law Studies* 1

McConvill, James "Part 2F.1A of the Corporations Act: Insert a New s.242(2) or Give it the Boot?" (2002) 30 *Australian Business Law Review* 309

McConvill, James, "Ensuring Balance in Corporate Governance: Parts 2F.1 and 2F.1A of the Corporations Law" (2001) 12 *Australian Journal of Corporate Law* 293

McConvill, James and M. Bagaric, "Towards Mandatory Shareholder Committees in Australian Companies" (2004) 28 *Melbourne University Law Review* 125

McDonough, Darryl, "Proposed New Statutory Derivative Action: Does it Go Far Enough?" (1996) 8 *Bond Law Review* 47

McPherson, B. H., "Duties of Directors and the Powers of Shareholders" (1977) 51 *Australian Law Journal* 460

McQueen, Rob, "Company Law as Imperialism" (1995) 5 *Australian Journal of Corporate Law* 187

Macey, J. R. and J. P. Miller, "The Plaintiffs' Attorney's Role in Class Action and Derivative Litigaiton: Economic Analysis and Recommendations for Reform" (1991) 58 *University of Chicago Law Review* 1

Maloney, M. A., "Whither the Statutory Derivative Action?" (1986) 64 *Canadian Bar Review* 309

Mantziaris, Christos, "The Member's Right to Inspect the Company Books: Corporations Act, s.247A" (2009) 83 *Australian Law Journal* 621

Mason H. H., "Possible Alternatives to an Australian Securities and Exchange Commission: Contingent Fees and Derivative Actions by Shareholders" (1976) 50 *Australian Law Journal* 26

Mayanja, J., "Standing to Challenge the Implementation of Improper Defensive Measures" (1995) 5 *Australian Journal of Corporate Law* 66

Mezzanotte, Felix E., "The Unconvincing Rise of the Statutory Derivative Action in Hong Kong: Evidence from its First 10 Years of Enforcement" (2017) 17 *Journal of Corporate Law Studies* 469

Monichino, Albert, "Costs in Statutory Derivative Actions: The Lingering Ghost of Wallersteiner" (2015) 33 *Company and Securities Law Journal* 104

Myers, Minor, "The Decisions of the Corporate Special Litigation Committees: An Empirical Investigation" (2009) 84 *Indiana Law Journal* 1309

Nettle, Justice Geoffrey, "The Changing Position and Duties of Company Directors" (2018) 41 *Melbourne University Law Review* 1402

von Nessen, Paul, Say H. Goo and Chee Keong Low, "The Statutory Derivative Action: Now Showing Near You" (2007) 7 *Journal of Business Law* 627

Osunbor, O. A., "A Critical Appraisal of 'The Interests of Justice' as an Exception to the Rule in *Foss v. Harbottle*" (1987) 36 *International and Comparative Law Quarterly* 1

Payne, Jennifer, "Clean Hands in Derivative Actions" (2002) 61 *Cambridge Law Journal* 76

Pender, Kieran, "The 'Price" of Justice? Costs-conditional Special Leave in the High Court" (2018) 42 *Melbourne University Law Review* 149

Piercy, Lara Jane, "Comparison of the law Concerning Implied Terms of Good Faith in Australia and in England" (2017) 6 *Journal of Civil Law and Practice* 163 du Plessis, Jean J., "Directors' Duty to Act in the Best Interests of the Corporation: 'Hard Cases Make Bad Law'" (2019) 34 *Australian Journal of Corporate Law* 3

du Plessis, Jean J., "Open Sea or Safe Harbour? American, Australian and South African Business Judgment Rule Compared" (2011) 32 *Company Lawyer* 378–382

Poole, J. and P. Roberts, "Shareholder Remedies: Corporate Wrongs and the Derivative Action" (1999) *Journal of Business Law* 99

Prentice, Dan D., "Creditors' Interests and Director's Duties" (1990) 10 *Oxford Journal of Legal Studies* 265

Prince, Peter, "Australia's Statutory Derivative Action: Using the New Zealand Experience" (2000) 18 *Company and Securities Law Journal* 493

Puchniak, Dan W., "The Derivative Action in Asia: The Complex Reality" (2012) 9 *Berkeley Business Law Journal* 1

Puchniak, Dan W. and Masafumi Nakahigashi, "Japan's Love for Derivative Actions: Irrational Behavior and Non-economic Motives as Rational Explanations for Shareholder Litigation" (2012) 45 *Vanderbilt Journal of Transnational Law* 1

Puchniak, Dan W. and Cheng Han Tan SC, "Company Law" (2015) 16 Singapore Academy of Law Annual Review 255

Ramsay, Ian M. and Ben Saunders, "Litigation by Shareholders and Directors: An Empirical Study of the Australian Statutory Derivative Action" (2006) 6 *Journal of Corporate Law Studies* 397

Ramsay, Ian M., "An Empirical Study of the Use of the Oppression Remedy" (1999) 27 *Australian Business Law Review* 23

Ramsay, Ian M., "Corporate Governance, Shareholder Litigation and the Prospects for a Statutory Derivative Action" (1992) 15 *University of New South Wales Law Journal* 149

Ramsay, Ian M., "Enforcement of Corporate Rights and Duties by Shareholders and the Australian Securities Commission: Evidence and Analysis" (1995) 23 *Australian Business Law Review* 174

Reisberg, Arad, "Promoting the Use of Derivative Actions" (2003) 24 *Company Lawyer* 250

Reisberg, Arad, "Funding Derivative Actions: A Re-examination of Costs and Fees as Incentives to Commence Litigation" (2004) 4 *Journal of Corporate Law Studies* 345

Reisberg, Arad, "Theoretical Reflections on Derivative Actions in English Law: The Representative Problem" (2006) 3 *European Company and Financial Law Review* 69

Reisberg, Arad, "Access to Justice or Justice not Accessed: Is There a Case for Public Funding of Derivative Claims?" (2012) 37 *Brooklyn Journal of International Law* 1021

Romano, Roberta, "The Shareholder Suit: Litigation Without Foundation" (1991) 7 *Journal of Legal Economics and Organisation* 55

Saenger, Ingo, "The Best Interests of the Corporation: Procedural Questions of Enforcing Individual and Corporate Rights and Legal Actions Against Board Members" (2015) 26 *European Business Law Review 13* 13

Sealy, Len S., "The Rule in Foss v. Harbottle: The Australian Experience" (1989) 10 *Company Lawyer* 52

Sealy, Len S., "Foss v. Harbottle: A Marathon Where Nobody Wins" (1981) 40 *Cambridge Law Journal* 29

Stapleton, Geoff P, "Locus Standi of Shareholders to Enforce the Duty of Company Directors to Exercise the Share Issue Power for Proper Purposes" (1990) 8 *Company and Securities Law Journal* 213

Stoop, Helena H., "The Derivative Action Provisions in the Companies Act 71 of 2008" (2012) 129 *South African Law Journal* 530
Sullivan, G. R., "Restating the Scope of the Derivative Action" (1985) 44 *Cambridge Law Journal* 236
Summers, Robert, "'Good Faith' in General Contract Law and the Sales Provisions of the Uniform Commercial Code" (1968) 54 *Virginia Law Review* 195
Tang, Samantha S., "Corporate Avengers Need not Be Angels: Rethinking Good Faith in the Derivative Action" (2016) 16 *Journal of Corporate Law Studies* 471
Tang, Samantha S., "Shareholder Remedies: Demise of the Derivative Claim?" (2012) 1 *UCL Journal of Law and Jurisprudence* 178
Taylor, Lynne, "Ratification and the Statutory Derivative Action in the Companies Act 1993" (1998) 16 *Company and Securities Law Journal* 221
Taylor, Lynne, "The Derivative Action in the Companies Act 1993: An Empirical Study" (2006) 22 *New Zealand Universities Law Review* 337
Thai, Lang, "Calling for Reform to the Statutory Derivative Action in Australia: Critical Analysis and Suggestions for Reform" (2013) 21 *Insolvency Law Journal* 242–262
Thai, Lang and Matthew Berkahn, "Statutory Derivative Actions in Australia and New Zealand: What Can We Learn from Each Other?" (2012) 25 *New Zealand Universities Law Review* 370
Thai, Lang, "How Popular Are Statutory Derivative Actions in Australia? Comparisons with USA, Canada, and New Zealand" (2002) 30 *Australian Business Law Review* 118
Thai, Lang, "Statutory Injunction: Call for Amendment to s 1324 of the Corporations Act" (2006) 24 *Company and Securities Law Journal* 41
Thai, Lang, "Commercial Litigation Funding: The Need to Impose Regulations to Improve the Outcome of the Shareholder Class Actions" (2011) 4 *Journal of the Australasian Law Teachers Association* 1
Thai, Lang, "Reconsideration of the "Good Faith" Requirement in Statutory Derivative Actions in Australia" (2020) 37 *Company and Securities Law Journal* 403
Thompson, Robert B. and Randall S. Thomas, "The Public and Private Faces of Derivative Lawsuits" (2004) 57 *Vanderbilt Law Review* 1747
Turner, Ryan J., "Directors' Fiduciary Duties and Oppression in Closely-Held Corporations" (2013) 31 *Company and Securities Law Journal* 278
Varzaly, Jenifer, "The Enforcement of Directors' Duties in Australia: An Empirical Analysis" (2015) 16 *European Business Organisation Law Review* 281
Varzaly, Jenifer, "Protecting the Authority of Directors: An Empirical Analysis of the Statutory Business Judgment Rule" (2012) 12 *Journal of Corporate Law Studies* 429
de Vere Stevens, K., "Should We Toss Foss? Toward an Australian Statutory Derivative Action" (1997) 25 *Australian Business Law Review* 127
Watkins, S., "The Common Law Derivative Action: An Outmoded Relic?" (1999) 30 *Cambrian Law Review* 40
Wedderburn, K. W., "Shareholders' Rights and the Rule in Foss v. Harbottle – Part 1" (1957) 15 *Cambridge Law Journal* 194
Wedderburn, K. W., "Shareholders' rights and the rule in Foss v. Harbottle – Part 2" (1958) 16 *Cambridge Law Journal* 93
Welsh, Michelle, "Realising the Public Potential of Corporate Law: Twenty Years of Civil Penalty Enforcement in Australia" (2014) 42 *Federal Law Review* 217
Whincop, Michael J., "The Role of the Shareholder in Corporate Governance: A Theoretical Approach" (2001) 25 *Melbourne University Law Review* 418

Wilson, J. D., "Attorney Fees and the Decision to Commence Litigation: Analysis, Comparison and an Application to the Shareholders' Derivative Action" (1985) 5 *Windsor Yearbook of Access to Justice* 142

Worthington, Sarah, "Corporate Governance: Remedying and Ratifying Directors' Breaches" (2000) 116 *Law Quarterly Review* 638

Yeung, Kenny, "Disentangling the Tangled Skein: The Ratification of Directors' Actions" (1992) 66 *Australian Law Journal* 343

BOOK CHAPTERS:

Berle, Adolf A. and Gardiner C. Means, "Chapter VI: The Divergence of Interest Between Ownership and Control", in *The Modern Corporation and Private Property* (Harcourt Publishing, 1932)

Blair, Margaret M., "Whose Interests Should Corporations Serve?" Chapter 6, in *Ownership and Control: Rethinking Corporate Governance for the Twenty-First Century* (The Brooking Institution, 1995)

Dixon, Olivia and Jennifer G. Hill, "Australia: The Protection of Investors and the Compensation for Their Losses", in Pierre-Henri Conac and Martin Gelter (eds.), *Global Securities Litigation and Enforcement*, pp. 1063–1100 (Cambridge University Press, 2019)

Hare, Christopher, "Shareholder Remedies: Personal Rights, Corporate Rights and the Derivative Action", in Peter Watts, Neil Campbell and Christopher Hare (eds.), *Company Law in New Zealand* (LexisNexis, 2011)

Finch, V., "Creditors' Interests and Directors' Obligation", in S. Shiekh and W Rees (eds.), *Corporate Governance and Corporate Control* (Cavendish, 1995)

Hill, Jennifer G., "Changes in the Role of the Shareholder" in Ross Grantham and Charles Rickett (eds.), *Corporate Personality in the 20th Century* (Hart Publishing, 1998)

Hill, Jennifer G., "Images of the Shareholder: Shareholder Power and Shareholder Powerlessness", in Jennifer Hill, Randall S. Thomas (eds.), *Research Handbook on Shareholder Power* (Edward Elgar Publishing, 2015)

Hill, Jennifer G. and Matthew Conaglen, "Directors' Duties and Legal Safe Harbours: A Comparative Analysis", in D. Gordon Smith and Andrew S. Gold (eds.), *Research Handbook on Fiduciary Law* (Edward Elgar, 2018)

Keay, Andrew and Joan Loughrey, "An Assessment of the Present State of Statutory Derivative Proceedings" in Joan Loughrey (ed.), *Directors' Duties and Shareholder Litigation in the Wake of the Financial Crisis* (Edward Elgar Publishing, 2012)

Legg, Michael, "Public and Private Enforcement: ASIC and the Shareholder Class Action", in Michael Legg (eds), *Regulation, Litigation and Enforcement* (Thomson Reuters, 2011)

Puchniak, Dan, "The Complexity of Derivative Actions in Asia: An Inconvenient Truth", (Chapter 2) in Dan Puchniak, Harald Baum and Michael Ewing-Chow (eds), *The Derivative Action in Asia: A Comparative and Functional Approach* (Cambridge University Press, 2012)

Redmond, Paul, "Safe Habours or Sleepy Hollows? Does Australia need the Statutory Business Judgment Rule?" in Ian Ramsay (ed.), *Corporate Governance and Duties of Company Directors* (Centre for Corporate Law and Securities Regulations, University of Melbourne, 1997)

Siems, Mathias, "Private enforcement of directors' duties: Derivative actions as a global phenomenon" in Stefan Wrbka, Steven Van Uytsel and Mathias Siems (eds.), *Collective Actions: Enhancing Access to Justice and Reconciling Multilayer Interests?* (Cambridge University Press, 2015)

Taylor, Lynne, "Derivative Action", in John Farrar (ed.) *Company and Securities Law in New Zealand* (Brookers, 2008)

Thai, Lang, "Class Action Procedure in Australia: Issues and Challenges" (Chapter 11) in Colin B. Picker and Guy I. Seidman (eds.), *The Dynamism of Civil Procedure: Global Trends and Developments* (Ius Gentium: Comparative Perspectives on Law and Justice, Springer International Publishing, 2016)

Wee, Meng Seng and Dan W. Puchniak, "Derivative action in Singapore: Mundanely non-Asian, Intrigingly non-American and at the forefront of the Commonwealth" in (Chapter 8) in Dan Puchniak, Harald Baum and Michael Ewing-Chow (eds.), *The Derivative Action in Asia: A Comparative and Functional Approach* (Cambridge University Press, 2012)

BOOKS:

Austin, Robert P. and Ian M. Ramsay, *Ford, Austin and Ramsay's Principles of Corporations Law* (17th Edition, LexisNexis Butterworths, 2018)

Austin, Robert P. and Ian M. Ramsay, *Ford, Austin and Ramsay's Principles of Corporations Law* (Looseleaf Services, 2019)

Bainbridge, Stephen M, *Corporate Law* (2nd edition, Foundation Press, 2009)

Berle, Adolf A. and Gardiner C. Means, *The Modern Corporation and Private Property* (Harcourt Brace and World Publishing, 1932).

Blair, Margaret M., *Ownership and Control: Rethinking Corporate Governance for the Twenty-first Century* (Brookings Institution, 1995)

Boros, Elizabeth, *Minority Shareholders Remedies* (Oxford University Press, 1995)

Boyle, AJ, *Minority Shareholder Remedies* (Cambridge University Press, 2002)

Brickman, Lester, *Lawyer Barons: What Their Contingency Fees Really Cost America?* (Cambridge University Press, 2011)

Charman, Andrew and Johan du Toit, S. C., *Shareholder Actions* (Bloomsbury Publisher, 2nd edition, 2018)

Chew, Margaret, *Minority Shareholders' Rights and Remedies* (2nd edition, LexisNexis, 2007)

Chiu, Iris H-Y., *The Foundations and Anatomy of Shareholder Activism* (Hart Publishing, 2010)

Coffee, John C., *Entrepreneurial Litigation: Its Rise, Fall and Future* (Harvard University Press, 2015)

Corkery, James, *Directors' Powers and Duties* (Longman Professional, 1987)

DeMott, Deborah A, *Shareholder Derivative Actions: Law and Practice* (Thomson Reuters Publisher, 2017–2018)

Dickerson, Robert, John Howard and Leon Getz, *Proposals for a New Corporations Law for Canada* (Volume 1, 1971)

Donald, David C., *A Financial Centre for Two Empires: Hong Kong's Corporate, Securities and Tax Laws in its Transition from Britain to China* (Cambridge University Press, 2014)

Dooley, M. P., *Foundation of Corporation Law* (Foundation Press, 1995)

Farrar, John, et al, *Farrar's Company Law* (2nd edition, 1988)

Girvin, Stephen, Sandra Frisby and Alastair Hudson, *Charlesworth's Company Law* (18th edition, Sweet & Maxwell, 2010)
Gospel, Howard and Andrew Pendleton, *Corporate Governance and Labour Management: An International Comparison* (Oxford University Press, 2006)
Greenfield, Kent, *Corporations are People Too (And They Should Act Like It)* (Yale University Press, 2018)
Hirsch, A. and Sheehey D., *Awarding Attorneys' Fees and Managing Fee Litigation* (Federal Judicial Center, Volume 19, 1994)
Kraakman, R, J. Armour, P. Davies, L. Enriques, H. Hansmann, G. Hertig, K. Hopt, H. Kanda and E. Rock, *The Anatomy of Corporate Law: A Comparative and Functional Approach* (2nd edition, Oxford University Press, 2009)
Kritzer, H. M., *Risks Reputations and Rewards: Contingency Fee Legal Practice in the United States* (Stanford University Press, 2004)
Lin, Shaowei, *Derivative Actions in Chinese Company Law* (Kluwer Law International, 2015)
Njoya, Wanjiru, *Property in Work: The Employment Relationship in the Anglo-American Firm* (Ashgate Publishing Limited, 2007)
Peterson, Dennis H. and Matthew J. Cumming, *Shareholder Remedies in Canada* (Looseleaf Services, 2nd edition, LexisNexis, 2009)
Puchniak, Dan, Harald Baum and Michael Ewing-Chow (eds), *The Derivative Action in Asia: A Comparative and Functional Approach* (Cambridge University Press, 2012)
Reisberg, Arad, *Derivative Actins and Corporate Governance: Theory and Operation* (Oxford University Press, 2007)
Stapledon, Geoff P., *Institutional Shareholders and Corporate Governance* (Clarendon Press, 1996)
Stout, Lynn, *The Shareholder Value Myth: How Putting Shareholders First Harms Investors, Corporations and the Public* (Berrett-Koehler Publishers, 2012)
Welling, Bruce, *Corporate Law in Canada: The Governing Principles* (Scribblers Publishing, 3rd edition, 2006)
Zouridakis, Georgios, *Shareholder Protection Reconsidered: Derivative Action in the UK, Germany and Greece* (Routledge, 2021)

REPORTS:

Access to Justice Taskforce, Federal Attorney-General's Department, *A Strategic Framework for Access to Justice in the Federal Civil Justice System* (September 2009)
American Law Institute, *Principles of Corporate Governance: Analysis and Recommendations* (1994)
Australian Government Treasury, *Treasury Laws Amendment (Measures for Consultation) Bill 2021: Litigation Funders: Draft Exposure* (October 2021)
Australian Law Reform Commission, *Integrity, Fairness and Efficiency: An Inquiry into Class Action Proceedings and Third Party Litigation Funders* (Report 134, January 2019)
Australian Law Reform Commission, *Inquiry into Class Action Proceedings and Third Party Litigation Funders* (Final Report, 21 December 2018)
Australian Law Reform Commission, *Inquiry into Class Action Proceedings and Third Party Litigation Funders* (Supplementary Note: Leave to Proceed, September 2018)
Australian Law Reform Commission, *Inquiry into Class Action Proceedings and Third Party Litigation Funders* (Discussion Paper, June 2018, and the Post-Submission Seminar Presentation, September 2018)

Companies and Securities Law Review Committee, *Enforcement of the Duties of Directors and Officers of a Company by means of a Statutory Derivative Action* (Discussion Paper No. 11, 1990)

Companies and Securities Law Review Committee, *Enforcement of the Duties of Directors and Officers of a Company by Means of a Statutory Derivative Action* (Report No. 12, 1990)

Companies and Securities Advisory Committee, *Statutory Derivative Action* (Report, July 1993)

Corporations and Market Advisory Committee, *Report on the Social Responsibility of Corporations* (2006)

Corporations and Markets Advisory Committee, *Shareholder Claims against Insolvent Companies: Implications of the Sons of Gwalia Decision* (Report, December 2008)

Corporations Law Simplification Task Force, *Commentary on Draft Provisions Dealing with Proceedings on Behalf of a Company by Members and Others* (Report, 1995)

Dickerson Committee Report, *Proposals for a New Business Corporation Law for Canada* (Ottawa, 1971)

Hong Kong Legislative Council, *Report of the Bills Committee on Companies (Amendment) Bill 2003, 30 June 2004, LC Paper No.: CB(1) 2264/03-04*

House of Representatives Standing Committee on Legal and Constitutional Affairs, *Corporate Practices and the Rights of Shareholders*, Final Report (Australian Government, November 1991)

House of Representatives, *Corporate Law Economic Reform Program Proposal, Proposals for Reform: Directors' Duties and Corporate Governance: Facilitating Innovation and Protecting Investors* (Paper No.3, 1997)

House of Representatives, *Explanatory Memorandum to the Corporate Law Economic Reform Program Bill* (C'th, 1998)

Law Commission, *Shareholder Remedies: Report on a Reference under Section 31(e) of the Law Commissions Act 1965* (Law Commission Report No. 246, Canada, 1997)

Law Commission of Ontario, *Class Actions: Objectives, Experiences, and Reforms*, Consultation Paper (Toronto, March 2018)

Lawrence Committee Report, *Which Influenced the Enactment of the Ontario's Business Corporations Act in 1970*

Organization for Economic Cooperation and Development (OECD), *Private Enforcement of Shareholder Rights: A Comparison of Selected Jurisdictions and Policy Alternatives for Brazil* (2020 Report)

Parliamentary Joint Committee on Corporations and Financial Services, *Corporate Responsibilty: Managing Risks and Creating Value* (2006)

Productivity Commission, *Access to Justice Arrangements* (Inquiry Report, No. 72, Volumes 1 and 2, 2014)

Second Reading Speech by the Australian Attorney-General, *Federal Court of Australia Amendment Bill 1991 (C'th), House of Representatives, Parliamentary Debates* (Hansard, 14 November 1991)

Senate Standing Committee on Legal and Constitutional Affairs, *Company Directors' Duties: Report on the Social and Fiduciary Duties and Obligations of Company Directors* (Discussion Paper, 1989)

Victorian Law Reform Commission, *Access to Justice: Litigation Funding and Group Proceedings* (Final Report, March 2018)

OTHER REPORTS

Australian Securities and Investment Commission Annual Report 2017–2018: https://asic.gov.au/Annual-report-2017-18/ASIC-AR-introduction.html (viewed 12 July 2019)

Bainbridge, Stephen M., "Shareholder Activism and Institutional Investors" (Law-Economic Research Paper No. 5-20, University of California Los Angeles, School of Law, 2005).

Bowley, Tim and Jennifer G. Hill, "Stewardship and Collective Action: The Australian Experience" (Working Paper No. 491/2020, ECGI Working Paper Series in Law, European Corporate Governance Institute, January 2020).

Hill, Jennifer G., "Good Activist/Bad Activist: The Rise of International Stewardship Codes" (Working Paper No. 368/2017, ECGI Working Paper Series in Law, European Corporate Governance Institute, September 2017)

Hedges, Jasper, Helen Bird, George Gilligan, Andrew Godwin and Ian Ramsay, "An Empirical Analysis of Public Enforcement of Directors' Duties in Australia: Preliminary Findings" (Working Paper No. 105/2016, Centre for International Finance and Regulation, Melbourne Law School, March 2016)

Katelouzou, Dionysia, The Rhetoric of Activist Shareholder Stewards (European Corporate Governance Institute – Working Paper No. 636/2022, King's College London Law School Research Paper, March 2022): https://papers.ssrn.com/sol3/papers.cfm?abstract_id=4057118 (viewed 12 July 2022)

Lee, Michael B. J., Varying Funding Agreements and Freedom to Contract: Some Observations (1 June 2017) published on the Federal Court of Australia website: www.fedcourt.gov.au/digital-law-library/judges-speeches/justice-lee/lee-j-20170601 (viewed 21 October 2020)

Morabito, Vince, An Empirical Study of Australia's Class Action Regimes: The First Twenty-Five Years of Class Actions in Australia (Fifth Report, July 2017): https://papers.ssrn.com/sol3/papers.cfm?abstract_id=3005901 (viewed 16 August 2020)

Safari, Neshat, *Reconsidering the role of the derivative claim in the United Kingdom: A comparative study with the United States and New Zealand* (PhD Thesis, School of Law, City University of London, May 2018)

Appendix A
Australia

Corporations Act 2001 (C'th)

Part 2F.1A—Proceedings on behalf of a company by members and others

236 Bringing, or intervening in, proceedings on behalf of a company

(1) A person may bring proceedings on behalf of a company, or intervene in any proceedings to which the company is a party for the purpose of taking responsibility on behalf of the company for those proceedings, or for a particular step in those proceedings (for example, compromising or settling them), if:
  (a) the person is:
    (i) a member, former member, or person entitled to be registered as a member, of the company or of a related body corporate; or
    (ii) an officer or former officer of the company; and
  (b) the person is acting with leave granted under section 237.

(2) Proceedings brought on behalf of a company must be brought in the company's name.

(3) The right of a person at general law to bring, or intervene in, proceedings on behalf of a company is abolished.

Note 1: For the right to inspect company books, see subsections 247A(3) to (6).

Note 2: For the requirements to disclose proceedings and leave applications in the annual directors' report, see subsections 300(14) and (15).

Note 3: This section does not prevent a person bringing, or intervening in, proceedings on their own behalf in respect of a personal right.

237 Applying for and granting leave

(1) A person referred to in paragraph 236(1)(a) may apply to the Court for leave to bring, or to intervene in, proceedings.

(2) The Court must grant the application if it is satisfied that:
  (a) it is probable that the company will not itself bring the proceedings, or properly take responsibility for them, or for the step in them; and
  (b) the applicant is acting in good faith; and

(c) it is in the best interests of the company that the applicant be granted leave; and
(d) if the applicant is applying for leave to bring proceedings—there is a serious question to be tried; and
(e) either:
(i) at least 14 days before making the application, the applicant gave written notice to the company of the intention to apply for leave and of the reasons for applying; or
(ii) it is appropriate to grant leave even though subparagraph (i) is not satisfied.

(3) A rebuttable presumption that granting leave is not in the best interests of the company arises if it is established that:
(a) the proceedings are:
(i) by the company against a third party; or
(ii) by a third party against the company; and
(b) the company has decided:
(i) not to bring the proceedings; or
(ii) not to defend the proceedings; or
(iii) to discontinue, settle or compromise the proceedings; and
(c) all of the directors who participated in that decision:
(i) acted in good faith for a proper purpose; and
(ii) did not have a material personal interest in the decision; and
(iii) informed themselves about the subject matter of the decision to the extent they reasonably believed to be appropriate; and
(iv) rationally believed that the decision was in the best interests of the company.

The director's belief that the decision was in the best interests of the company is a rational one unless the belief is one that no reasonable person in their position would hold.

(4) For the purposes of subsection (3):
(a) a person is a third party if:
(i) the company is a public company and the person is not a related party of the company; or
(ii) the company is not a public company and the person would not be a related party of the company if the company were a public company; and
(b) proceedings by or against the company include any appeal from a decision made in proceedings by or against the company.

Note: ***Related party*** is defined in section 228.

238 Substitution of another person for the person granted leave

(1) Any of the following persons may apply to the Court for an order that they be substituted for a person to whom leave has been granted under section 237:
   (a) a member, former member, or a person entitled to be registered as a member, of the company or of a related body corporate; or
   (b) an officer, or former officer, of the company.
(2) The Court may make the order if it is satisfied that:
   (a) the applicant is acting in good faith; and
   (b) it is appropriate to make the order in all the circumstances.
(3) An order substituting one person for another has the effect that:
   (a) the grant of leave is taken to have been made in favour of the substituted person; and
   (b) if the other person has already brought the proceedings or intervened—the substituted person is taken to have brought those proceedings or to have made that intervention.

239 Effect of ratification by members

(1) If the members of a company ratify or approve conduct, the ratification or approval:
   (a) does not prevent a person from bringing or intervening in proceedings with leave under section 237 or from applying for leave under that section; and
   (b) does not have the effect that proceedings brought or intervened in with leave under section 237 must be determined in favour of the defendant, or that an application for leave under that section must be refused.
(2) If members of a company ratify or approve conduct, the Court may take the ratification or approval into account in deciding what order or judgment (including as to damages) to make in proceedings brought or intervened in with leave under section 237 or in relation to an application for leave under that section. In doing this, it must have regard to:
   (a) how well-informed about the conduct the members were when deciding whether to ratify or approve the conduct; and
   (b) whether the members who ratified or approved the conduct were acting for proper purposes.

240 Leave to discontinue, compromise or settle proceedings brought, or intervened in, with leave

Proceedings brought or intervened in with leave must not be discontinued, compromised or settled without the leave of the Court.

241 General powers of the Court

(1) The Court may make any orders, and give any directions, that it considers appropriate in relation to proceedings brought or intervened in with leave, or an application for leave, including:
  (a) interim orders; and
  (b) directions about the conduct of the proceedings, including requiring mediation; and
  (c) an order directing the company, or an officer of the company, to do, or not to do, any act; and
  (d) an order appointing an independent person to investigate, and report to the Court on:
    (i) the financial affairs of the company; or
    (ii) the facts or circumstances which gave rise to the cause of action the subject of the proceedings; or
    (iii) the costs incurred in the proceedings by the parties to the proceedings and the person granted leave.

(2) A person appointed by the Court under paragraph (1)(d) is entitled, on giving reasonable notice to the company, to inspect any books of the company for any purpose connected with their appointment.
(3) If the Court appoints a person under paragraph (1)(d):
  (a) the Court must also make an order stating who is liable for the remuneration and expenses of the person appointed; and
  (b) the Court may vary the order at any time; and
  (c) the persons who may be made liable under the order, or the order as varied, are:
    (i) all or any of the parties to the proceedings or application; and
    (ii) the company; and
  (d) if the order, or the order as varied, makes 2 or more persons liable, the order may also determine the nature and extent of the liability of each of those persons.
(4) Subsection (3) does not affect the powers of the Court as to costs.

242 Power of the Court to make costs orders

The Court may at any time make any orders it considers appropriate about the costs of the following persons in relation to proceedings brought or intervened in with leave under section 237 or an application for leave under that section:

(a) the person who applied for or was granted leave
(b) the company
(c) any other party to the proceedings or application.

An order under this section may require indemnification for costs.

Appendix B
New Zealand

Companies Act 1993 (New Zealand)

165 Derivative actions

(1) Subject to subsection (3), the court may, on the application of a shareholder or director of a company, grant leave to that shareholder or director to—
  (a) bring proceedings in the name and on behalf of the company or any related company; or
  (b) intervene in proceedings to which the company or any related company is a party for the purpose of continuing, defending, or discontinuing the proceedings on behalf of the company or related company, as the case may be.

(2) Without limiting subsection (1), in determining whether to grant leave under that subsection, the court shall have regard to—
  (a) the likelihood of the proceedings succeeding:
  (b) the costs of the proceedings in relation to the relief likely to be obtained:
  (c) any action already taken by the company or related company to obtain relief:
  (d) the interests of the company or related company in the proceedings being commenced, continued, defended, or discontinued, as the case may be.

(3) Leave to bring proceedings or intervene in proceedings may be granted under subsection (1), only if the court is satisfied that either—
  (a) the company or related company does not intend to bring, diligently continue or defend, or discontinue the proceedings, as the case may be; or
  (b) it is in the interests of the company or related company that the conduct of the proceedings should not be left to the directors or to the determination of the shareholders as a whole.

(4) Notice of the application must be served on the company or related company.

(5) The company or related company—
  (a) may appear and be heard; and
  (b) must inform the court, whether or not it intends to bring, continue, defend, or discontinue the proceedings, as the case may be.

(6) Except as provided in this section, a shareholder is not entitled to bring or intervene in any proceedings in the name of, or on behalf of, a company or a related company.

166 Costs of derivative action to be met by company

The court shall, on the application of the shareholder or director to whom leave was granted under section 165 to bring or intervene in the proceedings, order that the whole or part of the reasonable costs of bringing or intervening in the proceedings, including any costs relating to any settlement, compromise, or discontinuance approved under section 168, must be met by the company unless the court considers that it would be unjust or inequitable for the company to bear those costs.

167 Powers of court where leave granted

The court may, at any time, make any order it thinks fit in relation to proceedings brought by a shareholder or a director or in which a shareholder or director intervenes, as the case may be, with leave of the court under section 165, and without limiting the generality of this section may—

(a) make an order authorising the shareholder or any other person to control the conduct of the proceedings:
(b) give directions for the conduct of the proceedings:
(c) make an order requiring the company or the directors to provide information or assistance in relation to the proceedings:
(d) make an order directing that any amount ordered to be paid by a defend- ant in the proceedings must be paid, in whole or part, to former and present shareholders of the company or related company instead of to the company or the related company.

168 Compromise, settlement, or withdrawal of derivative action

No proceedings brought by a shareholder or a director or in which a shareholder or a director intervenes, as the case may be, with leave of the court under section 165, may be settled or compromised or discontinued without the approval of the court.

Appendix C
Singapore

Companies Act 1993 (Chapter 50, 2006, revised edition) (Singapore)

Derivative or representative actions

216A – (1) In this section and section 216B —

"complainant" means —

(a) any member of a company;

(b) the Minister, in the case of a declared company under Part IX; or

(c) any other person who, in the discretion of the Court, is a proper person to make an application under this section.

(2) Subject to subsection (3), a complainant may apply to the Court for leave to bring an action or arbitration in the name and on behalf of the company or intervene in an action or arbitration to which the company is a party for the purpose of prosecuting, defending or discontinuing the action or arbitration on behalf of the company.

(3) No action or arbitration may be brought and no intervention in an action or arbitration may be made under subsection (2) unless the Court is satisfied that —

(a) the complainant has given 14 days' notice to the directors of the company of his intention to apply to the Court under subsection (2) if the directors of the company do not bring, diligently prosecute or defend or discontinue the action or arbitration;

(b) the complainant is acting in good faith; and

(c) it appears to be prima facie in the interests of the company that the action or arbitration be brought, prosecuted, defended or discontinued.

(4) Where a complainant on an application can establish to the satisfaction of the Court that it is not expedient to give notice as required in subsection (3)(*a*), the Court may make such interim order as it thinks fit pending the complainant giving notice as required.

(5) In granting leave under this section, the Court may make such orders or interim orders as it thinks fit in the interests of justice, including (but not limited to) the following:

(d) an order authorising the complainant or any other person to control the conduct of the action or arbitration;

(e) an order giving directions for the conduct of the action or arbitration by the person so authorised; and

(f) an order requiring the company to pay reasonable legal fees and disbursements incurred by the complainant in connection with the action or arbitration.

(6) Where the action has been commenced or is to be brought in the State Courts, an application for leave under subsection (2) shall be made in a District Court.

Evidence of shareholders' approval not decisive — Court approval to discontinue action under section 216A

216B – (1) An application made or an action brought or intervened in under section 216A shall not be stayed or dismissed by reason only that it is shown that an alleged breach of a right or duty owed to the company has been or may be approved by the members of the company, but evidence of approval by the members may be taken into account by the Court in making an order under section 216A.

(2) An application made or an action brought or intervened in under section 216A shall not be stayed, discontinued, settled or dismissed for want of prosecution without the approval of the Court given upon such terms as the Court thinks fit and, if the Court determines that the interest of any complainant may be substantially affected by such stay, discontinuance, settlement or dismissal, the Court may order any party to the application or action to give notice to the complainant.

(3) In an application made or an action brought or intervened in under section 216A, the Court may at any time order the company to pay to the complainant interim costs, including legal fees and disbursements, but the complainant may be accountable for such interim costs upon final disposition of the application or action.

Appendix D
Canada

Canada Business Corporations Act RSC 1985 Chapter C-44, ss.238-240

Definitions

238 In this Part,action
action means an action under this Act;complainant
complainant means

(a) a registered holder or beneficial owner, and a former registered holder or beneficial owner, of a security of a corporation or any of its affiliates,
(b) a director or an officer or a former director or officer of a corporation or any of its affiliates,
(c) the Director, or
(d) any other person who, in the discretion of a court, is a proper person to make an application under this Part. (*plaignant*)

Commencing derivative action

239 (1) Subject to subsection (2), a complainant may apply to a court for leave to bring an action in the name and on behalf of a corporation or any of its subsidiaries, or intervene in an action to which any such body corporate is a party, for the purpose of prosecuting, defending or discontinuing the action on behalf of the body corporate.

Conditions precedent

239 (2) No action may be brought and no intervention in an action may be made under subsection (1) unless the court is satisfied that

(a) the complainant has given notice to the directors of the corporation or its subsidiary of the complainant's intention to apply to the court under subsection (1) not less than fourteen days before bringing the application, or as otherwise ordered by the court, if the directors of the corporation or its subsidiary do not bring, diligently prosecute or defend or discontinue the action;

(b) the complainant is acting in good faith; and

(c) it appears to be in the interests of the corporation or its subsidiary that the action be brought, prosecuted, defended or discontinued.

Powers of court

240 In connection with an action brought or intervened in under section 239, the court may at any time make any order it thinks fit including, without limiting the generality of the foregoing,

(a) an order authorizing the complainant or any other person to control the conduct of the action;

(b) an order giving directions for the conduct of the action;

(c) an order directing that any amount adjudged payable by a defendant in the action shall be paid, in whole or in part, directly to former and present security holders of the corporation or its subsidiary instead of to the corporation or its subsidiary; and an order requiring the corporation or its subsidiary to pay reasonable legal fees incurred by the complainant in connection with the action.

Appendix E
British Columbia

British Columbia Business Corporations Act, SBC 2002, Chapter 57, ss 232-233

Derivative actions

232 (1) In this section and section 233,

"complainant" means, in relation to a company, a shareholder or director of the company;

"shareholder" has the same meaning as in section 1 (1) and includes a beneficial owner of a share of the company and any other person whom the court considers to be an appropriate person to make an application under this section.

(2) A complainant may, with leave of the court, prosecute a legal proceeding in the name and on behalf of a company

(a) to enforce a right, duty or obligation owed to the company that could be enforced by the company itself, or

(b) to obtain damages for any breach of a right, duty or obligation referred to in paragraph (a) of this subsection.

(3) Subsection (2) applies whether the right, duty or obligation arises under this Act or otherwise.

(4) With leave of the court, a complainant may, in the name and on behalf of a company, defend a legal proceeding brought against the company.

Powers of court in relation to derivative actions

233 (1) The court may grant leave under section 232 (2) or (4), on terms it considers appropriate, if

(a) the complainant has made reasonable efforts to cause the directors of the company to prosecute or defend the legal proceeding,

(b) notice of the application for leave has been given to the company and to any other person the court may order,

(c) the complainant is acting in good faith, and

(d) it appears to the court that it is in the best interests of the company for the legal proceeding to be prosecuted or defended.

(2) Nothing in this section prevents the court from making an order that th complainant give security for costs.

(3) While a legal proceeding prosecuted or defended under this section is pending, the court may,

  (a) on the application of the complainant, authorize any person to control the conduct of the legal proceeding or give any other directions for the conduct of the legal proceeding, and

  (b) on the application of the person controlling the conduct of the legal proceeding, order, on the terms and conditions that the court considers appropriate, that the company pay to the person controlling the conduct of the legal proceeding interim costs in the amount and for the matters, including legal fees and disbursements, that the court considers appropriate.

(4) On the final disposition of a legal proceeding prosecuted or defended under this section, the court may make any order it considers appropriate, including an order that

  (a) a person to whom costs are paid under subsection (3) (b) repay to the company some or all of those costs,

  (b) the company or any other party to the legal proceeding indemnify

    (i) the complainant for the costs incurred by the complainant in prosecuting or defending the legal proceeding, or

    (ii) the person controlling the conduct of the legal proceeding for the costs incurred by the person in controlling the conduct of the legal proceeding, or

  (c) the complainant or the person controlling the conduct of the legal proceeding indemnify one or more of the company, a director of the company and an officer of the company for expenses, including legal costs, that they incurred as a result of the legal proceeding.

(5) No legal proceeding prosecuted or defended under this section may be discontinued, settled or dismissed without the approval of the court.

(6) No application made or legal proceeding prosecuted or defended under section 232 or this section may be stayed or dismissed merely because it is shown that an alleged breach of a right, duty or obligation owed to the company has been or might be approved by the shareholders of the company, but evidence of that approval or possible approval may be taken into account by the court in making an order under section 232 or this section.

Appendix F
The United Kingdom

Companies Act 2006 (UK)

PART 11

DERIVATIVE CLAIMS AND PROCEEDINGS BY MEMBERS

CHAPTER 1

DERIVATIVE CLAIMS IN ENGLAND AND WALES OR NORTHERN IRELAND

260 Derivative claims

(1) This Chapter applies to proceedings in England and Wales or Northern Ireland by a member of a company—
  (a) in respect of a cause of action vested in the company, and
  (b) seeking relief on behalf of the company.
  This is referred to in this Chapter as a "derivative claim".
(2) A derivative claim may only be brought—
  (a) under this Chapter, or
  (b) in pursuance of an order of the court in proceedings under section 994 (proceedings for protection of members against unfair prejudice).
(3) A derivative claim under this Chapter may be brought only in respect of a cause of action arising from an actual or proposed act or omission involving negligence, default, breach of duty or breach of trust by a director of the company.
  The cause of action may be against the director or another person (or both).
(4) It is immaterial whether the cause of action arose before or after the person seeking to bring or continue the derivative claim became a member of the company.

(5) For the purposes of this Chapter—
(a) "director" includes a former director;
(b) a shadow director is treated as a director; and
(c) references to a member of a company include a person who is not a member but to whom shares in the company have been transferred or transmitted by operation of law.

261 Application for permission to continue derivative claim

(6) A member of a company who brings a derivative claim under this Chapter must apply to the court for permission (in Northern Ireland, leave) to continue it.
(7) If it appears to the court that the application and the evidence filed by the applicant in support of it do not disclose a prima facie case for giving permission (or leave), the court—
(a) must dismiss the application, and
(b) may make any consequential order it considers appropriate.
(8) If the application is not dismissed under subsection (2), the court—
(a) may give directions as to the evidence to be provided by the company, and
(b) may adjourn the proceedings to enable the evidence to be obtained.
(9) On hearing the application, the court may—
(a) give permission (or leave) to continue the claim on such terms as it thinks fit,
(b) refuse permission (or leave) and dismiss the claim, or
(c) adjourn the proceedings on the application and give such directions as it thinks fit.

262 Application for permission to continue claim as a derivative claim

(10) This section applies where—
(a) a company has brought a claim, and
(b) the cause of action on which the claim is based could be pursued as a derivative claim under this Chapter.
(11) A member of the company may apply to the court for permission (in Northern Ireland, leave) to continue the claim as a derivative claim on the ground that—
(a) the manner in which the company commenced or continued the claim amounts to an abuse of the process of the court,
(b) the company has failed to prosecute the claim diligently, and
(c) it is appropriate for the member to continue the claim as a derivative claim.
(12) If it appears to the court that the application and the evidence filed by the applicant in support of it do not disclose a prima facie case for giving permission (or leave), the court—

(a) must dismiss the application, and
(b) may make any consequential order it considers appropriate.

(13) If the application is not dismissed under subsection (3), the court—
(a) may give directions as to the evidence to be provided by the company, and
(b) may adjourn the proceedings to enable the evidence to be obtained.

(14) On hearing the application, the court may—
(a) give permission (or leave) to continue the claim as a derivative claim on such terms as it thinks fit,
(b) refuse permission (or leave) and dismiss the application, or
(c) adjourn the proceedings on the application and give such directions as it thinks fit.

263 Whether permission to be given

(15) The following provisions have effect where a member of a company applies for permission (in Northern Ireland, leave) under section 261 or 262.

(16) Permission (or leave) must be refused if the court is satisfied—
(a) that a person acting in accordance with section 172 (duty to promote the success of the company) would not seek to continue the claim, or
(b) where the cause of action arises from an act or omission that is yet to occur, that the act or omission has been authorised by the company, or
(c) where the cause of action arises from an act or omission that has already occurred, that the act or omission—
(i) was authorised by the company before it occurred, or
(ii) has been ratified by the company since it occurred.

(17) In considering whether to give permission (or leave) the court must take into account, in particular—
(a) whether the member is acting in good faith in seeking to continue the claim;
(b) the importance that a person acting in accordance with section 172 (duty to promote the success of the company) would attach to continuing it;
(c) where the cause of action results from an act or omission that is yet to occur, whether the act or omission could be, and in the circumstances would be likely to be—
(i) authorised by the company before it occurs, or
(ii) ratified by the company after it occurs;
(d) where the cause of action arises from an act or omission that has already occurred, whether the act or omission could be, and in the circumstances would be likely to be, ratified by the company;
(e) whether the company has decided not to pursue the claim;

(f) whether the act or omission in respect of which the claim is brought gives rise to a cause of action that the member could pursue in his own right rather than on behalf of the company.

(18) In considering whether to give permission (or leave) the court shall have particular regard to any evidence before it as to the views of members of the company who have no personal interest, direct or indirect, in the matter.

(19) The Secretary of State may by regulations—
(a) amend subsection (2) so as to alter or add to the circumstances in which permission (or leave) is to be refused;
(b) amend subsection (3) so as to alter or add to the matters that the court is required to take into account in considering whether to give permission (or leave).

(20) Before making any such regulations the Secretary of State shall consult such persons as he considers appropriate.

(21) Regulations under this section are subject to affirmative resolution procedure.

264 Application for permission to continue derivative claim brought by another member

(22) This section applies where a member of a company ("the claimant")—
(a) has brought a derivative claim,
(b) has continued as a derivative claim a claim brought by the company, or
(c) has continued a derivative claim under this section.

(23) Another member of the company ("the applicant") may apply to the court for permission (in Northern Ireland, leave) to continue the claim on the ground that—
(a) the manner in which the proceedings have been commenced or continued by the claimant amounts to an abuse of the process of the court,
(b) the claimant has failed to prosecute the claim diligently, and
(c) it is appropriate for the applicant to continue the claim as a derivative claim.

(24) If it appears to the court that the application and the evidence filed by the applicant in support of it do not disclose a prima facie case for giving permission (or leave), the court—
(a) must dismiss the application, and
(b) may make any consequential order it considers appropriate.

(25) If the application is not dismissed under subsection (3), the court—
(a) may give directions as to the evidence to be provided by the company, and
(b) may adjourn the proceedings to enable the evidence to be obtained.

(26) On hearing the application, the court may—

(a) give permission (or leave) to continue the claim on such terms as it thinks fit,

(b) refuse permission (or leave) and dismiss the application, or adjourn the proceedings on the application and give such directions as it thinks fit.

Index

Page numbers in *italics* mark figures, while page numbers in **bold** indicate tables.